W9-DAV-373

THE BRITISH MUSEUM

A–Z Companion

THE
BRITISH
MUSEUM

Marjorie Caygill

A–Z Companion

THE BRITISH MUSEUM PRESS

© 1999 The Trustees of the British Museum
All pictures © The Trustees of the British Museum

First published in 1999 by The British Museum Press
A division of The British Museum Company Ltd
38 Russell Square, London WC1B 3QQ

Ninth and Tenth impressions 2007

A catalogue record for this book is available
from the British Library

ISBN-13: 978-0-7141-2143-7

Designed by Andrew Shoolbred
Cover design by Carla Turchini
Typeset in Rotis and Minion by Wyvern 21
Printed and bound in Slovenia by Gorenjski Tisk
by arrangement with Korotan Ljubljana

Contents

The *British Museum A–Z Companion* is the latest in a very long line of guides to the Museum's collections reaching back to 1760, when an anonymous author, who had despaired of the Museum's publishing its own guide, produced a slim volume for 'Those who have a Mind to be acquainted with the principal Parts of it [the Museum]'. A year later appeared Edmund Powlett's *The General Contents of the British Museum: With Remarks Serving as a Directory In viewing that Noble Cabinet*. Powlett, like others after him, compiled a typically idiosyncratic selection, writing:

> I know it is impossible to please every body, consequently have no doubt but much Fault will be found with this little Performance: Some will think I have passed too slightly over the Fresco Paintings; or that I might have said more of the portraits... Many will imagine I have not been attentive enough to the Manuscripts or Medals; and others, perhaps, would have wished me to have filled twenty Pages, with a Description of the Mole Cricket.

The first illustrated guide was John and Andrew van Rymsdyk's *Musæum Britannicum* in 1778. Its index, beginning with 'Achate, natural History of' and ending with 'Zoology, Humming Birds', included such odditites as 'Fish, swimming in boiling hot Water' and 'Spear, a curious', but also references not far removed from those in this book.

The official 'Synopsis' first appeared in 1808 and ran to 63 editions. The guides continued in various forms over the years: improving texts for children (some surreptitiously plagiarized from the Trustees' publications), 'spurious guides' which undersold the official books, including a useful series produced by Henry G. Clarke (author of *Knitting, Netting and Crochet*), scholarly handbooks, texts aimed at the increasingly powerful working classes wishing to better themselves. Line drawings gradually gave way to grainy monochrome photographs and then to brilliant colour; Greece, Rome and Egypt ceded space to the British collections and the Orient as the horizons of the Museum staff and Trustees broadened.

This first *A–Z Companion* mirrors its predecessors inasmuch as it, too, cannot cover everything. Rather, it offers a reasonably representative taste of the inexhaustible variety contained under one roof. It is arranged alphabetically, rather than by gallery or Museum department. It is hoped that this arrangement will enable readers to find new and interesting juxtapositions of cultures and periods which will suggest new ways of looking at the Museum's collections.

Acknowledgements

This book is dedicated to the curatorial staff of the British Museum, without whose continuing research and scholarship a general guide such as this would not be possible. Their erudition is the foundation for the Museum's wide range of 'popular' publications, as well as for all displays of objects, permanent or temporary. I have drawn extensively on curators' published work and have benefited from their freely offered comments on each entry. They are too many to mention individually, but most are named in the 'Further Reading' sections.

Thanks are also due to my editors, Joanna Champness and Elisabeth Ingles, and to Jemima Scott-Holland who waded through vast photographic archives to obtain the illustrations. I am also beholden to Emma Way who initiated and supported the project, to Susanna Friedman who saw it through press, and to Teresa Francis who provided last-minute assistance. They have all contributed an immense amount to what is in every way a team effort.

About this guide

The intention is to give readers an impression of the vast holdings of the British Museum from all millennia and from all over the world. Virtually all of the Museum's major objects, or classes of objects, are described, and this book can therefore be used as a companion to a visit. In addition, the brief descriptions and suggestions for further reading are intended to stand alone as a useful introduction to many aspects of ancient and modern material culture.

Not all of the Museum's collections of approximately twelve million objects are on display. Many items, such as prints and drawings and a considerable part of the ethnographical collections, are fragile and can thus only be shown for short periods so as to protect them from deterioration. In some instances, such as the reference collection of half a million coins and medals, there would never be sufficient space for everything to be shown at the same time. The Museum has world-renowned and extensive archives of other study material, for example potsherds from excavations, vast quantities of flints and libraries of cuneiform tablets, which are primarily of interest to the scholar, although selections from these categories are on display and much is published.

Galleries are continuously rearranged and thus even major items may be temporarily absent. The Museum's Information Desk will be pleased to advise what is on show.

Colour coding has been used for the entries in the book to indicate which Department of the Museum cares for the objects shown. The key is printed opposite.

Key

Africa (Africa, Oceania and the Americas)

Americas (Africa, Oceania and the Americas)

Middle East (formerly Western Asiatic Antiquities)

Asia (formerly Oriental Antiquities, Japanese Antiquities)

Egypt (Ancient Egypt and Sudan, formerly
Egyptian Antiquities)

Europe (Prehistory and Europe, formerly Medieval
and Later Antiquities)

Greece and Rome (Greek and Roman Antiquities)

Money (Coins and Medals)

Pacific (Africa, Oceania and the Americas)

Prehistory (Prehistory and Europe, formerly
Prehistoric and Romano-British Antiquities)

Prints and Drawings

Roman Britain (Prehistory and Europe, formerly
Prehistoric and Romano-British Antiquities)

Other/inter-departmental entries

A'a, creator of Rurutu

A'a, principal deity of Rurutu, one of the main Austral Islands in French Polynesia, caught the attention of the sculptor Henry Moore when, as an impoverished student, he spent many hours in the British Museum in the 1920s. Moore, when he became successful, had a bronze cast of the statue in the hall of his home and later described it with a sculptor's eye:

> The little images, scattered all over the body like frogs jumping from a pool, are not stuck on but are all part of the same piece of wood – a remarkable technical achievement. And each figure is a separate piece of invention. The excitement of this piece comes from its sense of life-force, with all those small figures springing from the parent figure. The head, too, is marvellous. Its great round back repeats the shape of the full, round belly, but emphasizes, by contrast, the thinness and sharpness of the jaw ...

Wooden figure
representing the deity A'a
Rurutu, Austral Islands,
French Polynesia
18th century AD
ETH LMS.19
h. 1.17 m (3 ft 10 in)
Purchased from the
London Missionary
Society, 1911

The modern poet William Empson also wrote of A'a in 'Homage to the British Museum':

> There is a supreme God in the ethnological section,
> A hollow toad shape, faced with a blank shield ...

The European impact upon Polynesia from the eighteenth century AD onwards was often catastrophic. In some island groups such as the Australs, new diseases and missionary fervour devastated the local culture before the full significance of items such as this figure could be appreciated. This carving was given up to missionaries by converts to Christianity in the 1820s. Inside the detachable back is a cavity where smaller images were originally kept.

FURTHER READING
M.D. McLeod and J. Mack, *Ethnic Sculpture* (London, 1985)
H. Moore, *Henry Moore at the British Museum* (London, 1981)
S. Hooper, *Pacific Designs: Art and Divinity in Polynesia 1760-1860* (London, 2006)

On the right is a vessel from the great Achaemenid Empire which dominated the Near East from the sixth to fourth centuries BC. The inscription proclaims the power of Artaxerxes I (*r*.464–424 BC): 'Artaxerxes, the great king, King of Kings, King of countries, son of Xerxes the king, of Xerxes son of Darius the king, the Achaemenian, in whose house this drinking-cup/saucer of silver was made'. Below is another fine piece from the same period, a partially gilded fluted drinking horn said to have been found in eastern Turkey. It is made in two parts, the base in the form of a griffin.

The Achaemenid Empire began in 550 BC when the Persians under Cyrus the Great (*r*.550–530 BC) overthrew Astyages, King of the Medes, and established the Achaemenid dynasty (named after a legendary ancestor, Achaemenes). Cyrus considerably expanded his new empire, first conquering western Anatolia then the Neo-Babylonian Empire in 539 BC. He founded a capital at Pasargadae on the Iranian plateau.

The Persian Empire reached its greatest extent under Darius I (522–486 BC). A Royal Road ran from Susa in south-western Iran to Sardis in western Turkey, and a canal was dug from the Nile to the Red Sea. Construction also began at the great royal centre of Persepolis (p. 248) and royal tombs were cut into nearby cliffs. The Achaemenid kings continued to dominate the Near East and, through diplomacy, to influence events further west until 334 BC when Alexander the Great led his troops eastwards.

The Achaemenids built on the metalworking traditions of their predecessors and forged a distinctive style, which took elements from the varied cultures of their huge empire. Achaemenid metal wares were in great demand and examples have been found in Thrace, Egypt and Bactria (p. 237). The Museum's collection consists of sculptures, seals, metalwork and jewellery.

FURTHER READING

J. Curtis, *Ancient Persia* (2nd edn, London, 2000)
J. Curtis and N. Tallis (eds), *Forgotten Empire: The World of Ancient Persia* (London, 2005)

Inscribed bowl of Artaxerxes I
Persia (Iran)
Silver, mid–late 5th century BC
WA 1994–1–27, 1
diam. 29 cm (11⅖ in)
Purchased with the aid of the National Art Collections Fund, the British Museum Society and the Friends of the Ancient Near East

Silver drinking horn (rhyton)
?Turkey
5th–4th century BC
WA 124081;
1897–12–31, 178
h. 23 cm (9 in)
A.W. Franks Bequest

African textiles

One of the most obvious features of the material culture of Africa is cloth. Woven textiles and other fabrics, often with brilliant colours and intricate design, are available in almost every part of the African continent. Some are imported from Europe and India, but most are still locally manufactured by both industrial and traditional methods. The Museum has an extensive collection.

Particular colours, kinds of decoration or shapes of garment may have political or ritual significance. The tribal affiliation of a Moroccan Berber woman, for example, can be seen in the pattern of stripes of her cloak. In Benin, Nigeria, chiefs wear red cloth as part of their ceremonial court dress. Red, by its association with anger, blood, war and fire, is regarded as threatening, and by the wearing of such cloth a chief protects himself, and his king, from evil. The basic colour spectrum of Africa, red, black and white, usually carries some significance, although its precise nature varies from one people to another. Elsewhere in Nigeria, among the Ebira for example, red is a colour associated with success and achievement. In Madagascar the term 'red', *mena*, is applied to burial cloths, though with the sense of 'colourful', not because they are predominantly red in colour.

Weaving is organized in different ways. In most of West Africa, Ethiopia, East Africa and Zaire, for example, it is all done by men. Elsewhere, as in Berber North Africa and Madagascar, it is carried out by women. In other areas, such as Nigeria, Arab North Africa and the Sudan, both men and women weave. However, in the few cultures where both sexes weave they each use a different kind of loom.

Shown here is an Asante Kente cloth. The Asante people of Ghana are renowned for their silk and cotton textiles, woven in a great variety of patterns. The Kente cloth comprises narrow strips sewn together, each ending in a group of five rectangular design blocks. Traditionally, Asante cloths denoted the wearer's status, with certain types of cloth reserved for chiefs or for the Asantehene (king) himself.

Large royal Kente cloth
(detail)
Ghana, Africa
Woven silk,
mid-20th century AD
ETH 1947.Af.6.2
l. 2.96 m (9 ft 8½ in)

FURTHER READING
J. Gillow, *Printed and Dyed Textiles from Africa* (London, 2001)
A. Hecht, *The Art of the Loom: weaving, spinning and dyeing across the world* (London, 1989)
J. Picton and J. Mack, *African Textiles* (London, 1989)
C. Spring and J. Hudson, *North African Textiles* (London, 1995)
C. Spring and J. Hudson, *Silk in Africa* (London, 2002)

In the fifteenth century the Portuguese explored the coast of West Africa in search of trade, treasure and political influence. Where they encountered long-established traditions of artistic creativity, they commissioned luxury works for use in Europe. Out of this contact between radically different cultures developed one of the earliest and finest 'tourist' arts ever created, that of the elaborate and beautiful Afro-Portuguese ivories. These include great hunting horns, their surfaces covered with delicate carvings, and enigmatic lidded vessels, usually interpreted as salt cellars.

These complex works came from two main areas: the Sherbro or Bullom area of what is now Sierra Leone, and the city of Benin in modern Nigeria. The horns produced by Sherbro carvers are profusely decorated with European hunting motifs combined with African elements. The Sherbro 'salts' show a great delicacy of carving and combine such European motifs as the Madonna and Child with distinctly African forms such as crocodiles, snakes and fierce, toothed beasts. The Benin lidded vessels are less delicately carved; many show bearded Portuguese, some standing, others on horseback. Although relatively few have survived, the great technical skill of the carvers confirms that the ivories must have been made at the royal court.

The Museum has a dozen major examples of Afro-Portuguese ivories. To the right is an ivory salt cellar which depicts four Portuguese along the base and on top of the lid a fifth in a boat holding a telescope. The Portuguese are wearing a costume that dates to the 1520s–40s and their beards and short capes are based on Spanish fashions popularized by the Emperor Charles V (1500–58). Wood joinery seems to have been uncommon in traditional Africa, and when called upon to represent the planks of a Western ship, the carver interprets them as being fixed in the same way as the tiles on the King of Benin's palace roof.

FURTHER READING
P. Girshick Ben-Amos, *The Art of Benin* (London, 1995)

Ivory salt cellar
Benin, Nigeria
late 15th–early 16th
century AD
ETH 1878.11–1.48
h. 24 cm (9½ in)
Purchased from Major
General Augustus W.
Meyrick

The Aigina treasure is something of an archaeological mystery. The pieces were purchased in 1892 through Cresswell Brothers, a London firm of sponge-dealers with offices across the Mediterranean. The objects were said to have been found in a tomb on the island of Aigina in 1891. Further pieces were bought in 1914 from a former governess to the family of Cresswells' agent on Aigina. There are a number of accounts of the discovery but the exact circumstances are still uncertain.

The treasure is composed principally of gold objects: three diadems; two pairs of very elaborate earrings; five simple hoops (possibly earrings); many beads and pendants; two ornate pendants and part of a third; a chest ornament; a bracelet; four inlaid finger-rings; part of a plain finger-ring; decorated plaques and plain strips for sewing on garments; and an embossed cup. There are also beads and pendants of rock-crystal, amethyst, cornelian, green jasper and lapis lazuli. The quality of workmanship of some items suggests Cretan manufacture.

Below (bottom) is the most striking object from the treasure: a pendant which represents a Cretan god standing in a field of lotus flowers (common in Egyptian art), each hand holding a goose by the neck. Behind him are two curved objects, possibly sacred bulls' horns. He wears a tall feather headdress, large circular earrings, bracelets on his wrists and upper arms, a tightly fitting tunic and a tight belt with an embroidered tassel. This god is known to archaeologists as the 'Master of Animals', the male version of the universal Minoan goddess, the 'Mistress of Animals', who was to become Artemis to the later Greeks. Five gold discs suspended from the bottom of the ornament may represent the sun.

The two earrings above are hoops in the form of double-headed snakes which enclose pairs of facing greyhounds; below the snakes are pairs of monkeys set back to back. From the circumference hang fourteen pendants on gold chains, seven in the form of little owls and seven discs. Similar earrings are shown in Minoan art, but these are the largest and most elaborate examples to have been found.

TOP **Two gold earrings**
BOTTOM **The 'Master of Animals' pendant**
Greek Islands
Minoan, c.1700–1500 BC
GR 1892.5–20.10–13, 8;
Cat. Jewellery 762, 763, 765
h. (pendant) 6 cm (2⅓ in)

FURTHER READING
R. Higgins, *The Aegina Treasure* (London, 1979)

Alexander the Great

A lexander (356–323 BC) was regent of Macedonia at 16, king at 20 and died master of much of Europe and Asia at 32. His father Philip II unified his native Macedonia before extending his rule over the rest of mainland Greece. Alexander succeeded in 336 BC after his father's assassination, in which he may, or may not, have had a part. He then embarked on a programme of territorial expansion which was to extend the boundaries of the Greek world to Egypt and India and bring him enduring fame.

In 334 BC Alexander crossed the Hellespont (the Dardanelles) which divides Europe and Asia, going first to Troy. His defeat of the Persian army at the River Granikos, east of Troy, opened the gates of Asia Minor to him. A further victory at the Battle of Issos (late in 333 BC) was followed by the conquest of the Persian territories of Phoenicia, Palestine and Egypt. Returning from Egypt to Persia in October 331 BC, Alexander crushed the last stand of the Persian king at Gaugamela on the plains of Mesopotamia. He then swept eastwards until he met strong resistance from the inhabitants of Bactria and Sogdiana. In 327 BC Alexander advanced eastwards again to India and the River Hydaspes. His soldiers' reluctance to follow him further to the banks of the River Ganges forced him to return to Persia, where he died of a fever at Babylon.

The Museum has a number of objects connected with Alexander and his times and also with the subsequent legend. On the right is an idealized portrait head carved in the second or first century BC, which shows Alexander as the god he became after his eventual burial at Alexandria, where this head was found.

A direct link is a dedicatory inscription from the Temple of Athena Polias at Priene in Ionia. Alexander reached Priene in 334 BC when the temple, designed by the architect Pytheos, one of the architects of the Mausoleum at Halikarnassos (pp. 292–3), was still under construction. He left funds for its completion. His generosity was recorded in the inscription on the anta of the temple: 'King Alexander dedicated the temple to Athena Polias'.

Portrait of Alexander
Alexandria, Hellenistic
Egypt
Marble, 2nd–1st century BC
GR 1872.5–15.1;
Cat. Sculpture 1857
h. 38.1 cm (15 in)

FURTHER READING
Arrian (trans. A. de Sélincourt), *The Campaigns of Alexander* (new edn, New York, 1993)
A. Stewart, *Faces of Power. Alexander's Image and Hellenistic Politics* (Berkeley, Los Angeles and Oxford, 1993)

The Amaravati sculptures are probably the most important single collection of a particular school of Indian sculpture outside India. They consist of over 130 slabs from the great stupa at Amaravati, in Andhra Pradesh, south-eastern India. Most date from the first to the third centuries AD. A reconstruction of the stupa which would have housed relics of one or more Buddhist teachers is shown below.

From at least the last centuries BC relics of the Buddha and his successors were held to be sacred. These were enshrined in stupas which, because of their sanctified contents, became the focus of Buddhist ritual. The stupa at Amaravati was built during the rule of the Satavahana (or Andhra) dynasty, whose rulers emerged about the first century BC to hold power for three, perhaps even four and a half centuries. Around the fifth century AD Buddhism ceased to be the dominant religion in the area but its decline was gradual. The stupa fell into decay, only to be rediscovered in the eighteenth century.

RIGHT
Reconstruction of the
great stupa at Amaravati

OPPOSITE ABOVE
**Drum slab showing
events associated with
the birth of Prince
Siddhartha**
Amaravati, Deccan
(Andhra Pradesh), India
2nd century AD
OA BM 44
h. 1.57 m (5 ft 2 in)

OPPOSITE BELOW
**The footprints of the
Buddha** (*buddhapada*)
Amaravati, India
1st century BC
OA BM 57
h. 67.5 cm (26½ in)

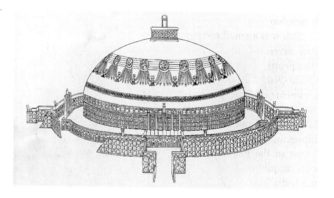

The dome was 18.25 m (60 ft) high with a diameter of 39.6 m (130 ft) and was carved from limestone. One hundred carved slabs were placed against it and the dome was decorated at its lower edge by a further series of high, rectangular carved slabs. At the summit was a square rail with sides. The dome was encircled at the base by an elaborate and richly decorated stone rail consisting of some 136 pillars 2.74 m (9 ft) high with three circular cross-bars between each. The inner faces of the railing slabs carried detailed sculptures illustrating stories from the life of the Buddha, which could be read by devotees as they processed around the monument by a wide grey limestone path. Entrances at the four points of the compass were crowned by seated lions. The rail was topped by thick coping stone and its inner face was elaborately carved.

On the next page is a drum slab showing four events associated with the birth of Prince Siddhartha, later to become the Buddha.

The **Amaravati sculptures**

The top right panel depicts Queen Maya, his mother, dreaming of the birth to come. The top left shows the interpretation of her dream in the court of her husband Shuddhodana. The bottom right panel shows Queen Maya standing under the *sal* tree immediately after the birth. The baby Siddhartha is depicted symbolically as a long cloth with a pair of footprints upon it. In the last panel, bottom left, Queen Maya takes the baby to the Sakya clan sage, the local deity Sakyavardhana, for presentation. When he recognizes the baby's Buddhahood to come he raises his hands in worship.

Below is a small rectangular slab carved with the *buddhapada* (footprints of the Buddha). At the centre of each foot is a finely spiked *dharmachakra* (Wheel of the Law), at the heel of each foot is a *triratna* (symbol representing the three Jewels of Buddhism).

The majority of the sculptures are shared between the British Museum and the Government Museum, Madras (Chennai). Those in the British Museum were acquired in 1880 when the India Museum in London was dispersed. They are now displayed in the Asahi Shimbun Gallery of Amaravati Sculpture. The reconstruction gives an impression of the path round the shrine walked by countless pilgrims.

FURTHER READING
R. Knox, *Amaravati: Buddhist Sculpture from the Great Stupa* (London, 1992)

In 1887 a number of clay tablets inscribed in cuneiform (p. 92) were discovered at el-Amarna in Egypt. Of the 382 known tablets the largest collections are in the Cairo Museum, the British Museum and the Berlin Museum.

All but 32 are diplomatic correspondence between Egypt and either the great powers in Western Asia such as Hittite, Mitannian and Babylonian kings, or the vassal rulers of Palestine, Phoenicia and Syria. The letters vividly depict the turbulent state of the region. They begin around year 30 of Amenhotep III (1390–1352 BC) and end no later than the first year of Tutankhamun's reign (1336–1327 BC). The majority date to the time of Amenhotep III's son Akhenaten (1352–1336 BC), the 'heretic' pharaoh who founded a new capital at el-Amarna. Most are written in the Babylonian language, which was used at the time for most formal diplomatic correspondence. Egyptian and Babylonian princesses are traded for gold and lapis lazuli, chariots and beds inlaid with precious materials. There are constant complaints on both sides about the way messengers and princesses are being treated, with the Kassite kings of Babylonia pointing out that the gold they had been sent was inferior.

Letter from Yapahu, ruler of Gezer, to Amenhotep III or Amenhotep IV (Akhenaten)
el-Amarna, Egypt
14th century BC
WA 29832;
1898–11–15, 218
h. 10.8 cm (4¼ in)

In the tablet shown above, Yapahu, King of Gezer, begs the pharaoh for help against the 'Apiru', roving bands of stateless people who were raiding cities (there is much debate as to whether there is a connection between the 'Apiru' and the later Israelites):

To the king, my lord, my god, my son, the sun in the sky. Thus [says] Yapahu, governor of Gezer, your servant, the dust at your feet, the groom of your horses. I surely fall at the feet of the king, my lord, my god, my sun, the sun in the sky, seven times and seven times, on the stomach and on the back. I have surely heard the words of the messenger of the king my lord. May the king, my lord, the sun in the sky, care for his land. Since the Hapiru are stronger than us, may the king, my lord, help me to escape from the Hapiru, so that the Hapiru do not destroy us.

FURTHER READING
W.L. Moran, *The Amarna Letters* (Baltimore and London, 1992)

Amazons

In Greek mythology the Amazons were female warriors whose legendary home was in Asia Minor on the boundaries of the civilized world. There they had founded a state, its capital, Themiskyra, ruled over by a queen. Men were not admitted but once a year the Amazons would go to their neighbours to form temporary unions. Of the children who resulted only the girls would be kept, the boys being killed or returned to their fathers. The name derives from the Greek word meaning 'without breast', since legend had it that the Amazons' right breasts were removed so that they could better draw a bow.

Amazons appear frequently in Greek myths: they were said to have come to the aid of Troy after Hector's death. On one of the Museum's finest vases (below) the hero Achilles is seen driving a spear into the throat of the Amazon Queen Penthesilea. It was said that as she died their eyes met and, too late, he fell in love with her.

The Amazons were also said to have invaded Attica following Theseus's abduction of the Amazon Antiope and were only repulsed after fierce fighting. In art at least the fact that they were invaders like the Persians is often emphasized by giving them dress and weapons of Persian type.

The Bassae frieze (p. 52) shows one of the Twelve Labours of Herakles, his expedition against the Amazons at Themiskyra when he was charged by Eurystheus, King of Argos or Mycenae, with bringing back the girdle of the Amazon queen. This she consented to, but Hera, wife of Zeus, started a rumour that Herakles was trying to carry off the queen herself and a bloody battle ensued.

They are also to be seen in combat on one of the friezes of the Mausoleum at Halikarnassos.

FURTHER READING
J. Boardman, 'Herakles, Theseus and Amazons'
in D. Kurtz and B. Sparkes (eds), *The Eye of Greece*
(Cambridge, 1982)
D. von Bothmer, *Amazons in Greek Art*
(Oxford, 1957)

Black-figured neck amphora (wine-jar) potted by Exekias and attributed to him as painter
Made in Athens; found at Vulci, Etruria
*c.*540–530 BC
GR 1836.2–24.127;
Cat. Vases B 210
h. 41.6 cm (16⅓ in)
Purchased (Chevalier Durand sale)

Nebmaatra Amenhotep III (1390–1352 BC) of the Eighteenth Dynasty was the son and successor of Thutmose IV (1400–1390 BC), his mother being Mutemwiya. He became king of Egypt at a time when the country's fortunes had reached their zenith. Her empire was secure, the country settled and prosperous. Foreign policy was restricted, in Nubia, to the fostering of Egyptian ways and civilization, accompanied by the extensive building of temples; in Asia, to the development of friendly relations with the rulers of the subject principalities of the empire and of the bordering countries. Relations with several of the foreign kings were cemented by marriages between Amenhotep III and their daughters. Some of his foreign correspondence has survived in the form of the Amarna Letters (p. 18). Within Egypt prosperity and the attendant settled conditions enabled Amenhotep III to devote himself to extensive building operations and to the fostering of the arts. Great temples were constructed, among which the temple of Luxor dedicated to Amun-Re was the most unusual and beautiful.

It seems likely that he chose the sun-disk, the Aten, as his personal god, whilst still honouring the other gods, thus anticipating the eventual religious revolution of his son Amenhotep IV (also known as Akhenaten, 1352–1336 BC).

The Museum has a number of representations of Amenhotep III, including a sandstone stela (below) of the king and Queen Tiy his principal wife, a woman of non-royal birth whose strong personality left a considerable mark on the reign. Amenhotep is shown as an old, obese man, slumping in his chair, an uncharacteristic pose for Egyptian kings. The conventional representation of the king appears in two colossal statues in the Egyptian Sculpture Gallery from his now destroyed mortuary temple in Western Thebes. Made of black granite, the statues show the king seated on a throne with his hands placed flat on his thighs, wearing the short *shendyt* kilt to which is attached a ceremonial bull's tail. On his head is the *nemes* headcloth fitted with an uraeus at the front. He also wears a false beard and a large ornamental collar.

Painted sandstone stela of Amenhotep III and Queen Tiy
el-Amarna, Egypt
18th Dynasty, c. 1350 BC
EA 57399
h. 30.5 m (12 in)
Given by the Egypt Exploration Society

FURTHER READING
A. Kozloff and B. Bryan, *Egypt's Dazzling Sun. Amenhotep III and his world* (Cleveland, 1992)

Amitabha Buddha

In Buddhist teaching, Amitabha rules over the Western Paradise, a heavenly land into which all who call upon his name will be reborn. In China this doctrine was central to the Pure Land sect, which was very popular during the sixth and seventh centuries AD. This monumental figure of the Buddha Amitabha was produced during the Sui dynasty in China (AD 581–618) and is dated to the fifth year of Kaihuang (corresponding to AD 585). It was dedicated, according to the inscription at the base, in Chongguang Temple, Hancui Village. Hancui Village can no longer be identified, but it is thought that its location was south-west of Baoding in Hebei Province, a region associated with white marble sculpture.

White marble figure of the Buddha Amitabha
Hancui, China
Sui dynasty, AD 585
OA 1938.7–15.1
h. 5.78 m (18 ft 11¼ in)
Presented by C.T. Loo to the Chinese Government and by them to the Museum, 1938

The hands, now missing but formerly fixed into the arm sockets by dowels, would have been carved in prescribed gestures, the right hand raised in the gesture of fearlessness (*abhaya-mudra*) and the left lowered in the gesture of bestowal (*varada-mudra*), both appropriate to a saviour. The model for such figures may have been Indian bronze statuary brought to China by pilgrims or trade.

The sculpture was presented in 1938 to commemorate the International Exhibition of Chinese Art which took place in London in 1935–6.

FURTHER READING
W. Zwalf (ed.), *Buddhism: Art and Faith*
(London, 1985)

21

Amulets

Selection of Egyptian amulets dating from the Old Kingdom to the Ptolemaic period, c.2300–100 BC

BELOW
Glazed-composition winged funerary scarab with holes for attachment to mummy-wrappings
EA 58993
w. 11.8 cm (4⅔ in)

BELOW CENTRE
Red jasper 'tit' amulet, sacred to Isis
EA 20639
l. 6.8 cm (2⅔ in)

A n amulet, talisman or charm is a personal ornament which because of its shape, the material from which it is made, or even just its colour, is believed to endow its wearer magically with certain powers or capabilities. At the very least, it is held to afford some kind of magical protection.

The Museum has amulets from almost all periods and all societies. The Egyptian collection is particularly rich in such material. The first recognizable amulets in Egypt occur as early as the Badarian Period, a thousand years before the First Dynasty. Although all have been found in burials, their magical properties were obviously intended primarily to give aid in life. Amulets also acted as substitutes in the afterlife, for example for bodily parts which might be damaged or destroyed. Amulets shaped like possessions were wrapped with the mummy and could magically replace real clothing, personal accoutrements, goods and equipment included in the burial for use in the afterlife, should these be subsequently stolen or destroyed. Amulets of various deities were worn in life as a token of devotion so as to afford their wearer patronage and protection, and were put into the tomb in the hope that this might continue in death. Five-thousand-year-old amulets have been found in Mesopotamia.

In early medieval times in Europe magical gems (p. 198) with protective properties were worn. Amulets continue to be worn or carried today, for example in the form of St Christopher medals, four-leaved clovers and rabbits' feet.

FURTHER READING
C. Andrews, *Amulets of Ancient Egypt* (London, 1994)

Faience hand
EA 22991
l. 3.1 cm (1¼ in)

Polychrome glazed-composition 'wedjat-eye', the 'sound' eye of Horus, with rows of seated frontal cats
EA 26300
w. 8.8 cm (3½ in)

Faience papyrus amulet
EA 7435
l. 5.6 cm (2⅕ in)

Red glass flat-backed heart amulet
EA 8088
l. 5.3 cm (2 in)

Below is a bronze head with intensely gazing, deep-set eyes which would at one time have been inlaid with precious stones or enamel. This is the goddess Anahita, shown in the guise of Aphrodite. The head was found at Satala in north-east Asia Minor (Armenia Minor). A left hand holding drapery was also discovered, indicating that the head belonged to a full-length clothed or semi-clothed figure. On first viewing it the then Keeper of Greek and Roman Antiquities at the Museum described it as the finest bronze he had ever seen.

Anahita was the goddess of waters, fertility and procreation. Possibly of Mesopotamian origin, she was widely worshipped in Achaemenid times (p. 11). Her cult was introduced by Artaxerxes II, and statues and temples were set up in her honour throughout the Persian Empire. The widespread cult persisted in Asia Minor long after the empire had been destroyed. Anahita is sometimes identified with the planet Venus and in Greece was associated with Athena and Aphrodite.

FURTHER READING
D. Haynes, *The Technique of Greek Bronze Statuary* (Mainz am Rhein, 1992)
A. Stewart, *Greek Sculpture* (New Haven and London, 1990)

Bronze head of Anahita
North-east Asia Minor
200–100 BC
GR 1873.8–20.1;
Bronze 266
h. 38.1 cm (15 in)
Purchased (Castellani Collection)

Anatolian silver

Anatolia is the area also known as Asia Minor and now called Turkey. Mountain ranges in the east divided round an immense, high plateau and extended westwards into the Mediterranean to form the Aegean Islands. The land is well-watered and fertile, with abundant natural resources including metals. Anatolia has always been a land bridge for peoples moving west from Central Asia, south from Russia, east from Europe or north through the Taurus mountains from Syria and Mesopotamia (now Iraq). These peoples have left traces of their passage through Anatolia; many settled there. Among the items in the Museum from these ancient civilizations are a distinctive two-handled silver cup found near Troy, similar in shape to items of pottery from a number of sites in central and coastal Anatolia, the Balkans and the Aegean; and (left) a silver bull with gold inlay on a copper stand, which perhaps came from the canopy pole of a rich burial.

Between 3000 and 2000 BC there is evidence for large settlements, often walled, in this area, and for increasing contact between Anatolia and its neighbours. Trade with Syria and Mesopotamia flourished along the Rivers Euphrates and Tigris, and there were maritime connections with the Aegean and the Balkans.

Anatolia exported copper and arsenical bronze, and research has shown that there may have been tin mines in the Taurus that were exploited for the casting of tin bronzes. Rich tombs south of the Black Sea and at Alaca Hüyük provide evidence for elaborate creations in a variety of metals, including distinctive standards topped by stags and bulls. Excavations at the historic site of Troy in the west have shown that textiles were also important in the economy.

Silver bull with gold inlay
Central Antolia
(probably from Alaca Hüyük)
Early Bronze Age,
c.2300 BC
WA 135851; 1973–1–20,1
h. 24 cm (9½ in)

FURTHER READING
S. Lloyd, *Early Highland Peoples of Anatolia* (London, 1967)

24

With the discovery of the Sutton Hoo treasure (pp. 312–13) in 1939 the rich traditions of Anglo-Saxon art were more fully appreciated. Much fine metalwork had survived, as well as magnificent illuminated manuscripts such as the Lindisfarne Gospels, and elaborately carved stone sculpture and ivories; but wall paintings, stained-glass windows, secular painting and wood carving, at which the Anglo-Saxons excelled, rarely survive. The objects in the Museum remind us of what we have lost. Overleaf are six silver brooches (two pairs and two singles), only one of which seems to have been worn. They may therefore be a silversmith's hoard buried during the 840s' Viking raids on East Anglia. They were found during the digging of a grave in Pentney churchyard, Norfolk, in 1977. Their discovery doubled the tally of known Late Saxon silver disc brooches. On the right is the 'Fuller brooch' (named after its part donor), one of the greatest achievements of late-Saxon metalwork. It is one of a series of large silver disc brooches in fashion from the ninth to the eleventh centuries. The design represents the Five Senses: Sight in the centre; Taste on the left; Smell on the right. Below are Hearing (left) and Feeling (right). Below is a pen case made of walrus ivory with glass inlays, carved with men, animals, birds and monsters. Its shape suggests that it was used to hold quill pens.

The beginnings of Anglo-Saxon England are poorly documented. After the Roman legions had been withdrawn, by 410, the whole structure of the Roman state rapidly disintegrated. During the fifth century a large part of lowland Britain passed to Anglo-Saxon control. The newcomers – Franks and Frisians, as well as the Angles, Saxons and Jutes from north-western Germany and Denmark – brought their own pagan gods, whose cult appears to have very largely replaced Christianity in lowland Britain by the end of the sixth century. The grave-goods of these pagan tribes, dating from the fifth to the

The 'Fuller brooch'
England
late 9th century AD
MLA 1952,4–4,1
diam. 11.4 cm (4½ in)
Purchased with the aid of
Captain A.W.F. Fuller

Walrus ivory pen case
City of London, England
mid-11th century AD
MLA 1870,8–11,1
l. 23.2 cm (9⅛ in)

Anglo-Saxon art

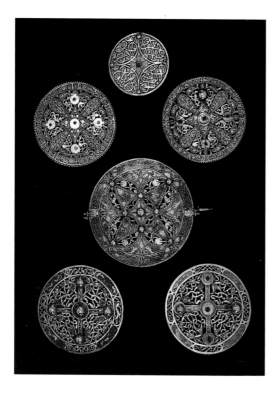

Six disc brooches (the
Pentney hoard)
Pentney, Norfolk, England
early 9th century AD
MLA 1980,10–8,1–6
diam. (largest brooch)
10.2 cm (4 in)
Treasure trove

seventh centuries, are exceptionally well represented in the Museum, supplemented by material from modern settlement excavations.

After the conversion of the English to Christianity following the arrival of St Augustine in 597, the practice of burying personal possessions with the dead gradually came to an end. Although from the mid-seventh century onwards fewer objects have survived, the finds include a high proportion of personal possessions, such as jewellery and weapons. In the sixth and seventh centuries there were many smaller kingdoms, but by the later eighth century three were predominant: Northumbria, Mercia and Wessex. In the ninth century territory was lost to the Viking raiders. Gradually the kings of Wessex took control, although between 1016 and 1042 the country was ruled by a succession of Scandinavian kings. The native dynasty was restored in the person of Edward the Confessor (1042–66), but after Edward's death came the Norman Conquest and the end of Anglo-Saxon England.

The roots of Anglo-Saxon art lie in Celtic, Mediterranean and Germanic tradition and display a strong emphasis on pattern, often based on animal and plant motifs and with highly stylized human figures. Particularly from the century before the Norman Conquest we find, however, a uniquely English style.

FURTHER READING
J. Backhouse, D.H. Turner, L. Webster (eds), *The Golden Age of Anglo-Saxon Art, 966–1066* (London, 1984)
L. Webster and J. Backhouse (eds), *The Making of England: Anglo-Saxon Art and Culture AD 600–900* (London, 1991)
D.M. Wilson, *Anglo-Saxon Art: from the 7th century to the Norman Conquest* (London, 1984)

Ankhwa the ship-builder

Alongside the massive and regal statues of the pharaohs of Egypt in the Museum's collections are to be found more intimate images of ordinary people, so-called 'private' sculptures, the earliest of which date to the Third Dynasty. Below is the red granite seated figure of the ship-builder Ankhwa, depicted holding a carpenter's adze over his shoulder. Private statuary was intended for the tomb and its main development follows closely the conventions set by royal sculpture. It was static, frontally posed, the features idealized.

The design was first marked out in red ochre on a rough block of stone of the size required, then the basic shape of the figure was blocked out without distinguishing face, arms or legs. This process and the modelling of the features were carried out with the use of guide lines in subsequent stages. Hardstone modelling was done by pounding with a ball of dolerite, and by rubbing with stones of various sizes in conjunction with an abrasive, probably quartz sand. Sawing and drilling with copper tools were also done with an abrasive. The final stages of the work consisted of modelling the features by light bruising and burnishing, followed by the addition of inscriptions and paint.

The figure bears a second name, probably to be read 'Bedjmes', carved to one side of the main line of text. It is likely that both names belonged to the same man.

FURTHER READING
T.G.H. James and W.V. Davies,
Egyptian Sculpture
(London, 1983)

The ship-builder Ankhwa
Probably from Saqqara, Egypt
late 3rd or early 4th Dynasty, *c.*2600 BC
EA 171
h. 64 cm (25⅛ in)
Purchased from Henry Salt, 1835

The **Armada Service**

The 'Armada Service' is the earliest known surviving set of English dining silver. It consists of 26 silver dishes, each having a rim engraved with the arms of Sir Christopher Harris of Radford, near Plymouth, Devon (*c.*1553–1625), and those of his second wife Mary Sydenham.

The name comes from a family tradition that it was made from New World silver captured from Spanish treasure ships around the time that the great armada of 1588 was sent by King Philip II of Spain against England. There is, however, no proven connection. Harris safeguarded booty from the Spanish ship *Madre de Dios* in 1592 for Sir Walter Raleigh (1552–1618), and a document appointing Harris commissioner of the booty signed by Lord Cecil (1520–98), Raleigh and Drake (*c.*1540–96), could be the basis for the tradition that Harris was repaid in kind.

The service was discovered on a farm near Brixton, Devon, in 1827. In 1645 Sir Christopher's heir, his great-nephew John Harris, was a Major-General of the royalist army unsuccessfully besieging Plymouth during the Civil War of 1640–49. Perhaps he, or a retainer, hid the family plate from the victorious Parliamentarians.

Dishes from the Armada Service
England
Silver, 1581, 1599, 1600, 1601
MLA 1992,6–14, 1–26
diam. 12.1–39.8 cm
(4¾–15⅔ in)
Purchased 1992 with the aid of the National Heritage Memorial Fund

The 'Armada Service', made by four different goldsmiths, bears London silver hallmarks for 1581, 1599, 1600 and 1601. The dishes are deep, a characteristic late sixteenth-century form. Much dining silver is recorded in the inventories of families both in England and on the Continent, but as most items were melted down this is the largest and most important group to survive from this period.

FURTHER READING
D. Thornton and M. Caveli, 'The "Armada Service": a set of late Tudor dining silver', *The Antiquaries Journal*, 76 (1996), pp. 153–80

The **Armento Rider**

The 'Armento Rider', which was found at Armento, Basilicata, southern Italy, is one of the most remarkable examples of Greek bronze-work of the sixth century BC. It is a reminder that the city-states of southern Italy were frequently at war, both amongst themselves and with the native Italic peoples whose territory they had usurped. On mainland Greece heavily armed cavalry was rare, but in southern Italy the wide plains allowed the rearing of fine horses and their deployment in battle. This beardless cavalryman would originally have held a spear in his left hand and carried a shield in his right, which would also have guided the reins. Stirrups were not yet in use. His helmet was once topped by a crest running from side to side.

Trade and the search for raw materials, especially metal, first brought the Greeks into contact with the rich natural resources of Italy. It was not until after c.730 BC that they also began to exploit the agricultural potential of the coastal plains of southern Italy and Sicily and began to found colonies as independent city-states. With them the settlers brought their language and writing, their art and craftsmanship (including skilled bronze-working), their religion and their way of life. Many of the colonies prospered greatly, and later Greeks were to call the area Megale Hellas (Great Greece).

The 'Armento Rider'
Basilicata, southern Italy
Bronze, c.550 BC
GR 1904.7–3.1
h. 23.6 cm (9¼ in)

This well-preserved bronze with its beautiful light green patina is solid cast, as hollow-casting was not yet in common use. It was probably made in Taranto, Apulia. The horse and the rider are separately modelled and detachable. The Museum has a rich collection of bronze statuettes from southern Italy, of which this is one of the finest.

FURTHER READING
C. Rolley, *Greek Bronzes*
(London, 1986)

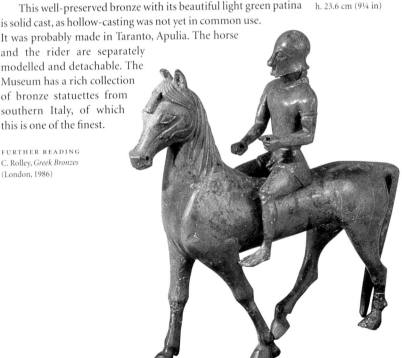

Armour

Armour is body covering designed for protection in combat, and since men have fought from the earliest times it is one of the oldest of artefacts. For the greater part of its history only excavated fragments of armour survive, although its appearance is indicated by drawings. Greek vases and Assyrian reliefs are a particularly rich source among the Museum's holdings. Although the Museum does not have a systematic collection of armour from more modern times, a number of ancient items are to be found in the collections. Below is a Greek helmet of Corinthian type, familiar from vase paintings, with nose-guard and cheek pieces, made from a single sheet of bronze. It was apparently lost by a member of the Etruscan forces defeated by the Syracusans and their allies at the naval battle

Bronze helmet
Corinth, Greece
c.460 BC
GR 1824.4–7.32;
Bronze 251
h. 25.4 cm (10 in)
Richard Payne Knight
Bequest

Suit of armour
Japan
17th/18th/19th century AD
(Momoyama/Edo period)
OA+ 13545
h. 1.25 m (4 ft 1¼ in)

Armour

that took place off Cumae in 474 BC; the inscription on the helmet records its dedication to Zeus at Olympia by Hieron, ruler of Syracuse, and his people, as Etruscan spoils from Cumae. From Egypt comes one of the strangest sets of armour in the collection, a crocodile-skin suit found in the so-called crocodile grottoes in Middle Egypt near modern Manfalut. This is not an article of everyday wear, but a parade suit for special ceremonial occasions associated with the crocodile cult, which was popular with Roman soldiers in the area. The Ribchester parade helmet (p. 269) from Britain was also designed for ceremony, not battle. Another elaborate piece is the helmet from the Sutton Hoo treasure (p. 313).

From more modern times comes a suit of Japanese armour (previous page) with a thick steel-plate bullet-proof cuirass.

Below is a set of African horse armour taken during or shortly after the Battle of Omdurman in the Sudan (1898). Such quilted armour, padded with the fibre of the silk cotton tree, was traditionally worn by the heavy cavalry of the great Sudanic African empires.

FURTHER READING
C. Spring, *African Arms and Armour* (London, 1993)
M. Pfaffenbichler, *Medieval Craftsmen: Armourers* (London, 1991)

Quilted horse armour taken during or shortly after the battle of **Omdurman**
Sudan
c.AD 1898
ETH 1899.12–13.2
h. 135 cm (53 in)
Given by Major Maxse

In 1888, at Hawara, the excavator W.M. Flinders Petrie described 'a procession of three gilt mummies . . . glittering in the sun'. Below is one of the three, a haunting portrait of a young man named Artemidorus. This is a face from the past, almost certainly a good likeness of the young man before his premature death, probably around AD 100–120. The portrait is painted on limewood in encaustic (a mixture of pigment and beeswax) with a hardening agent such as resin or egg, the exact technique of which has been lost. The portraits were made to cover the heads of the elaborately bandaged, mummified bodies of the dead.

The largest number of such portraits has been found in the Egyptian Fayum. The individuals depicted were probably the descendants of Greek mercenaries who had fought for Alexander the Great and his successors, the early Ptolemies, and who were granted land in the Fayum after it had been drained for agricultural use. The colonists settled and married local women, adopting Egyptian religious beliefs. By the time of the Roman conquest in 31 BC the population of the area was very mixed. To Roman eyes the descendants of the colonists were Egyptians, but in their own view they were Greeks. It was, however, Egyptian beliefs and burial practices which they adopted. Among the scenes shown on this coffin is the Egyptian god Anubis attending the mummy, which is laid out on a bier in the form of a lion, probably with the goddesses Nephthys at the head and Isis at the foot. Beneath, Thoth and Re-Horakhty flank the fetish of Osiris associated with his cult-centre at Abydos. Below, the god Osiris, on a funerary bier, reawakens to a new life. The inscription is in Greek and though misspelled reads 'Farewell Artemidorus'.

Painted stucco
mummy portrait of
Artemidorus
Hawara, Egypt
AD 100–120
EA 21810
h. 171 cm (67⅓ in)
Presented by H. Martyn
Kennard, 1888

FURTHER READING
S. Walker and M. Bierbrier, *Ancient Faces. Mummy Portraits from Roman Egypt* (London, 1997)

Asante goldwork Africa (Ghana)

The wealth of the great kingdom of Asante in Ghana on the west coast of Africa was based on its vast gold deposits. Gold casting was well established there by the late fifteenth century. T.E. Bowdich visited the capital at Kumase in 1817 and described the scene thus:

> The sun was reflected, with a glare scarcely more supportable than the heat, from the massy gold ornaments ... Some wore necklaces reaching to the navel entirely of aggry beads; a band of gold and beads encircled the knee, from which several strings of the same depended; small circles of gold like guineas, rings, and casts of animals, were strung round their ancles; ... manillas, and rude lumps of rock gold, hung from their left wrists, which were so heavily laden as to be supported on the head of one of their handsomest boys.

Ceremonial umbrella fitting
Asante, Ghana
Wood covered in sheet gold, 19th century AD
ETH Af.1934,1
h. 26.5 cm (10⅖ in)
Purchased (Christy Fund)

Bowdich collected a number of items which came to the Museum – gold castings, pottery, leatherwork and a wooden stool. Other superb pieces were acquired later in the century. Virtually all royal insignia made use of cast gold, using the 'lost-wax' method.

The most striking items of regalia were the multi-coloured umbrellas (*kyinie*) used to shade senior chiefs in public; they had probably been used in Asante long before 1817. They were used to keep the chief physically cool but also to promote a condition of spiritual peace and coolness and to create around him a particular symbolic space. The *Asantehene* (king) was covered with an umbrella whenever he left the palace and when he moved from one part to another, even at night. When a chief walked, his umbrella-bearer made the umbrella 'dance' to the music of the drums and horns that accompanied his chief, sounding his praise-names and recounting his deeds.

The umbrellas seen and described by Bowdich were topped by a variety of detachable images (*kyinie akyi*) – war horns, pelicans, elephants, barrels, swords. Shown here is an umbrella top in the form of a carving of five *sankofu* birds.

FURTHER READING
M.D. McLeod, *The Asante* (London, 1981)

The excavator Austen Henry Layard wrote on the discovery of one of these creatures:

> They had awed and instructed races which flourished 3000 years ago. Through the portals which they guarded, kings, priests, and warriors had borne sacrifices to their altars. . . . For twenty-five centuries they had been hidden from the eye of man, and they now stood forth once more in their ancient majesty. . . . Above the spacious hall in which they stood, the plough had passed and the corn now waved.

Until the 1840s the cities of Assyria, in what is now Iraq but was then part of the Ottoman Empire, had long been buried and forgotten. The first major excavations were carried out by the French Consul at Mosul, Paul-Emile Botta (1802–70), who dug at Kuyunjik (ancient Nineveh) and Khorsabad (Dur Sharrukin). He was followed by Austen Henry Layard (1817–94), working for the Museum, who during the years 1845–7 and 1849–51 discovered at

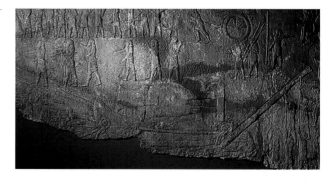

Relief of a winged bull
for Sennacherib's palace
South-West Palace,
Nineveh, Assyria
*c.*700 BC
WA 124823; 1859–9–2, 3
h. 1.35 m (4 ft 5½ in)

Nimrud (Kalhu) the North-West Palace of King Ashurnasirpal, the adjoining temples of Ishtar and Ninurta and the Central Palace of Tiglath-pileser III. At Nineveh (Kuyunjik) he discovered the South-West Palace of King Sennacherib. He also excavated at Ashur, Khorsabad and Nebi Yunus.

The Museum now has six gateway figures – a pair of lions and a bull and a lion from different doorways, from the North-West Palace at Nimrud (*c.*865–860 BC), and a pair of bulls from Khorsabad (*c.*710 BC). The Khorsabad pair, one of which is seen opposite, were purchased for the Museum in 1846 by Henry Creswicke Rawlinson (1810–95). The figures from Nimrud are from Layard's excavations.

A human-headed winged or wingless bull is a common motif in Mesopotamian art from the Early Dynastic period through to Neo-Babylonian times (the sixth century BC). During the time of the Assyrian Empire, as in earlier times throughout Mesopotamia,

Assyrian gateway figures

doors and gateways were looked on as vital points through which both evil and beneficial influences might find entry. The building of entrances was accompanied by elaborate ceremonies and names of good omen were bestowed upon them. The annals of the Assyrian kings make it clear that the colossal figures, half-man, half-animal, which were set up on either side of important palace entrances from the time of Ashurnasirpal II (*r*.883–859 BC) to Esarhaddon (*r*.680–669 BC), were there not only to adorn the building and impress the visitors but also to guard. An inscription of Esarhaddon records:

> Protecting colossal figures of stone which by their appearance ward off evil, guarding the footfall, protecting the path of the King their maker, I placed to the right and left of the thresholds.

The figures are thought to have been called by the Assyrians *alad-lammu* or *lamassu*. They were carved out of a single block of marble (gypsum), roughly shaped in the quarry and then transported to their final destination for the finished carving to be done. Reliefs from Sennacherib's South-West Palace at Nineveh show the quarrying of an immense piece of marble and (opposite) the transport of a roughly carved winged bull. The figures wear ropes, like other protective spirits, and a horned cap, the distinctive headdress of divinity. They have five legs: seen from the side, four; from the front, two. Beside or behind each colossal figure there was frequently a winged spirit carved in stone carrying the magic cone and bucket. The statues most probably were painted.

Human-headed winged bull and attendant genie
Khorsabad (Dur Sharrukin), Assyria
c.710 BC
WA 118809;
1850–12–28, 4
h. 4.42 m (14 ft 6 in)
Purchased (Henry Rawlinson)

FURTHER READING
D. Collon, *Ancient Near Eastern Art* (London, 1995)
A.H. Layard, *Nineveh and its Remains* (London, 1853)
J. Reade, *Assyrian Sculpture* (2nd edn, London, 1998)

The origins of the great Assyrian Empire lie in the old trading and cult centre of Ashur, built on a hill overlooking the River Tigris in what is now northern Iraq. It became independent from the Sumerian Empire around 2000 BC. About 300 years later Shamshi-Adad took over the city and extended its territory north-wards to Nineveh and westward as far as the Euphrates, creating a formidable kingdom.

From *c*.1300 BC a succession of able kings began to transform Ashur into a first-rate political power. Strategically situated on main trade routes, Assyria was always at risk from her neighbours. In the mid-thirteenth century under Tukulti-Ninurta I the Assyri-

Relief of Tiglath-pileser III
South-West Palace, Nimrud
(Kalhu)
730–727 BC
WA 118908; 1851–9–2, 498
h. 1.88 m (6 ft 2 in)
Excavated by A.H. Layard

ans temporarily conquered Babylon and reached the Persian Gulf. In the twelfth century the great Tiglath-pileser I revived his coun-try's fortunes, his armies victorious in Syria and Babylon. His murder put an end to this glorious period.

Assyria re-emerged in 911 BC with the advent of Adad-Nirari II who recovered lost territories, advancing into Kurdistan and defeating Babylon. At his death the king's territories covered all of what is now northern Iraq. Almost every year the terrible Assyrian armies would set out with fire and sword, putting down rebellion, amassing booty and extending the territories subservient to their god Ashur.

Stela of Ashurnasirpal II
Temple of Ninurta,
Nimrud (Kalhu)
865–860 BC
WA 118805; 1851–9–1, 32
h. *c*.2.94 m (9 ft 7¾ in)
Given by King Edward VII

The king was absolute monarch. Access to his presence was limited, but he might concern himself with decisions at any administrative level. He was not a mere secular ruler; he was high priest of the god Ashur, and his traditional duty was to maintain and extend the borders of the god's territory.

As Assyria became stronger these territories began to encroach upon those of powerful neighbours – Urartu, Iran, Elam and Egypt. In *c*.875 BC King Ashurnasirpal's armies reached the Mediterranean coast. His successor Shalmaneser III secured the inland cities of Syria and suppressed a Chaldean rebellion to the south.

Assyrian kings

In 879 BC Ashurnasirpal II moved the capital from Ashur to Kalhu (Nimrud). There was a pause after 825 BC and by 745 BC the empire was under threat from the expanding northern power of Urartu (classical Armenia). During the reign of Tiglath-pileser III Assyria recovered lost territories and by the king's death the empire extended from the borders of Egypt to southern Babylonia. Assyria tended to avoid direct rule but was merciless in putting down revolt and in transporting entire populations. The capital moved briefly to Khorsabad in *c.*710 BC. Sennacherib's capital with its 'Incomparable Palace' was from *c.*700 at Nineveh. For most of the seventh century BC Assyria controlled the Middle East; Egypt was conquered at last, albeit briefly. Ashurbanipal defeated Elam to the south and Babylon, but the empire became increasingly vulnerable to internal and external threats. The final collapse came in 614 BC when a joint force of Medes and Babylonians attacked Ashur. In 612 this alliance captured and sacked Nineveh.

The story of these years, the triumphs of the Assyrian kings in war and peace, their exploits in the hunting field, and the gods who watched over them, were recorded in stone on the walls of the royal palaces. The king can usually be distinguished by his royal hat, reserved for him alone. From the side its shape is that of a truncated cone, with a diadem around it and a smaller cone or knob on top. The Museum has an outstanding collection of reliefs and statues of the kings of Assyria. They include (opposite) a relief of Tiglath-pileser III (745–727 BC) standing in his state chariot under a parasol. Above is a fortified city on a mound. The cuneiform inscription identifies it as Astartu, the Biblical Ashtaroth Karnaim in Gilead. This capitulation probably took place in 733–732 BC when Tiglath-pileser invaded Syria and Israel (II Kings xv.25–29). There is also (below) a court scene showing Ashurnasirpal II, and (opposite) a stela of the same king (883–859 BC), erected 879–878 BC or possibly later, in which the helmet decorated with horns represents the supreme god Ashur; the winged disc to its left stands for the sun god Shamash; the crescent within a full circle is the emblem of the moon god Sin; the undulating forked line is the thunderbolt of Adad the storm god; Astarte, the planet Venus, signifies Ishtar, goddess of love and war.

Court scene: Ashurnasir-pal II enthroned between attendants, flanked by a pair of winged protective spirits
Traces of paint remain on the sandals
North-West Palace, Nimrud (Kalhu)
*c.*865–860 BC
WA 124564–6;
1850–12–28,8, 9
h. 269.24 cm (8 ft 10 in)
Excavated by A.H. Layard

FURTHER READING
P. Bienkowski and A. Millard (eds), *British Museum Dictionary of the Ancient Near East* (London, 2000)

Astrolabes

The astrolabe was the most important astronomical instrument of the Middle Ages. One of its chief uses was to tell the time, but it was also used for terrestrial measurements. Astrolabes are complex disc-shaped instruments, usually made of brass. They comprise mathematical models of the heavens used to compute (1) the position of the sun and selected stars; (2) the apparent daily and yearly movements of the sun and selected stars; (3) the altitude of the heavenly bodies and thence, by calculation, the time of day; and (4) the height of terrestrial objects.

The astrolabe has four basic parts. The mater or mother is a thick circular plate. On the back of it, which is marked with calendar and zodiacal as well as hour and degree scales, the alidade (rotating rule) is used for sighting an object or star. On the front is a circular recess into which fit the two other parts. These are plates engraved for different latitudes and the rete, a pierced plate with a stereographic projection of the celestial sphere and the chosen fixed stars indicated by decoratively cut pointers, which fits over the plate.

The astrolabe was first described by the Greeks, but the earliest surviving examples are Arabic versions of the ninth and tenth centuries AD. The oldest known dates from AD 984/5 (374 AH). By the thirteenth century the astrolabe was known from India to Islamic Spain. From the Arabs the knowledge of making and using astrolabes was brought back to Europe. The Museum has a considerable collection of some 50 astrolabes. Its founding collection included what is probably the most beautiful example in the Museum, the fine brass astrolabe with silver inlay constructed by Abd al-Ali, son of Muhammed Rafi al Juzil, and decorated by his brother Muhammed Baqir for the Safavid ruler Shah Sultan Husayn, dated AD 1712/13 (left). The collections include the earliest recorded European dated scientific instrument with a signature, an astrolabe made in England in 1342 and inscribed *Blakeni me fecit Anno.Do. 1342* ('Blakene made me, AD 1342').

Brass astrolabe with silver inlay
Persia
AD 1712/13
OA. OA+ 369
h. 53 cm (20¾ in)
Sir Hans Sloane Bequest

FURTHER READING
R.T. Gunther, *Astrolabes of the World*, vols I–II (reprinted London, 1976)
H. Michel, *Traité de l'Astrolabe* (Paris, 1947)
H.N. Saunders, *All the Astrolabes* (Oxford, 1984)

Athenian tombstones

Since burial within the walls of Athens itself was forbidden, cemeteries lined the roads outside the city walls, where graves were designed to impress passers-by. In the walled garden plots of wealthy families were tombstones (*stelai*) of various shapes: tall shafts with floral crowns, sculptured figures with shrines (*naiskoi*) and marble copies of clay funerary vases. Figure scenes in relief often decorated these *stelai*. Family groups were popular, many including the theme of the clasping of hands, a gesture whose significance might be either parting at death or the hope of reunion beyond the grave. Family plots were expensive: one cost 2500 times the daily wage of an oarsman in the fleet. The less wealthy tried to copy the rich by having the furnishings of a costly memorial carved on a single tombstone, but in 317/316 BC the use of all but the simplest was banned.

Stele of Melitta
Athens,
4th/2nd century BC
GR 1909.2–21.1;
BM Inscriptions 942
h. 94 cm (37 in)
Given by Messrs Cubitt

The Museum has a number of these tombstones. Especially touching is the relief of a woman (Sculpture 2232) who sits and gazes off into the distance as a nurse holds the baby she has left behind. The tombstone shown here has a particularly poignant inscription which commemorates Hippostrate's nurse. The original stone was made in Athens in the fourth century BC and reused for Melitta in the second century BC. Melitta is shown seated with the word 'nurse' below. The inscription reads:

Here the earth covers Hippostrate's best
    nurse
and now she longs for you. When you were
    alive I used
to love you and even now you are below the
    earth I honour you.
I shall honour you as long as I live. And I
    know that if there
is a reward for the best people even below
    the earth, the first
honours in the house of Persephone and
    Pluto will be given, nurse, to you.

FURTHER READING
C.W. Clairmont, *Classical Attic Tombstones*
(Kilchberg, 1993)
R. Garland, *The Greek Way of Death* (London, 1985)
D.C. Kurtz and J. Boardman, *Greek Burial Customs*
(London, 1971)

Portraits of **Augustus**,
Emperor of Rome

Rome, late 1st century BC–early 1st century AD

S uetonius described the Emperor Augustus thus:

Throughout his life, his appearance was distinguished and graceful. He did not dress extravagantly and cared little about his hair. . . . He had few teeth, which were small and dirty . . . his eyebrows and his nose jutted out and then turned inwards. He was . . . rather short but with well-proportioned limbs. On his body were spots, birthmarks and calluses caused by excessive use of the strigil. . . . He sometimes limped.

Augustus was born in 63 BC as Gaius Octavius (Octavian), great-nephew and adopted son of Julius Caesar. After Caesar's murder in 44 BC, Octavian founded a triumvirate with Mark Antony and Lepidus (42 BC); he subsequently defeated Antony and Cleopatra of Egypt in a civil war, leaving him with supreme power. He was given the name 'Augustus' by the Roman Senate in 27 BC and died in AD 14.

Augustus considered his image a matter of importance and no attempt was made to portray him as described by Suetonius. The earliest portraits show him bearded in mourning for his murdered great-uncle. In the ensuing years of civil war Octavian's portrait became influenced by images of Hellenistic rulers of the Eastern Mediterranean. After he took the name Augustus the emperor's portrait was modified to reflect political changes at Rome.

Over 250 statues of Augustus have survived. He appears larger than life, with perfect proportions based upon Classical Greek notions of ideal human form. Above is a bronze head from an over-life-sized statue found at Meroë in the Sudan. It was probably made in Egypt, decapitated by raiding Meroitic tribesmen and carried off for burial under the steps of a temple commemorating the successful raids. On the right is a three-layered sardonyx cameo portrait of Augustus wearing the protective *aegis* of Zeus with the heads of Phobos (Fear) and Medusa. The Museum has a number of other portraits, including those on coins of his reign.

ABOVE **Head of Augustus**
Meroë (Nubia)
*c.*27–25 BC
GR 1911.9–1.1
h. 47.75 cm (18¾ in)
Given by the Sudan Excavation Committee aided by the National Art Collections Fund

RIGHT **Cameo portrait of Augustus**
Roman
*c.*AD 14–20
GR 1867.5–7.484;
Gem 3577
h. 12.8 cm (5 in)
Purchased (Strozzi and Blacas Collections)

FURTHER READING
S. Walker, *Greek and Roman Portraits* (London, 1995), pp. 61–71
P. Zanker (trans. A. Shapiro), *The Power of Images in the Age of Augustus* (Ann Arbor, 1988)

Australian Aboriginal paintings Australia, 20th century AD

The Aboriginal people of Australia lived by hunting, gathering and, in some areas, fishing; for the most part they moved in small bands across vast territories, living off the land as they went. To survive they developed a subtle and deep understanding of their natural environment. European impact had a devastating effect on Aboriginal societies, dispossessing and destroying many, and radically affecting most of the remainder. However, there has been a recent revival of Aboriginal culture. The Museum has acquired a number of collections of contemporary Aboriginal art which, although it often employs modern materials, also uses motifs that refer back to the long-standing Aboriginal concern with the land. Land in Aboriginal thinking is significant not simply as a resource but also as physical evidence of the formative Dreamtime period, during which Ancestral Beings are thought to have travelled across the country, creating its distinctive features and allocating it to different groups. Below is an acrylic painting from Yuendumu in the Western Desert area of Australia's Northern Territory.

The Museum also has a substantial collection of Australian Aboriginal ethnography dating back as far as 1798. Much of this includes weapons, tools and hunting equipment which reflect the material culture of the country's original inhabitants.

FURTHER READING
Australian Gallery Directors' Council,
Aboriginal Australia (Sydney, 1981)
W. Caruana, *Aboriginal Art*
(London, 1993)
P. Sutton (ed.), *Dreamings: The Art of Aboriginal Australia* (Victoria, 1988)

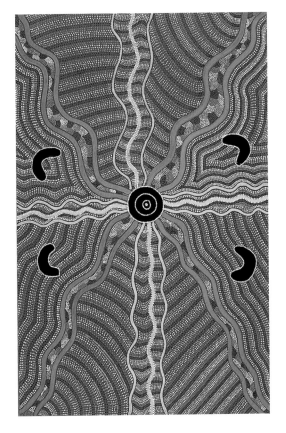

Bush Potato Dreaming
Yuendumu, Northern
Territory, Australia
Acrylic paint on canvas,
1986
ETH 1987.Oc.4.7
145 × 94 cm (57 × 37 in)
Purchased
(Warlukurlangu Artists'
Association)

Possibly the best-known Kassite artefacts are the so-called 'boundary stones' or *kudurru*, irregularly shaped stone boulders, with a text and divine symbols or figures of kings. These formed permanent records of land ownership and privileges. They occur from the fourteenth century BC onwards and are most plentiful in the twelfth century BC.

Little is known of their language, but the Kassites seem to have entered Babylonia by 1500 BC from the mountains to the northeast. For over two centuries the Kassite empire was one of the great powers of the Near East, exchanging ambassadors with the Hittites and Egyptians. It fell to the Elamites from south-west Iran under King Shutruk-Nahhunte I in *c.*1157 BC.

Stone *kudurru*
Babylonia
1099–1082 BC
WA 90841; 1863–8–26,1
h. 61 cm (24 in)
Given by Sir Arnold
Kemball

While the form of the *kudurru* suggests that it originated as a field marker, most examples were elaborately carved, and they have usually been found in temples where they were deposited for safekeeping. The sun, moon and star symbolize Shamash, Sin and Ishtar (Venus), major Mesopotamian sky-gods who witness and guarantee the legal grant. Additional symbols refer to other gods and celestial powers, including precursors of the signs of the zodiac (p. 366).

The Museum has 24 *kudurru*. On the left is an example from the reign of Marduk-nadin-ahhe (*r.*1099–1082 BC) which records a purchase of land by a royal officer, Marduk-naṣir. The value is given in silver, but was paid in the form of a chariot, equipment, clothes, animals and food. Curses are invoked on anyone who attempts to invalidate the sale or damage the stone. The name of the stone, carved just to the right of the figure of the king, was 'The Establisher of the Boundary for ever'. King Marduk-nadin-ahhe holds a bow and two arrows and wears quilted slippers and a feather-topped Babylonian crown, decorated with rosettes, winged bulls and a tree. Above the king are divine symbols and a snake which divides the scene from the text on the back and sides.

FURTHER READING
L.W. King, *Babylonian Boundary-Stones and Memorial Tablets in the British Museum*, 2 vols (London, 1912)

Baccarat glass ewer

This dramatic ewer was among the star pieces shown by the firm of Baccarat at the Paris Universal Exhibition of 1878. The exhibition, the largest held up to then, was attended by 13 million paying visitors and was an event which signalled France's recovery from the war against Prussia of 1870–1.

The ewer is free-blown, its spout the gaping mouth of a grotesque sea-monster's mask. Wheel-engraved decoration suggests the monster's scaly body terminating in entwined tails wreathed with ivy. This ewer was created as a show-off piece, combining technical virtuosity with a stunningly original design. The inspiration comes from the engraved rock-crystal vessels with fantastic ornament in the so-called 'Mannerist' taste of the early seventeenth century displayed at the Louvre since the Napoleonic period. The finished result is, however, entirely nineteenth-century in conception. Baccarat, based in Paris with factories in Lorraine, was known for its high-quality cut and engraved glassware.

This is part of a choice collection of nineteenth-century decorative art, much, although not all, acquired in recent years. The collection is international in scope and comprises ceramics, glass, metalwork and jewellery, fields in which the Museum has traditionally collected (furniture and textiles of this period are to be found in the Victoria and Albert Museum). Strengths of the collection include an outstanding group of work by Christopher Dresser and a remarkable selection of material illustrating the nineteenth-century passion for earlier historic styles. The Gothic and Renaissance revivals can be studied through objects from many European countries, while the influence in the West of the arts of Islam and the Far East takes in America as well, with a fine group of jewellery and silver in the Japanese taste by Tiffany of New York.

Engraved glass ewer
Baccarat, Lorraine, France
c.AD 1878
MLA 1991,7–2, 1
h. 31.9 cm (12½ in)

FURTHER READING
J.-L. Curtis, *Baccarat* (London, 1992)
J. Rudoe, *Decorative Arts 1850–1950. A Catalogue of the British Museum Collection* (2nd edn, London, 1994), cat. 363
D. Sautot, *Baccarat, une histoire 1764 …* (Paris, 1993)

'America Needs
Goldwater and Miller'
political campaign badge
USA
Aluminium, 1964
CM M8913
6.3 × 8.2 cm (2½ × 3¼ in)
Given by
W. W. Woodside

'England expects every
man to do his duty'
patriotic badge
England
Aluminium disk with
brass pin, 1900
CM 1906–6–28–1
diam. 2.1 cm (⅘ in)
Parkes-Weber Gift

The badge – political and apolitical – is an important and increasingly nostalgic symbol of the late twentieth century with its succinct and often witty text or illustration: Ban the Bomb, Save the Whale, Rats have Rights, Stop Acid Rain, and many more, some obscure, some still relevant. The badge chronicles major and minor events such as the Vietnam War and the Olympic Games, strikes and protest marches, consumer goods and fashions, elections and jubilees, sporting triumphs and failures, changes of government and governments trying to avoid change.

The forerunner of the political button badge, the election medal, first appeared in 1807, handed out to voters in the Parliamentary election for the constituency of Yorkshire. It was the brainchild of the manufacturer Edward Thomason, whose Birmingham factory turned out 50,000 in cheap metal alloy. The election medal enjoyed great popularity during the following two decades and continued in use throughout the nineteenth century until it was superseded in the United States by the cheaper plastic button badge in the 1880s and 1890s. Campaign medals had been in use in America since the 1820s, when Andrew Jackson had been labelled the 'Hero of New Orleans'. In 1860 Abraham Lincoln was the first politician to use badges incorporating photographic portraits of himself.

The Museum has a series of American presidential campaign badges beginning with Horatio Seymour in 1868, and including Taft, Hoover, Eisenhower, Kennedy and Nixon. Another type was the mass-produced enamelled badge. One of the earliest party organizations to make use of these was the Primrose League, founded in 1883 and named after Disraeli's favourite flower.

Although the Museum had been collecting badges since 1861 it was not until the 1970s and 1980s that a concerted attempt was made to acquire an extensive collection. This does not aim to be either comprehensive or especially representative, but it does reflect the major political and social changes, particularly in Britain and the United States, of those years.

'Perestroika' political
badge
USSR
Brass, early 1989
CM 1990–6–28–1
diam. 2.9 cm (1⅕ in)

FURTHER READING

P. Attwood, *Badges* (London, 2004)

P. Attwood, *Acquisition of Badges (1978–1982)*, British Museum Occasional Paper No. 55 (London, 1985); *Acquisition of Badges (1983–1987)*, British Museum Occasional Paper No. 76 (London, 1990)

F. S. Setchfield, *The Official Badge Collector's Guide from the 1890s to the 1980s* (Harlow, 1986)

The **Balawat gates**

The Assyrian kings often speak of setting up 'gates of shining bronze'. In the Museum are replicas of the great gates from the palace of Shalmaneser III (858–824 BC) at Balawat (Imgur-Enlil), a small but unique site in Iraq near Mosul, where there was also a temple to Mamu, god of dreams. Tablets inform us that the gates were made of fragrant cedar wood; they were hung on huge cedarwood trunks capped with bronze and turning in stone sockets. Several different workmen were involved – the designs show great variety in the details and workmanship. When they were discovered in 1878 by Hormuzd Rassam the wood had completely rotted away, leaving the bronze fragments now in the Museum.

The original gates, perhaps 6.8 m (7½ yd) high, had 16 horizontal bronze bands approximately 27 cm (10½ in) high, eight on each doorleaf. They are embossed with two friezes representing Shalmaneser's campaigns during the first ten years of his reign, identified by cuneiform inscriptions. Enemies are defeated in open battle or attacked in their towns, prisoners are executed or led away under escort, the Assyrians offer sacrifices and set up memorial stelae. The campaigns include the submissions of the princes of Urartu (in the area of Lake Van in eastern Turkey) (p. 343), the Aramaeans of Bit Adini on the Upper Euphrates, the city of Hamath in Syria, and the princes of southern Babylonia.

Replica of one band from the gates of the palace of Shalmaneser at Balawat
Bronze, 858–824 BC
WA 124658
h. c.27 cm (10½ in)

Rassam also found a second smaller pair, set up by Ashurnasirpal II (883–859 BC), evidently also belonging to another small residence. Each doorleaf consisted of eight bands, decorated by embossing and chasing, the subjects being either military or hunting. From cuneiform inscriptions we learn that royal hunts of the wild ox took place on the Euphrates, lion-hunts on the river Balih in North Syria. The appearance of the Aramaeans – bearded bowmen wearing short kilts – is of particular interest; it is the oldest illustration of that people, hitherto only to be found depicted in later Assyrian sculptures of Tiglath-pileser, Sennacherib and Ashurbanipal, showing Chaldaeans.

Detail of the capture of the city Kulisi from the Balawat gates
Balawat, near Nimrud, Assyria
858–824 BC
WA 124656
Excavated by H. Rassam

FURTHER READING
R.D. Barnett, *Assyrian Palace Reliefs* (London, 1970)

Balinese kites

K ite-flying in Bali is traditionally an important social and religious occupation. On the religious plane it marks the linking of earth and heaven and protects the rice crop; socially, it involves furious competition between young men's groups in different villages. Traditional Balinese kites are of three kinds: *bebean* ('fish' kites), *pecukan* ('pinched' kites) and *janggan* ('dragon' kites). *Bebean* tend to be between 2.75 and 4.5 metres (9–15 ft) long, of cloth-covered bamboo, and are normally flown by a team of some 15 men. Their chief attraction is the incorporation of two bull-roarers that emit a loud whirring sound as the kite flies. *Pecukan* are usually about 2.75 metres (9 ft) across and leaf-shaped. They are more acrobatic than *bebean*, have a different 'voice', and are much harder to control and launch. *Janggan* are the rarest and most sacred; their tails may stretch for 18 metres (60 ft) and they incorporate the head of a dragon at the front.

Modern kite in the form of a sailing ship
Bali, Indonesia
Wood, bamboo and nylon
ETH 1997.As. 41.3
l. approx. 1 m (3¼ ft)

Small boys' kites often fight against each other directly, each seeking to cut through the opponent's strings, and it is the skills acquired here that are used later in men's kites. As well as the traditional rivalry between small communities, the Lomba Layang-Layang kite-flying festival is an annual event that attracts a large international audience from all over South-East Asia. The competition includes a section for fantasy kites that are judged by aesthetic criteria, although they may retain religious connotations. Balinese kites take incredibly ingenious forms: a three-masted schooner, giant flies, a Saturn V rocket with rotating engines, Hindu deities riding in helicopters, dragonflies, frogs, multiple windmills, butterflies.

The Museum's recently acquired collection of Balinese kites, together with photographs and descriptions of their use, typifies the work of the Department of Ethnography which aims to preserve a record of the activities of traditional societies in a changing world.

Balkan costume

In 1971 the Museum acquired a major ethnographic collection of over 300 items from Bulgaria, including metalwork, pottery, woodwork, ritual masks, domestic textiles and jewellery. Most striking are 12 complete costumes dating from the end of the nineteenth or early twentieth century which come from all the main regions of the country. Since 1992 a number of purchases and gifts have contributed further Bulgarian costumes, with, in addition, outstanding examples from the former Yugoslavia (particularly FYR Macedonia). These date from the late nineteenth century to the 1970s.

Almost all the Museum's current holdings of Balkan costume are women's festive outfits, some now very rare, worn at weddings and on church feast days. Many are extraordinarily elaborate and adorned with fine embroidery; a complete bride's outfit from Mariovo in FYR Macedonia, for example, is made up of 11 separate garments and weighs almost 50 kg (110 lb). Men's outfits, however, are traditionally more restricted in variety of style and ornamentation.

The majority of the garments were made from locally produced materials – flax, hemp, cotton and wool – which would largely have been processed, woven, dyed, sewn and decorated in the home by women. The basic form of traditional Balkan dress is similar across a wide region, but the immense variety in detail, which marks out the wearer's region, village of origin or ethnic group, is astonishing. The finest women's costumes would have been passed down from mother to daughter, the younger generation adding decorative details to personalize the garments.

FURTHER READING
E. Ivancich Dunin, *Dance Occasions and Festive Dress in Yugoslavia* (Los Angeles, 1984)
E. Kwasnik (ed.) *Bulgaria: tradition and beauty* (Liverpool, 1989)
N. Pantelic, *Traditional Arts and Crafts in Yugoslavia* (Belgrade, 1984)

Woman's festive costume
Kyustendil, Bulgaria
early 20th century
P&E 1993.Eu.7.34–40
Waller Lumley Collection
Purchased with the support of the British Museum Society (East European Purchase Fund)

Banquets

Although most of the objects in the Museum portray, or belong to, people long dead, they are by no means gloomy but in many instances demonstrate the pleasures of life. A particular human enjoyment is eating and drinking in company, to the accompaniment of entertainment and talk. Shown opposite is an Egyptian banquet from the tomb of Nebamun (*c*.1325 BC) (p. 225). At the beginning of the feast guests would be offered flowered garlands by servants. They were also given scented cones of wax for their hair. Guests sat at small tables at which they were served with fruit and wine, the hosts and honoured guests on chairs, others on stools or cushions. During the meal musicians played, singers sang and dancers would perform.

A more sinister occasion is that portrayed in the Assyrian relief below, which shows what at first appears to be a royal party in a peaceful garden with birds and a locust on the trees. The king has left his weapons on a table. He reclines on a sofa below a trellised vine and his queen sits facing him. They are drinking and there are refreshments, including perhaps a bunch of onions, on the table.

Ashurbanipal's garden party
North Palace, Nineveh, Assyria
Gypsum relief, *c*.650 BC
WA 124920; 1856–9–9, 53
h. 56 cm (22 in)
Excavated by H. Rassam.

Eunuchs and court ladies fan the royal couple. Others, shown on other slabs in the sequence, bring food or play music, using harps, a lyre, drums, pipes and a lute. The queen wears a crown like a castle, decorated with towers and crenellations, and a richly ornamented, fringed dress. In her left hand she holds a bunch of flowers and in her right an ornamental cup. The king lies on a couch decorated with leaping and reclining lions. At either end of this stand incense burners, perhaps a precaution against the stench, for on the tree in front of the harpist hangs a human head, that of the Elamite king Teumman, defeated at the battle of Til Tuba (p. 328). High-ranking Elamites are among those forced to wait on the king. This is the earliest securely dated example of a reclining banquet, which the Greeks and Romans adopted from the east.

Banquets

Below is a Greek bronze of the sixth century BC depicting a reclining banqueter. It probably once formed a decorative element of a tripod support for a bronze bowl. The word 'symposium' means literally 'drinking together'. In particular it is used of the after-dinner drinking party which was so important a feature of Greek social life. A feast or symposium might take place at a sanctuary as part of the celebrations for a religious festival, or in one of the official dining rooms of a city on some important civic occasion. More often, however, symposia were held in private houses; a group of friends and acquaintances coming together for conversation and merriment.

Guests at a banquet
Tomb of Nebamun,
Thebes, Egypt
18th Dynasty, c.1450 BC
EA 37986
h. 76 cm (30 in)

Bronze figurine of a reclining banqueter
Said to be from the sanctuary of Zeus at Dodona, Greece
6th century BC
GR 1954.10–18.1
l. 10 cm (4 in)
Purchased with the aid of the National Art Collections Fund

FURTHER READING
A. Dalby and S. Grainger, *The Classical Cookbook* (London, 1996)
M. Berriedale-Johnson, *The British Museum Cookbook* (London, 1995)
M. Berriedale-Johnson, *Festive Feasts Cookbook* (London, 2003)

The **Barone Tomb**

The so-called Barone Tomb, named after the first owner of the finds, was discovered in September 1847 at Capua in Campania, Italy. It consisted of a square stone box in which was placed a large bronze cauldron (*lebes*), holding the ashes of the dead. Next to it were two Athenian vases, a red-figured cup and a black-figured neck amphora, which date the burial to the early fifth century BC. The cauldron was acquired by the Museum in 1855, the red-figured cup only in 1920. The black-figured neck amphora passed to the Bibliothèque Nationale in Paris.

Originally intended for mixing wine and water, the bronze cauldron is surmounted by statuettes of a man and a woman dancing, surrounded by mounted archers. Engraved on the shoulder is a narrow frieze showing Herakles driving away the cattle of Cacus, and scenes from funeral games. (Cacus, a three-headed, fire-breathing giant, stole four cows and four oxen from the herd that Herakles had taken from Geryon. Herakles discovered the missing cattle and killed Cacus.)

Greek colonies had been established along the coast of southern Italy after *c.*730 BC and Greek merchants penetrated deep into Campania, sometimes settling at such places as Capua, Suessula and Nola, and coming into contact with existing inhabitants such as the Etruscans. One of the finest products of the merging of Greek and Etruscan traditions is the series of large bronze bowls, used as cremation urns, of which this is an example.

FURTHER READING
S. Haynes, *Etruscan Bronzes* (London, 1985), pp. 269–70, no. 64, pls 64 and 64b

Bronze cauldron (*lebes*)
Made in Campania, found at Capua, Italy
*c.*480 BC
GR 1855.8–16.1;
Bronze 560
h. 67.3 cm (26.5 in)
Purchased (Raffaele Barone)

Baskets

Materials such as bark, withes, roots, canes and grasses are available almost all over the world for the making of baskets. There is evidence that baskets pre-date Neolithic times and may be very much earlier, and there are similarities between basketry today and that produced in the third millennium BC. Baskets can be classified according to the arrangement of the foundation (the standards) and the moving element. In coiled construction a single element or standard is wound in a spiral, the coils being kept in place by thread. In non-coiled baskets the standards form a foundation that predetermines the shape and dimensions of the finished article. There are three main groups: wattle (or twined) construction, in which a single layer of rigid, passive, parallel standards is held together by flexible threads; lattice construction, in which a frame made of two or three layers of passive standards is bound together by wrapping the intersections with a thread; and matting or plaited construction, in which standards and threads are indistinguishable.

The largest group of baskets in the Museum – some four thousand – is in the Department of Ethnography. These include storage baskets, baskets for making beer, for cooking, for fishing, for gathering food, for serving food, for straining liquids, and for transport and/or ceremonial purposes. Some of the finest come from the Americas. Among them (shown on the right) is perhaps the earliest surviving example of a Cherokee basket, which has been in the Museum since 1753.

Plaited river-cane basket, probably Cherokee
South Carolina, USA
Before 1753
ETH Sl.1218
l. 53.3 cm (20⅘ in)
Sir Hans Sloane Bequest

There are also a considerable number of Egyptian baskets and basket fragments. In Egypt, as elsewhere in much of the ancient world, baskets were, after clay pots, the most common form of household container, used to store fruit, seeds, linen-cloth and bronze tools. Many have survived because of the dry climate, and some fragments of basketwork in the collection date from as early as the Predynastic period.

FURTHER READING
D. Wright, *The Complete Book of Baskets and Basketry* (Newton Abbot, 1977)

The **Bassae frieze**

A t Bassae, near Phigaleia in south-western Arcadia, lies the temple of Apollo Epikourios (Apollo the Helper). Pausanias, the Greek traveller who visited it in the second century AD, wrote: 'Of all the temples in the Peloponnese this one could be considered second only to the temple at Tegea for its proportions and the beauty of its stone'. Work is thought to have begun *c.*420 BC and the temple to have been constructed over a long period, with the sculptured frieze completed around the turn of the century.

The site of the temple was first noted by western travellers in 1765, but it was not until 1811 that a group of architects and artists discovered the sculpture. The frieze shows the triumph of Greek civilization over barbarians. There are twenty-three surviving blocks and various fragments of the metopes from the porches. The sequence of their placement remains somewhat uncertain: each slab was carved separately, with hardly any sculptural overlap, while severe modifications to some slabs even suggest that the frieze may not have been installed as originally planned.

On the south and east sides of the frieze is arranged a series of slabs showing the battle fought by Herakles and the Greeks against the Amazons (p. 19). Above is one of the most accomplished of all

Part of the frieze from the Temple of Apollo Epikourios
Bassae, Arcadia, Greece
*c.*400 BC
GR 1815.10–20.95 and 217
h. 64 cm (25⅕ in)
Purchased by the British Government from an auction at Zakynthos

the slabs, which shows Herakles, wearing his lion skin and wielding a club, matched against Hippolyte. On the left an Amazon rides down a fallen Greek, while on the right a Greek unseats an Amazon. The north and west sides show the fight between the Lapiths and Centaurs (p. 181). The battles are a brutal, fast-moving swirl of animals and fighters.

FURTHER READING

J. Boardman, *Greek Sculpture. The Late Classical Period* (London, 1995)
D. Williams and I. Jenkins, 'The arrangement of the sculptured frieze from the Temple of Apollo at Bassae' in O. Palagia and W. Coulson (eds), *Sculpture from Arcadia and Laconia* (Oxford, 1993)

The two 'Basse-Yutz' flagons, named from their find-place at Basse Yutz, Lorraine, eastern France, are amongst the finest survivals of Early Celtic art of the so-called La Tène period (p. 182). They were found with two Etruscan bronze *stamnoi* (vessels used for mixing wine) in 1917. Unfortunately, the excavation was illicit so there is little information about the find, but it seems likely that the objects came from a grave.

Fine vessels like these would have belonged to a wealthy family in Gallic society, a society whose love of southern wine exposed it to Greek art, and whose native artists were particularly receptive to new ideas. Made of bronze, the flagons are virtually identical and are inlaid with precious coral from the Mediterranean coast (now faded to white) and red enamel (opaque red glass, probably from Asia Minor). The handles are in the form of a dog or wolf standing with forepaws on the rim; a duck appears to float on the stream of wine pouring from the spout. The vessels show a mixture of styles. Their overall shape follows Etruscan beaked flagons; the palmette decorations under the spouts are a popular Celtic motif derived ultimately from Egypt and more immediately from Greece; the 'oriental' dogs that form the handles were also transmitted by way of Greek or Etruscan art. The duck is a native element.

FURTHER READING
R. and V. Megaw, *The Basse-Yutz Find: Masterpieces of Celtic Art* (London, 1990)

One of the Basse-Yutz flagons
Basse Yutz, Lorraine, France
*c.*400 BC
PRB 1929 5–11 1
h. 39.6 cm (15½ in)
Purchased with the aid of Oscar Raphael, Mr Szarvasy and the Earl of Cawdor

Benin bronzes

The Kingdom of Benin is famous for its brass castings, the finest dating from the fifteenth and sixteenth centuries AD. Benin was a powerful state in West Africa, from at least the thirteenth century AD. Under various Obas (rulers) it gained or lost domination over many subject kingdoms in the course of the centuries. At times it included Yoruba towns such as Owo, and its borders extended west as far as Lagos and east as far as the River Niger. Its core has always been the Edo people of southern Nigeria.

Brass plaque depicting an Oba
Benin, Nigeria
16th century AD
ETH 1898.1–15.44 [XIV.4]
h. 40 cm (15¾ in)

Traditional state religion centred on the Oba, who lived in a huge palace compound and whose well-being was associated with that of the whole kingdom. Among the brass castings produced for the court were plaques which at one period were used to cover the wooden pillars of the Oba's palace. Brass goods were a royal prerogative in Benin, associated with wealth, power and foreign trade. They were made by the 'lost wax' technique by a guild of casters under royal supervision in Benin City. Mostly they depict officials and retainers engaged in the complex ritual of courtly life. Some show the Portuguese who made the first European contacts with the kingdom in the late fifteenth century. The bronzes are, however, wholly African: stylistic analyses and local oral tradition combine to assign them to between 1550 and 1650.

At the beginning of 1897 Benin forces attacked and massacred a British diplomatic mission. In a wave of nationalist outrage the British organized a punitive expedition against Benin and took the capital. Some 900 brass plaques were found half-buried in a storehouse. It was decided to sell them to provide compensation for those injured and killed. The bronzes were rapidly disseminated through the museum collections of the world and eventually around 300 came to London, some of which remain in the Museum.

Above is a plaque showing the Oba returning from battle, riding side-saddle in the manner exclusive to him. The smaller figures are court retainers. The background designs represent river leaves, associated with Olokun, god of the waters. The leaves are used by Olokun priestesses in curing rites.

FURTHER READING
P.G. Ben-Amos, *The Art of Benin* (London, 1995)
M.D McLeod and J. Mack, *Ethnic Sculpture* (London, 1985)

The **Bible** in the British Museum

The collections of the Museum are rich in material which helps to illuminate the peoples and events of the Bible. There are the material remains of Hebrews and Hittites, Assyrians, Elamites and Egyptians, Persians, Babylonians and others who appear in its pages. In the nineteenth century there was a revolution in knowledge of the Biblical world, as a result both of excavation and the decipherment of ancient texts. The Museum was closely involved in both.

The first serious study of Mesopotamian antiquity was conducted by Claudius James Rich (1787–1821), the East India Company's Resident in Baghdad, whose collections were acquired by the Museum. The Museum funded early excavations in Assyria by Austen Henry Layard and his successors, who brought back thousands of texts from Ashurbanipal's library of cuneiform tablets at Nineveh; these form the core of a collection which has made the Museum the world centre for cuneiform studies.

Among the items in the Museum which refer to Biblical characters are the Black Obelisk of Shalmaneser (p. 57) and the Nabonidus cylinder (above), one of four found at the four corners of the ziggurat at Ur which mentions Belshazzar, a prominent figure in the Book of Daniel. A clay prism containing the final edition of Sennacherib's annals, dated to 691 BC, gives an account of the campaign against King Hezekiah. Various documents and inscriptions refer to the mysterious 'Hapiru' of the second millennium (the statue of Idrimi, p. 160; the Amarna letters, p. 18), who probably included the wandering Hebrews. In the Assyrian reliefs we glimpse the Hebrews, for example in the siege of Lachish and its aftermath (pp. 178–9), and there are many representations of the terrible Assyrian army. The Egyptian text known as the *Teachings of Amenemope*, c.1000 BC, has many parallels to the sayings in the Book of Proverbs ascribed to King Solomon. The Flood Tablet from Mesopotamia (p. 125) relates a story akin to that in Genesis. There are coins in circulation during Biblical times, and busts of Roman emperors of the New Testament period.

Cylinder inscription of Nabonidus
Babylon
6th century BC
WA 91125; K.1689
l. 10.16 cm (4 in)
Excavated by A.H. Layard

Limestone relief showing men of Lachish in the Assyrian royal guard
Nineveh, Palace of Sennacherib
WA 124901;
1856–9–9,9
h. 160 cm (5ft 3in)

FURTHER READING
R.D. Barnett, *Illustrations of Old Testament History* (London, 1977)
T.C. Mitchell, *The Bible in the British Museum: Interpreting the Evidence* (2nd edn, London, 2004)
J.N. Tubb, *Canaanites* (London, 1998)
J.N. Tubb and R.L. Chapman, *Archaeology and the Bible* (London, 1990)

Buddhism is today a world religion with an historical founder who, by becoming enlightened (the *Buddha* in ancient Indian languages means the Enlightened One), discovered and taught a way to salvation (p. 65).

The first independent evidence for Buddhism comes from the reign of Emperor Ashoka (273–232 BC) of the Maurya dynasty, whose stone inscriptions are the earliest Indian historical records. His reign promoted Buddhism and the construction of monuments was encouraged. The chief monument, the stupa, was a round, solid, domed brick- or stone-built structure, originally a tumulus, that became the hallmark of Buddhism and a potent symbol. From at least the late centuries BC, relics of the Buddha and his successors were held to be sacred. These were enshrined in stupas which, because of their sanctified contents, became the focus of Buddhist ritual.

The Bimaran reliquary is one of the most notable finds from a stupa; it bears the earliest known representation of the Buddha. It was discovered inside an inscribed stone box together with pearls, coins and beads. Framed by arcades formed with the Indian pointed arch (typical of Gandhara architecture, p. 130) are the Buddha flanked by Indra and Brahma, both gods of early Indian religion. They are shown twice, separated by a worshipper whose headdress, earrings and armlets suggest a *bodhisattva* (p. 319). Between the arches are eagles and, above and below, garnets.

The inscription refers to relics of the Buddha dedicated by one Shivarakshita. If the base silver coins of King Azes which were discovered nearby (*c.*60 AD) are contemporary, this dates the reliquary to the first century AD.

Gold reliquary inset with rubies
Bimaran, Afghanistan
1st–2nd century AD
OA 1900.2–9.1
h. 6.5 cm (2½ in)

FURTHER READING
W. Zwalf (ed.), *Buddhism: Art and Faith* (London, 1985)

The **Black Obelisk** of Shalmaneser III

This obelisk of black stone erected in 825 BC in the city of Nimrud by the Assyrian King Shalmaneser III (*r.*858–824 BC) includes the earliest surviving picture of an Israelite: the Biblical Jehu, King of Israel, bringing tribute *c.*841 BC. Set up at a time of civil war in Assyria, the obelisk glorifies the achievements of the king and his chief minister, their campaigns of 31 years and the tribute they exacted from their neighbours.

The tribute bearers are in five rows and are identified by captions. The places from which the tribute comes are (from top): 1. Gilzanu, in West Iran; 2. House of Omri (ancient Israel); 3. Musri (Egypt?), probably a gift which includes an Indian elephant, monkeys and other exotic animals; 4. Suhi, on the Euphrates; 5. Patina, in south Turkey.

Ahab, son of Omri, king of Israel, lost his life in battle in 850 BC, fighting against the king of Damascus at Ramoth-Gilead (I Kings xxii. 29–36). His second son (Joram) was succeeded by Jehu, a usurper, who broke the alliances with Phoenicia and Judah, and submitted to Assyria. The caption above the scene, written in Assyrian cuneiform, can be translated 'The tribute of Jehu, son of Omri: I received from him silver, gold, a golden bowl, a golden vase with pointed bottom, golden tumblers, golden buckets, tin, a staff for a king [and] *purukhti* fruits.' The Assyrians in this period used the term 'House of Omri' to cover both the Kingdom of Israel, governed from Omri's capital, Samaria, and the family of Omri, in which they apparently included Jehu.

The obelisk was discovered by Austen Henry Layard in 1846. The decipherment of the cuneiform script as used in Assyria, in which the Museum was much involved, was greatly helped by this well-preserved text.

LEFT **The Black Obelisk of Shalmaneser III**

ABOVE **Detail showing Jehu, son of Omri**
Nimrud, Assyria
*c.*825 BC
WA 118885; 1848–11–4,1
h. 1.98 m (6 ft 6 in)
Excavated by A.H. Layard

FURTHER READING
J.E. Reade, *Assyrian Sculpture* (2nd edn, London, 1998)

Board games

Board games of one kind or another are played all over the world. They tend to fall into categories associated with man's perennial preoccupations: divination, the hunt, the battle and the race. Chess, for example, is at least as old as the sixth century AD and probably much older. Originally a four-handed game involving the use of dice, it simulated the battles of real armies, but gradually evolved into a game of unsurpassed strategy and challenge. The Museum has, for example, a nineteenth-century set from India which shows green and red colours, not black and white as in Europe. The finest chess pieces in the Museum, however, are undoubtedly the group of twelfth-century AD chessmen found on the Isle of Lewis (p. 183).

The best games spread from culture to culture, carried by soldiers or traders in their travels, played for amusement or gain, or both. Backgammon, for example, developed from the medieval game of Tables, which in turn derived from the popular Roman board game *ludus duodecim scriptorum*, the 'Game of Twelve Lines'. Ludo, popular in England since the nineteenth century, is merely a westernized version of the traditional Indian race game of *pachisi*, or *chausar*, whose origins are as yet unestablished.

Board and counters for the Royal Game of Ur
Mesopotamia
*c.*2600 BC
WA 120834;
1928–10–9, 378
l. 30.1 cm (11⅞ in)
Excavated by Sir Leonard Woolley

One of the oldest boards for a game in the Museum is that found in the Royal Cemetery at Ur, shown below, dating from *c.*2600 BC. Several were found (of which this is the finest) with designs of rosettes, paired eyes and patterns of five dots on the twenty squares. It was a race game for two players, who competed to move their pieces from one end of the board to the other. There were normally seven pieces for each player, and moves were

Board games

Detail from the 'Satirical Papyrus'
Deir el-Medina, Thebes, Egypt
late New Kingdom, c.1500–1200 BC
EA 10016/1
h. 15.5 cm (6 in)
Purchased from Joseph Sams, 1834

controlled by the use of tetrahedral or stick dice. Game boards of this general type were being made in a workshop in Syria well before 3000 BC. Others broadly contemporary with the Ur example have been found in Iran and probably in Pakistan.

This game of Twenty Squares was played all over the Near East for millennia. Scratched at the base of one of the colossal winged bulls (pp. 34–5) which guarded the entry to the Assyrian King Sargon's palace at Khorsabad in c.710 BC is a rough grid for playing the same game, probably incised by guards or those waiting to gain admittance. After the fall of Babylon in 539 BC Jewish refugees may have carried it to India, where a version was played until recently. The game was introduced into Egypt c.1700 BC.

Another ancient game is the Egyptian *senet*, the game of Thirty Squares. Above is a scene from the 'Satirical Papyrus' (late New Kingdom), in which an antelope plays a game with a lion. *Senet* required a playing surface divided into thirty squares arranged in three rows, and playing pieces, half of a conical form and half shaped like spools or reels. In time it was regarded as one of the pleasures to be enjoyed by the deceased in after-life. Later still, the game was played to decide the fate of the player in the Underworld.

The Museum now has a wide and expanding collection of board games from the ancient to the modern, ranging from chess to snakes and ladders and including *mancala* (right), of which it has the most extensive collection in the world. The origin and antiquity of this game remains obscure. Today it is played in Africa, Asia, the Middle East and the Americas. Players move pieces around the board and these are captured by calculation and strategy.

Wooden statue representing Shyaam aMbul aNgoong, the founder of the Kuba Kingdom, Zaire, seated with a *mancala* board before him
Mushenge, Zaire, Africa
ETH Af.1909.12–10
h. 55 cm (21⅔ in)
Given by Emil Torday

FURTHER READING
R.C. Bell, *Board and Table Games from many Civilizations* (New York, 1979)
H.J.R. Murray, *A History of Board Games other than Chess* (Oxford, 1952)
J. de Voogt, *Mancala Board Games* (London, 1997)

Bookplates, or *ex-libris*, are printed to be pasted into books to denote ownership. They are of interest for their artistic, genealogical, bibliographical and heraldic evidence and are also fascinating as one of the very few artistic works or examples of printing employed by people not given to private patronage.

It is thought that bookplates originated in Germany, after the invention of printing by Johannes Gutenberg in the mid-fifteenth century. The earliest bookplate known may be that of Johannes Knabensberg, called Igler (from the German word for hedgehog), which has been dated to 1450. Albrecht Dürer designed book-plates, and other well known artists include Lucas Cranach the Elder, Hans Burgkmair and Hans Holbein the Younger.

The earliest plates were woodcuts. By the end of the sixteenth century these were largely superseded by copperplate engraving. The subjects were predominantly armorial. After 1800 copper-plates gave way to engravings on the end grain of wood blocks, although the tradition of engraving on metal continued. With the invention of cheaper and more versatile photo-engraving, hand-engraving was almost completely supplanted by 1900.

The largest section of the Museum's collection was bequeathed by A.W. Franks (1826–97), Keeper of British and Medieval Antiq-uities and Ethnography. There are 35,098 British and American plates, 4752 German, 8908 French and many others from else-where. For over 90 years collectors of British bookplates have annotated the items in their collections with either F (followed by the relevant number) or NIF (not in Franks).

Franks was never able to acquire the earliest-known English bookplate, dated 1574, used in *c.*70 volumes presented to the University of Cambridge by Sir Nicholas Bacon (1509–79), father of Francis; but a copy was acquired later. Nine of these book-plates remain in books and the only other recorded print is that in the Museum.

Two other major collections were those of Max Rosenheim (1932; 11,000 plates) and George Heath Viner (1955; 8000 plates).

FURTHER READING
E.R.J. Gambier Howe, *Catalogue of British and American Book Plates bequeathed to the Trustees of the British Museum by Sir Augustus Wollaston Franks*, 3 vols (London, 1903–4)
F. Johnson, *A Treasury of Bookplates from the Renaissance to the Present* (New York, 1977)
B.N. Lee, *British Bookplates: A Pictorial History* (Newton Abbot, 1979)

Bookplate (Guest) of Canford Manor
Printed in gold and colour, no date
PD 13034
11.8 × 8.1 cm
(4⅔ × 3¼ in)
A.W. Franks Bequest

CANFORD MANOR.

The 'Book of the Dead' is the name given by Egyptologists to sheets of papyrus covered with magical funerary texts and accompanying illustrations called 'vignettes'. The ancient Egyptians placed these with their dead in order to help them pass through the dangers of the Underworld and attain an afterlife of bliss in the Fields of Reeds, the Egyptian heaven.

These papyri contain altogether nearly two hundred individual spells, or chapters, although no one example has all of them. The texts were known to the ancient Egyptians as the Chapters of Coming Forth by Day, for they largely concerned the freedom granted to the spirit forms to come and go as they pleased in the afterlife.

The earliest Books of the Dead date to the mid-fifteenth century BC, but many of the texts can be traced back more than a thousand years earlier. Some of the spells originated in the Pyramid Texts, which first appeared carved in hieroglyphs in the pyramid of King Wenis, last ruler of the Fifth Dynasty, about 2345 BC; many were clearly centuries older.

During the Middle Kingdom (c.2040–1786 BC) funerary beliefs and practices were democratized: a guaranteed afterlife became open to all. From the New Kingdom onwards Books of the Dead became a regular part of the funerary equipment and every Egyptian who could afford a copy was buried with it close at hand. The wealthy might commission an expert scribe to produce their own personal choice of chapters. Some made do with a prepared text with spaces for the insertion of their name and titles. The papyri were then placed on or in the coffin, inside a wooden statuette of the funerary god Osiris, or even inside the statuette's hollow plinth or among the folds of the mummy's bandages.

The Museum has over 200 Books of the Dead, most of which are fragmentary. Among the finest are those of Ani, Hunefer, Anhai and Nesitanebtashru. Below is a scene from the funerary papyrus of Hunefer. Here we see Chapter 125, the judgement of the

The Book of the Dead of the Royal Scribe and Steward of King Sety I, Overseer of Royal Cattle and Scribe of Divine Offerings, Hunefer (detail)
Memphis, Egypt
19th Dynasty, c.1275 BC
EA 9901/3
h. 45 cm (17¾ in)

Books of the Dead

The Book of the Dead
of the Royal Scribe,
Accounting Scribe for
Divine Offerings of all
the gods, Overseer of the
Granaries of the Lords of
Tawar, Ani (detail)
Tomb of Ani, Thebes,
Egypt
19th Dynasty, c.1250 BC
EA 10470/17
h. 42 cm (16½ in)
Given by Sir Wallis Budge

deceased before the god Osiris, found in most Books of the Dead. This chapter is often accompanied by a vignette showing the weighing of the heart before the 42 assessor-gods. Anubis introduces Hunefer to the Weighing of his Heart against the feather of Maat. Anubis, depicted a second time, checks the accuracy of the balance; Thoth stands ready to write down the result, watched by the monster Ammit, who gobbles down sinful hearts. Vindicated, Hunefer is introduced by falcon-headed Horus-avenger-of-his-father to Osiris, who is enthroned in an elaborate booth with Isis and Nepthys and the Four Sons of Horus. Above squat 14 gods and goddesses who are witnesses to the judgement. In the spell Hunefer declares:

> I have not caused pain, I have not made hungry, I have not
> made to weep, I have not killed, I have not commanded to kill,
> I have not made suffering for anyone.

In Spell 92 (above) from the funerary papyrus of Ani, we see Ani's human-headed soul carrying a *shen*, a symbol of eternity, as it hovers protectively over his mummy, which wears a mummy mask and lies on a lion-shaped bed between two tall stands containing flames.

FURTHER READING
C. Andrews (ed.), *The Ancient Egyptian Book of the Dead* (London, 1984)

British coinage

The earliest gold coins, used in south-east England, were made in the area of modern north-east France and Belgium, and their design was ultimately derived from the gold stater of Philip II of Macedon (351–336 BC). After c.75 BC the first anonymous coins were made in Britain and then, from c.30 BC, coins inscribed with the names of successive kings were produced. After the Roman invasion of AD 43, however, Roman coins superseded native issues.

In the late sixth century Frankish gold coins began to circulate in small numbers in the south-east of England. Similar gold coins (shillings) were issued in southern England from around the beginning of the seventh century, but by about AD 670 these had been replaced by silver *denarii* (pennies). These were issued by all the major Anglo-Saxon kingdoms. The tenth century saw the unification of England under the Wessex dynasty, and by the end of the reign of Edgar (AD 959–75) a single coinage, based on the silver penny, was established throughout the kingdom.

The Norman conquest made little initial impact on the English coinage, but Norman influence led to the introduction of coinage in Wales, Scotland and Ireland. Under Edward I (AD 1272–1307) the range of English coinage was significantly expanded for the first time, to include halfpennies and farthings and the groat (fourpence). Under Edward III (1327–77), from 1351 the groat and half-groat (twopence) became essential parts of the currency. Edward III also introduced a successful gold coinage, based on the noble of 6s. 8d., equal to both a third of a pound and half a mark, in the two main medieval units for reckoning money. At this time the purchasing power of the pound was equal to something like £300–400 in modern terms.

Under the Tudors the English coinage shifted to fit closely the £sd system (the pound of 20 shillings, the shilling of 12 pence), rather than the medieval mark. Henry VII introduced the sovereign, the first pound coin, in 1489, and Henry VIII added 10, 5 and 2½ shilling coins (the last two being the crown and half-crown). Henry VII also introduced the first 12-penny shilling, which was the first English coin to have a realistic portrait of the ruler on it.

Silver penny of Alfred of Wessex
London
c.AD 880
BMC 92.1838–7–10–285
diam. 20 mm (¾ in)

British coinage

Gold sovereign of Henry
VII
England
AD 1489
CM E4841
diam. 44 mm (1¾ in)

Elizabeth II fifty pence
piece
Britain
AD 1971
CM 1978–7–16–9
diam. 30 mm
(1⅕ in)
Presented by
the Royal Mint

Under Elizabeth I there were more denominations than at any other time in English history.

Because the value of gold against silver could change, the coinage had to respond accordingly. Charles II introduced the guinea as the pound coin in 1663; its value was allowed to shift along with gold prices, and eventually it stabilized at 21 shillings, where it remained for much of the eighteenth century. Only in 1816–17 was a proper pound coin restored, in the shape of the gold sovereign. In 1660 a proper copper coinage of halfpennies and farthings was produced by the Royal Mint for the first time, coins which were the first English issues to bear the figure of Britannia. Scottish coinage had been aligned with the English by James VI and I in 1604 at a ratio of 12:1, so that the main gold coin (called a unite, to symbolize the union of the crowns) was worth a pound in England and £12 Scots. Under Queen Anne a separate Scottish coinage ceased to be struck, creating a single currency for the whole of Great Britain.

The nineteenth century British coinage was plentiful and stable, but in the early twentieth century pressures from economic disruption and war saw gold displaced by paper banknotes from 1917, the silver coinage debased to 50% fine after the First World War and replaced by cupro-nickel after the Second, and the low denominations provided by brass and bronze. By the 1970s the advantages of a decimal system, above all in the ease of calculation that it provided, were irresistible, and Britain went decimal in 1971. The one link to the ancient £sd system was the pound, as one decimal pound equalled the older pound, giving validity to the survival of the £ sign (Latin: *libra* = pound).

The Museum has a comprehensive collection of ancient British pieces, medieval and modern coins and banknotes.

FURTHER READING
H.A. Grueber, *Handbook of the Coins of Great Britain and Ireland* (2nd edn, London, 1972)
J. Kent, *2000 Years of British Coins and Medals* (London, 1978)
J. Williams (ed.), *Money. A History* (London, 1997)

The life and teachings of the **Buddha**

The Buddha is believed to have been born in the mid-sixth century BC into a royal house in northeastern India. Called Siddhartha Gautama, of the Sakya tribe in the border country between the modern states of India and Nepal, he probably lived between the end of the sixth and the beginning of the fifth century BC. After witnessing sickness, hunger and death, his desire to understand the reason for human suffering led him to abandon his privileged life and adopt the life of an ascetic. His studies provided him with no satisfactory system of belief, and finally in deep meditation he achieved Enlightenment by understanding the connection between desire and suffering.

As in Hinduism, the belief in an endless cycle of rebirths lies at the base of Buddhist thought. The Buddha's message was the means of release from this cycle. He taught that all existence is suffering, that suffering is caused by desire and that by practising conduct which lessens attachment to the physical world, desire can be reduced. Attachment leads to a lower existence in the next life; non-attachment leads to a better rebirth. The final release from the chain of rebirths is the state of nirvana ('being extinguished'), which results from total non-attachment and the accumulation of positive karma.

Following his Enlightenment under the sacred tree at Bodh Gaya the Buddha went to the Deer Park at Sarnath, where he preached his first sermon. There he 'set in motion the Wheel of the Law' symbolized in this statue from Gandhara (right) of the Buddha preaching, his hands in *dharma-chakramudra*. After his death his relics were distributed amongst his disciples; this is the beginning of the long process of his veneration.

Scenes from the life of the Buddha can be seen throughout the oriental galleries (see Amaravati sculptures, pp. 16–17). Some of the earliest images of him came from Gandhara, and the Museum has a particularly fine collection from this region.

Schist statue of the Buddha preaching
Gandhara, from Hoti Mardan, Mardan District, NWFP, Pakistan
2nd–3rd century AD
OA 1895.10–26.1
h. 95 cm (37⅖ in)
Given by Eustace Smith

FURTHER READING
W. Zwalf (ed.), *Buddhism: Art and Faith* (London, 1985)
D. Pemberton, *Buddha* (London, 2002)

Below is a sculpture of the Buddha shown in the position of meditation and holding a myrobalan in his hand; this fruit has medicinal properties and identifies the Buddha as a healer. The figure is made of dry lacquer, shell inlay and gilding. It was produced in Burma in the late eighteenth or early nineteenth century AD.

The figure is one of the Museum's earliest acquisitions from Asia and is known to have been displayed in Montagu House before the present Museum building was constructed in the 1830s. Paradoxically, it is accompanied by one of the Museum's more recent acquisitions. Images of the Buddha in Burmese shrines often stand on elaborate thrones, *palin*. There was no record of this figure having been accompanied by a throne and so, in 1994, a commission was placed by the Museum with the foremost wood-carver and lacquerer of Mandalay – Saya Win Maung – to provide a new throne (*palin*). This was made of lacquered teak and is of a tiered eight-sided design. It is decorated with inset glass and also with raised lacquerwork, or *thayo*. This is a method whereby lacquer sap is mixed with fine ash and then moulded. The pieces are fixed on to the throne using lacquer as a glue. Around the edge runs a Burmese inscription recording the names of the craftsmen involved, and the fact that it has been offered by them in homage to the Buddha image.

Buddha and throne
Buddha: Rangoon, Burma
Gilded lacquer, wood and
textile, late 18th or early
19th century AD
OA 1826.2–11.1
h. 2.04 m (6 ft 8⅓ in)
Given by Captain
Frederick Marryat
Throne: Burma
(Myanmar)
AD 1994
OA 1995.5–13.1
h. 1 m (3 ft 3⅓ in)

FURTHER READING
J. Lowry, *Burmese Art* (London, 1974)
S. Fraser-Lu, *Burmese Lacquers* (London, 1985)
R. Isaacs and T. R. Blurton, *Visions from the Golden Land: Burma and the Art of Lacquer* (London, 2002)
A. Green and T. R. Blurton (eds), *Burma: Art and Archaeology* (London, 2002)

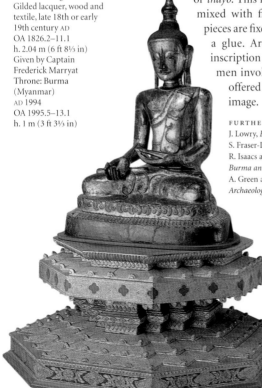

Byzantine ivories

In AD 330 the Emperor Constantine the Great (c.AD 274–337) adopted as his seat of power Byzantium (modern Istanbul), renaming it Constantinople. In AD 337 ivory carvers were among the craftsmen excused public service by the emperor, on condition they devoted their time to learning their craft. The brilliant results of such encouragement can be seen in later fourth- and fifth-century AD carved elephant ivory panels, boxes and diptychs.

Below (left) is an example of this craftsmanship, an early diptych leaf showing the deification of a prominent figure, perhaps an emperor, who is seated on his elephant-drawn funeral carriage. Immediately above is a funeral pyre, from which a god drives heavenwards accompanied by two eagles, probably symbolizing departing spirits. The dead man is borne upwards by two personifications of winds, to be greeted by five robed figures, probably ancestors. The Latin monogram at the top of the panel, 'SYMMACHORVM' (of the Symmachi), may refer to a member of the immensely gifted senatorial family; the most likely candidate is Quintus Aurelius Symmachus, Prefect of Rome AD 384/5, who died in AD 401 or 402.

In AD 395 the Roman Empire was divided, with separate emperors ruling in Constantinople and Rome. Byzantine art enjoyed a golden age under Justinian I (AD 527–65). On the far right is a masterpiece of this period, the largest surviving Byzantine ivory panel, a leaf from a sixth-century AD diptych with the commanding figure of an archangel, perhaps Michael. The Greek inscription, which would have continued on the other leaf of the diptych, may be translated 'Receive the suppliant before you, despite his sinfulness'.

After two periods of iconoclasm (during which religious images were prohibited) in c.AD 726 and 815–43, Byzantine art became increasingly influenced by local traditions.

FURTHER READING
D. Buckton (ed.), *Byzantium:
Treasures of Byzantine Art and Culture*
(London, 1994)
R. Loverance, *Byzantium* (2nd edn,
London, 2004)

LEFT **Ivory diptych leaf**
Rome
AD 402
MLA 1857,10–13,1
h. 30.1 cm (11⅞ in)
Purchased (Gheradesca
Collection)

RIGHT **Ivory panel with
archangel**
Constantinople (Istanbul,
Turkey)
2nd quarter of 6th
century AD
MLA OA 9999
h. 42.8 cm (16⅞ in)
Acquired before 1856

The treasure was found on the hill of St Louis, Carthage (in what is now Tunisia). It dates from the late fourth or early fifth century AD and comprises eight bowls or dishes, twelve spoons and eight items of jewellery. It was probably owned by the Cresconius family, whose name, preceded by a Christian symbol, appears on one of the dishes. The Cresconii were a well-known and important family in North Africa in the late fourth and fifth centuries who held a number of prominent positions at a time when Carthage was still, after Rome, the second city in the Western Roman Empire. The reason for the burial of the treasure is not known. It may have been concealed in c.AD 400 when a long-standing local religious feud flared up, but it is more likely to have been hidden from the Vandals who in AD 429 crossed the Straits of Gibraltar

Set of three silver bowls
Carthage (modern Tunisia)
late 4th/5th century AD
MLA AF 3280–3282
h. 11.4 cm (4½ in)
A.W. Franks Bequest

from Spain and swept into Africa. In 439 Gaiseric, king of the Vandals, captured Carthage and established a kingdom.

Above are three elegant silver bowls, probably the finest pieces in the treasure and indeed considered to be among the finest surviving examples of silver from this period. One has a cover which can also be used as a dish. The other pieces include two inscribed dishes, one reading LOQVERE FELICITER ('talk happily') preceded by a divine monogram, an alpha and omega; the other is marked D D ICRESCONI CLARENT. A shallow dish with a handle (*patera*) is embossed with the figure of a frog. Two bowls are decorated with country scenes, showing the survival of classical taste in the Christian period. Of the spoons, four are plain with pear-shaped bowls, seven have a small cross where the bowl joins the handle, while another, more elaborate, is engraved with a wreath and the Christian *chi-rho* symbol flanked by an alpha and omega.

Caryatid from the Erechtheion

According to Vitruvius the name 'caryatid' was derived from the women of the city of the Carya (or Caria) in Laconia, which sided with the Persians at Thermopylae. The victorious Greeks destroyed the city and made the women slaves, leading them into captivity still wearing the clothes and jewellery from their former lives. However poignant the legend, it cannot be true, since such statues appeared before the Persian Wars. A more likely derivation of the name is from the young women of Sparta who danced every year in honour of Artemis Caryatis (Artemis of the Walnut Tree).

This is one of six caryatids from the Porch of the Maidens (*korai*) of the Erechtheion in Athens. On her head is a basket and at one time she held a *phialai* (offering bowl) in her hands.

The Erechtheion was an Ionic temple on the north side of the Acropolis. The west end contained the tomb of Erechtheus, a legendary king of Athens. At the east end was a broad porch consisting of six Ionic columns (one of which is also, in the Museum). Another porch projected from the south side, its flat roof supported by six statues of maidens known as 'caryatids'.

Construction of the Erechtheion was perhaps begun *c.*421 BC, and in 409 BC a commission was appointed to survey the building and superintend its completion. Fragments of the inscribed marble stelae recording the commission's first report and the decree appointing it are in the Museum's collections.

Between 1800 and 1803 G.B. Lusieri, acting on behalf of Lord Elgin, removed the caryatid which stood second from the left on the front of the South Porch. During the Greek War of Independence (1821–33) the temple was reduced to ruins, although the caryatids survived. It has now been reconstructed.

Caryatid from the Erechtheion
Athens
*c.*415 BC
GR 1816.6–10.128;
Cat. Sculpture 407
h. 2.31 m (7 ft 7 in)
Purchased by the British Government from Lord Elgin

FURTHER READING
R.J. Hopper, *The Acropolis* (London, 1971)
A. Stewart, *Greek Sculpture* (New Haven and London, 1990)

69

Cats

It is not known when cats were first domesticated. Skeletons are quite frequently found at archaeological sites from the early prehistoric period, but these are presumably from wild animals. There may, however, have been tamed kittens that grew into adult cats and stayed near human habitation long before evidence of felines appears in the archaeological record.

The remains of cats have been found at a number of early sites in different parts of the world. These include Jericho, where a cat's tooth was identified from the Pre-Pottery Neolithic level dating to around 9000 years ago, and Harappa in the Indus valley, where another was found from around 4000 years ago. Remains of a cat have been identified from the Pre-Pottery Neolithic levels of a site in Cyprus dated to around 7000 years ago. It is generally assumed that the cat was first domesticated by the ancient Egyptians, but if this is so it was remarkably late, and long after all the other major domesticates had become fully established. There are no remains of cats from the prehistoric period in Egypt, but remains dating from the Old Kingdom (2686–2181 BC) have been found. There are pictorial representations of cats, one famous one is the ginger cat attacking birds in the scene from the tomb of Nebamun (18th Dynasty, c.1400 BC; p. 225).

The cat was sacred for the Egyptians. It represented the living form of the goddess Bastet, as seen in the bronze 'Gayer-Anderson' cat of c.600 BC (right). A vast number of cats were embalmed in ancient Egypt. Although this might be regarded as a mark of affection, studies have shown that many of the cat mummies are of young animals, deliberately killed to be mummified and presented as votive offerings.

By the first millennium BC the cat was beginning to be found in Europe and Asia as a domestic animal. During the Roman period it spread rapidly throughout Europe. Pawprints were found embedded in a tile from Roman Silchester. Today the domestic

Red-figured *skyphos* (detail); a youth and a woman playing with a ball, a cat and a bird
Attributed to the Tarporley painter
Apulia, Italy
c.400 BC
GR 1867.5–8.1175;
Vase F 126
h. 15.24 cm (6 in)
Purchased
(Blacas Collection)

The 'Gayer-Anderson' cat
Memphis or Saqqara, Egypt
Late Period, after 600 BC
EA 64391
h. 42 cm (16½ in)
Given by John Gayer-Anderson (Pasha) and Mary Stout, 1939

Cats

cat (*felis catus*) is found in all places where humans have lived.

Thus the Museum has representations of cats of all shapes, sizes and types. On a Greek vase of the sixth century BC (far left) a spotted cat leaps towards a white pigeon. In one of the most famous of all prints of cats, Cornelis Visscher's stolid seventeenth-century tabby (below) sits comfortably, its whiskers alert, giving the impression of being unaware of an approaching mouse. A nineteenth-century black and white Japanese cat crouches watchfully, awaiting its prey (right).

In addition to cats in its collections, the Museum had a tradition of providing a home for cats on its site. These included Mike, who in the 1920s and 30s was the protégé of the Keeper of Egyptian Antiquities, and more recently Susie and Maisie.

FURTHER READING
J. Clutton-Brock, *The British Museum Book of Cats* (London, 1988)
J. Malek, *The Cat in Ancient Egypt* (London, 1993; rev. edn 2006)

Cat amongst flowers
Ran'ei (*fl. c.*1840)
Japan
Hanging scroll, ink and colours on silk, 19th century AD
JA 1881.12–10.0.804; JP 2039
h. 56.75 × 30.25 cm (22⅓ × 12 in)
Purchased from William Anderson

The Large Cat
Cornelis Visscher (1628/9–58)
Engraving, *c.*1657
PD 1868–8–22–881
13.9 × 18.4 cm (5½ × 7¼ in)
Slade Bequest, 1868

Early Celtic art is the name given to the decorative styles of Europe, from Ireland to Romania, between 500 BC and AD 100. Inspired by the formal motifs – palmettes and lotus buds – ornamenting imports from Greece and Italy, metalworkers rapidly evolved their own abstract, flowing patterns of scrolls, swirls and whirligigs.

Early Celtic art is also a haunted region where stylized faces may be seen peering out of a tangle of plant ornament on torcs and bracelets. Even the precisely patterned ornament on the Battersea shield (below) suddenly reveals owl-like faces with great, round, squinting eyes. The Museum's collection of metalwork produced in the British Isles between the sixth century BC and AD 100 is outstanding. Within the framework of a European tradition British workshops developed their own distinctive styles, and their creations are amongst the greatest artistic achievements.

The Battersea shield
The River Thames at Battersea, London
1st century BC
PRB 1857.7–15,1
l. 77.7 cm (30½ in)

The art is one of display in warfare, personal ornament and possessions. Many fine pieces accompanied their owners to the grave, and others were carefully deposited in the ground in hoards. A remarkable number of weapons have been recovered from lakes, rivers and bogs, evidence of water-cults, whose details are obscure since the Britons of this period left no written history. Some of the finest examples of British art were dredged from the River Thames in the vicinity of London. Other rivers have yielded treasures such as the magnificent Witham Shield, from the River Witham, near Lincoln, swords and scabbards from the River Nene near Peterborough, and a unique bronze shield found in a former watercourse at Chertsey, Surrey, in 1985.

One of the great finds from the Thames, at Battersea, in 1857, is the decorated bronze facing of a shield, with flowing palmette and scroll ornament enhanced with red enamel. The shield, made between 300 and 100 BC, was of wood or leather.

The Aylesford bucket was made of wood; its bronze fittings were found in 1886 in a cremation burial of the second half of the first century BC, the richest grave in a cemetery at Aylesford, Kent. The bucket might have been used as part of a wine service, together with an Italian bronze jug and pan found in the same grave. The handle mounts are in the form of

Early **Celtic art** in Britain

Bronze armlets
AD 100–250
LEFT Castle Newe,
Strathdon, Aberdeenshire
1838 7–4 3a and b
Given by Lord and Lady
Willoughby
RIGHT Pitkellony Castle,
Perthshire
1946 4–2 1 and 2
Given by Oscar Raphael
diam. 14.1 and 14.7 cm
(5½ and 5¾ in)

human heads, each wearing a cap or helmet. The decoration on the upper band includes pairs of stylized horses.

Above are two massive armlets, that on the right found with another in 1837 in Perthshire, Scotland, the other one of a pair from Aberdeenshire. Cast in brass and bronze respectively, their terminals contain roundels of red and yellow glass. Fourteen similar armlets have been found in Scotland and one in Ireland.

Below is a sheet bronze horse mask from Stanwick, North Yorkshire. It was part of a hoard of harness found in the mid nineteenth century, the acquisition of which led to the active formation of the British collections by the Museum.

FURTHER READING
S. James and V. Rigby, *Britain and the Celtic Iron Age* (London, 1997)
R. and V. Megaw, *Early Celtic Art in Britain and Ireland* (Aylesbury, 1994)
I. Stead, *Celtic Art* (2nd edn, London, 1996)

Bronze horse mask
Stanwick, North
Yorkshire
c.AD 50–100
PRB 1847 2–8 82
h. 10.1 cm (4 in)
Given by Lord Prudhoe,
1847

Central Asian textiles

The region called 'Central Asia' is often simply defined by the former Soviet republics of Kazakhstan, Turkmenistan, Uzbekistan, Tajikistan and Kyrgyzstan. However, at its broadest extent it spreads from the eastern borders of the Caspian Sea in the west into the Xinjiang province of China in the east, in a belt some 1000 miles wide from north to south. Most of the population of this vast area of desert, oasis, steppe and high mountains was traditionally nomadic. These peoples are particularly noted for their 2500-year history of using felt, a non-woven wool textile which is waterproof and insulating.

The Museum's two finest collections of textiles from Central Asia, both acquired through fieldwork, come from Kyrgyzstan and north-eastern Iran. Although the Kyrgyz were forcibly settled on to

Felt floor cover *(shyrdak)*
Made by Kapipa Kasmaliyeva from Tash Tokum village, Naryn region, Kyrgyzstan
AD 1965
OA 1995.As.20.6
3.29 × 1.51 m
(10 ft 9 in × 4 ft 11 in)
Acquired with the aid of the British Museum Society

collective farms in the 1930s, the extraordinary floor felts are an echo of their nomadic heritage. The Museum's collection is largely contemporary, but these brightly coloured 'carpets' were traditionally made for circular tents, or yurts. The felts, made by women, are produced either in the form of *ala ki'iz* ('bright felts', with patterns embedded into the textile) or *shyrdak* ('mosaic felts', with appliquéd designs). Historically, felt was used in Kyrgyzstan for many purposes: tent covers, interior fittings, bags, saddle-cloths and clothing.

The Turkman collection from north-eastern Iran features tent felts but also includes a complete yurt with interior fittings, flat- and pile-woven carpets and storage bags, animal regalia, jewellery and costume, from the late nineteenth and twentieth centuries. Examples of the most striking Turkman garment, the married woman's *chyrpy* (a silk mantle), have been added recently.

FURTHER READING
M. Burkett, *The Art of the Felt Maker* (Kendal, 1979)
J. Harvey, *Traditional Textiles of Central Asia* (London, 1996)
J. Kalter, *The Arts and Crafts of Turkestan* (London, 1984)

The **Chaourse treasure**

This hoard, discovered in 1883 at Chaourse, a village near Montcornet in north-eastern France, is one of the most important and nearly complete table services to survive from antiquity. It was probably buried c.AD 260 at a time of severe disturbances in Gaul.

The hoard comprises some 39 objects, all silver apart from five small vessels and a mirror of silvered bronze. There are large serving platters, some with contrasting niello (silver sulphide) decoration, including one with a central roundel containing a swastika; another platter features a gilded figure of Mercury; jugs and cups fitted with elegant projecting collars finely decorated with scrolling designs of leaves and heads; plain and decorated cups and bowls including a vessel for washing the hands; a statuette of Fortuna; a pail decorated with a magnificent acanthus-scroll frieze between heavy beaded borders; an ingeniously designed and beautifully made combination funnel and strainer; and a pepper-pot in the shape of a squatting black slave-boy. The treasure contains silver drinking-cups, though at this period glass was often preferred for drinking vessels, as it imparted no taste.

Despite its size the date and context of the hoard are uncertain. A few objects are of second-century date, but most date to the third century AD. The names inscribed on the vessels, such as Genialis and Cavarianus, probably represent owners of part or all of the service, perhaps its final owners before it was buried.

FURTHER READING
D. Strong, *Greek and Roman Gold and Silver Plate* (London, 1966)

The Chaourse treasure
Chaourse, France
2nd–3rd century AD
GR 1889.10–19.1–19;
1890.9–23.1–20;
Silver 144–82
diam. (of Mercury plate)
23.4 cm (9⅕ in)

Although bronze was the Greek sculptor's favourite medium, very few large Greek bronzes have survived, the great majority having been melted down and the metal reused throughout antiquity and later. The bronze statue, slightly over life-size, to which the head below belonged survived entire until 1836, when peasants found it while digging for water near the site of ancient Tamassos in central Cyprus. Sadly, it was then largely destroyed, the torso and limbs being broken up for scrap.

The statue may represent the god Apollo, son of Zeus and Leto, brother of Artemis (see p. 86). Apollo symbolized light and beauty and was associated with music, archery, medicine, prophecy and the care of flocks and herds. This rare head has long locks of hair knotted over the forehead and clusters of curls falling round the neck (cast separately), characteristic of the 'golden-haired' god. The eyes were originally inlaid. The lips may have been painted to produce a more realistic appearance.

The bronze is known as the 'Chatsworth Apollo', since it was formerly in the possession of the Dukes of Devonshire, whose home is at Chatsworth in Derbyshire.

Bronze head
Found at Tamassos,
Cyprus
*c.*470–460 BC
GR 1958.4–18.1
h. 31.6 cm (12½ in)
Given by H.M. Treasury

FURTHER READING
D. Haynes, *The Technique of Greek Bronze Statuary* (Mainz am Rhein, 1992)
C. C. Mattusch, *Greek Bronze Statuary* (Cornell, 1988)

Chelsea porcelain

Shown here are two of the finest pieces produced by the Chelsea porcelain factory – the 'Cleopatra' vases. They were donated anonymously in 1763, a year after their manufacture. The painted panels show the death of Cleopatra and the death of Harmonia (daughter of Cleopatra and Mark Antony's patron deities) and, in contrast, colourful exotic birds. The Chelsea porcelain manufactory specialized in luxury products: it alone among English porcelain was rated as comparable to that of Meissen or Sèvres.

England was a relative latecomer to porcelain manufacture. A formula which imitated the hardness and translucency of oriental porcelain was discovered at Meissen in Germany about 1709, but no porcelain was made in England until c.1745. The earliest factories were in London, at Stratford-le-Bow, Chelsea and Limehouse, shortly followed by Newcastle-under-Lyme (Staffordshire), Derby, Longton Hall (Staffordshire), Vauxhall (London) and Liverpool.

The Chelsea factory may well have been in operation as early as 1742, but the first tangible proof of its existence is provided by the 'goat and bee' pattern jugs. One in the Museum composed of a pair of reclining goats supporting a jug with a twig handle and a bee moulded in relief under the lip is incised with a triangle, *Chelsea* and *1745*. A Huguenot silversmith from Liège, Nicholas Sprimont (1716–71), assumed the factory's direction in c.1750 and it remained under his charge for most of its life. The business was a precarious one, menaced by high costs, technical problems, imports and the vagaries of fashion. It was eventually sold to William Duesbury, proprietor of the Derby porcelain concern, in 1769 and closed in 1784.

Chelsea can be identified by the following incised, relief or painted marks (the dates are approximate and there may be some overlap): Triangle (c.1745–9), Raised Anchor (to 1752), Red Anchor (to 1756) and Gold Anchor (1756–69). The Museum has some 200 pieces of Chelsea porcelain, including tewares, tablewares and figures and groups.

FURTHER READING
E. Adams, *Chelsea Porcelain* (2nd edn, London, 2001)

The 'Cleopatra' vases
Chelsea, London
1762
MLA 1763,4– 15,1 and 2;
Pottery Catalogue II,28
h. 50 cm (19¾ in)
Anonymous gift through
James Empson

The bequest of over one million cigarette and other trade cards by Edward Wharton-Tigar (1913–95) has given the Museum the world's definitive collection. This gift continues a Museum tradition of acquiring such material. In 1818 Sarah Sophia Banks (1744–1818), sister of Sir Joseph Banks, bequeathed a collection of visiting cards, admission tickets and a large number of trade cards, the highly decorated sheets issued as advertisements by shopkeepers in the eighteenth century. Sir Ambrose Heal's (1872–1959) bequest of 9000 items includes also newspaper cuttings, letters, shop bills, headed paper and reproductions, formed as part of his research into the history of London shops and trades.

Edward Wharton-Tigar, the world's greatest cartophilist, began collecting at the age of seven in 1920. His collection covers the early 1870s to the present, with the great mass of cards belonging to the years between the 1890s and World War II. His first card was part of the Will's British Birds series and depicted a corncrake.

'Trade cards' comprise cards of all types distributed by commercial organizations as inducements to the public to buy their wares. The largest single group of such cards was issued by cigarette manufacturers, but almost every other trade was involved to some degree. Cards were issued in all countries of the world, in a large range of sizes, in a variety of printing techniques and with a huge range of subject-matter. The Wharton-Tigar collection includes such splendidly diverse topics as Boer War Heroes, Australian Rugby Football Players, the Humming Birds of Hawaii, Nineteenth-Century Serving Girls, the History of Hungary and the Preservation of Poultry.

Since the same set of cards was frequently issued with different backs for different purposes, the Wharton-Tigar bequest is arranged in two series: the type series shows one card of each edition of each set; the other contains one complete example of each series of cards. It includes many very rare cards, including a card issued by a cigarette company that was immediately withdrawn on orders from its subject, the American baseball player Honus Wagner, a fanatical anti-smoker.

Cigarette card, 'A Kitchen in Tibet, Ogden's Guinea Gold Cigarettes'
PD Box 29–2950
Wharton-Tigar Collection

Cigarette card, 'Types of Lemco Cattle: Aberdeen Angus'
PD Box 49–4901
Wharton-Tigar Collection

TYPES of LEMCO CATTLE

Aberdeen Angus

FURTHER READING
A. Heal, *London Tradesmen's Cards of the XVIII Century, an account of their origin and use* (London, 1925)
E.C. Wharton-Tigar (ed.), *Cartophilic Reference Book* (St Albans, 1942–)

The tombstone of
G. Julius Alpinus **Classicianus**

Below is the tombstone of the procurator (finance minister) of Britain, who was appointed by the Emperor Nero in the aftermath of the rebellion of Queen Boudicca and the Iceni in AD 60–61 to correct the financial abuses that had been largely responsible for sparking off the conflict.

His activities are known from the Roman historian Tacitus, an unusual instance at this period where an historical personage can be linked to a burial monument. His name shows him to have been a member of the Gallic aristocracy but, for all his importance, we have no record of the date or circumstances of his death, only that another procurator was appointed in AD 65. From the inscription, which is incomplete but which can be read as follows, we presume he died in office:

> DIS·/[M]ANIBUS/IG(AI) IUL(I) G(AI) F(ILI)
> F]AB(IA TRIBU) ALPINI CLASSICIANI /—-/—-/
> PROC(URATORIS) PROVINC(IAE) BRITA[NNIAE]
> IULIA INDI FILIA PACATA I[NDIANA(?)]/
> UXOR [F(ECIT)]

['To the spirits of the departed (and) of Gaius Julius Alpinus Classicianus, son of Gaius of the Fabian voting tribe . . . Julia Pacata I[ndiana], daughter of Indus, his wife, had this built.']

The tombstone comes from Trinity Place, Trinity Square, London, and was reused in the fourth century AD in a bastion of the Roman town wall. Part was found in 1852 during excavations and further sections were discovered in 1885, when an underground railway was cut through the site, and in 1935.

Tombstone of
G. Julius Alpinus
Classicianus
London
Oolite, 1st century AD
PRB 1852 8–6 2/
1935 7–12 1
l. 2.28 m (7 ft 5¾ in)
Given by W. J. Hall and
the London Passenger
Transport Board

FURTHER READING
R.G. Collingwood and R. P. Wright, *The Roman Inscriptions of Britain*, vol. 1, no. 12 (Oxford, 1965)
P.R. Sealy, *The Boudiccan Revolt Against Rome* (Aylesbury, 1997)
G. Webster, *Boudicca: the British Revolt against the Romans*, AD 60 (London, 1978)

Claude Gellée, called Claude Lorrain (1604/5–82), was born of humble parents and moved from his native Lorraine to Rome at an early age. There he was apprenticed to the landscapist and painter of illusionistic architectural decorations Agostino Tassi (*c*.1580–1644). He returned briefly to Lorraine in 1625 but a year later moved back to Rome and lived there virtually without interruption for the rest of his life. His career as a landscape painter almost certainly began only after his return to Rome from Nancy, but within a few years he rose to fame and by 1637 he was the leading landscapist in Italy, with commissions from the Pope, the French ambassador and the king of Spain. Thereafter he enjoyed an unbroken success with both Roman and foreign patrons and secured himself a modest fortune. Initially influenced not only by his master, Tassi, but also by Paul Bril and by other artists working in Rome, he evolved an idealized, classically inspired compositional formula that won him international renown.

The Museum's collection of some 500 drawings by Claude Lorrain is the largest in existence. Most of them are sketches of an astonishing freedom and poetry made directly from nature in the Roman Campagna; distinct from these are his composition drawings, including the 195 in the *Liber Veritatis*, which was acquired in 1957 from the Chatsworth Collection. These were made by the artist as a record of his oeuvre, since his works were extensively forged and imitated even in his own lifetime. As well as being a pictorial document, the *Liber Veritatis* is also a work of art. The drawings were removed in 1976 from the album to which they had been transferred in the early eighteenth century and were mounted separately, making them more easily available to the public. Shown here is a *Landscape with Tobias and the Angel* which records a painting now in the State Hermitage, St Petersburg, executed for a Flemish patron, Henri van Halmade, in 1663.

Landscape with Tobias and the Angel
From the *Liber Veritatis*
Pen, brown-wash, white heightening on blue paper, AD 1663
PD 1957–12–14–166;
RD 916
19.8 × 25.9 cm
(7¾ × 10⅛ in)

FURTHER READING
A.M. Hind, *Catalogue of the Drawings of Claude Lorrain in the Department of Prints and Drawings in the British Museum* (London, 1926)
M. Kitson, *Claude Lorrain:* Liber Veritatis (London, 1978)
J.J.L. Whiteley, *Claude Lorrain. Drawings from the Collections of the British Museum and the Ashmolean Museum* (London, 1998)
P. Stein, *French Drawings: Clouet to Seurat* (London, 2005)

Clocks

Neither the inventor, the date nor the place of the first mechanical clock is known, but by about AD 1300 most European countries had mechanical clocks. At first the driving force was provided by weights. The mechanism for slowing down the speed at which the weights drop and evening out the spending of the power created by weights is known as an 'escapement'. The 'verge' escapement, the earliest surviving form, was in general use until about 1670, when alternative forms evolved.

By the middle of the fifteenth century, probably in Burgundy or Flanders, clocks were being made with a new driving force – the spring. The successful application of the spring resulted from the invention of the 'fusee' to even out its motive power. This revolutionized clockmaking, for without the necessity for weights, portable table clocks became a practical proposition.

In the second half of the sixteenth century a new 'plated' movement evolved. In this the movement is placed horizontally, with the dial (at least at first) on top, and all the mechanism, except the balance-wheel, contained between the two plates.

A dramatic change was brought to European clockmaking by Christian Huygens's invention of the pendulum clock in 1657. Subject to the law of gravity, this has inherent time-keeping properties and is less dependent on variations in force within the clockwork mechanism. Far more consistent time-keepers were now produced, including the 'long-case' or grandfather clock.

The Museum has one of the world's finest horological collections – some 7000 items. On the right is a clock made in *c.*1689 by the master clockmaker Thomas Tompion for the Royal Bedchamber in Kensington Palace. It is the earliest English pendulum-controlled spring-driven clock to go for one year without rewinding and has a pull repeating mechanism that sounds the last quarter and the last hour struck.

Perhaps the most popular clock in the Museum was made by 'French' and based on an 1808 patent by William Congreve. The clock is controlled by a steel ball which takes 30 seconds to roll from one end of the table to the other.

FURTHER READING
D. Thompson, *Clocks* (London, 2005)

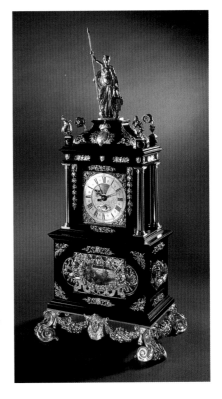

Thomas Tompion's Royal Clock (the 'Mostyn Tompion')
London
1689
MLA 1982,7–2, 1
h. 71 cm (28 in)
Purchased with the aid of the National Heritage Memorial Fund, the National Art Collections Fund and the Katharine Goodhart Kitchingman Bequest

Coin hoards

Most savings hoards have failed to come down to us, having been recovered by the owners or their heirs. The same does not always apply to emergency hoards buried, in wartime or during civil unrest, by persons who were unable to return to the place of concealment or perhaps even could not find it again. In most instances we can only speculate as to why and by whom the coins were buried.

The earliest known coin hoard comprises 19 electrum coins from the seventh century BC, found at the Temple of Artemis at Ephesus by a British Museum excavation in 1904–5. A hoard of 37 Roman gold *aurei* from Bedgar, Kent, for example, probably belonged to an officer with the Roman invasion of Britain in AD 43. The largest British hoard of Roman coins – about 55,000, mostly *antoniniani* of c.200–274 AD – was discovered at Mildenhall in Wiltshire in 1978 and is called after the town's Roman name

Part of the Hoxne hoard
Hoxne, England
4th–5th century AD
CM 1994–4–1
Treasure trove, acquired with the aid of the National Heritage Memorial Fund, the National Art Collections Fund, Lloyds Private Banking, private donations

Cunetio (the largest recorded hoard – 81,000 coins – was discovered in Bulgaria in 1929). Another recently discovered large hoard, almost 15,000 coins (above), was found at Hoxne (p. 154) in 1992.

Each year hoards of various sizes are unearthed and brought to the Museum, where they are cleaned and identified. Under the ancient laws of Treasure Trove the Museum had the right of first refusal for items of precious metal buried with the intention of recovery. The law was changed by the Treasure Act (1996) which removed the *animus revertendi* requirement, clarified the amount of gold or silver that objects must contain in order to be 'treasure' and enabled the Museum also to acquire containers associated with the hoard.

FURTHER READING

E. Besly and R. Bland, *The Cunetio Treasure, Roman Coinage of the Third Century AD* (London, 1983)

R. Hobbs, *Treasure: Finding our Past* (London, 2003)

The earliest **Coins**

Before the invention of coinage, metals, grains and shells appear to have been used by ancient peoples to make payments. Metals were valued as the raw materials for tools, weapons and ornaments. Shells were highly regarded as ornaments, while grains had universal value as storable foodstuffs. Each of these things could be measured when offered and accepted in payment – metals by weight, grains by volume, shells by number.

Early Mesopotamian and Chinese inscriptions record that payments could be made with ornaments and tools produced from metal. Other ancient peoples cast metal into distinctive ingots which did not resemble functional objects but had a form specific to their use as money. In some cases they were decorated, perhaps to make their monetary function and value more recognizable.

Coins were metal objects specifically developed for use as money, their size and shape making them easily portable and recognizable. The first coins in the West appeared in Lydia in Western Asia Minor in the seventh century BC, small versions of ingots stamped with designs indicating quality and weight. During the late sixth century BC coins were adopted by neighbouring peoples of Asia Minor, such as the Lycians, and from there they spread through the Greek world. The Greeks and subsequently the Romans were responsible for the widespread use of coinage throughout Europe, Asia and Africa. The empires of the Achaemenids and Alexander the Great brought the idea to India while the Romans, through both trade and conquest, ensured the adoption of coinage in the Western world.

In China a simultaneous but entirely separate tradition of coinage developed which spread throughout the Far East. The first coins were standardized imitations of tools and shells, decorated and inscribed to indicate their role as money. From the fourth century BC round coinage was introduced and standardized in 221 BC by China's first emperor. The growth of Chinese rule in the Far East spread Chinese coinage in the standard size and form established by the Han dynasty. During the Tang dynasty the use of coins spread to Korea, Vietnam and Japan.

The Western and Chinese traditions eventually met in the first century AD in Khotan, China.

Electrum coin
Lydia
*c.*575 BC
BMC.13
diam. 13 mm (½ in)

Bronze spade coin
China
Zhou dynasty, *c.*600 BC
CM 1996–6–11–1
l. 123 mm (4¾ in)

FURTHER READING
J. Williams (ed.), *Money. A History*
(London, 1997)

The indigenous peoples in the Americas regarded gold as being charged with the energizing, fertilizing powers of the sun. Skilled goldworking preceded the coming of the Spanish in the fifteenth century AD, and the earliest evidence of metalworking in South America has been traced back to *c.*2000 BC, in the Peruvian Andes. Through trade, exchange and invention, knowledge of metallurgy spread north to Ecuador, Colombia and Central America, and south to Bolivia, Argentina and Chile. A variety of metals was exploited in the Andes, but gold was specially prized for its

Gold pectoral
Calima, Colombia
AD 100–1500
ETH 1900.5–17.1
w. 36 cm (14⅙ in)

durability and solar association. Native goldsmiths independently discovered many of the principal techniques of goldworking known elsewhere in the world, including hammering, casting, soldering and gilding. Gold's lustrous qualities were employed to stunning effect in fashioning masks, figurines and ritual regalia.

The Museum has gold objects from a number of early peoples in this region, but a particularly fine collection of gold from Colombia. Shown here is a hammered and embossed gold pectoral (chest ornament) from Calima. The design may allude to a powerful bird of prey such as an eagle, the high-flying master of the sky, widely associated in Amerindian religion with the masculine, generative powers of the sun. The eyes are closed, and this may be a device to convey the idea that the gaze is not directed outward to the visible world but rather focused 'inwardly' on the spirit realm and the sources of ancestral inspiration.

FURTHER READING
C. McEwan (ed.), *Pre-Columbian Gold: Technology and Iconography* (London, 1999)

Coptic textiles

The word 'Copt' originally applied to the indigenous population of Egypt, as distinct from foreign settlers, but gradually it came to mean specifically those who had embraced Christianity. With the defeat of the Egyptian navy at the battle of Actium in 30 BC, the ensuing death of Antony and the suicide of Cleopatra VII, Egypt was drawn firmly into the Roman Empire and remained part of this, and later of the Byzantine Empire, until the Muslim invasion of AD 641. There is a tradition that the Church at Alexandria was founded by the evangelist St Mark, but it was not until the middle of the third century that it began to expand rapidly, providing the impetus for the development of Coptic, the language of the original inhabitants written in a mainly Greek script.

Undyed linen textile
decorated with coloured
wools
Akhmim, Egypt
4th–5th century AD
EA 43049
h. 1.8 m (5 ft 11 in)

The Museum possesses a good collection of Coptic textiles, including wool tapestries with mythological motifs and floral designs. The majority date from the fourth century AD onwards, particularly those from the cemeteries of Antinoopolis and Akhmim. Subjects of a purely Christian nature do not become common until the eighth century; they continue until the twelfth, when the textiles themselves disappear and with them the last vestiges of pharaonic civilization. The bulk of the surviving textiles of the fourth to sixth centuries consists of costume ornaments with tapestry-woven designs, usually of dyed wools, with linen threads for small details. Above is a tapestry with two large divine figures, set against an open background studded with decorative rosettes between vertical bands of decoration formed of coloured wool on a linen base. The male figure on the left wears a pointed cap of western Asiatic origin which is a mark of divine or heroic status; the female with bow and arrow may be Artemis.

FURTHER READING
A. Baginski and A. Tidhar, *Textiles from Egypt, 4th–13th centuries* (Israel, 1980)

The **Corbridge Lanx**

In 1735 Isabel Cutter, the nine-year-old daughter of the local cobbler at Corbridge, Northumberland, discovered this silver dish on the bank of the River Tyne. Other late Roman silver vessels were recovered in the vicinity between 1731 and 1760, and though none survived some were sketched or described. From this it would seem that gradual erosion of the river bank was washing out part of a fourth-century silver hoard, at least one item of which bore Christian symbols. Corbridge (Corstopitum) was a Roman garrison town.

Lanx was a term used in antiquity to denote a type of serving dish and this is one of the finest surviving late Roman silver 'picture' plates.

The scene shows the god Apollo at the entrance to a shrine, holding a bow, his lyre at his feet. His twin sister Artemis (Diana), the hunter goddess, enters from the left, and the helmeted goddess with her hand raised to indicate conversation is Athena (Minerva). The two female figures in the centre are less obvious. The entire scene is clearly a shrine of Apollo. The Greek island of Delos was the birthplace of Apollo and Artemis, and Athena was also worshipped there. If the Delian shrine is depicted then the older woman sitting spinning may be Leto, the mother of the twins, and the standing woman her sister Ortygia, who was transformed into the island of Delos. In the foreground stands an altar flanked by Artemis's hound and fallen stag and a griffin, a mythical beast associated with Apollo.

The decoration of the platter and its style indicate a fourth-century AD date. Its place of manufacture is unknown but may have been a major city in the Mediterranean, North Africa or Asia Minor. Ephesus has been suggested because of its links with the cults of Artemis, Apollo and Leto.

The Corbridge *Lanx*
Probably made in the Mediterranean area
Silver, 4th century AD
PRB.P 1993 4–1 1
l. 50.6 cm (20 in)
Given by the Secretary of State for National Heritage with the aid of the National Heritage Memorial Fund, the National Art Collections Fund and the British Museum Society

FURTHER READING
T. W. Potter, *Roman Britain* (2nd edn, London, 1997)

John Sell **Cotman**

John Sell Cotman (1782–1842) is one of the finest English land-scape watercolourists of the early nineteenth century. He was born in Norwich, trained and worked in London and then returned to his birthplace, where he became a leading member of the 'Norwich School'. He had travelled widely throughout Britain, sketching, and from 1811 to 1823 lived on the coast in Yarmouth, where he produced some very good paintings. In 1834 he left the area to become drawing master of King's College, London.

In September 1805 Cotman spent a week or so in Durham and was impressed by the picturesque position of the cathedral tower-ing over the River Wear. The watercolour below is the best of five known drawings of the view and it was probably the one exhibited at the Royal Academy in 1806. The cathedral, described as 'half church of God, half castle 'gainst the Scot', was begun in 1093 and is considered to be one of the finest Romanesque buildings in existence.

The Museum has an outstanding collection of Cotman's work, amounting to over 500 drawings and watercolours and a complete holding of his etchings.

'Durham Cathedral from the South-East'
Watercolour over pencil, 1805–6
PD 1859–5–28–119
43.6 × 33.1 cm
(17¹⁄₁₀ × 13 in)

FURTHER READING
A.M. Holcomb, *John Sell Cotman* (London, 1978)

Credit cards

The ancients valued gold and silver, the late twentieth century values plastic. In the West the earliest coins were of precious metal, often adulterated. Bronze fiduciary money, that is, money whose value depends on trust rather than on the worth of its constituent material, increased in the nineteenth century, as did paper currency. The economic consequences of World War I challenged the dominance of gold and silver coinages. The rising price of precious metals and the influence of new economic theories led to their replacement by paper money and token coins of base metal with values determined by political policies and international exchange rates.

The twentieth century has seen the transformation of all circulating coins into fiduciary money, but also developments away from the use of actual money. The first cash-dispenser machines in the world were introduced in Britain in 1967. Now, in the late twentieth century, we see a growing tendency to make payments without cash in any physical form. Historically such transactions have long been familiar to merchants and bankers using letters of credit and bills of exchange. Internationally accepted credit cards and immediate electronic transfer of funds between accounts have now brought the invisible movement of money into the everyday life of millions of people. Gold and silver are no longer the prime symbols of money or exchange value, and neither cash nor credit cards are conceived of as substitutes for specific amounts of precious metal. However, a strong symbolic association between gold and currency endures, for example in the designation of those with the highest spending power as 'gold' cards. On the left is a selection of bank cards, debit cards, store account cards and credit cards from the Museum's growing collection of such items from around the world.

Credit and other cards
late 20th century AD

FURTHER READING
Credit Card Research Group, *Understanding Credit and Debit Cards* (London, July 1995)
G. Davies, *A History of Money from Ancient Times to the Present Day* (Cardiff, 1994)
J.K. Galbraith, *The World Economy since the Wars* (London, 1995)

Cretan bull acrobat

This bronze statuette, made in Crete c.1600 BC, shows a slim, long-haired acrobat somersaulting dangerously over the horns of a massive bull that plants its feet squarely on the ground and throws back its head. The bull-leaping game or ritual also appears on frescoes from the palace at Knossos, and is illustrated on engraved gems. It is probably an element in the legends of the Cretan King Minos and the Minotaur, part man, part bull, to whom seven young Athenian men and seven young girls were sacrificed regularly and who Theseus eventually confronted and killed in the labyrinth within the palace.

Around 2000 BC the comparatively primitive culture of the Cyclades was eclipsed by the spectacular Bronze Age civilization that developed on Crete. This was centred round the elaborate palaces, perhaps of priest-kings, at Knossos, Mallia, Phaistos and Zakro, and is now called 'Minoan' after the legendary King Minos. The earliest palaces were destroyed in c.1700 by an earthquake, but were rebuilt. Around 1450 all the palaces except Knossos were destroyed again, most probably by Mycenean invaders from mainland Greece. Knossos survived until around 1375 BC.

FURTHER READING
L. Burn, *Greek Myths* (London, 1990)
S. Hood, *The Arts in Prehistoric Greece* (Harmondsworth, 1978)

Cretan bull acrobat
Said to be from near
Rethymnon, western
Crete
Bronze, c.1600 BC
GR 1966.3–28.1
h. 11.4 cm (4½ in)
Purchased with the aid of
the Shaw Fund

The **Crystal Skull**

Whatever its origins, this skull, carved from a single piece of rock crystal, is a spectacular piece of skilled craftsmanship. All that is certain is that it is at least one hundred years old, since it was purchased by the Museum from Tiffany in New York at the end of 1897. By then it had passed through a number of hands. It was said in a publication by Tiffany's manager in 1890 to have been brought originally from Mexico by a Spanish officer 'some time before the French occupation of Mexico' (which took place in 1862–7).

For many years it was accepted as a rare survival of Aztec or Mixtec art, made in Mexico before the Spanish Conquest of the sixteenth century. The skull bears some, but not close, resemblance to smaller carvings of skulls in Mixtec or Aztec style made prior to the Conquest. Examinations under high magnification have, however, indicated that a European jeweller's wheel was used to produce some of the incised lines forming the teeth. This could demonstrate that the piece is post-Conquest, perhaps an example of Colonial Spanish cathedral art from Mexico. Alternatively, it could be an earlier object reworked after the coming of the Spaniards. Yet another possibility is that the skull is of much more recent manufacture, and even from an entirely different geographic region. It has been suggested that the rock crystal used is Brazilian, which makes a pre-Conquest date less likely, since this source of rock crystal has apparently only recently been exploited.

Rock-crystal skull
Origin and date uncertain
ETH Am.1898–1
h. 21 cm (8¼ in)
Purchased 1897 (Tiffany and Co.) with funds bequeathed by Henry Christy

FURTHER READING
M. Jones (ed.), *Fake? The Art of Deception* (London, 1990), pp. 296–7
F. Kunz, *Gems and Precious Stones of North America* (New York, 1890), pp. 285–6
J. Maclaren Walsh, 'Crystal Skulls and Other Problems' in A. Henderson and A.L. Kaeppler (eds), *Exhibiting Dilemmas, Issues of Representation at the Smithsonian* (Washington, 1997), pp. 116–39

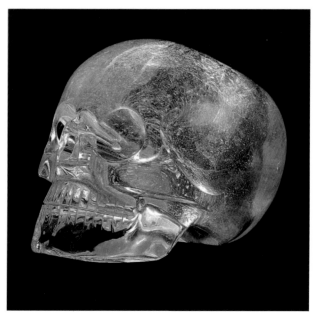

The **Cuerdale hoard**

The Cuerdale hoard was found on the bank of the River Ribble near Cuerdale Hall, Lancashire, in 1840. With over 7000 coins and more than 1300 items of silver, weighing 90 lb (40 kg), it is by far the largest Viking hoard ever found in northern or western Europe. The coins in the hoard date its deposition to c.905 or a little later.

The first Viking raid on Britain is recorded in the Anglo-Saxon Chronicle for AD 793: 'on 8 January, the ravages of heathen men miserably destroyed God's church of Lindisfarne with plunder and slaughter'. Between then and c.1050 the Vikings made raids around most of the British Isles. From the late ninth century Danes settled in large numbers in the north and east of England, founding or revitalizing a number of towns, the most important of which was York. Norwegian settlers predominated in Scotland and the Isles, and all around the Irish Sea.

As well as land for settlement, the Vikings sought wealth in precious metals, reflected in the numerous hoards which have been found in Britain and Ireland. Jewellery, often cut up into 'hack-silver', appears in these hoards alongside coins as another form of portable wealth. The composition of the silver items demonstrates the wide-ranging activities of the Vikings, who sailed around Spain to the Mediterranean, and travelled across Russia as far as Constantinople. Although the coins in the Cuerdale hoard predominantly come from the Danelaw (the Viking-controlled area of England), there are also Islamic, Anglo-Saxon and Continental examples. The hack-silver includes fragments of penannular and thistle brooches of Hiberno-Norse origin, Anglo-Saxon metalwork, Carolingian silver-gilt belt mounts and other exotic scraps.

The Cuerdale hoard (detail)
England
10th century AD
MLA 1841,7–11, 1–741;
1873,11–1, 1;
1954,2–3, 1–2
CM 1838–7–10–1436;
1442; 1168; 1203
Given by H.M. Queen Victoria

Objects from the hoard were acquired by a number of institutions and private collections, with a major portion being presented to the Museum.

FURTHER READING
G. Williams (ed.), *World of Money* CD-ROM (London, 1998)

Cuneiform

At one time it was thought that writing was invented in southern Iraq in c.3000 BC, but it now appears that its invention was a gradual process, accomplished over a wide area. Its purpose appears to have been to record business activities for officials of palaces and temples. On the very earliest texts pictures (sometimes called pictographs) were drawn on damp clay. But the scribes found it quicker to produce a stylized representation of an object by making a few marks rather than attempt a naturalistic impression. These stylized representations then had to be standardized so that everyone could recognize them. The tool employed, the end of the wooden or reed stylus, which struck the clay first, made a wider mark than the shaft, producing the wedge-shaped impression after which this writing system came to be known – cuneiform (from the Latin *cuneus*, wedge).

Cuneiform was pioneered by the Sumerians and Babylonians and over 3000 years was used by many peoples, among them Elamites, Hittites, and Urartians, and for some 15 languages. It was last used in c.AD 75.

Pictographic tablets from Tell Brak
c.3300–3100 BC
WA C.0206–7
(Originals in Deir es-Zor Museum, Syria)

Part of the 'standard inscription' of King Ashurnasirpal II
North-West Palace, Nimrud, Assyria
c.865–860 BC
WA 124584–5;
1851–9–2,499–500
h. 2.17 m (7ft 0¼in)
Excavated by A.H. Layard

The Museum has a large collection of cuneiform tablets spanning many centuries, but the cornerstone of the study and continued decipherment of cuneiform is the Kuyunjik (or K.) collection of 25,000 tablets. Between 1845 and 1851 Austen Henry Layard discovered the palaces of the Assyrian kings at their capitals of Kalhu/Nimrud (the Biblical Calah) and Nineveh (the modern Kuyunjik). At Kuyunjik two libraries of clay tablets were found by Layard in the palace of Sennacherib and by Hormuzd Rassam in the palace of Ashurbanipal. Many were inscribed with the name of Ashurbanipal, grandson of Sennacherib (r.668–627 BC). These tablets, gradually deciphered and pieced together in a process which is still continuing, have proved crucial to our grasp of Mesopotamian thinking and literature.

Above left are early pictographic tablets from Tell Brak, and left is the so-called 'standard inscription' of King Ashurnasirpal, carved across the centre of every wall panel in the North-West Palace at Nimrud. It begins 'Palace of Ashurnasirpal, priest of Ashur, favourite of Enlil and Ninurta, beloved of Anu and Dagan, the weapon of the great gods, the mighty King, King of the world, King of Assyria….'

FURTHER READING
C.B.F. Walker, *Reading the Past: Cuneiform* (London, 1987)

Cycladic figurines

W e can only speculate about the meaning of the Cycladic figurines, since they come from a society that left no written records. Many come from graves and it has been suggested that they were made particularly for funerary use. Not all Early Cycladic graves contain figurines, although some have more than one. Some have been found on settlement sites. Most are female but some are male. The majority are single but there are pairs and groups including musicians, drinkers and occasional warriors or hunters.

In the third millennium BC (the Early Bronze Age) relatively prosperous and well-populated settlements flourished in the Cyclades. The inhabitants were dependent on farming and fishing, but they also learned to use metal, especially copper, silver and lead, and their sculptors carved works of simple form and line using the local marble. Early Cycladic material is broadly divided into three groups: the Grotta-Pelos culture (3200–2800 BC), the Keros-Syros culture (2800–2300 BC) and the Phylakopi I culture (2300–2000 BC), named after islands or sites where typical material has been found; they overlap and the dates are approximate.

Cycladic sculptures invite comparison with modern art, and indeed those in the Museum were among the objects which influenced the sculptor Henry Moore (p. 214) during his visits in the 1920s. Moore wrote.

> If I was asked to explain to students what it is I mean by 'a sense of form' perhaps I would start off with the Cycladic Room of the British Museum, for what the Cycladic sculpture has got is an unbelievably pure sense of style, of unity of form.

Pictured here is a figurine of a woman bearing traces of black and red paint on the face, indicating eyes, eyebrows and a diadem, along with a dotted pattern on at least one of the cheeks.

Marble figurine of a woman (early Spedos type)
Cyclades, Greece
Keros-Syros culture, c.2700–2500 BC
GR 1971.5–21.1
h. 76.8 cm (30¼ in)

FURTHER READING
J.L. Fitton, *Cycladic Art* (2nd edn, London, 1999)

Cypriot sculpture

Cyprus is tucked into the eastern corner of the Mediterranean at the crossroads between the major civilizations of the ancient world. The name comes from the Latin for copper, *Cyprium aes* (metal of Cyprus), and the island was renowned for copper in antiquity. The first traces of human occupation date back to about 8800 BC. Settlers from the Greek world arrived in large numbers around 1100 BC and Phoenicians (from modern Lebanon) about 250 years later. In the earlier Iron Age the island, now internally organized into autonomous city kingdoms, was subjected to foreign rule by Assyria (*c.*707–612 BC); it was then in close alliance with, if not controlled by, Egypt (570–526/5 BC) and later under Persian authority (526–333 BC). The Cypriot kings voluntarily submitted to Alexander the Great in 333 BC, but this was to lead to their demise, and in 294 BC Cyprus became part of the large Hellenistic monarchy of Egypt. Rome first annexed the island in 58 BC and again in 30 BC. Events of the fourth century AD marked the beginning of a new period in Cyprus' history.

Upper part of a colossal limestone statue
Sanctuary of Apollo at Idalion, Cyprus
*c.*490–480 BC
GR 1917.7–1.233;
Cat. Sculpture C154
h. 104 cm (41 in)
Excavated by Sir Robert Hamilton Lang

It was not until about 640/630 BC that numerous limestone figures were produced for dedication in sanctuaries, a tradition that flourished until the imposition of Roman rule. The earliest style was essentially a Cypriot creation, but Cyprus' involvement with other Mediterranean powers soon led to the development of a new style showing influence from the Greek East, Egypt and the Near East. Increased contact between Cyprus and East Greek cities after 526/525 BC led to greater dependence on East Greek models, while other statues wore Egyptian crowns and kilts reflecting Phoenician taste. Sculpture of the Hellenistic (333–30 BC) and Roman periods adopted styles that were universal throughout the Greek-dominated eastern Mediterranean, and in the Roman period statues of gods and rulers proliferated and adorned public buildings.

FURTHER READING
V. Tatton-Brown, *Ancient Cyprus* (2nd edn, London, 1997)

Cyrene, the original capital of ancient Cyrenaica (now eastern Libya), was one of the greatest of Greek colonies. Herodotus (c.485–425 BC) relates that King Grinius of Thera consulted the oracle of Apollo at Delphi and was told to found a city in Libya. On his protesting that he was too old, the oracle pointed to a young man named Battus. After many vicissitudes and another visit to the oracle Battus arrived on the Libyan mainland and was taken by the local inhabitants to high ground, from various points of which issued springs. The Greeks settled in this fertile oasis between the Mediterranean and the Libyan desert some time in the seventh century BC. They dedicated the spring that sustained their community to the god Apollo, whose oracle had encouraged their expedition. The city they built was called Cyrene, after the nymph Κυιana who nourished the spring waters.

Cyrene remained a monarchy under descendants of its founder until the Persian invasion of c.450 BC. This was followed by a republic which submitted to Alexander the Great (p. 15) in 331 BC, and then by a local dynasty of the Ptolemies. The Romans took over in 96 BC, administering the region as a province with Crete. Although Cyrene was prosperous, religious unrest led to the Jewish revolt of AD 115 in which 20,000 lives were lost. After order was restored the Emperor Hadrian (r.AD 117–38) encouraged the reconstruction of Cyrene and sent new settlers. The settlers asserted the Greek origins of Cyrene, a sentiment reflected in contemporary sculpture and architecture.

The cult of Apollo was extremely important to the inhabitants of Cyrene from the Archaic period onwards, since it was the oracle of Apollo at Delphi which had been responsible for the colony's foundation. Following the devastation of the sanctuary of Apollo during the Jewish revolt, the programme of rebuilding included a temple in the Doric style which was finally dedicated during the joint reign of Marcus Aurelius and Commodus (AD 176–80). The cult statue of Apollo playing the *kithara* (lyre) (above) was probably completed and dedicated at the same time as the temple.

The sculpture was found during excavations carried out for the Museum in 1860–1 by R. Murdoch Smith (Royal Engineers) and E.A. Porcher (Royal Navy). It was discovered broken in many

Marble statue of Apollo
Cyrene, Libya
2nd century AD Roman copy of Hellenistic original of c.200–150 BC
GR 1861.7–25.1;
Cat. Sculpture 1380
h. 228.6 cm (7ft 6 in)
Excavated by R.M. Smith and E.A. Porcher

Cyrene

Bronze head of a North African
Cyrene, Libya
c.300 BC
GR 1861.11–27.13;
Bronze 268
h. 30.5 cm (12 in)
Excavated by R.M. Smith
and E.A. Porcher

pieces in the temple floor, close to a large base on which it had originally stood. The god combines features of Dionysos (p. 105) and Apollo. The statue is a Roman copy of a Hellenistic original, one of a dozen surviving copies of a work attributed to the second-century BC Athenian sculptor Timarchides.

Also found on the temple site, beneath the *cella* (main room), was the bronze head (left) whose distinctive features suggest a North African, possibly a native Libyan. The head was found with fragments of bronze horses, and may therefore have belonged to an equestrian group. To give a multi-coloured effect the lips, made separately, were originally overlaid with copper sheet; the teeth are of bone, now blackened with age. The pupils of the eyes were originally of glass and the whites of magnesium carbonate. The eyelashes were separately cast and attached.

FURTHER READING
J. Huskinson, *Corpus of the Sculptures of the Roman World, Great Britain*, Vol. II Fascicule I, *Roman Sculpture from Cyrenaica in the British Museum* (London, 1975)
R.M. Smith and E.A. Porcher, *History of Recent Discoveries in Cyrene* (London, 1864)

Richard **Dadd**

Richard Dadd (1817–86) was one of the most idiosyncratically talented of nineteenth century artists. He is mainly known today for his painting 'The Fairy-Feller's Master Stroke' (Tate Gallery) and for the fact that many of his finest works were painted after 1842 when he murdered his father in a fit of insanity and was committed to an asylum for life.

'Halt in the Desert' (shown below) was painted in *c*.1845. One of Dadd's most important early works and among the most impressive watercolours of the period, it was exhibited in Manchester in 1857 but subsequently thought to have been lost. It re-emerged in 1986 when it was brought for an opinion to the television programme the *Antiques Roadshow* and was subsequently purchased by the Museum.

In 1842 Dadd's patron, Sir Thomas Phillips, took him as draughtsman on his expedition to Greece, Turkey, Palestine and Egypt: it was from this journey that Dadd returned insane. The party toured the Holy Land for two weeks, finishing up in Jerusalem, only to set out next day to visit Jordan and the Dead Sea, returning across the wilderness of Engaddi by moonlight. Dadd shows the travellers temporarily camped by the Dead Sea for two hours after sunset, before continuing their journey through the mountains. Dadd himself is at the far right of the camp fire.

Almost all of Dadd's works are carefully signed and dated, frequently bearing long inscriptions describing the subjects. On the back of this watercolour the scene is described: 'Ici on voit clair de lune peigné des recollections qui existent dans la tête du peinteur, et des certains marques et lines dans la livre petit que je crois de n'avoir pas été dans le possession du Sir Thos. Phillips. C'est sur le bord de la Mer Morte tout près un petit rousseau, entre le Jordan Fleuve et les Montagnes sur le route à St Sabre.'

FURTHER READING
P. Alderidge, *Richard Dadd* (London, 1974)

'Halt in the Desert'
Watercolour and body-colour, after 1842
PD 1987–4–11–9
37 × 70.7 cm
(14½ × 27¾ in)
Purchased with the aid of the National Heritage Memorial Fund

The *dakinis* are fierce minor goddesses, more revered than their male counterparts, the *dakas*. Their Tibetan name, *mkah-hgro*, which translates as 'walking in the sky', indicates their sphere of activity. Their fearsome weapons, the skull cap filled with blood, the skull necklace and their terrifying expressions ensure that they are frequently propitiated. Shown here in painted clay is Sarvabuddhadakini, 'the *dakini* of all the Buddhas'.

Buddhism was first introduced into Tibet from India in the seventh century AD, but only became fully established in the tenth. Different schools of Mahayana Buddhism entered Tibet at this time, including the school of tantric teachings popular in eastern India at the turn of the first and second millennium AD. Other traditions emphasizing the role of monastic life and its disciplines were also established. Tibet's location in the highest habitable terrain of Asia, the Tibetan plateau bounded on the south by the Himalayas and on the north by the Takla Makan desert, ensured a degree of isolation in which a distinctive culture flourished.

FURTHER READING
W. Zwalf (ed.), *Buddhism: Art and Faith* (London, 1985)
W. Zwalf, *Heritage of Tibet* (London, 1981)

Sarvabuddhadakini
Tibet
19th century AD
OA 1948.7–16.24
h. 40.6 cm (16 in)
H.G. Beasley Bequest

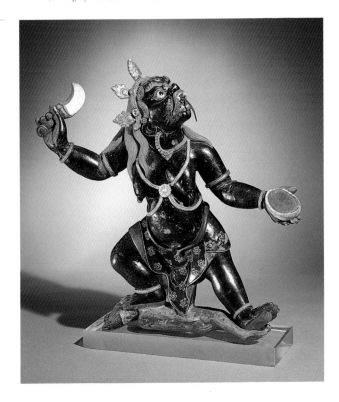

In Mexico, when the souls of the dead return to this world for a few brief hours each year, they are welcomed with a feast. The festival of Todos Santos (All Saints), also called Dia or Dias de los Muertos, is neither sombre nor macabre, but much enjoyed as a time of family and community reunion. It takes place mostly between 31 October and 2 November and is a mixture of customs and beliefs from Catholic Europe and indigenous Mexico from colonial and modern times.

On the Day, or Days of the Dead (1 and 2 November), each family sets up a table lavishly decorated with flowers, leaves, fruits, candles and pictures or images of the saints. The souls are attracted by the colour and aromatic scent of the *cempasuchil*, a type of marigold, as well as the burning of copal incense. Both have been associated with festivals of the dead since pre-Hispanic times. The souls arrive to the tolling of church bells; their presence is sensed by the family. First the souls of young children are offered suitable food and toys on 1 November, and the following day it is the turn of the adults. The souls take up the essence of the offerings until, on the day after, the living of the family will eat and drink from them, perhaps sharing with relatives, godparents, neighbours and friends. Thus the living and dead come together as one community in the sharing of the feast.

'The Atomic Apocalypse – Will Death Die?'
Papier mâché ensemble
Made by the Linares family
of Mexico City
ETH 1989.Am.13

The Museum has a unique collection of these offerings, gathered together over many years. It includes brilliantly coloured sugar skulls, sugar coffins with pop-up skeletons, pottery toys of skeletons engaged in everyday activities, beautifully made masks, textiles and costumes, altars, tableaux, carvings and papier-mâché sculptures, of which a selection is seen above. In this tableau, King Death sits on the world while War gallops on a red horse and Famine rides a locust.

FURTHER READING
E. Carmichael and C. Sayer, *The Skeleton at the Feast: The Day of the Dead in Mexico* (London, 1992)

Dr **Dee's magic**

In the sixteenth century the line between science and magic was unclear. There was a widespread conviction that there was no rational explanation for the laws of nature and that there was a magical principle at the basis of the universe. John Dee (1527–1608/9) was a scholar in this tradition. He was competent in mathematics and astronomy but also deeply involved in magic and astrology.

According to his lengthy entry in the *Dictionary of National Biography*, on 10 March 1574/5 Queen Elizabeth I visited Dr Dee's home at Mortlake where she 'requested Dee to bring out his famous magic glass and describe its properties, which he accordingly did to her majesty's satisfaction'.

The *DNB* also relates: 'he possessed a crystal globe which he believed had the quality, when intently surveyed, of presenting apparitions and even emitting sounds... Only one person, having been named as seer, could see the spirits and hear the voices, concentrating all his faculties on the crystal.' Dee also used a magic mirror into which to call his spirits.

The Museum has a collection of Dee's relics. The obsidian mirror is Aztec. It was preserved in a leather case and at one time belonged to Horace Walpole (1717–97), who wrote the label. The crystal ball is thought to have been one of Dr Dee's 'shewstones', said by Dee to have been given him by an angel. The gold disc is engraved with a representation of the Vision of the Four Castles seen during a session at Krakow in Poland in 1584. The three wax discs with magicial inscriptions supported Dee's magical table.

FURTHER READING
P. J. French, *John Dee* (London, 1972)
H. Tait, '"The devil's looking-glass": the magical speculum of Dr John Dee' in W.H. Smith (ed.), *Horace Walpole. Writer, Politician and Connoisseur* (New Haven and London, 1967), pp. 195–212.

Obsidian mirror
14th–16th(?) centuries AD
MLA 1966,10–1, 1
diam. 18.4 cm (7¼ in)
Gold disc
late 16th century AD
MLA 1942,5–6, 1
diam. 8.8 cm (3½ in)
Given by the National Art
Collections Fund
Crystal ball
date unknown
MLA Sloane 232
diam. 6 cm (2⅓ in)
Sir Hans Sloane Bequest
Three wax discs
late 16th century AD
MLA OA, 105–7
diam. (max.) 23 cm (9 in)
Cottonian Library

Mrs **Delany's flower collages**

In 1772, in her seventy-third year, Mrs Delany (1700–88) wrote to her niece 'I have invented a new way of imitating flowers'. Over a period of ten years, until her eyesight failed, her remarkable skill with scissors created a collection of nearly one thousand paper pictures of plants, of botanical accuracy unsurpassed in that medium. Years later she recalled how she had begun her new recreation: she noticed the similarity of colour between a geranium and a piece of red paper that was on her table. Taking her scissors, she cut out the scarlet paper and, using more coloured paper for the leaves and stalk, she created a picture so realistic that a friend mistook the paper petals for real ones.

The variety of species and their complexity did not deter her – the flamboyant 'Barbadoes Flower Fence' has stamens two inches long with the anther at the tips; the diminutive 'Eyebright' measures three inches but includes eleven flowers amongst the leaves and roots; *Mimosa latisliqua* has 543 leaves cut in different shades of green and 120 stamens in a single bloom. Below is 'Rosa Spinosissima, Burnet Rose' (*Rosa pimpinellifolia*), with 65 thorns cut in one piece together with the stem.

As her collection grew, so did Mrs Delany's fame, bringing explorers and botanists to her with gifts of rare plants. George III and Queen Charlotte were admirers of her albums of 'paper mosaicks' and ordered new plants growing at Kew to be sent to her.

Her skill continues to amaze. Occasionally she dyed pieces to obtain the exact shade she required, or used watercolour to indicate shading, but mostly this was achieved by placing minute pieces layer upon layer. The adhesive is so effective that after two hundred years and much handling the tiny pieces are still in place.

'Rosa Spinosissima, Burnet Rose'
England
Paper collage, undated
PD 1897–5–5–746
24.3 × 20.3 cm (9½ × 8 in)
Given by Lady Llanover

FURTHER READING
R. Hayden, *Mrs Delany: her Life and her Flowers* (3rd edn, London, 2000)
C.E. Vulliamy, *Aspasia: the Life and Letters of Mary Granville, Mrs Delany (1700-1788)* (London, 1935)

Demeter of Knidos

Asia Minor (Caria), mid-4th century BC

Marble figure of Demeter
Knidos, Anatolia, Turkey
c.350–330 BC
GR 1859.12–26.26;
Cat. Sculpture 1300
h. 147 cm (4ft 9⅞ in)
Excavated by Charles
Newton

Demeter was the goddess of fertility, who governed the cycle of the seasons and the growing of grain. When her daughter Persephone was abducted by Hades and carried off to the Underworld, Demeter went searching for her, her absence making the earth sterile. Although Persephone had eaten seven pomegranate seeds, thereby binding herself to Hades, a compromise was reached allowing her to return to earth, bringing the spring, but when she goes back to Hades it is winter.

Knidos was a Dorian city on the south-west coast of Asia Minor. The sanctuary of Demeter was situated beneath a cliff in which were cut niches for statues and votive offerings. This sanctuary was laid out about the same time as the refounding of the city, in c.350 BC.

The statue below was made of Parian marble, the head and body carved from separate blocks. The goddess wears a heavy mantle which is drawn over her head like a veil, at least one hand probably held a libation bowl or torch. The throne originally had arms and a high back. It has been suggested, on the basis of a similarity with a portrait of Alexander the Great attributed to him, that the sculptor may be Leochares, who may have worked on the Mausoleum in the nearby city of Halikarnassos (pp. 292–3).

The site was excavated by Charles Newton in 1857–8. As well as sculpture, a number of other objects were recovered including terracotta figures and numerous lamps and glass bottles, ranging in date from the middle of the fourth century BC to the Roman period. In addition there was a group of curses inscribed on lead tablets. One was inscribed with a dedication to Demeter, Kore (Persephone) and Plouton (Hades) by a woman named Antigone in the second century BC, attempting to clear her name after she was accused of trying to poison a certain Asklepiades.

FURTHER READING
Sir C. Newton, *Travels and Discoveries in the Levant* (London, 1865)
B. Ashmole, 'Demeter of Cnidus', *JHS*, 71 (1951)
J. Boardman, *Greek Sculpture, The Late Classical Period* (London, 1995)

Devi, the Great Goddess

I n Hinduism many different goddesses are worshipped. They are generically known by the name of Devi, which means 'goddess'. Because of the connection between the fertility of the earth and female reproduction, the goddess is often referred to as 'Mother'. In her manifestation as fertile mother, Devi is recognized by many Hindus as incarnate in the life-providing rivers of the subcontinent. The soil can be seen as the body of the goddess, the features of the landscape being her own physical features. There are also other goddesses whose role is more specific, and less obviously concerned with productivity. A characteristic common to most

Painting on paper of Gajalakshmi, Lakshmi bathed by elephants
Punjab Hills, India
c.AD 1775
OA 1924.4–1.02

Sandstone panel of Chamunda
Orissa, India
9th century AD
OA 1872.7–1.83
h. 1.19 cm (46½ in)
Bridge Collection

goddesses is their connection with life-giving blood. Many require blood-offerings.

The goddess as a rule, when worshipped alone, is fierce, but when she is the consort of a male deity she is benevolent.

The great male gods are usually attended by a goddess; Sarasvati, the goddess of learning and the arts, is consort of Brahma. The consorts of Vishnu are Sridevi or Lakshmi, the goddess of fortune (above), who appears on his right, and Bhudevi, the goddess of the earth, on his left. Parvati is the consort of Shiva. The divine consorts are in some way considered versions of the same vital female force, which is Devi. Parvati is also called Durga, the Unapproachable. She sometimes displays her sinister side; in this form she may be Kali, Chamunda (right) or Sitala.

FURTHER READING
T.R. Blurton, *Hindu Art* (London, 1992)

The Sacred Way at
Didyma
Didyma, western Asia Minor, 6th–5th century BC

A long the Sacred Way at Didyma sat a series of impressive monumental statues, usually larger than life-size, dedicated by rich and powerful people as gifts to the god Apollo. Many of the statues represent seated men and women, sometimes identified by inscriptions as members of aristocratic families. One now in the Museum proclaims: 'I am Chares, Son of Kleisis, Ruler of Teichioussa, the statue belongs to Apollo.' These are not portraits, since although there are differences in clothing, the body of each statue resembles those of its companions. The fact that the statue belongs to the god is more important than the fact that it commemorates a human personage. It is, for example, a symbol of Chares, but not a portrait, because it lays no stress upon the attributes which belonged to him alone. Another statue is inscribed with the name of the sculptor, 'Eudemos made me'.

Seated marble male figure weaving a sleeved chiton (long linen tunic) and a himation (mantle)
Didyma, Ionia, Turkey
c.560 BC
GR 1859.12–26,5;
Cat. Sculpture B 278;
Inscription 933
h. 1.49 m (4 ft 10½ in)
Excavated by C.T. Newton

The temple of Apollo at Didyma in western Asia Minor was the site of a famous oracle. During the sixth century BC the sanctuary was one of the richest in what was then East Greece. The temple, which belonged to the city of Miletus, stood near the sea and the Sacred Way led to a small harbour about a mile and a half away. The statues all date to the period before 494 BC when the Persians destroyed the sanctuary.

The Sacred Way was excavated in 1857 by Charles Newton, British Vice-Consul at Mytilene, later to become the first Keeper of Greek and Roman Antiquities at the Museum. Ten of the figures and two lions were acquired by the Museum.

FURTHER READING
J. Boardman, *Greek Sculpture. The Archaic Period* (London, 1978)

Dionysos or Bacchus

To the Greeks Dionysos, also called Bacchus, was the god of wine and mystic ecstasy, son of Zeus and Semele. The Romans acquired his cult from Greece and linked him with the Italian god Liber Pater. First shown as a bearded man, he later appeared as a beautiful youth with dark eyes and flowing locks, crowned with vine and ivy. In peace his robe was purple, in war a panther's skin. He led his followers, the maenads or bacchants, in a triumphal journey across Asia and eventually to Greece, a progress which was a popular subject in art. Bacchus was worshipped in tumultuous revels and mystic rites, the Bacchanalia. In Athens the dramatists produced their plays as part of the spring festival of the Great Dionysia.

Bronze mask of Bacchus
Roman
1st century AD, perhaps from a Hellenistic original
GR. 1989.1–30.1
h. 21.4 cm (8⅓ in)
Purchased with the aid of the National Heritage Memorial Fund

Below is a bronze mask of the god which may have served originally as a decorative attachment below the handles of a special kind of pail (*situla*) used in the rites of the goddess Isis. Bacchus is shown with long hair and a curly beard, wearing a crown of ivy. A band across the forehead is inlaid with iron, the centres of the ivy-berries and the lips with copper, and the whites of the eyes with silver. The horns are probably seventeenth-century Italian additions, perhaps made in an attempt to represent the god Pan. The mask was once in the collection of Dr Richard Mead, an early pioneer in the fields of poisons and smallpox, who perhaps acquired it in Italy in 1695–6.

Bacchus/Dionysos is seen in many guises in the Museum: in the wedding procession on the Sophilos vase (p. 306), on the Andokides vase, and he may be the reclining figure in the east pediment of the Parthenon (pp. 245–6). In post-classical times the god and symbols associated with him were often used by Western artists.

FURTHER READING
T.H. Carpenter, *Dionysian Imagery in Archaic Greek Art* (Oxford, 1986)
F.W. Hamdorf, *Dionysos Bacchus* (Munich, 1986)
E. Simon, *Festivals of Attica* (Wisconsin, 1983), pp. 89–108
A. Dalby, *Bacchus: A Biography* (London, 2005)

Dogs

For at least 14,000 years, perhaps longer, humans and dogs have lived together. In the Museum, as elsewhere, they appear in all shapes and sizes, from the vicious mastiffs of the Assyrian lion-hunt (pp. 186–7) to the delicate marble greyhounds of the Townley collection (p. 332).

Below a dog with massive neck muscles, dragged back by a heavy collar, stands ready to spring at any desperate lion which might try to escape the spears and arrows of the Assyrian king and

Lion-hunt of Ashurbanipal
Nineveh, Assyria
c.645 BC
WA 124892 (detail)
h. of slab 157 cm
(13 ft 0⅓ in)
Excavated by Hormuzd Rassam

his followers. Opposite, by contrast, two Roman greyhounds nuzzle each other playfully. The pair were found at Monte Cagnolo, near the ancient Lanuvium.

The Museum's foundation collection, bequeathed by Sir Hans Sloane, includes an inscription found near the Pincian Gate in Rome in 1726 which speaks across the centuries of the grief felt by humans on the death of a much-loved pet, in this case a dog called Margarita ('pearl'). In 12 lines of verse it describes how the dog was born in Gaul and named by 'the shell of rich waters'. Although she was trained to hunt in the hills and forests she was unaccustomed to chains and beatings:

> *molli namque sinu domini dominaeque iacebam*
> *et noram in strato lassa cubare toro*

Dogs

Part of a set of protective clay dogs
North Palace, Nineveh, Assyria
*c.*645–635 BC
WA 30001–5;
1856–9–3, 1505–9
l. (max.) 7.5 cm (3 in)
Excavated by W.K. Loftus

('for I used to lie on the soft lap of my master and mistress and knew what it was to sleep when tired on a well strewn couch')

et plus quam licuit muto canis ore loquebar
nulli latratus pertimuere meos

('and I used to speak more than was right with the speechless mouth of a dog; no one was frightened by my barks').

Also from Assyria comes a set of clay dogs, painted in various colours – red, yellow, black, green-blue – which were buried at a doorway to provide magic protection. Their inscribed names would fit the hounds of Ashurbanipal – 'Enemy-catcher', 'Loud barker', 'Enemy-biter', 'Don't think – bite', 'Remover of evil'.

FURTHER READING
J. Rawson (ed.), *Animals in Art* (London, 1977)

The Townley greyhounds
Monte Cagnolo, Latium, Italy
Marble, 1st–2nd century AD
GR 1805.7–3.8;
Cat. Sculpture 2131
h. 65 cm (25½ in)
Purchased (Townley collection)
Excavated by Gavin Hamilton

Silver dollar
USA
1794
CM SSB 168–69
diam. 39 mm
(1½ in)
Given by Sir
George
and Lady
Banks

In 1512 rich deposits of silver were discovered in the kingdom of Bohemia (the modern Czech Republic) at St Joachimsthal (St Joachim's valley, modern Jachymov), in the territory of the Counts of Schlick. A mint was opened nearby which used this silver for a recently introduced type of coin, a very large silver piece worth the same as the small gold pieces known as *gulden* which were previously used. These silver coins were about 30 grams (1 oz) in weight, and were known at first as *guldengroschen*. The version from St Joachimsthal was known as the *Joachimsthaler guldengroschen*. The output of the mine and mint, especially in the 1520s, was so large that the coinage eclipsed earlier *guldengroschen* from Tyrol and Saxony, and gave its name – shortened to *thaler* – to this whole class of coin across much of Europe.

Many countries used a derivation of the word *thaler* for their own similar-sized silver issues, as the use of this type of coin became widespread during the sixteenth century and later. The Scandinavian version was the *daler*, in the Netherlands it was the *daalder*, and in Italy the *tallero*. In England native coins of this size were always called crowns, as they replaced a gold coin of that name, but the term *dollar* was adopted to describe most foreign equivalents.

Silver trade dollar
(obverse and reverse)
USA
1875
CM 1935–4–1–9323
diam. 38 mm
(1½ in)
T. B. Clarke-
Thornhill
Bequest

Most of the silver which made these coins came, not from Bohemia, but from Spanish-ruled Mexico and Alto Peru (modern Bolivia). Much American silver came to Europe struck into the large silver coins of the Spanish denominational system, *ocho-reales*, or pieces of eight (p. 254). These, by extension, became widely known as 'dollars', especially in the British colonies in the Caribbean and North America, where they were the principal coinage available. Thus the first official coinage under the Constitution of the United States, authorized in 1792 and struck in 1794, was based on a large silver dollar, divided into 100 copper cents.

The Spanish 'dollar' (sometimes called the Pillar dollar, from its design of the Pillars of Hercules) became one of the great world trading coinages of the early modern period, with similar roles played by the Dutch *leeuwendaalder* (lion dollar) in the Far East, and (from the late eighteenth century) the Austrian Maria Theresa *thaler* in the Levant, Ethiopia and Arabia.

FURTHER READING
J. Williams (ed.), *Money. A History* (London, 1997)

This bronze flesh hook, designed for lifting chunks of meat out of a stew, was found in a bog at Dunaverny, Co. Antrim, in 1829. The hollow, three-part metal handle would have fitted round an oak shaft. It was decorated with a family of swans and their cygnets and a pair of ravens. The function of the pendant rings is not known, but they were perhaps used to effect rotation of the birds.

From *c.*1300 BC European metalworkers developed a variety of sheet bronze vessels whose manufacture required special skills and much time. These highly prestigious vessels would have emphasized social roles at important events. The larger vessels could be used for cooking or the dispensing of food or beverages. Serving utensils and personal bowls were generally made of wood and pottery. Cauldrons were a special feature of Western Europe, as were bronze flesh hooks such as this. They were highly crafted and sometimes ornately adorned, as in this example. In Britain and Ireland certain sites known as 'burnt mounds' were established cooking areas. They feature large quantities of burnt stone, the result of roasting meat or heating stews. The associated cooking pits are large enough to suggest communal cooking.

The Dunaverny flesh hook
Dunaverny, Co. Antrim, Ireland
Bronze, 950–750 BC
PRB 1856 12–22 1
l. 56.3 cm (22⅛ in)
Purchased from H.O. Careton

The **Dunhuang paintings**

The sands of Central Asia have preserved the remains of the cities that were linked by the Silk Route along the foothills of the Tianshan and the Kunlun ranges, either side of the Taklamakan desert north of Tibet. The rulers and peoples of these cities were Iranian or Indian in origin. At different periods the Chinese appointed their own officials to regulate affairs alongside local rulers. At all times the culture of these cities was a mixture of Chinese elements, local Central Asian practices, and beliefs and traditions from further west. Here, early in the twentieth century, the explorer Sir Aurel Stein (1862–1943) uncovered wooden buildings, official documents, seals and remnants of daily life such as combs and shoes, all preserved from the time of the Silk Route's greatest days up to the Tang (AD 618–906) and Five Dynasties (AD 907–960) periods.

At Dunhuang, where the northern and southern branches of the Silk Route around the desert meet to travel down the Gansu corridor to the Chinese heartland, a brackish stream provides a patch of trees and small millet fields at the foot of high dunes. Here lies the valley of the Thousand Buddhas, so-called from the legend of a monk who dreamt he saw a cloud with a thousand Buddhas floating above one side of the valley. Here in the gravel conglomerate cliff, almost a mile long, hundreds of cave-temples were from the fourth century AD onwards hollowed and filled with wall paintings and with painted images in stucco. From a hidden deposit in one of them, sealed since the early twelfth century AD, Stein acquired thousands of manuscripts and hundreds of paintings on silk, hemp cloth and paper. They are valuable sources for the history of Chinese figure painting and architecture, and contain some fine examples of early landscape painting in the scenes of the life of the Buddha.

On the left is a painting of the Guardian King of the North, Vaisravana, riding across the waters. He is one of the four Devarajas or kings of the points of the compass, who are accompanied by large forces of supernatural warriors.

Vaisravana riding across the waters
Dunhuang, China
Ink and colours on silk,
Five Dynasties, mid-10th century AD
OA 1919.1–1.045
61.8 × 54.7 cm
(24⅓ × 22½ in)
Acquired by Marc Aurel Stein

FURTHER READING
R. Whitfield and A. Farrer, *Caves of the Thousand Buddhas: Chinese art from the Silk Route* (London, 1990)
S. Whitfield, *Aurel Stein on the Silk Road* (London, 2004)

This woodcut by Albrecht Dürer (1471–1528) and others is printed from 192 separate blocks. Measuring nearly 3 metres (10 ft) square, it is one of the largest ever made. Above the central arch, entitled Honour and Might, is a genealogy of Maximilian I (1459–1519), Holy Roman Emperor from 1493, who was described as 'the foremost knight of the age'. Above the left arch, Praise, and the right arch, Nobility, are represented events from his life. These are flanked by busts of emperors and kings to the left and a column of Maximilian's ancestors to the right. The outermost towers on either side show scenes from the emperor's private life.

The Triumphal Arch of
the Emperor Maximilian I
Germany
Woodcut mounted on a
linen backing, 1517–18
PD E. 5–1
h. 3 m (10 ft)
Bequeathed by Joseph
Nollekens (1737–1823)
subject to the life
ownership of Francis
Douce

Albrecht **Dürer**

Elk
Germany
Pen and brush with black
ink and watercolour
PD Sloane 5261–101
21.3 × 26 cm
(8⅓ × 10¼ in)
Sloane Bequest (1753)

The architect and painter Jörg Kölderer designed the overall appearance of the structure and Dürer designed the individual scenes and architectural elements, some of which he subcontracted to his pupils Hans Springinklee and Wolf Traut, and Albrecht Altdorfer of Regensburg. The blocks were cut by Hieronymus Andreä of Nuremberg between 1515 and 1517. The descriptive programme, devised by the court historian Johann Stabius, is printed in five columns along the bottom. This was one of a number of massive woodcut prints commissioned by Maximilian, and the only one to be completed in his lifetime. The impression in the Museum comes from the first edition, issued in 1517–18. About 700 sets were printed but they are today very rare.

The Museum's collection of Dürer drawings is one of the largest in the world, and has good examples of his watercolour landscapes and portrait drawings. The foundation of the collection is an album which came from the collections of Sir Hans Sloane (pp. 304–5).

Dürer was born at Nuremberg and in 1512 became Court Painter to Maximilian I, retaining this appointment under Charles V. He is regarded as the greatest of all German artists, his work as an engraver on metal ranking as highly as his skill as a painter. He also produced a large number of brilliant woodcuts.

FURTHER READING
G. Bartrum (ed.), *Albrecht Dürer and his Legacy* (London, 2002)
J.K. Rowlands, *Drawings by German Artists in the Department of Prints and Drawings at the British Museum* (London, 1993)
J.K. Rowlands, *The Age of Dürer and Holbein, German Drawings 1400–1550* (London, 1988)

John **Dwight** and **English stoneware**

One of the finest portrait busts in the Museum's choice collection is that shown below of Prince Rupert of the Rhine (1619–82) wearing the collar and mantle of the Order of the Garter. Rupert was the son of Charles I's sister Elizabeth of Bohemia. In 1645, during the English Civil War, he was appointed chief of the Royalist forces against Parliament. This lifesize stoneware portrait was produced by the manufacturer John Dwight. The sculptor Edward Pearce (*d*.1695) or his workshop probably moulded and extensively hand-finished the bust at Dwight's factory. It remained with Dwight's descendants until the year 1861.

Stoneware is a term describing clay that has been fired to a temperature (over 1200°C) at which it becomes extremely hard and impervious to liquids. The technique was perfected in the Rhineland during the early fourteenth century AD, and its industries supplied Europe with stoneware vessels for the next 400 years.

The commercial success of the stoneware trade stimulated several attempts to manufacture the ware for domestic use in Britain. In 1672 John Dwight of London was granted a patent for the sole right of producing 'the Stone Ware vulgarly called Cologne Ware'. Excavations in the 1970s at the site of his Fulham pottery confirmed that he concentrated on copying Rhenish ware for the tavern trade. In 1974 excavations at Woolwich, downstream from Fulham, revealed the remains of a kiln producing German-type stoneware 30 to 35 years before Dwight's patent, but Dwight was the first in Britain to put the manufacture of stoneware on a firm commercial footing.

Among Dwight's most remarkable achievements were his experimental porcelains, some of the first such attempts in northern Europe, and his stoneware statuary, of which the finest piece is the Prince Rupert bust. The Museum also has four small mythological figures imitating bronzes, a figure of Flora, a sportsman and companion, a small portrait bust of Mrs Dwight, a hand of a child and brass stamps for reliefs used on Dwight's tankards.

Stoneware portrait of Prince Rupert of the Rhine, partly gilded
Fulham, London
c.1673–5
MLA Pottery Catalogue
F.3
h. 60 cm (23½ in)

FURTHER READING
R.J.C. Hildyard, *Brown Muggs* (London, 1985)
A. Oswald, R.J.C. Hildyard, R.G. Hughes, *English Brown Stoneware 1670–1900* (London, 1982)

Easter Island statue
(Hoa Hakananai'a)

Easter Island, 11th–17th centuries AD

Basalt statue called Hoa Hakananai'a
Orongo, Easter Island, Chile
11th–17th centuries AD
ETH 1869.10–5.1
h. 2.64 m (8 ft 8 in)
Given by H.M. Queen Victoria to whom it was presented by the Lords of the Admiralty

Easter Island or Rapu Nui, 2,300 miles west of South America, was settled by Polynesians between 400 and 800 AD. The first known contact with Europeans took place in 1722, when the Dutchman Jacob Roggeveen sighted the island on Easter Sunday. A Spanish expedition followed in 1770 and in 1774 Captain Cook's ship *Resolution* made a brief visit. The visitors noted with amazement the monolithic statues (the *moai*) then still standing on their platforms or *ahus*. In the nineteenth century there was more sustained contact, with terrible consequences for the island's population and traditional culture.

The statue cult flourished from *c.*1000 until the second half of the seventeenth century when it was replaced by the birdman cult, the ceremonial centre of which was Orongo on the edge of the island, high up between the sea and the crater of an extinct volcano. The birdman cult revolved around a universal creator god and provider called Makemake, who became incarnate in the birdman.

Hoa Hakananai'a was probably produced late in the statue cult phase; the carving style is similar to the earlier statues but the designs on the back, probably added later, link it to the birdman cult. These designs include the so-called 'ring and girdle' motif; above it are two birdmen with a bird higher up flanked by ceremonial paddles; a third paddle is on the left ear; on the right ear are four vulva symbols with two or more on the top of the head.

The statue was collected during a surveying voyage of HMS *Topaze* in 1868. It may have once stood on a ceremonial platform and was eventually transferred, perhaps for safety, to one of the stone houses in Orongo.

FURTHER READING
J.A. Van Tilburg, *Easter Island: Archaeology, Ecology and Culture* (London, 1994)
J.A. Van Tilburg, *HMS* Topaze *on Easter Island: Hoa Hakananai'a and Five Other Museum Sculptures in Archaeological Context*, British Museum Occasional Paper no. 73 (London, 1992)
J.A. Van Tilburg, *Hoa Hakananai'a*, British Museum Objects in Focus (London, 2004)

The beginning of Egyptian jewellery-making can be traced 4000 years before the birth of Christ, when men of the Badarian culture wrapped around their hips massive girdles of bright green, glazed stone beads. Even before the beginning of the First Dynasty in 3100 BC the craftsmen of the Naqada II period had progressed to fashioning beads from highly coloured semi-precious stones and precious metal, skilfully combining them in a diadem for a non-royal female. For the next 3000 years the products of the jewellery-maker's workshop delighted the living and afforded amuletic protection to the dead until, in the twilight of the Greco-Roman period, Greek forms prevailed.

Jewellery might signify rank or office, but was also worn for decoration by everyone from the meanest peasant to the pharaoh himself. Men and women, even sacred animals, wore jewellery on many parts of their body. It was put into the tomb for use in the Afterlife. Most basic types were established in form as early as the end of the Old Kingdom, *c.*2200 BC; only earrings made a relatively late appearance. In paintings and statues the Egyptians were depicted in all their finery – ear plugs, diadem, pectoral, choker and collar. A few items of jewellery are known only in such representations but, for the most part, examples of almost every type can be seen in the Museum's collection.

Bracelet of Prince Nemarath
Sais, Egypt
Gold inlaid with lapis lazuli and glass, 22nd Dynasty, *c.*940 BC
EA 14595
h. 4.2 cm (1⅔ in)

Above (right) is one of a pair of gold bracelets depicting Harpocrates (Horus-the-child). A hieroglyphic inscription inside says that they were made for the king's son and general, Nemarath (son of the Libyan pharaoh Sheshonq I, founder of the 22nd Dynasty) in *c.*945 BC.

Bracelet
Thebes, Egypt
Gold, carnelian and lapis lazuli, Middle Kingdom, *c.*2000–1500 BC
EA 14691
l. 20.5 cm (8 in)

FURTHER READING
C. Andrews, *Ancient Egyptian Jewellery* (London, 1990)

Egyptian script and writing

The main script of ancient Egypt was a set of pictorial signs now known as hieroglyphs, from the Greek *hieros* (sacred) and *glyphos* (carved sign). Hieroglyphs are pictorial signs of two types: signs that represent sounds, like the letters of the alphabet, or parts of words and signs that represent objects or ideas.

The oldest surviving hieroglyphic texts date to *c*.3200 BC. The signs are incised or painted on ivory labels and pottery vessels, imprinted on jars with cylinder seals or carved on ceremonial palettes. They record names, especially those of the kings, which were written in a *serekh* (rectangular panel with niched section). The motif of niched walls and the use of cylinder seals derive from Mesopotamia, where it is thought the idea of writing originated. The hieroglyphic script had a religious significance and was designed for lasting inscriptions on wood, ivory and particularly on stone. Hieroglyphic texts are usually read from the direction towards which the animal or human figures are looking.

Hieroglyphs were in use until the end of the fourth century AD. The last known hieroglyphic inscription, on the island of Philae, dates to 394 AD (the latest in the Museum is dated 296 AD).

In addition to hieroglyphs the Egyptians employed two other scripts, both descended from hieroglyphs, called by the Greeks hieratic (priestly writing) and demotic (people's writing). In contrast to hieroglyphs, which could be written in either direction, hieratic and demotic were always written from right to left, usually in ink on papyrus, potsherd or limestone flake with a rush brush. They could also be carved on stone. Hieratic at first differed from hieroglyphs only because it was written with a rush brush instead of a pointed tool. Sporadic examples on stone are known from the first three dynasties. The oldest texts on papyrus still in existence are administrative documents of *c*.2500 BC.

By the Eleventh Dynasty hieratic had developed into a much more distinctive and cursive script and texts were usually written in vertical columns. During the Twelfth Dynasty scribes began to write texts in horizontal lines, a practice which encouraged hieratic to become even more cursive.

By the Eighteenth Dynasty a clear distinction existed between the well-formed hieratic used for literary purposes and the more cursive hieratic employed for business documents, a divergence which progressed throughout the New Kingdom.

Quartzite statue of the chamberlain Pesshuper, who holds a papyrus roll in his left hand in the attitude of a scribe
Provenance unknown
25th or 26th Dynasty
EA 1514
h. 53 cm (20¾ in)

Egyptian script and writing

From the business hieratic of the late New Kingdom developed two other even more cursive scripts, abnormal hieratic and the demotic already mentioned. Only about 45 documents in the former script have been identified; demotic documents extend over a period of one thousand years, from the 21st year of Psammetichus I (643 BC) to the middle of the fifth century AD.

The Museum has an extensive collection of Egyptian writing in all media, the best known being the Rosetta Stone (pp. 272–3). The collection of Egyptian papyri (p. 244) is the finest in existence.

FURTHER READING
M. Collier and B. Manley, *How to Read Egyptian Hieroglyphs* (London, 1997)
W.V. Davies, *Egyptian Hieroglyphs* (London, 1987)
N. Spencer and C. Thorne, *The British Museum Book of Egyptian Hieroglyphs* (London, 2003)

Detail from the Book of the Dead of Hunefer, showing Thoth and Hunefer
Egypt
Painted papyrus,
19th Dynasty, *c.*1285 BC
EA 9901/3
h. 39.5 cm (15½ in)

Queen **Elizabeth I**

Elizabeth I gold medal:
obverse
England
c.AD 1580–90
CM M6903
5.6 × 4.4 cm (2⅕ × 1¾ in)

BELOW **Burse panel**
London
c.1596–1603
MLA 1997,3–1, 1
l. 52 cm (20½ in)
Purchased with the aid of
the National Art Collec-
tions Fund, the Heritage
Lottery Fund and the
British Museum Society

Elizabeth I (AD 1533–1603) has a special place in English history; no other English sovereign has made so indelible an impression upon the popular memory and imagination. Daughter of King Henry VIII and his second wife, Anne Boleyn, who was beheaded for adultery, she survived the intrigues of the reigns of her half-brother Edward VI and half-sister Mary I to become queen in 1558. During her reign the 'virgin queen' carried out a delicate game of diplomacy, playing off suitors from all over Europe and avoiding permanent entanglements at home. England was drawn towards a policy of energetic expansion which was to peak in the reign of another queen – Victoria.

On the left we see the queen in magnificence portrayed on one of the finest of the Museum's collection of medals. It was designed by Nicholas Hilliard (1547–1619) during the period of greatest threat to England from the Spanish in the 1580s, as a gift or award. The obverse with the portrait of the queen bears the legend DITIOR . IN . TOTO . NON . ALTER . CIRCVLVS . ORBE ('no other circle in the whole world more rich'), an allusion to the crown and its power. On the reverse is a bay-tree uninjured by lightning and winds, flourishing upon an island, inscribed NON . IPSA . PERICVLA . TANGVNT ('not even dangers affect it'). The design refers to the supposed virtues of the laurel or bay-tree, impervious to lightning and protective of the places where it grew or the persons who wore it. The lightning probably represents the wrath of heaven, which is deflected from the island (Britain) by the bay-tree (Elizabeth) and instead threatens the ships of the Spanish Armada in the distance.

The Museum has other likenesses of the queen in the collection of prints. Also associated with Elizabeth is the recently acquired burse or purse panel (left) made to contain the massive silver Great Seal of England. Of red silk velvet, it is embroidered with the Tudor arms and the Elizabethan royal cypher, and would have been made in London around 1596 for Sir Thomas Egerton, the last of Elizabeth's five Keepers of the Great Seal.

Watercolour painting originated on the continent of Europe, but it was in England that its possibilities were explored and it came to maturity. There are various reasons why watercolour became the 'English medium'. Not only does the damp and misty climate seem best captured by coloured washes on paper, but the particularly English fascination with travel, nature and viewing landscape meant that watercolour was eagerly adopted as the most portable medium for working quickly and out of doors. In the Museum's Department of Prints and Drawings the collection of British drawings is larger than any other school represented, and contains examples from the sixteenth century to the present day.

Some of the earliest watercolours in the collection are those executed by John White (*fl. c.*1585–93) (p. 359), who produced a detailed series illustrating the flora, fauna and native inhabitants of Virginia and Florida. It was not until the second half of the eighteenth century that the British school of watercolour painting was firmly established. This period is represented in the Museum by artists such as Thomas Hearne (1744–1817) and the brothers Paul (1725–1809) and Thomas (1721–98) Sandby, who produced topographical 'stained' drawings of scenes around the British Isles. The landscapes artists made while travelling abroad during the Grand Tour provide the collection with awe-inspiring views of the Alps and poetic visions of Italy's 'Classic Ground'; John Robert Cozens (1752–92), John 'Warwick' Smith (1794–1831) and Francis Towne (1740–1816) produced some of the finest. At the turn of the century, Thomas Girtin (1775–1802) and John Sell Cotman

The Parade, St James's Park, with the Ceremony of Trooping the Colour
Thomas Rowlandson (1756–1827)
England
Pen, ink and watercolour, *c.*AD 1808
PD 1880–11–13–2323
18.5 × 30 cm
(7¼ × 11⅘ in)
Purchased (Crace Collection)

English watercolours

Stonehenge
John Constable
(1776–1837)
England
Watercolour over
black chalk, squared for
transfer, c.AD 1836
PD 1888–2–15–38
16.8 × 25 cm (6⅔ × 10 in)
Presented by Miss Isabel
Constable

(1782–1842) (p. 87) were interpreting the scenery and ruins of Britain and France with new techniques and colours.

J.M.W. Turner (1775–1851) (p. 334) is justifiably the most famous of all English watercolourists, but three other accomplished watercolourists of the nineteenth century whose works are well represented are David Cox (1783–1859), Peter de Wint (1784–1849) and Richard Parkes Bonington (1802–28). John Constable (1776–1837), although better known as a painter in oils, used watercolour for marvellous nature and sky impressions painted from Hampstead Heath.

The collection also includes watercolours illustrating contemporary life. The careful draughtsmanship and sharp wit of Thomas Rowlandson (1756–1827) (previous page) make him one of the most skilled satirists of the period, while the watercolours of George Scharf (1788–1860) document everyday life in the Regency and early Victorian periods.

FURTHER READING
M. Clarke, *The Tempting Prospect: A Social History of English Watercolours* (London, 1981)
L. Stainton, *Nature into Art: English Landscape Watercolours* (London, 1985)
A. Wilton and A. Lyles, *The Great Age of British Watercolours 1750–1880* (London, 1993)

The **Esquiline treasure**

The most spectacular item in the Esquiline treasure is the so-called 'Projecta Casket' (below). The inscription on the rim of the lid reads: SECVNDE ET PROIECTA VIVATIS IN CHRISTO ('Secundus and Projecta, may you live in Christ'). The top of the casket has portraits of a couple in a wreath held by cupids. The other four panels of the lid have mythological scenes: (front) Venus, the goddess of love, attended by sea-creatures and cupids; (both ends) a nereid (p. 227) riding a sea-monster; and (back) a procession to a domed Roman bath, with attendants carrying caskets. On the lower front panel is a woman dressing her hair; there are also servants carrying utensils.

The Projecta Casket is thought to have formed part of a wedding present for the couple named Secundus and Projecta. Monograms on the treasure indicate that it may have belonged to the Turcius family. The identity of the couple is not known for certain, but it has been suggested that Projecta was a young married Christian woman whose death on 30 December 383 is commemorated in an epitaph by Pope Damasus (AD 366–84). The procession may represent a Roman bride's ceremonial toilet on the eve of her marriage.

The treasure, dating from the second half of the fourth century AD, was found in 1793 at the foot of the Esquiline hill in Rome. It was almost certainly buried accidentally, probably in an earthquake.

The Projecta Casket
Rome
Gilded silver,
4th century AD
MLA 1866,12–29, 1
l. 55.9 cm (22 in)
Purchased (Duc de Blacas)

No inventory of the find survives, although 61 items are identified today, two of them in other museums. The Museum's holding also comprises a ewer inscribed 'Pelegrina use [this vessel] to good fortune'; a flask with cupids, two furniture ornaments in the form of hands grasping rods with finials, and various dishes. There are also four cast and partially gilt figures representing the protectresses of the major cities of the late Roman Empire (Rome, Constantinople, Antioch and Alexandria). Another spectacular piece is the so-called 'Muse Casket', similar to one shown on the back of the Projecta Casket. This holds five silver canisters and is decorated with the figures of eight of the nine Muses.

FURTHER READING
K.J. Shelton, *The Esquiline Treasure* (London, 1981)

Fakes

There can be few museums or collectors who have not at some time acquired objects that are not quite as they seem. The British Museum is no exception. Not only does it own objects, languishing in its reserve collections, which have been removed from display as fakes, but conversely, with advances in authenticity testing, items once believed to be 'fake' have been restored to respectability.

Shown here (no longer on display) is one of the most splendid of the Museum's undoubted fakes – a 'sixth-century BC Etruscan' terracotta sarcophagus manufactured in Italy in the nineteenth century. The sarcophagus came to the Museum in pieces in 1871, was assembled there and bought two years later from the dealer Alessandro Castellani, who had acquired it from one Pietro Pennelli. The inscription on the lid was shortly condemned as a copy from one on a gold brooch in the Louvre. In 1875 Pietro's brother Enrico claimed that he had made the sarcophagus. This was strongly denied, and it continued to be displayed in the Museum until 1935, appearing in countless popular books on the Etruscans and their art. Today we can appreciate that the pose of the figures on the lid and the nudity of the man are unparalleled in Etruscan art and the woman, wearing something suspiciously like nineteenth-century underwear, is unlike anything known from antiquity.

'Fake' is, however, a relative term. Many of the objects in the Townley Collection (p. 332), while of ancient origin, have since been drastically recut; the Piranesi vase (p. 255) is a *mélange* of ancient and modern pieces. Some suspect items such as the Shabako stone (p. 294) are now so old that they are of interest in themselves. An exhibition held in 1990 brought out many old favourites from the Museum and elsewhere. Among the 400 or more objects were a furry fish and a vegetable lamb, nineteenth-century 'medieval' forgeries by 'Billy and Charley', Piltdown Man, Moche-style vessels from Peru, a merman – all evidence of the ingenuity of forgers and the frequent fallibility of experts.

'Etruscan' terracotta
sarcophagus
Italy
19th century AD
GR 1873.8–20.643;
Cat. Terracottas B 630
l. 160 cm (13 ft 1½in)
Purchased
(Castellani Collection)

FURTHER READING
M. Jones (ed.), *Why Fakes Matter: Essays on Problems of Authenticity* (London, 1993)
M. Jones (ed.), *Fake? The Art of Deception* (London, 1990)

False doors

In Egyptian tombs and mortuary temples the false door served as a link between the living and the dead. Before it would be placed regular offerings to the deceased, essential for his or her survival in the Afterlife. The *ka*, the spiritual double of the dead person, would emerge through the false door to eat and drink the essence of the offerings.

Egyptian tombs consisted of two elements, the burial place itself and the funerary chapel, in which these offerings were presented. The earliest built offering places so far recorded date from the First Dynasty (*c.*2900 BC). At first the tomb superstructures were decorated on all sides with deep recesses, probably in imitation of the façades of palaces and other great secular buildings. Later the recesses were reduced to two, at the north and south ends of the eastern side. They served as false doors, the southern one being made larger and more elaborate to act as an offering chapel; it was here that a stele was set as a focus for the offerings.

Carved on the stele would usually be a figure of the deceased seated before an offering table upon which were loaves of bread, with texts enumerating the various food and drink offerings and the name and titles of the deceased. These representations were really only a reserve supply; ideally the relatives of the deceased, or employed mortuary priests, were supposed to bring offerings regularly. The false door was gradually superseded by a new, smaller type of funerary stele on which it was not uncommon to include an account of the career of the dead person.

Limestone false door and architrave of Ptahshepses
Saqqara, Egypt
5th Dynasty, *c.*2400 BC
EA 682
h. 3.66 m (12 ft) in total

The Museum has many good examples of Old Kingdom false doors, the most elaborate being the limestone false door and architrave of the Fifth Dynasty from the tomb of Ptahshepses (right). The panelled slabs on each side of the door are inscribed with his biography, recording his birth in the reign of King Menkaure of the Fourth Dynasty, his marriage to a princess, Khamaat daughter of Shepseskaf, and his career under four kings of the Fifth Dynasty.

FURTHER READING
S. Quirke and J. Spencer (eds), *The British Museum Book of Ancient Egypt* (London, 1992), pp. 112–14

Fans

Fans have been used since earliest times – the oldest in the Museum come from Egypt and the Near East. They can be divided into two groups: the rigid or screen fan and the folding fan. The latter is composed of sticks held together at the handle. In some instances the leaf is pleated, in others the sticks are wider and overlap, connected at the top with a ribbon or thread.

Ceremonial fans are known from ancient times; two were found in King Tutankhamun's tomb. The use of elaborate personal fans is however best documented in China and Japan. Rigid fans were the first to be used; the folding technique appears to have been invented by the Japanese in the seventh century AD. Folding fans reached Europe from the East in the sixteenth century. From Italy they were introduced to France, possibly by Catherine de' Medici (1519–89). The fashion spread to England; there is a portrait of Queen Elizabeth I of around 1592 with a folding fan attached by ribbons to her waist. The eighteenth century was the grand age of fans in Europe – some exquisitely painted, others cruder. The fashion for printed fan leaves first appeared in England in the 1720s with an enormous variety of subjects – maps, almanacks, games, riddles, dances, commemorative and political themes. After the middle of the nineteenth century the printed fan was largely overtaken by fans made from textiles, embroideries, lace or feathers. Their use declined in the twentieth century after the First World War.

The Museum has a number of Egyptian fan handles and fragments. Below is a fan from New Kingdom Egypt; the handle of ivory and wood bears the head of the goddess Hathor. There are around 500 in the Department of Ethnography, many rather primitive. The Oriental Departments have a number of elaborate fans from China and Japan. The collection of 687 European fans put together by Lady Charlotte Schreiber, given to the Museum in 1891, is housed in the Department of Prints and Drawings.

Mounted fan entitled
'The Garden'
Etching, coloured by hand, and mounted on ivory sticks, with gilt and coloured ornaments, signed 'According to Act of Parliament, 1741'
PD Schreiber 29
Schreiber Collection

Hathor-headed fan handle of ivory and wood, modern ostrich feathers attached
Thebes, Egypt
New Kingdom, c.1300 BC
EA 20767
l. (handle) 16 cm (6¼ in)

FURTHER READING
L. and I. Wheatley, *The Indispensable Fan: The Story of the Fan in Society* (Edinburgh City Art Centre, 1984)
Fans and Fan Leaves Collected and Described by Lady Charlotte Schreiber: English (London, 1888), *Foreign* (London, 1890).

The most famous of all cuneiform tablets is the eleventh tablet of the Epic of Gilgamesh (below). In 1878 George Smith, an assistant in the Museum, discovered on an incomplete tablet from the library of Ashurbanipal at Nineveh a version of the story of the Deluge which closely resembled that in the Book of Genesis. The *Daily Telegraph* newspaper paid Smith's expenses for an expedition to Nineveh where he located part of a related epic. A revelation at the time, both epics have since been duplicated and completed by tablets found elsewhere.

The Assyrian version of the Flood legend is preserved near the end of the epic poem. Gilgamesh, seeking to restore his dead friend Enkidu to life, finds Utnapishtim, who tells him how he obtained eternal life. Mankind had angered the storm-god Enlil who decided to drown them all with a mighty flood. Ea, the god of wisdom, took pity on one man, Utnapishtim, and whispered a warning to the reeds of his hut, whereupon he took his family and other living things into a great ark. When the rains descended, mankind was destroyed. After six days the waters sank and Utnapishtim's ship touched ground. A bird was released but found no resting place. Then a swallow was sent out, but returned; finally a raven was released but did not return, showing that the water had receded to reveal land. Utnapishtim thereupon disembarked and sacrificed to the gods, who, though angry at this escape, were persuaded to grant him divine honours and a dwelling-place at the mouth of the River Euphrates.

The story closely follows the lines of that of Noah, though there are distinct differences, particularly in the multiple gods of the Mesopotamian account. Clearly there was some point of contact between the two legends, but how and when the story became known to the Hebrews is not fully agreed.

Clay tablet with the Babylonian account of the Flood
Nineveh (Iraq)
7th century BC
WA K3375
13.5 × 15.3 cm (5¼ × 6 in)
Excavated by A.H. Layard or H. Rassam

FURTHER READING
J.B. Pritchard (ed.), *Ancient Near Eastern Texts relating to the Old Testament* (3rd edn, Princeton, 1969)
E. Sollberger, *The Babylonian Legend of the Flood* (3rd edn, London, 1971)

Flowers

Primitive man was a hunter whose first drawings were of animals; it was not until he began to cultivate plants for food or medicine that he scratched on some slivers of bone a few lines that could conceivably have been a crude representation of a plant. But as settlements grew into towns, personal ornaments became more sophisticated, frequently drawing inspiration from plants. The tombs of the second Early Minoan period of *c.*2800–2400 BC, for example, contained gold jewellery of daisies, lilies, roses and sprays of olives. The lotus was seldom absent from New Kingdom necklaces in Ancient Egypt.

Plants have always been symbolic of both spiritual and secular concepts. The Egyptians linked the lotus with the sun-god Horus, as a symbol of regeneration; in association with Isis it symbolized fertility. A species of acanthus evolved into one of the most common ornamental features in European decorative art. Its formalized leaves distinguish the capitals of the Corinthian and Composite Orders in Greek and Roman architecture. In Hindu art the lotus represents both Brahma and Lakshmi; for Buddhists it is a sacred emblem of purity. The Madonna lily (*Lilium candidum*), one of the oldest cultivated flowers, was adopted as a royal flower by the Minoans; Christians made it a symbol of the Virgin Mary. Another symbol of the Virgin Mary, the *fleur-de-lis*, a stylized lily, was incorporated in the royal arms of France in the twelfth century AD. The cypress tree which Persians and Mughals always planted in

Ducks fly out of a papyrus thicket on a fragment of painted pavement
el-Amarna, Egypt
18th Dynasty, *c.*1380 BC
EA 55617
h. 93 cm (36⅔ in)
Excavated by the Egypt Exploration Society

Flowers

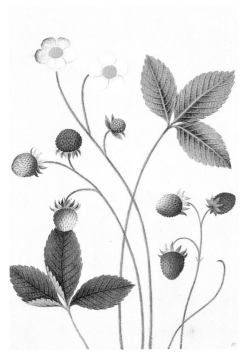

Hautbois strawberry (*Fragraria moschata*)
Jacques le Moyne de Morgues (*c.*AD 1500–88)
France
Watercolour, *c.*1533–88
PD 1962–7–14–1 (12); cat PH47
21.2 × 14.7 cm (8⅓ × 5¾ in)

Porcelain vase with *famille rose* enamel decoration, peach branch and flowers
China
Qing dynasty, Qianlong mark and period (AD 1736–95)
OA 1936.4–13.44
h. 52 cm (20½ in)
Reginald R. Cory Bequest

their gardens was a hopeful reminder of immortality. The 'four noble plants' in Chinese paintings – plum, orchid, chrysanthemum and bamboo – denoted the four seasons. Turkish Iznik ware (p. 167) displays adaptations by sixteenth-century Turkish potters of Chinese motifs such as the peony and lotus, sometimes transformed into fantastic shapes. In nineteenth-century England the symbolic language of flowers, as seen in the Hull Grundy jewellery gift (p. 156), was a frivolous means of communication between lovers.

Flowers can be seen throughout the Museum – in stone, metal, ivory, wood and other materials. Sometimes colourful, sometimes austere, symbolic or frivolous, naturalistic or stylized, they have appealed to artists throughout the ages.

FURTHER READING
L. Manniche, *An Ancient Egyptian Herbal* (3rd edn, London, 2006)
J. Rawson, *Chinese Ornament: the Lotus and the Dragon* (London, 1984)
A. Scott-James, R. Desmond and F. Wood, *The British Museum Book of Flowers* (London, 1989)
M. Caygill, *Flowers* (London, 2006)

The Folkton drums, three of the most extraordinary relics of prehistoric Britain, are unique. They have no obvious function and their combination of form and decoration is unmatched elsewhere. They were found in 1889 by Canon William Greenwell when he opened a round barrow on Folkton Wold, East Yorkshire. They were placed behind the head and hips of the unburnt body of a child in a shallow grave, one of a number of burials in the same mound. That the drums were made locally seems probable since all three are solid cylinders carved from magnesian limestone, an outcrop of which occurs nearby.

The continuous decoration on the sides is divided into two broad and two narrow panels. The top in each case has a raised decorated area surrounded by a plain band; the flat bases are plain. The panels consist of elaborate geometric designs, repeated in essentially the same order on each drum. An eye motif occurs on two and is perhaps represented by a generalized squiggle on the third. Circles and concentric rings appear on the upper surfaces, extended by a star pattern on the largest. The decoration has similarities with the pottery of the Later Neolithic Grooved Ware style, datable between c.2600 and 2100 BC, and also with Beaker pottery and Passage Grave art.

The Folkton drums
Britain
Late Neolithic,
c.2600–2000 BC
PRB 1893 12–28 15–17
(large drum) diam.
14.8 cm, h. 12.2 cm (5⅞, 4⅞ in); (medium drum)
diam. 12.75 cm, h. 10.7 cm
(5, 4¼ in); (small drum)
diam. 10.6 cm, h. 8.7 cm
(4⅛, 3½ in)
Given by Canon William
Greenwell

As to their purpose, we can only speculate. They might perhaps be durable versions of carved wooden objects. Graves of the period tend to contain goods of a personal character, either possessions in life or objects made specifically for burial with the deceased. In terms of their craftsmanship the drums must have been highly valued, and yet there were no other obvious signs of distinction in the burial mound.

FURTHER READING

D.V. Clarke, T.G. Cowie and A. Foxton, *Symbols of Power at the Time of Stonehenge* (Edinburgh, 1985)

I. Kinnes and I.H. Longworth, *Catalogue of the Excavated Prehistoric and Romano-British Material in the Greenwell Collection* (London, 1985)

The Franks Casket is unique. Carved from whale bone in eighth-century Northumbria, it bears the longest runic text known on a portable object. It is named after Augustus Wollaston Franks (1826–97), one of the Museum's greatest curators.

It is possible that the casket was taken to France by the mid-tenth century. It was discovered being used as a work-box by a farmer's family in the nineteenth century in Auzon, Haute-Loire. One side reached the Museo Bargello, Florence. Franks purchased the rest in Paris, giving it to the Museum in 1867.

From at least the second century AD the runic alphabet of 24 letters was used by some Germanic nations. The sides and lid of the casket are intricately decorated with scenes from Christian, Germanic and Roman tradition with accompanying runic inscriptions in Old English and, at one point, Latin, in both Roman lettering and runes. On the top is a scene showing an archer defending a stockade against armed enemies. Above him, carved in runes, is his name, 'ÆGILI'. On the front are two scenes, depicting respectively the Germanic hero Weland and the Adoration of Christ: in a small panel above the latter is the title 'MÆGI' (Magi). The left side depicts the wolf suckling Romulus and Remus, the founders of Rome. The back depicts the Emperor Titus's capture of Jerusalem in AD 70. The enigmatic right side has an encrypted inscription, compounding its mystery.

The Anglo-Saxons were fond of riddles and the inscription on the front can be translated 'the fish beat up the seas on to the mountainous cliff; the king of terror became sad when he swam on to the shingle'. The answer is given as 'HRONÆSBAN' (whale's bone). In other words, the box was made from the bone of a beached whale.

The casket may have been made for an Anglo-Saxon king, perhaps to house a gospel book.

The Franks Casket
Northumbria, England,
found at Auzon, Haute-
Loire, France
8th century AD
MLA 1867,1–20, 1
l. 23 cm (9 in)
Given by A.W. Franks

FURTHER READING
M. Caygill and J. Cherry (eds),
*A.W. Franks. Nineteenth-century
Collecting and the British Museum*
(London, 1997)
R.I. Page, *Reading the Past: Runes*
(London, 1987)
L. Webster and J. Backhouse (eds),
*The Making of England: Anglo-Saxon
Art and Culture* AD 600–900 (London,
1991), cat. no. 70

Gandhara sculpture

Gandhara is the ancient name for part of the North-West frontier province of Pakistan and the valley of the Kabul river. After its annexation by the British East India Company in 1849, great quantities of Buddhist cult images and reliefs in grey-blue and green schist and lime plaster gradually came to light. They were found in ruined Buddhist complexes largely abandoned in the seventh century AD.

Buddhism had reached Gandhara in the third century BC. At the time the sculpture was produced, largely from the first to the sixth century AD, the prosperous Gandhara region was in the heartland of the powerful Kushan Empire, controlling some of the principal Asian trade-routes. Numerous shrines and monasteries were constructed or renewed and provided with great quantities of cult images and narrative reliefs in stone, clay and stucco.

To its European discoverers and students the most striking and intriguing feature of the sculpture was an undeniable, if modified, relationship with Western classical art. Various explanations have been put forward for this, invoking the Greek successor states which flourished in this region following the invasions of Alexander the Great, and their relationship to the Roman Empire; also the commercial and cultural links that persisted well into the Christian era between Gandhara and the Hellenized East, both within the Roman Empire and in the territories lying in between.

The Museum's collection of Gandhara sculpture is one of the finest in the world. Large and small cult images in stone and stucco portray the Buddha and the other benevolent deities (*bodhisattvas*). There are two rare, standing Buddhas in bronze. Stone friezes depict vivid scenes of the main incidents of the Buddha's life and previous existences (p. 65). Below is a scene in which the Buddha-to-be prostrates himself before the figure of the Buddha of a previous age, Dipankara.

Dipankara jataka (story)
Gandhara, Pakistan
Schist, 2nd–3rd century AD
OA 1880.68
h. 40.5 cm (16 in)

FURTHER READING
W. Zwalf, *A Catalogue of the Gandhara Sculpture in the British Museum* (London, 1996)
W. Zwalf, *The Shrines of Gandhara* (London, 1979)

Ganesha

Ganesha is the Hindu Lord of Beginnings, the placer and remover of obstacles. The son of Parvati, consort of Shiva (p. 301), he is depicted as elephant-headed, with a large pot-belly and often with chubby, childlike limbs.

In the most common story of his origins Ganesha was created by Parvati alone from the unguents and dirt rubbed from her legs as she washed. At the time Shiva, the greatest of the gods, was away from home. On returning and finding an unknown young man guarding his wife's bathroom, he challenged him and cut off his head. When Parvati explained the circumstances, Shiva undertook to restore Ganesha to life, and ordered one of his retinue to bring him the head of the first being he met. This was an elephant, but as compensation Ganesha was appointed Lord of the Ganas (Shiva's rowdy and dwarfish retinue).

In recognition of his courage in defending his mother's chamber, Ganesha is given custody over all doorways. Before any new undertaking is commenced, his name is invoked. He is honoured with flowers and coloured powders in most Hindu temples: on entering, a visitor will acknowledge Ganesha before any other god.

Like his father he dances, but ponderously. His attributes are an elephant goad and a noose and, above all, a bowl of sweetmeats from which he lifts delicacies to his mouth with his trunk. Sometimes he carries his broken tusk. This he detached to use as a pen, when acting as scribe for the sage Vyasa while he recited the Mahabharata epic. He is often depicted mounted upon a rat, his customary vehicle.

There are many statues of Ganesha in the Museum and he is also frequently seen in the collection of Indian paintings, both old and modern.

Crowned Ganesha sitting on a lotus, painted in the Basohli style
Punjab Hills, India
c.AD 1720
OA 1966.2–12.3
Purchased with the aid of the Brooke-Sewell Fund

FURTHER
READING
T.R. Blurton, *Hindu Art* (London, 1992)

131

This is the only surviving major English musical instrument from the Middle Ages. Prior to its acquisition by the Museum in 1963 it was known as the 'Warwick gittern' since it was for many years owned by the Earls of Warwick. Research and reappraisal are among the responsibilities of the Museum's curators and thus in 2005 the so-called 'gittern' was identified as a citole. Both musical instruments were widespread by the fourteenth century. A basic distinction, however, is that a citole has a flat back made of a single piece of wood whereas a gittern's back is made of several pieces: flat wooden ribs curve its back into a pear shape, as with the lute. Citoles were probably secular instruments used to accompany feasts, plays and dance. Once commonplace, they had all but vanished by the end of the fourteenth century.

Citole
England
c. AD 1290–1330
MLA 1963,10-2,1
h. 76 cm (30 in)
Purchased with the aid of the Pilgrim Trust and the National Art Collections Fund

The Museum's citole is a unique survival, with an interesting history. At some point it was remodelled as a violin by the addition of finger board and sounding board. From the royal arms and Leicester's badge engraved on the silver-gilt cover for the peg box (a later addition), we know that in 1578 it was in the

possession of either Queen Elizabeth I (p. 118) or her favourite Robert Dudley, Earl of Leicester (*c.*1532–88).

The style of the elaborately carved decoration is similar to English manuscript illumination and sculpture of the period *c.*1290–1330. At the top is a monster with webbed wings, claws and a scaly body, biting foliage. The eyes are formed by green inlay and the wavy hair on its head is subtly transformed into an openwork vine with a central stem and bunches of grapes. At the base of the vine are two goats nibbling at the stem. They stand on a pair of lions which are curled around a contorted human face. Elsewhere the carver has shown dense foliage inhabited by animals, hybrids and human figures, engaged in hunting or husbandry.

FURTHER READING
Carey Fleiner, 'Dulcet tones', *British Museum Magazine*, 53 (Autumn/Winter 2005), p.45
M. Remnant and R. Marks, 'A Medieval "gittern"' in *Music and Civilisation*, British Museum Yearbook, 4 (1980), pp. 83–134

Glass was first manufactured in Mesopotamia in the middle of the third millennium BC. The initial stages produced only beads and other small objects, formed or cast using simple tools and finished by stoneworkers' techniques. Few glass items of any kind are known from anywhere until the first vessels were made in western Asia some time before 1500 BC. Shortly afterwards, in the fifteenth century BC, the Egyptian industry was born. The Egyptians are thought to have learned the craft of glass-making from the East, but they quickly developed a distinctive and highly skilled industry which reached its height in the late Eighteenth Dynasty (*c*.1410–1320 BC). The oldest pieces of glass in the Museum are Egyptian and date to *c*.1460 BC. Below is a selection from the Museum's collection, including (second from left) a vessel from Thebes bearing the name of Thutmose III, which is one of the earliest datable Egyptian glass pieces.

Towards the end of the first century BC the technique of glass-blowing was invented, probably by Phoenician craftsmen working on the coast of Syria. The discovery that glass could be blown revolutionized the industry. Glass tableware became as widespread as fine pottery. Glasshouses, principally in the Levant, were making glass vessels by older techniques such as casting when new factories were founded in Italy in the first century BC. Initially these produced particularly colourful cast vessels. Free-blown glassware was first made in quantity towards the end of the first century BC, and thereafter glasshouses were established throughout the Roman Empire. The finest surviving piece of Roman glass is the Portland vase (p. 259).

Glass containers for
unguents and cosmetics
Egypt
18th Dynasty,
c.1450–1336 BC
FROM LEFT TO RIGHT
EA 24391
h. 6.3 cm (2½ in)
EA 47620
h. 8.7 cm (3⅗ in)
EA 55193
h. 14.5 cm (5¾ in)
Given by the Egypt
Exploration Society
(1921)
EA 4741
h. 8.7 cm (3⅖ in)
Purchased from Henry
Salt (1835)

FURTHER READING
H. Tait, *Five Thousand Years of Glass* (2nd edn, London, 1995)

The elephant tusk has always been prized for its texture and the colour it takes when polished. In the early Middle Ages ivory was rare, but suddenly, in the middle of the thirteenth century AD, it became available in quantity in northern Europe for the first time since the fourth century AD. The ivory trade-route seems to have run chiefly from North Africa to the coasts of Italy and southern France.

The new availability of ivory coincided with the emergence of the 'High Gothic' style in northern France. The term is an invention of the early eighteenth century, when the word 'Gothic' was adopted by antiquaries to describe the 'pointed style' of architecture. Just as the Goths were considered to have been the agents of the downfall of the Roman Empire (Alaric the Goth sacked Rome in AD 410), so the architecture of the great European cathedrals of the later Middle Ages was seen as supplanting classical canons of taste.

The first Gothic ivories were produced in the Paris of Louis IX (AD 1226–70), and during the period from c.1250 to 1400 Paris was a focus for the ivory trade. Although other cities, such as Cologne, have also been claimed as centres of production, attribution is difficult, since artists were mobile and no Gothic ivory is either signed or dated. In the fourteenth century, particularly, ivory became one of the major vehicles of expression for the Gothic sculptor. Since ivory, unlike precious metals, cannot be melted down for gain, a remarkable quantity of Gothic ivories has survived.

On the left is a seated Virgin and Child trampling the devil in the form of a dragon, the ivory's shape reflecting the curve in the tusk from which it is carved.

One of the greatest of all Gothic ivory carvers is known as the Master of Kremsmünster after his best-known work in the abbey of that name in Austria. Below is a fragment of a plaque from a diptych carved by the Master showing the funeral procession of the Virgin Mary. The left leaf is in the Staatliche Museen, Berlin.

Virgin and Child
Paris
c.1320–30
MLA 1978,5–2, 3
h. 33.8 cm (13⅓ in)
Sir Harold Wernher
Bequest

Fragment from a diptych
The Master of
Kremsmünster
Upper Rhine
late 14th century AD
MLA 1978,5–2, 5
h. 7.9 cm (3 in)
Sir Harold Wernher
Bequest

FURTHER READING
D. Gaborit-Chopin,
Ivoires du Moyen Age
(Fribourg, 1978)

Francisco **Goya**

Francisco José de Goya y Lucientes (1746–1828) was born in Fuendetodos. He travelled in Italy and then returned to work in Spain, becoming Principal Painter to the King in 1799. In 1792 he became deaf following an illness; this no doubt increased his introspection and inclination to the production of works which he said were 'to make observations for which commissioned works generally give no room, and in which fantasy and invention have no limit'. He was both a portrait painter and a brilliantly inventive etcher. In 1824 he went to Paris and then settled in voluntary exile in Bordeaux.

'Arthur Wellesley, first Duke of Wellington'
Spain
Red chalk over pencil,
AD 1812
PD 1862–7–12–185
23.5 × 17.8 cm (9¼ × 7 in)

The Museum has seven drawings by Goya. The earliest, 'The Garrotted Man', dates from the 1780s. The others include the red-chalk sketch of the Duke of Wellington (1769–1852), above, done from life after the victory over the French at the Battle of Salamanca on 23 July 1812, which served as a basis for all Goya's painted portraits of the Duke, and a brush drawing of a group of victims of the Inquisition, 'For Being of Jewish Ancestry', which can be dated after 1814.

The series of etchings that he produced: *Los Caprichos* (1799), a series of satirical prints on the vices of his times, *The Disasters of War* (1810–13), on the atrocities of the Napoleonic invasion of Spain and the reaction after the restoration of the royal family, the mysterious *Proverbios* or *Disparates* (Follies), and the *Tauromaquia* (1816), are unique in their powerful and unforgettable combination of satirical bitterness, fantastic imagination, brutality and compassion. The Museum has a very large collection of his prints, its great strength lying in the completeness of its holdings of the published editions of Goya's four main series. On the right is the disturbing 'The Sleep of Reason Produces Monsters' from the *Caprichos*.

'The Sleep of Reason Produces Monsters'
Spain
Etching and aquatint, 1799
PD *Caprichos*, pl. 43
21.5 × 15 cm (8½ × 6 in)

FURTHER READING
J. Wilson Barreau, *Goya's Prints: The Tomás Harris Collection in the British Museum* (London, 1981)
J. Wilson Barreau, A. Griffiths et al., *Disasters of War* (London, 1998)

The Museum has a collection of several thousand Greek vases; among the earliest to enter the collection were those purchased from Sir William Hamilton in 1772.

Greek vase techniques include: *Black-figure* – a technique invented in Corinth *c*.700 BC. The figures are painted in black silhouette against the natural colour of the clay, details being incised through the black surface with a sharp engraving tool. *Red-figure* – a technique invented *c*.530–520 BC in Athens, perhaps in the workshop of Andokides the potter. The figures are produced by filling in the background with black glaze and leaving them reserved in the natural orange-red of the clay, details being added with a brush. The technique declined at the close of the fourth century BC. *Bilinguals* – some vases at the end of the sixth century

CLOSKWISE FROM TOP RIGHT

Skyphos attributed to the Painter of Naples 2074, showing two nymphs
Campania, Italy
c.380–370 BC
BM Cat. Vases F 129
h. 21.5 cm (8½ in)

Hydria attributed to the Painter of London F 90, showing Aphrodite and Peitho in a chariot drawn by Erotes
c.390–380 BC
BM Cat. Vases F 90
h.39 cm (15⅓in)

Cup attributed to the Meleager Painter, showing Dionysos and Ariadne
Athens
c.390–380 BC
BM Cat. Vases E 129
h. 8 cm (3¼ in)

Hydria attributed to the Revel Painter, showing a Dionysiac revel
Campania, Italy
c.380–370 BC
BM Cat. Vases F 156
h. 38 cm (15 in)

Skyphos attributed to the Painter of Naples 2074, showing a satyr and a maenad
Campania, Italy
c.380–370 BC
BM Cat. Vases F 130
h. 22.5 cm (8¾ in)

All from the Blacas Collection

BC are decorated in both red- and black-figured techniques. *Coral red* – a pinky-red slip, infrequently used, perhaps because it was hard to control and had a tendency to flake off. *'Six' technique* – named after Jan Six who first studied it. Complete figures are rendered in thickly applied whitish clay slip, inner details being marked with incision or added red, the remainder of the vase being black. *White ground* – a thin layer of white clay applied to the whole vase, on which figures are drawn, partly in outline, partly with washes of colour. *Gnathian* – a style developed shortly before the middle of the fourth century BC, perhaps in Apulia (South Italy), in which colour, usually white, yellow or red, is added on top of the black-glaze vase.

FURTHER READING

B. Sparkes, *The Red and the Black* (London, 1996)
D. Williams, *Greek Vases* (2nd edn, London, 1999)

Grimes Graves

Grimes Graves is the name given to a massive flint-mine complex near Brandon in Norfolk. The name probably derives from the Old Norse *grimr* (Grim), a nickname of the god Odin. Large ancient earthworks and prehistoric sites might be attributed to supernatural hands because of their size. In later times they were often regarded as works of the Devil, with whom Grim was equated.

Flint and stone axes formed an essential part of the Neolithic tool-kit. Of the flint mining sites (more than 20 of which are known in Britain) the earliest are on the Sussex downs. Grimes Graves came into production during the later Neolithic period after production had ceased in Sussex.

The site has three main layers of flint which prehistoric flint-users would have employed: topstone, wallstone and floorstone. Topstone and wallstone occur in lumps or nodules which can be useful, but are sometimes small and sparse. The floorstone occurs in a more or less continuous seam of separate, large nodules which are roughly hemispherical in section and have a tabular structure; this was particularly prized by the Neolithic miners.

The mine shafts are clustered on a low chalk hill. The higher up the hill, the deeper the mine had to be sunk to reach the floorstone. More than 600 pits and shafts have been counted. On the hill slope, flint was exploited by sinking mine shafts to the level of the floorstone and driving galleries radially outward from the base. Antler picks were the chief mining tool, of which hundreds were used and discarded on site.

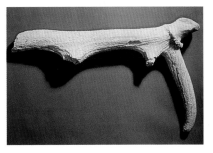

Antler 'pick'
Grimes Graves, Norfolk
Late Neolithic, *c.*2500 BC

One deep mine, the Greenwell Pit, was excavated by Canon Greenwell between 1868 and 1870. The shaft was about 40 feet deep and there was an extensive gallery system. The complex was re-excavated by the British Museum in 1974–6 with the help of a Dutch mining research team. It was calculated that some 58,200 kg (over 57 tons) of floorstone could have been extracted from these workings, which have been dated to *c.*2500–2400 BC.

Axes formed an important part of the product, and these were probably transported away from the site in the form of 'roughouts' to be finished elsewhere.

FURTHER READING
R. Holgate, *Prehistoric Flint Mines* (Aylesbury, 1991)
I.H. Longworth and G. Varndell, *Excavations at Grimes Graves, Norfolk 1972–1976
Fascicule 5: Mining in the deeper mines* (London, 1996)

Guardian Kings
of the Choson dynasty
Korea, late 14th–early 20th centuries AD

The four guardians of the cardinal points and defenders of Buddhism are found as paintings and sculptures at the entrance to Korean temples. The huge size of the painting shown below of the Guardian King of the West (erroneously labelled South on the painting), the dynamic depiction and the green and red mineral colours are typical of Choson dynasty Buddhist paintings. It bears signatures of later devotees, as well as the original red dedicatory cartouches. The painting, one of a pair in the Museum, comes from Taegu in South-East Korea. Although the name of the temple and the exact date have been erased, enough remains to show that the painting was completed in the Chinese Jiaqing period (AD 1796–1820).

The Choson dynasty is usually divided into two halves by the Japanese invasions of 1592 and 1597. During the early Choson there was much trade with China and Japan and this is regarded as a Golden Age, largely due to the enlightened rule of King Sejong (r.1418–50). The eighteenth century brought a cultural flowering under Yongjo (r.1724–76) and his grandson Chongjo (r.1776–1800). However, in the latter half of the nineteenth century an isolationist policy was adopted by the *Taewon'gun* (Prince Regent). A Bureau of Painting (*Tohwawon*) was established in 1392 and painters recruited through government examinations. The bureau was attached to the Ministry of Rites and its central role was to record state rituals.

By the eighteenth century a truly Korean school of landscape painting had emerged, the 'Real Place Landscape' (*chin'gyong sansu*). Portraiture also flourished during the Choson period, partly because of the Confucian emphasis on lineage.

FURTHER READING
B. McKillop, *Korean Art and Design* (London, 1992)
K. Pratt, *Korean Painting* (Oxford, 1995)
J. Portal, *Korea: Art and Archaeology* (London, 2000)

Guardian King of the West
Taegu, South-East Korea
Colour on textile (linen), late 18th–early 19th century AD
OA 1920.3–17.2
h. 3 m (9¾ ft)

Gudea, ruler of Lagash, *c.*2120–2100 BC, records that he brought stone from Magan (probably modern Oman) to make statues of himself for dedication in his temples. Many such diorite statues were found at Girsu, near Lagash (present-day Iraq) and are now in the Louvre, Paris. The Museum also has some related examples, one inscribed with Gudea's name, while another shows a shaven-headed man, probably Gudea, with hands clasped. His robe, its border marked by fine diagonal incisions, is draped over one shoulder but the other arm is left bare.

Raids by barbarian mountain tribesmen from the north-east known as the Guti resulted in the collapse of Akkadian government in southern Mesopotamia, *c.*2159 BC. Once again the area was divided into city-states under local Akkadian or Sumerian rulers. Finally, Utuhegal (2123–2113 BC), king of Uruk, expelled the Guti from southern Mesopotamia. Once an Akkadian provincial centre, the town of Girsu, in the far south-east, seems to have prospered under a Sumerian dynasty. Its most celebrated ruler was Gudea, during whose reign Sumerian literature flourished and hymns praising him have come to be regarded as supreme classics. Gudea claimed to have brought timber and silver from the Mediterranean coast to rebuild the shrine of his city-god Ningirsa, and to have provided it with other goods from far afield.

Diorite statue, probably of Gudea of Lagash
Mesopotamia
*c.*2100 BC
WA 122910; 1931–7–11,1
h. 73.6 cm (29 in)
Purchased with the aid of the National Art Collections Fund

FURTHER READING
D.O. Edzard, *Gudea and his Dynasty. The Royal Inscriptions of Mesopotamia, Early Periods 3/1* (Toronto, 1997)

Gu Kaizhi scroll painting
China, 6th–7th century AD

The Museum's most important Chinese painting is an early copy of a handscroll attributed to the figure-painter Gu Kaizhi (*c.*AD 344–*c.*406). Called 'Admonitions of the Instructress to Court Ladies', it illustrates advice on correct behaviour given to ladies of the imperial harem by the court preceptress.

Gu Kaizhi, a native of Wuxi in Jiangsu province, gained a reputation as a painter at the Jin court in Nanjing. He was famous for his portraits and figures, but he also painted landscapes. A number of important paintings are today attributed to him, but they were not associated with him in texts until the Song dynasty (AD 960–1279), so the relationship is tenuous. The handscroll 'Admonitions of the Instructress' is a copy which exists in two versions; the earlier, thought to be painted in the 6th century AD, is in the Museum. (The other is in the Palace Museum, Beijing.) It illustrates a moralizing text by Zhang Hua (AD 232–300), and consists of quotations from the text followed in each case by figure illustrations with no background, or at most slight suggestions of setting. The Museum scroll, in ink and colour (mainly vermilion) on silk, contains nine of the eleven scenes originally illustrated.

'Admonitions of the Instructress to Court Ladies' (scene 7) Copy of original attributed to Gu Kaizhi (*c.*AD 344–*c.*406) China 6th–7th century AD OA 1903.4–8.1 h. 25 cm (10 in)

Scene 7 (below) shows a court lady advancing towards the emperor, who repulses her with a gesture of his raised hand. The drapery is portrayed with long, continuous, even brushstrokes; movement is shown through the vitality of the swirling draperies.

The Museum has a collection of 1,400 Chinese paintings, including a small number of calligraphies, dating from the Tang dynasty (AD 618–906) to the present day. It is one of the finest collections of Chinese paintings in the West.

FURTHER READING
J. Rawson (ed.), *The British Museum Book of Chinese Art* (London, 1992)
S. McCausland, *First Masterpiece of Chinese Painting: The Admonitions Scroll* (London, 2003)
S. McCausland (ed.), *Gu Kaizhi and the Admonitions Scroll* (London, 2003)

Haida totem pole

Originally this red cedar pole stood as part of the Goose House in the nineteenth-century village of Kayang on Haida Gwaii or the Queen Charlotte Islands off north-west Canada. Most of the twenty communal houses had been abandoned by the time the pole was acquired for the Museum in 1902–3.

The term 'totem' originally referred to an individual spirit helper. On the north-west coast, stretching from Alaska to Washington state, 'totems' are the crests of high-ranking families. Poles such as this one are carved with clan crests and illustrate origin myths of the lineage of the family or house.

This pole portrays two myths. In the first, Raven, the creator of all things, steals fish from a village at the bottom of the ocean. He is caught and loses the top half of his beak, but succeeds in retrieving this and obtaining all the food he needs by turning himself into a chief, sitting amongst high-ranking people where food is plentiful. At the top of the pole is a chief or young mythical hero holding a staff. Below is a mythical creature, a seabear or the Raven with a broken beak.

The second story concerns a poor young man married to the daughter of a high-ranking chief. His mother-in-law, who is a shaman, criticizes him for over-eating, so he retreats into the forest where he gains supernatural powers. At his behest a whale is washed up. He climbs into it and beaches it in front of the village. His mother-in-law has dreamed of this and when the villagers cut up the whale the young man emerges, to her shame and the approval of the villagers. Below the mother-in-law, who holds two rattles, is a large whale, then a bear with a small human (the son-in-law) on its head and a killer whale in its stomach.

FURTHER READING
M. Halpin, *Totem Poles* (Vancouver, 1981)
P. Nuytten, *The Totem Carver* (Vancouver, 1982)
J. C. H. King, *First Peoples, First Contacts: Native Peoples of North America* (London, 1999)

Haida pole of red cedar
Queen Charlotte
Islands, Canada
19th century AD
ETH 1903.3–4.1
h. 11 m (36 ft)

Hallstatt pottery

Europe, mid-8th–mid-5th centuries BC

The large cemetery excavated at Hallstatt near Salzburg, Austria, in the nineteenth century gives its name to the first phase of the European Iron Age. The cemetery, which was used from c.750 to c.450 BC, belonged to a community whose wealth was based on local deposits of salt and copper, conveniently sited on an important trade route. Almost 1000 burials, both cremations and inhumations, were excavated between 1846 and 1863 by J.G. Ramsauer; later in the 1860s more were unearthed by John Evans and John Lubbock, who gave most of their finds to the Museum.

Graves of the Hallstatt Iron Age were rich in attractive pottery. Potters fully understood how firing and after-firing conditions affected ceramics; consequently they were able to decorate pots with patterns combining red, black and white. These vessels were highly prized and became important offerings in burials. Their size, shape and colour illustrate the degree of experimentation and range of skills achieved between 900 and 600 BC.

Large pottery dish from the 'Degerfeld' Barrow cemetery
Albstadt-Tailfingen, Zollernalbkreis, Germany
c.700–600 BC
PRB 1908 8–1 240
diam. 39 cm (15⅓ in)
Excavated in 1890

Fabrication methods were simple. Having shaped the vessel by coiling a sausage of clay the potter carefully smoothed off the surfaces to an even finish. Geometric patterns were incised, combed, stamped or furrowed. Powdered graphite was applied to the outside before firing in smoky conditions to produce the iridescent finish reminiscent of bronze. When black and red patterning was required the potter coated different areas with graphite and haematite, an iron-rich pigment which retains its red colour even in light smoke. Finished pots were fired in an open fire at 500–600°C. After firing, the incised patterns were inlaid with a white pigment or sheet metal to heighten the contrast.

FURTHER READING
I. Freestone and D. Gaimster (eds), *Pottery in the Making* (London, 1997)

142

The Harpy Tomb is named from the four female-headed birds at the corners that bear small-scale human figures. Once described as 'harpies' who carried off children and souls, they are now identified as Sirens, escorts to the dead, who sing in the Isles of the Blessed.

The Harpy Tomb was found in 1838 at Xanthos in south-west Asia Minor (pp. 360–1), the principal city of ancient Lycia. Although the tomb was commissioned by Lycians, a non-Greek people, the links between the Lycians and the Greek cities of western Asia Minor were always close, and the carving is probably by Greek sculptors. The Harpy Tomb is typical of Lycian tombs, being basically a stone box, originally perched on top of a pillar of grey-blue limestone. A series of Parian marble relief slabs surmounted by a heavy stepped coping formed a hollow chamber to contain the body, and a small opening was made on the west side in the belief that the soul could come and go. It was originally coloured – traces of paint can be seen on the background and on the thrones and costumes of the west side.

The four sides bear sculptured scenes apparently showing offerings or ceremonies in honour of gods or deified ancestors. The sculpture has Greek elements – the Sirens, the procession of girls in their finely pleated drapery bearing birds or flowers, and the youth who doffs his helmet before a seated elder. But there are Lycian influences too. One figure has been seen as Harpagos, founder of the Lycian dynasty, and another as the warrior king Kybernis, perhaps the occupant of the tomb. Above the opening or doorway is a cow suckling its calf, a motif that appears on the coins of Sppndaza, ruler of Lycia from 475 to 469 BC.

The Harpy Tomb
Xanthos, Lycia, Turkey
c.480 BC
GR 1848.10–20.1;
Cat. Sculpture B 287
total h. c.8.84 m (29 ft)
Excavated by Charles Fellows

FURTHER READING
A. Shapur Shahbazi, *The Irano-Lycian Monuments* (Tehran, 1975)
E. Slatter, *Xanthus, Travels and Discovery in Turkey* (London, 1994)

Hawaiian wood carving

Captain Cook's three voyages of exploration (1768–79) brought Polynesia to the notice of the West and were also the origin, both directly and indirectly, of many of the most important pieces in the Museum's collections, which include magnificent carvings and featherwork. Accompanying Cook on his first voyage were Joseph Banks (1743–1820), a Trustee of the Museum, and a staff member, the botanist Daniel Solander (1736–82). Cook was killed in Hawaii (the Sandwich Islands) in 1779. Further important early material from the Hawaiian islands, some of which came to the Museum, was collected by W. George Goodman Hewett, surgeon's mate on Captain Vancouver's voyage of 1791–5.

Above is a wooden bowl for preparing or drinking *kava* ('*awa* in Hawaiian), collected on Captain Cook's third voyage (1776–9). It is probably that given to Captain Clarke, Cook's second-in-command, by a chief of Kauai when he paid Clarke a visit aboard the *Discovery* on 23 January 1778. Cook wrote in his journal:

> He was a young man, cloathed from head to foot and accompanied by a young woman, suppos'd to be his wife. Captain Clarke made him some suitable presents and in return he gave him a large cava bowl, that was supported by two car[v]ed men, neither ill designed nor executed.

Wooden bowl for preparing or drinking *kava*
Hawaii
18th century AD
ETH Haw.46
l. 50.5 cm (19⁹⁄₁₀ in)
Given by Sir Joseph Banks, who inherited it from Captain Clarke

On the right is a temple image of the Hawaiian war god Ku in his aspect as Kuka'ili moku or the Snatcher-of-Land, presented to the Museum in 1839. Ku was the personal god of King Kamehameha I and as such assumed particular importance during the latter's rise to power, which culminated in the unification of the islands in 1795. Hawaiian images of gods were not idols or portraits but receptacles or dwelling places which became sacred only when, through prayer and appropriate ritual, gods were induced to enter them. This image, made of breadfruit (*Artocarpus* sp.) wood, was probably carved during the time of Kamehameha I. It was presented to the Museum 20 years after the king's death and the ensuing collapse of the traditional religious system of Hawaii.

Breadfruit wood image of the war god Ku
Hawaii
late 18th or early 19th century AD
ETH 1839.4–26.8
h. 2.08 m (6 ft 10 in)
Given by W. Howard

FURTHER READING
D.C. Starzecka, *Hawaii: People and Culture* (London, 1975)

By the beginning of the New Kingdom the Egyptian priesthood had become exclusively male, but women of high rank, some of whom were married to the priests, were allowed to serve as musicians. The role of these women was to play the sistrum, as accompaniment to the ritual chants or cult hymns, and sometimes even to provide the chants themselves. On the right is the gilded wooden inner coffin of a Theban priestess, Henutmehyt, bearing her title, 'Chantress of Amun'.

The coffin provided physical protection for the body and was heavily endowed with religious symbolism, intended to assure the deceased's rebirth and well-being in the Afterlife. The elevation of the deceased to a state of divinity was emphasized through the inclusion of attributes characteristic of the god Osiris, such as the crossed arms. The gilded inner coffin would have been placed inside a nest of wooden coffins, each fitting neatly within the next right down to an innermost two-piece cover or mummy board in openwork which lay immediately over the wrapped body. The centre of the lid carries a winged figure of the goddess Nut sitting beneath a representation of Henutmehyt adoring Re in a boat. The text below, following the lines of bandages on the mummy, framed figures of Isis, Nephthys and the Four Sons of Horus. The last are shown also on the side walls with Thoth and Anubis.

In addition to the inner coffin the Museum also has the richly decorated wooden outer coffin. This too depicts Henutmehyt partly shrouded in her mummy wrappings.

Henutmehyt was also provided with four wooden boxes containing *shabti* figures (p. 295). One of these is decorated with a picture of her receiving food and drink for the Afterlife from the goddess Nut, who stands within the branches of a tree. The *shabtis* of Henutmehyt are typical of those made for a high-ranking lady of the later New Kingdom.

FURTHER READING
C. Andrews, *Egyptian Mummies* (2nd edn, London, 1998)

Gilded inner coffin of
Henutmehyt
Thebes, Egypt
19th Dynasty,
c.1295–1186 BC
EA 48001
h. 1.88 m (6 ft 2 in)

The **Hinton St Mary mosaic pavement**

In a roundel in this mosaic lies what is thought to be the earliest representation of Christ yet found in Britain, and the only such portrait on a mosaic floor discovered in the Roman Empire. The central figure is portrayed as a fair-haired, clean-shaven man with dark, rather penetrating eyes. He wears an inner garment (*tunica*) and outer mantle (*pallium*). Behind his head is the chi-rho symbol, made up of the first letters of the Greek word *Christos* (Christ). The young man's hair is combed forward and falls in curly locks and he has a slightly cleft chin. To each side is a pomegranate – the symbol of immortality.

The pavement was discovered in 1963 buried beneath a field in the village of Hinton St Mary, Dorset. Its style indicates that it was laid in the fourth century AD. There were traces of a substantial building complex, probably including the remains of a villa. The mosaic was part of the best-preserved wing. The walls on either side had been demolished, probably after the departure of the Roman legions in AD 410.

The mosaic comes from a pair of rooms joined by a narrow opening, perhaps a *triclinium* (a room containing a dining table with couches along three sides). The single design runs through both rooms.

The Hinton St Mary
mosaic pavement (detail)
Dorset, Britain
4th century AD
PRB 1965 4–9 1
total l. 8.6 m (28 ft 2 in)

As often happened in Roman Britain, the old pagan beliefs were juxtaposed with the new religion of Christianity. While the portrait is the focus of the larger room, the smaller had a roundel portraying Bellerophon mounted on Pegasus thrusting a spear into the Chimaera. In the four corners of the larger section are portraits thought to be the four winds or the four evangelists. The half-circles show hunting scenes and a great tree with grey-blue leaves.

FURTHER READING
M. Henig, *The Art of Roman
Britain* (London, 1995)
K.S. Painter, 'The Roman site
at Hinton St Mary, Dorset',
British Museum Quarterly, vol.
31 (1967), pp. 15–31
J.M.C. Toynbee, 'A new Roman
mosaic pavement found in
Dorset', *Journal of Roman Studies*
lxiv (1964), pp. 7–14

Hispano-Moresque pottery

The Museum's collection of Valencian lustreware (the pottery of Moorish Spain) is one of the world's richest. The technique of applying lustre to a previously fired glaze was first used in Iraq in the ninth century AD. It was adopted in Egypt, where it attained new pictorial heights under the Fatimids (AD 969–1171). Potteries making lustred wares were established by potters from Fatimid Egypt in Moorish Spain, probably in the twelfth century AD, notably in Murcia and Málaga, and it was Moorish potters who brought the technique to Valencia in c.AD 1300.

Fine Spanish pottery was exported throughout Europe. The arms painted on some pieces identify special commissions from royal, noble or mercantile families. Florentine merchants ordered sets of lustred tableware direct from Valencia, to which Tuscan banks and trading companies were linked by trade. Spanish imports were a major factor in raising the status of pottery from the utilitarian to that of an art form in Renaissance Italy. Pottery had long been a luxury commodity in the Islamic world, and Valencian wares, which were more highly valued than native pottery, were imitated by Italian potters.

Lustre is a very thin coat of silver or copper on the surface of a glaze, producing an iridescent effect. Metal salts were ground with fired clay and painted on to the surface of the vessel, which had been previously glazed and fired. The pot was then fired at a relatively low temperature, when the salts broke down, diffused into the surface and were reduced to metal. Great skill was needed to control the lustre firing and the failure rate is likely to have been high. Because of its complexity, lustre appears to have been produced in only a few centres by a limited number of potters, who guarded their secrets.

On the right is a lustred pottery vase bearing the arms of the Medici family, probably made for Piero 'the Gouty' (d.1469) or his son Lorenzo the Magnificent (d.1492), successive rulers of Florence.

FURTHER READING
T. Wilson, *Ceramic Art of the Italian Renaissance* (London, 1987)

Vase
Valencia, Spain
c.AD 1465–75
MLA G 619
h. 57 cm (22½ in)
Miss Edith Godman
Bequest

The Museum has many thousands of prints depicting historical events. These range from contemporary records commemorating such occurrences as naval and military battles, ceremonies, notable trials, natural phenomena (such as the frozen Thames, below), scientific invention, political scandals and triumphs, to imaginary depictions of events long past. There are prints illustrating British history, for example, from the time of Julius Caesar's invasion of 55 BC (not, of course, contemporary), and continuing through the Roman and medieval periods. In Britain, contemporary prints began to appear from the seventeenth century onwards. Some prints were a reflection of events, others (p. 284) were satirical. From the mid-nineteenth century the role of the historical print was increasingly taken over by photography.

The collection also includes numerous prints depicting foreign history, mostly German, Dutch or French in origin, with a few from Italy, Spain and elsewhere. Some are rare, particularly the seventeenth-century German broadsheets, of which the Museum's collection is outstanding.

FURTHER READING
A. Griffiths, *The Print in Stuart Britain 1603–1689* (London, 1998)
A. Griffiths and F. Carey, *German Printmaking in the Age of Goethe* (London, 1994)

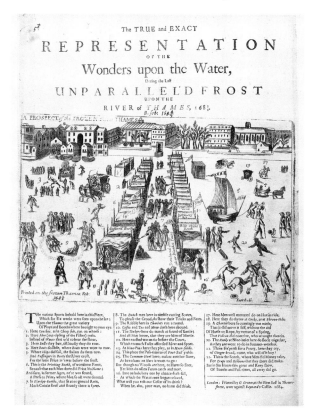

'The True and Exact Representation of Wonders upon the Water, During the Last Unparallel'd Frost upon the River Thames 1683/4'
11 February 1684
Anonymous
Broadsheet printed on the frozen Thames by G. Croom
PD 1880–11–13–1770
44.2 × 32.1 cm
(17½ × 12⅔ in), with an engraved view
21.1 × 31.7 cm
(8⅓ × 12½ in)
Purchased (Crace Collection)

Hittite ornaments

Anatolia, c.1400–1200 BC

The Hittites entered Anatolia before 2000 BC, and between c.1400 and 1200 BC they established one of the great empires of the ancient Near East, extending into Syria, which was partly under Egyptian control. By the time of the Assyrian colonies they were well integrated and may have been involved in a widespread destruction of cities c.1740 BC. A century later, however, King Hattusili I rebuilt Hattusa (now Boğazköy) and made it his capital.

The Hittites wrote in hieroglyphs and also adapted the cuneiform script for writing Hittite, the earliest attested Indo-European language. Most of the information about them and the artefacts which have survived relate to the period of the Hittite empire. Population movements in the Aegean, such as the Trojan War and the invasion of the Sea Peoples and Kashka, led to the empire's collapse in c.1200 BC.

The Museum's most remarkable example of Hittite workmanship is a series of miniature figures (below) representing Hittite deities and dignitaries. These were found in a grave at Carchemish on the Euphrates, a town which long retained aspects of Hittite culture. They were buried in about 605 BC, probably during the siege of Carchemish by Nebuchadnezzar of Babylon. The grave contained a cylinder of lapis lazuli and gold tassels from the ends of a belt. Minute gold beads, which had fused together because of the heat of the cremation, had probably been stitched to a garment. Also found were a gold disc and strip with openwork decoration.

Two of the 30 small figures show the Hittite sun-god wearing royal robes, carrying the curved rod which was an emblem of kingship, and identified by the winged sun-disc on his head, another symbol of kingship imported from Egypt via Syria. The figures may have been heirlooms as they resemble thirteenth-century BC deities carved near the Hittite capital for King Tudhaliya IV at the rock-cut shrine at Yazılıkaya.

Hittite figures of gold, steatite and lapis lazuli
Carchemish, south-east Anatolia, Turkey
c.1300–1200 BC
WA 116232;
1922–5–11,365
h. (largest) 1.75 cm
(1¹⁄₁₆ in)
Excavated by Sir Leonard Woolley

FURTHER READING
D. Collon, *Ancient Near Eastern Art* (London, 1995)

149

William **Hogarth**

From an apprenticeship to a silver engraver and training in the informal drawing academies of the day (one of which was run by Sir James Thornhill, Sergeant Painter to the King, whose daughter he married), William Hogarth (1697–1764) became the leading artist of his generation. The Museum has one of the finest collections of Hogarth's prints, including many rare early impressions. The well-known 'Gin Lane' (1751), below, shows in the background the steeple of St George's Church, Bloomsbury, just to the south of the Museum, two years before the Museum was founded, when the area was occupied by one of London's notorious slums. The print portrays the gin craze of the mid-eighteenth century, epitomized by the innkeeper's slogan – 'Drunk for a penny, dead drunk for tuppence'.

The advancement of Hogarth's career went hand-in-hand with a wider promotion of British art: in 1735 he set up a drawing academy in St Martin's Lane, London, which formed a focus for the development of the rococo style in Britain; in the same year he was largely responsible for the passing of the Engravers' Copyright Act. Although a fine portrait-painter, he is best remembered for his 'Modern Moral Subjects', engravings which gave him a large income. These contain amusing and realistic detail, usually set in recognizable parts of London, and portray the often sordid life of the period. Of them he wrote, 'I have endeavoured to treat my subjects as a dramatic writer; my picture is my stage, and men and women my players, who by means of certain actions and gestures, are to exhibit a dumb show'. His first great success came in 1732 with *A Harlot's Progress*, showing the downfall of a country girl in London. 1240 sets of the first edition were sold at one guinea (£1.05). Other series were the *Rake's Progress* (1733–5), *Marriage à la Mode* (1743–4), *Industry and Idleness* (1747) and the *Election* (1754). Since Hogarth's paintings were mainly worked directly on to the canvas and his studies from life often took the form of thumbnail sketches, only about 100 drawings survive, more than half of which belong to the Museum.

'Gin Lane'
London
Etching and engraving, 1751
PD 1868–8–22–1595
37.9 × 31.9 cm
(15 × 12½ in)
Felix Slade Bequest

FURTHER READING
D. Bindman, *Hogarth and his Times: Serious Comedy* (London, 1997)

Katsushika Hokusai (1760–1849) was the leading ukiyo-e (p. 339) artist of the later Edo period. He had the longest career of any of them – more than 70 years – and, as his art name 'Gakyojin' suggests, he was indeed 'mad with painting'.

By the early 1830s Japanese woodblock prints had been flourishing for some 150 years, and were popular in Kyoto, Osaka and Edo (Tokyo). These prints had not generally included landscape, the pigments available were not suitable and the lack of a strong blue which would not fade was a particular handicap. In the 1820s Prussian blue began to be imported in quantity and Hokusai, already over 60 years old, saw its potential. In the early 1830s he designed his great series *36 Views of Mount Fuji*, which fully utilized Prussian blue and at the same time established the landscape as a major print form. Hokusai realized that the new pigment was too powerful for the traditional palette of colour prints and strengthened the other colours to match it. The resulting brilliant and distinct pigments produced a new attitude among Japanese artists. Prints become a graphic art in their own right, using colour and design in a starker and more immediately striking way than before.

Hokusai included Japan's highest mountain, with its perfect volcanic shape, in all of the 36 prints seen from the south of the central mountains. Later he added another ten views from the north. The print below shows the mountain from the sea of Kanagawa, on the coast to the south-west of Tokyo. The vulnerability of the seamen is emphasized by the little Shinto shrine at the stern of the boat to the right marked by its *torii*, or symbolic gateway.

FURTHER READING
T. Clark, *100 Views of Mount Fuji* (London, 2001)
M. Forrer, *Hokusai, Prints and Drawings* (London, 1991)
R. Lane, *Hokusai, Life and Work* (London, 1989)

'The Hollow of the Deep Sea Wave off the Coast of Kanagawa'
(*Kanagawa oki nami-ura*)
Edo (Tokyo), Japan
*c.*1829–33
JA 1937.7–10.0147
25.9 × 37.7 cm
(10⅛ × 14⅜ in)

Horses

The horse is prized above most other animals. In India in Vedic times (*c.*1200 BC), for example, the horse was a symbol of royal authority, and its sacrifice consecrated the power of the king. The early history of the horse is obscure; there were at least two species

Detail from the Onager-hunt of Ashurbanipal
North Palace, Nineveh, Assyria,
*c.*645 BC
WA 124876 (detail)
h. of figure on horse
51.5 cm (20¼ in)
Excavated by Hormuzd Rassam

Lead-glazed horse
Luoyang, China
Tang dynasty, first half of 8th century AD
OA 1936.10–12.227
h. 85 cm (33½ in)
Purchased (from George Eumorfopoulos)

of wild horse, the Tarpan and the Przewalski, but there may have been others, including the ancestors of the Arab breed. Wild horses first appear in cave paintings, probably hunted for food. By *c.*1700 BC domesticated horses were used for transport throughout the Near and Middle East. In the first millennium BC the horse became more widely used for riding, and reliefs in the British Museum depict Assyrian cavalry in the ninth century BC. It was about this time that the nomadic inhabitants of Central Asia took to riding to a significant degree, striking fear into the settled lands of China, Western Asia and Europe. To combat this menace the Chinese and Greeks also became riders, and cavalry came into use in these areas as well. In later centuries the mounted Arabs had the same advantages as the earlier Central Asian nomads, and speed on horseback was one of the foundations of their military success. Horses were introduced

Horses

Horses
Mori Shuho (1738–1823)
Japan
Four-fold screen, ink and
gofun on paper,
Edo period, late 18th
century AD
JA 1988.10–18.1
136 × 264.8 cm
(53½ × 104¼ in)
Given by Mr K. Kishimoto

into the Americas by the Spanish Conquistadors in the sixteenth century AD.

Horses are to be seen throughout the Museum, among them the proud, prancing horses of Ashurbanipal's lion-hunt (pp. 186–7), which epitomize the warhorse described in the Bible (Job xxxix.21, 25):

> He paweth in the valley and rejoiceth in his strength, he goeth on to meet the armed men ...
> he saith among the trumpets Ha, ha, and he smelleth the battle afar off, the thunder of the captains, and the shouting ...

Horses are featured in mythology, among them the chariot horses of the sun-god Helios, drawing the sun up into the heavens, and the horses of the moon-goddess Selene sinking down exhausted, most beautifully recreated in the east pediment of the Parthenon (pp. 245–6).

On the left is an alert horse from the Tang dynasty tomb of Liu Yinhxun (*d.* AD 728) at Luoyang, while the herd of horses on a Japanese screen (above) cavorts free from harness.

FURTHER READING
C. Johns, *Horses: History, Myth, Art* (London, 2006)

The Hoxne (pronounced 'hoxon') hoard, discovered in 1992 in Suffolk, contains a staggering 15,000 coins – five times the size of the biggest coin hoard found previously in Britain. It consists of 574 gold *soldidii* of eight different emperors from Valentinian I (AD 364–75) to Honorius (AD 393–423), 61 large silver *miliarenses* and over 14,000 small silver *siliquae* spanning 14 reigns from Constantius II (AD 337–61) to Constantine III (AD 407–11). They come from 16 imperial mints. The two most recent coins in the hoard – two *siliquae* of the usurper Constantine III, a governor who removed large detachments of troops from Britain in order to defeat the Emperor Honorius – indicate that the hoard must have been buried after AD 407 during the time of political upheaval when Rome effectively abandoned control of Britain.

In addition there are 78 spoons, 98 if the round-bowled ladles are included – by far the largest collection of spoons in any late Roman hoard. There are four pepperpots, gold jewellery and a silver tiger inlaid with niello (p. 325). Many of the spoons are engraved with personal names and other symbols such as the Christian monogram. Nineteen have gilded decoration on a marine theme – a sea-god, dolphins and mythical sea-creatures.

FURTHER READING

R. Bland and C.M. Johns, *The Hoxne Treasure, an illustrated introduction* (London, 1993)

C.M. Johns and R. Bland, 'The Hoxne late Roman treasure', *Britannia* 25 (London, 1994), pp. 165–73

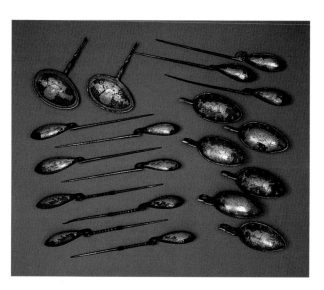

Matching set of 19 silver spoons with gilded figural decoration
Buried in the 5th century AD
PRB P1994 4–8 62–80
l. (of long-handled spoons) approx. 20 cm (7¾ in)
Acquired with the aid of the National Heritage Memorial Fund, the National Art Collections Fund, Lloyds Private Banking and private donations

Huguenot silver

On 17 October 1685 King Louis XIV revoked the Edict of Nantes which since 1598 had secured for the Protestants some freedom of worship and complete liberty of conscience in Catholic France. Protestant pastors were given 15 days to leave, and up to 200,000 people emigrated to Protestant Europe. Many were skilled craftsmen whose loss weakened France and enriched England, the United Provinces and Brandenburg, which received the refugees.

The Huguenots who settled in England, in Spitalfields, were particularly noted for their skill in silk weaving and silversmithing. The style of Huguenot silver was not in the English tradition; the hostility of the London silversmiths meant that the Huguenots were ostracized, and so initially their silver retained a separate identity. Instead of thin-walled embossed shapes, they introduced much heavier silver with many cast elements. They also brought to England many French shapes, for example the helmet ewer and the *écuelle* (broth bowl). The major silversmiths such as Paul Crespin and David Willaume were immensely successful and native English silversmiths soon had to follow their example.

In 1969 the Museum received a splendid bequest from Peter Wilding consisting of some 30 items of Huguenot silver of the highest quality and importance, made in London between 1697 and 1723. Shown here is a sideboard dish from the bequest. It was made for the Hon. George Treby MP (*c.*1684–1742) by Paul de Lamerie, who ran the most successful London silversmith's firm of the first half of the eighteenth century. By 1723 he was taking orders from the Russian court, the English nobility and the wealthy middle classes. A business such as his would have employed designers, chasers, modellers and engravers and sub-contracted work out to other craftsmen.

Sideboard dish made by Paul de Lamerie (detail)
London
Silver, 1723–4
MLA 1969,7–5, 25
diam. 60.8 cm (24 in)
Peter Wilding Bequest

FURTHER READING
P. Glanville, *Silver in England* (London, 1987)
T. Schroder, *The National Trust Book of English Domestic Silver 1500–1900* (London, 1988)

The **Hull Grundy Gift** of jewellery

One of the fascinations of the Hull Grundy Gift of 1200 pieces of jewellery is that it was put together by one woman who spent much of her life bedridden at her home in Hampshire.

The importance of the gift lies in its wealth of signed and documented works by leading European and American jewellers, designers and gem-engravers, such as Burges, Castellani, Tiffany and Lalique. There are items bearing dates, marks, signatures, inscriptions, many preserved in the original cases in which they left the jeweller's shop. The gift is therefore an invaluable research tool, its range extending from sixth-century Byzantium to the 1950s. Its greatest strength is in the eighteenth and nineteenth centuries. The Museum had an unparalleled collection of jewellery before the gift was made – including fine examples from the ancient world and from non-European peoples – but with little European jewellery after 1700.

The collection is now shown to best advantage alongside related material, but below is one of Anne Hull Grundy's 'Gardens': two hanging wall cases of botanical and sentimental 'message' jewellery, dating from the Romantic to late Victorian, selected by her husband.

FURTHER READING
C. Gere, J. Rudoe, H. Tait (ed.), T. Wilson, *The Art of the Jeweller: A Catalogue of the Hull Grundy Gift to the British Museum; Jewellery, Engraved Gems and Goldsmith's Work*, 2 vols (London, 1984)
H. Tait and C. Gere, *The Jeweller's Art: An Introduction to the Hull Grundy Gift to the British Museum* (London, 1978)

Pompeian-style necklace
Eugène Fontenay
Paris
Gold, painted enamel and diamonds, 1867–73
MLA Jewellery Cat. no. 983
l. (of central pendant) 2.95 cm (1¹⁄₁₀ in)

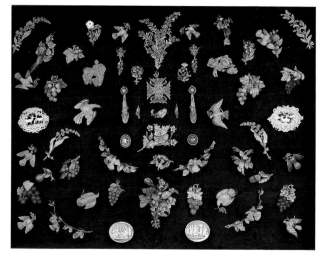

One of Anne Hull Grundy's 'Gardens'
Europe
AD 1820–90
Given by Professor and Mrs John Hull Grundy

To the Greeks Hypnos was the personification of sleep, twin brother of Thanatos, Death. In some myths the twins were either considered the sons of Nyx (Night) and Erebus, or were reared by Nyx as their nursemaid. Hypnos's home was variously located. Homer made him an inhabitant of Lemnos and described how he and Thanatos carry dead warriors from the battlefield. To Virgil he was an inhabitant of the Underworld. Ovid, in *Metamorphoses* II, described his home as a magic palace in the land of the Cimmerians where everything was asleep.

Unlike his brother, Hypnos was beneficial to men. His wings allowed him to travel rapidly over land and sea, touching the foreheads of the weary with his magic wand or fanning them with his wings to bring them sleep. His son was Morpheus, the god of dreams.

This bronze head is possibly a Roman copy, one of many versions of the same Greek original which was probably made during the Hellenistic period.

Hypnos was rare in sculpture until the late Classical/early Hellenistic period (late fourth century BC), although he appears with Thanatos on classical vases, especially *lekythoi* (oil jars).

FURTHER READING
C.C. Mattusch,
Classical Bronzes
(Cornell, 1996)

Bronze head of Hypnos
Roman, found at Civitella
d'Arno, Venezia, Italy
*c.*1st–2nd century AD
GR 1868.6–6.9;
Bronze 267
h. 21 cm (8¼ in)
Purchased (from
Alessandro Castellani)

According to Russian chronicles, the decisive consideration in Russia's conversion to Orthodox Christianity was the effect produced on tenth-century emissaries from Kiev by Constantinople's great church of Hagia Sophia. There, the visitors were said to have reported, 'we knew not whether we were in heaven or earth, for on earth there is no such vision nor beauty, and we do not know how to describe it; we know only that there God dwells among men'. Among the treasures of the Eastern Church were, and are, icons – compelling pictures of sacred persons or events which are largely found on the iconostasis, a screen separating the sanctuary from the nave in Eastern churches. In the eighth and ninth centuries AD there were bitter conflicts in the Byzantine Church between the iconoclasts, who opposed the use of religious images, and those who clung to them. When the conflict was resolved the Eastern Church established a doctrine of veneration and formulated a set of technical rules for the production of icons. Today they are considered an essential part of the Church, serving as objects of instruction and contemplation.

The Museum holds over 100 icons. One, below, known as *The Triumph of Orthodoxy*, celebrates the restoration of holy images in AD 843. In the centre of the upper register is a representation of the icon of the Mother of God, *Hodeghetria*, which it was claimed had been painted by St Luke. To the left stand the rulers at the time, the

Icon of the Triumph of Orthodoxy
Constantinople (Istanbul, Turkey)
Wooden panel faced with linen and gesso and painted in egg tempera on gold leaf, *c.*AD 1400
MLA 1988,4–11, 1
39 × 31 cm
(15⅓ × 12¼ in)
Purchased with the aid of the National Art Collections Fund
(Eugene Cremetti Fund)

Icons

Icon of St George
(the 'Black George')
Pskov, Northern Russia
Egg tempera and gold on
gesso on cloth and a
wooden panel,
late 14th century AD
MLA 1986,6–3, 1
77 × 57 cm
(30⅓ × 22½ in)

Regent Empress Theodora and her young son, the Emperor
Michael III. To the right stand Methodios, the Patriarch of
Constantinople (AD 843–7), and three supporters of the
Iconophile cause. The lower register comprises eleven historical
Iconophile figures, some of them holding images. In some
instances their names can be read.

Above is the icon of St George, painted in Pskov, found in a
village on the River Pinega, a tributary of the Severnaya Dvina,
which flows into the White Sea at Archangel in the extreme north-
west of Russia. The representation of St George on a black horse is
so rare that this icon has been known as the *Black George* since its
discovery in 1959.

FURTHER READING
D. Buckton (ed.), *Byzantium: Treasures of Byzantine Art and Culture* (London, 1994)

Idrimi, King of Alalakh

Idrimi was a vassal king of the Mitannian Empire which flourished c.1550–1325 BC, stretching right across north Syria and northern Mesopotamia. He ruled at Alalakh c.1500 BC, where he built a palace. His life can be reconstructed from the long inscription in cuneiform script in the Akkadian language which covered his statue.

Idrimi claimed descent from the kings of Iamhad (Aleppo) of the eighteenth century BC, and he may be wearing a version of the dress worn by them on the seal impressions found there. The inscription tells how, following a dispute, Idrimi and his family were obliged to flee from Iamhad to his mother's family at Emar (now Meskene), on the Euphrates. Determined to restore the family fortunes, Idrimi left Emar and went to Canaan, where he found other refugees from his father's kingdom; he mounted a seaborne expedition to recover his territory and eventually became a vassal of the Mitannian king Barattarna, who installed him as king in Alalakh. Idrimi had been reigning 30 years when he had his statue inscribed by the scribe Sharruwa. The inscription ends with curses on any who would desecrate it and blessings on those who honour it.

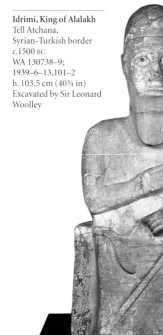

Idrimi, King of Alalakh
Tell Atchana,
Syrian-Turkish border
c.1500 BC
WA 130738–9;
1939–6–13,101–2
h. 103.5 cm (40¾ in)
Excavated by Sir Leonard
Woolley

The statue is carved of hard white dolomitic magnesite and the pupils are inlaid glass. The king wears a round-topped headdress with band and neck-guard, and a garment with narrow borders, perhaps fur-trimmed. It has been suggested that the inscription is in fact a later addition, carved to bolster national pride by providing evidence of the city's glorious past. At the time of the final destruction of Alalakh the statue was toppled from its base and its head and feet were broken off.

FURTHER READING
D. Collon, *Ancient Near Eastern Art*
(London, 1995)

Inro

Inro are containers for seals and seal paste, or sometimes medicines. They are usually composed of between two and six compartments which fit together and are held in place by a silk cord passing through a lengthwise hole at either side. The cord is tightened by a sliding bead (*ojime*). *Inro* were carried hanging from the sash of traditional Japanese dress, and kept in place by an ornamental toggle called a *netsuke* (p. 228). This system was used to suspend other containers from the sash such as purses, writing sets, smoking pipes and tobacco pouches.

Three lacquerware *inro* **from Japan**
LEFT 18th century
JA 1945.10–17.405
l. 7.7 cm (3 in)
Oscar Raphael Bequest

CENTRE late 16th century
JA 1945.10–17.403
l. 9 cm (3½ in)
Oscar Raphael Bequest

RIGHT late 18th–early
19th century
HG 348
l. 7.8 cm (3 in)
Given by Mrs Hull
Grundy

From around the end of the sixteenth century AD *inro* of lacquered wood became highly decorative. The Museum has some 355 specimens, one of the largest collections being that given by Mrs Hull Grundy (p. 156), which has exceptionally fine *inro* of the eighteenth and nineteenth centuries, exhibiting a range of techniques in gold and coloured lacquer, and inlay of shell, coral and metal.

Above are three lacquerware *inro*, each with four compartments. That on the left is decorated with shellfish in gold and black; in the centre, with boats on a lake and with chrysanthemums in relief over a black lacquer ground; on the right, with a peacock in gold and mother-of-pearl inlay on a gold ground.

FURTHER READING
J. Hutt, *Japanese Inro* (London, 1997)
M. and B. Jahss, *Inro and Other Miniature Forms of Japanese Lacquer Art* (London, n.d.)

Calligraphy is regarded as the supreme art in the Islamic world, the means by which the Qur'an, the word of God as revealed to the Prophet Muhammad, is conveyed. The language of the Qur'an is Arabic, and its alphabet derives from the Aramaic language used by the Nabateans (before the fourth century BC to the second century AD), whose kingdom extended from southern Syria to north-west Arabia and who had their capital at Petra (southern Jordan). Until the sixth century AD Arabic was a purely spoken language. Although colloquial Arabic today shows great diversity, the written language can be read anywhere in the Arab world, its unbroken literary tradition going back about 13 centuries. The Museum has an extensive collection of objects demonstrating the beauty of Islamic calligraphy – coins, paintings, pottery, amulets.

Portions of the Qur'an were probably written down in the time of the Prophet upon such materials as were to hand. Under 'Uthman (AD 644–50) its codification gave an impetus to the development of script in books. At this time the Qur'an was probably produced in codex form, as leaves of parchment bound in covers of wood and leather. The first versions do not appear to have survived, and the earliest Qur'ans probably date from the eighth century.

Very early scripts of the Muslim era are represented on the monuments of the Umayyads (AD 661–750). In the early years Mecca, Medina, Kufah and Basrah were all renowned as centres of calligraphy. Kufic, named after the town of Kufah in Iraq where this elegant, angular script was perfected in the first century of Islam (seventh century AD), was only one of four branches but, in the absence of sufficient manuscripts to distinguish these, it has proved convenient to group the angular styles of this and later ages together as 'Kufic' in contrast to the more curvilinear styles, which are usually named individually. Square, elegant Kufic scripts were used from earliest Islamic times, in Qur'ans written on vellum with gold illumination, carved on tombstones, or starkly written in black against a white ground on the tenth- and eleventh-century ceramics of the Samanid dynasty of eastern Iran. Above is a fine Kufic inscription painted in black slip on an eleventh-century bowl from Nishapur, Iran, reading 'He who speaks his speech is silver, but silence is a ruby: with good health and prosperity'.

Curvilinear scripts for secular purposes were developed in the chanceries of the Umayyads and the 'Abbasids. By the ninth century AD they had proliferated; Kufic was particularly suited to stone and mosaic and curvilinear scripts to the reed pen or brush.

Shallow bowl painted in black slip with a Kufic inscription
Nishapur, Iran
late 11th century AD
OA 1958.12–18.1
diam. 34.6 cm (13⅔ in)

Calligraphy of the **Islamic world**

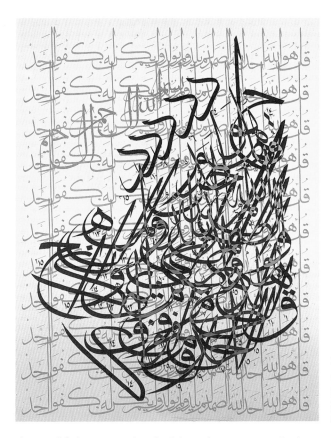

The Psalmody of
Qur'anic chapter Al-Iklas
Ahmed Mustafa
London
Screen print, 1983
OA 1987.6–4.4

Ibn Muqlah (AD 886–940) revised the scripts so as to make them suitable for copying the Qur'an. He established a system that was used to create the *aqlam-al-sitta*, the six major cursive styles (*thuluth, naskh, muhaqqaq, rayhani, riqa* and *tawqi*). The most enduring was the plain scribal hand, *naskhi*, developed in the twelfth and thirteenth centuries, which is now usually used in printing. Other variations derive from the generous *thuluth* style used by the Mamluk metalworkers of Egypt and Syria in the fourteenth century. Later scripts included *nasta'liq*, used from the sixteenth century in Iran, India and Central Asia, and the *tughra'i* script used from the fifteenth century in the Indian states of Bengal and Jaunpur.

The continuing inspiration of Arabic letter forms is seen in the work of the Egyptian calligrapher Ahmed Mustafa (above).

FURTHER READING
V. Porter, *Word into Art: Artists of the Modern Middle East* (London, 2006)

The first Islamic coins, adding Islamic inscriptions and imagery to the original designs, were copied from the Byzantine and Sasanian coins current in the areas that the Arabs conquered: the gold *dinar* (Latin *denarius*) from the Byzantine *solidus*, the copper *fals* from the Byzantine *follis* and the silver *dirham* from the Sasanian *drachm* (Greek *drachma*).

The Islamic faith was hostile to the use of pictorial representations, and although many pictures, even of the Caliph himself, appeared on early coin issues, from AD 696 the Umayyad Caliphate (AD 661–750) introduced a new, purely inscriptional Islamic coinage, boldly inscribed with a proclamation of the Muslim faith. Below is a gold *dinar*, probably minted at Damascus in AD 696–7, the first issue struck by the Caliph Abd-al-Malik as part of his reform of the coinage. Modified under the 'Abbasid caliphs (AD 750–1258) and their successors, this model later included the name of the ruler, the date according to the Hijra calendar (beginning with the year of the Prophet Muhammad's flight to Medina in AD 622) and the mint. The side generally called the obverse had a text stating the unity and uniqueness of God. The reverse initially bore a text controverting the Christian doctrine of the Trinity. This was replaced in AD 750 by a statement of Muhammad's role as the messenger of God. It remained a standard throughout the succeeding centuries and was used wherever the followers of Muhammad carried his faith.

Within this tradition designs did not remain static. From the earliest non-pictorial issues inscriptions were placed within defined areas. The proclamation of faith was arranged in a square space in the centre of the coin and the rest in a border round it. In the eighth century AD a frame sometimes separated the two areas, creating a new decorative element not to be fully exploited until the thirteenth century. Following a period of experiment where the Arabic words themselves formed the frame, square, lobed or star-shaped frames came to be the most important ornamental feature of Islamic coin design. Below is a gold *dinar* of Abu Zakariya Yahya II al-Wathiq (AD 1277–9), Hafsid ruler of North Africa, with a Kufic inscription within a square, a fine example of Maghribi script evolved in North Africa and Spain.

Departures from the rule against pictures were unusual and, where they occurred, tended to be on bronze coins. During the twelfth century AD a new fashion, free

Gold *dinar*, probably minted at Damascus in
AD 696–7
Dated AH 77
CM 1874–7–6–1;
BMC 186
19 mm (¾ in)

Gold *dinar* of Abu
Zakariya Yahya II
al-Wathiq (AD 1277–9)
North Africa
CM 1886–5–3–1
29 mm (1¼ in)

Coins of the **Islamic world**

of religious restraints, was developed on the copper coins of the Turkish rulers of Syria, northern Iraq and south-eastern Turkey. Under Byzantine and Crusader influences coins were issued with a variety of pictorial designs, many copied from other coins, both contemporary and ancient. Indian influence also played a part in encouraging the use of pictorial designs. On the right is a gold *mohur*, a presentation coin of the Mughal emperor Jahangir (*r.*1605–27), struck at Ajmir in northern India, showing the emperor seated cross-legged on his throne with a goblet in his hand. The main function of the images was to identify the issues, but astrological and mythological designs also appeared.

Coins are important for the political and religious history of the Islamic world. The ruler's right to issue coinage (*sikka*) and the invocation of his name in the Friday sermon (*khutba*) were the ultimate vindications of his independent status. The Museum's collection is extensive, ranging from the earliest coins to modern issues.

Gold *mohur* of the Mughal emperor Jahangir (*r.* AD 1605–27) Struck at Ajmir, northern India AH 1023 (AD 1614–15) India Office Collection no. 1908 21 mm (¾ in)

FURTHER READING
M. Broome, *A Handbook of Islamic Coins* (London, 1985)
M. Mitchiner, *Oriental Coins and their Values: the World of Islam* (Sanderstead, 1976)
J. Williams (ed.), *Money. A History* (London, 1997)

The Museum has one of the finest collections in existence of medieval Islamic metalwork, drawn from the distinctive metalworking traditions in the lands which came under the influence of Islam after AD 622, the first year of the Islamic era.

Two categories of metalwork common to other cultures are absent: figurative sculpture, since this was too reminiscent of the icons of Christianity, Buddhism and other religions which Islam sought to replace, and liturgical vessels, which were not necessary to the Islamic religion.

The major categories of metalwork include vessels and utensils, jewellery, arms and armour, tools and scientific instruments. All of these have separate traditions – different craftsmen and workshops, demands and techniques. Although the Museum's display may give the impression that Islamic metalwork consists almost entirely of highly decorated brass vessels, this is an accident of survival. Gold and silver vessels were made but have tended not to survive, being melted down for re-use.

The 'Blacas ewer'
Mosul
AD 1232
OA 1866.12–29.61
h. 30.4 cm (12 in)
Purchased (collection of
the Duc de Blacas)

Gold, silver, copper, iron, lead and tin were used, although some strict Muslims shunned the use of vessels made of precious metals. Metals could be used alone but were usually combined to form alloys, of which the most common was brass (an alloy of copper and zinc). Inlay, the laying of materials into the metal, was particularly popular. Precious metals were often inlaid with niello (a hard shiny black substance made from a mixture of metallic sulphides) to enhance their engraved designs. Base metals were inlaid with gold, silver and copper, to add colour, or black material such as bitumen, to give contrast to their increasingly complex designs.

On the left is the 'Blacas ewer', made of sheet brass, engraved and inlaid with silver and copper. The ewer was decorated in the workshop of Shuja'b Man'a in Mosul, which must have been one of the best in the city.

FURTHER READING
R. Ward, *Islamic Metalwork* (London, 1993)

Iznik pottery

Pottery produced at Iznik (ancient Nicaea) from the end of the fifteenth to the seventeenth century AD, when the factories had passed their peak, is one of the great glories of Ottoman art, and the Museum has one of the greatest collections in the world.

There are still many unexplained questions regarding Iznik pottery. One is the source of the large number of pieces which came on to the market from around 1860 onwards, to be snapped up by collectors. Iznik pottery had been prized in late sixteenth-century Europe but there is little evidence of its continuing popularity. One suggestion is that the later pieces came from palace treasuries in Istanbul or Edirne, abandoned by the Ottoman sultans for palaces on the Bosphorus.

The terms first used by nineteenth-century art historians are also confusing, largely referring to locations where examples of pottery were found rather than to their place of manufacture. The earliest pottery attributed to the Iznik kilns is fifteenth-century so-called 'Miletus ware', a coarse blue and white type named for the large quantity found at Miletus. Fragments have also been recently excavated at Iznik. The fine pottery of Iznik, blue and white ware catering for a demand for Chinese porcelains fashionable at the time but in short supply in Turkey, is first recorded in inventories of the Topkapi Saray in AD 1479. The earliest group – 'Abraham of Kutahya' ware – is named after an Armenian deacon who ordered a cruet datable to AD 1510. It would, however, appear that this particular piece may have been made in Kutahya rather than Iznik. Another group of blue and white wares decorated with spiral scrolls is known as 'Golden Horn' ware, deriving its name from a quantity of broken examples and sherds dug up at Sirkeci on the south shore of the Golden Horn at the beginning of the twentieth century. This was also produced at Kutahya and Iznik, probably from the 1520s. 'Damascus' ware was perhaps manufactured around AD 1560–80, the last 15 years producing some of the finest Iznik pottery ever made.

The so-called 'Rhodian group' comes from c.AD 1555–70, when tile manufacture came to the fore. The distinctive colour is Armenian bole, an iron-rich earth, which when fired gives a vivid tomato red.

FURTHER READING
J. Carswell, *Iznik Pottery* (rev. edn, London, 2006)

Footed basin decorated with hyacinths, lotuses and leaves
Iznik, 'Damascus' group, c.AD 1550–70
OA G 1983.67
h. 27.3 cm (10¾ in)
Miss Edith Godman Bequest

In China jade and bronze have always been regarded as superior to the bright metals, gold and silver, and to the cut gems valued in the West. From early times jade was thought to possess magical qualities and was also valued for its artistry.

Jade is the name given to two different minerals, nephrite and jadeite. Jade is one of the hardest stones known, almost as hard as diamond. Among the most important and precious objects in ancient China were ceremonial jade sceptres and discs. During the Neolithic period axes and knives of jade and other fine stones replaced ordinary stone tools for ceremonial, religious and political use.

Jade was likened to the man possessing the five cardinal virtues of benevolence, justice, wisdom, courage and modesty. It was believed that by listening to the delicate tinkling sounds produced by jade pieces one could prevent evil thoughts from controlling the mind.

Cong is the name given to a type of jade object of unknown purpose found in burials of the Neolithic period in south-east China. The *cong* has a square cross-section with a cylindrical hole and is often decorated at the corners with faces, each shown with simple eyes; the two horizontal bars above represent the hairline, with a shorter bar below for the nose.

Jade discs, known by the ancient name *bi*, were used from the Neolithic period, *c.*5000 BC, particularly in south-eastern China in the region of Shanghai. Their significance is not known.

FURTHER READING
J. Rawson, *Chinese Jade: From the Neolithic to the Qing* (London, 2002)

A group of *cong* and *bi* in jade and other hard stones
South-east China
Neolithic (mainly Liangzhu type), *c.*2500 BC
BACK ROW, FROM LEFT TO RIGHT
OA 1945.10–17.157
h. 20.3 cm (8 in)
Raphael Bequest
OA 1884.4–5.1
diam. 12.5 cm (5 in)
Given by C.H. Gould
OA + 100
h. 15 cm (6 in)
FRONT ROW
OA 1945.10–17.139
diam. 17 cm (6⅔ in)
Raphael Bequest
OA 1937.4–16.162
diam. 21.5 cm (8½ in)
OA 1937.4–16.142
diam. 11.7 cm (4½ in)
OA 1937.4–16.183
h. 6.7 cm (2⅔ in)

Jainism is founded on the teachings of an historical figure, Mahavira, who was probably born in the mid-sixth century BC in eastern India and was a contemporary of the Buddha. He, like the Buddha, found the constraints of orthodox sacrificial religion too rigid and sought a more humanistic approach to existence.

As in all Indian religions, release from the continuous cycle of births was the basis of the teaching of Mahavira. He taught the necessity of a measured lifestyle, especially the avoidance of all life-taking. Any killing, even of an insect, would mean an accumulation of bad karma and a lower rebirth in the next life. Jains therefore consider vegetarianism to be essential.

The Jains have a pantheon of 16 goddesses, of which the most important is the goddess of learning, Sarasvati or Shruta Devi. They seek inspiration from their 24 teachers or *tirthankaras*, of whom Mahavira is considered to be the last. Some of the other important teachers include his predecessor Parshvanatha (identified by the protective cobra hood over his head) and Rishabhadeva, the first of the 24. When one of them is depicted on sculpture the other 23 are often arranged in miniature around the central figure. They are usually shown naked, a symbolic indication of the sundering of all ties with worldly existence.

The bronze image of Parshvanatha (right) shows him sitting in meditation on a lion-throne under the sheltering hood of a cobra in a miniature shrine, around the arch of which are flying garland-bearers and musicians. On either side is a standing 'saviour'. Flanking the throne are the tutelary deities Sarvanahuti and Ambika, the latter holding a branch of mangoes and nursing a child, and two male fly-switch (*chauri*) bearers. On the pedestal supporting the throne are eight heads and a snake, representing the Nine Planets.

Bronze figure of
Parshvanatha, inlaid with
copper and silver
North Gujarat, western
India
*c.*1050 AD
OA 1974.4–11.1
h. 35.5 cm (14 in)
Purchased with the aid of
the Brooke Sewell Fund

FURTHER READING
P. Pal (ed.), *The Peaceful Liberators: Jain Art from India* (London and New York, 1995)

The **Jericho skull**

Jericho is a large tell or mound (now called Tell es-Sultan) which lies in the fertile Jordan valley, beside a road leading from a crossing of the river up into the Judaean hills and to Jerusalem. Long before the existence of the Biblical city of Jericho the site had been used for the flimsy huts of hunters who camped around a natural spring and some 12,000 years ago built a small sanctuary there. By about 7000 BC the descendants of the Jericho hunters had settled in more substantial mud-brick houses and were experimenting with the domestication of plants and animals.

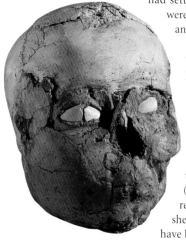

Excavation of the earliest levels revealed that the early inhabitants, who did not yet know pottery, felt the need to protect themselves behind huge walls and ditches dug out of the bedrock. An impressive round tower, perhaps one of several, was excavated; it was 10 m (33 ft) in diameter, stone-built, and its surviving height was 8.5 m (28 ft); it had a stairway inside.

The skull shown here, which was found at the slightly later Pre-Pottery Neolithic B level (6000 BC or earlier), has had the lower jaw removed and the face modelled in lime plaster with shells placed in the eye sockets. Red and black paint have been used to represent hair and moustaches. Six other skulls were found with this one during excavations in the 1950s led by Dame Kathleen Kenyon (later a Trustee of the Museum). Similar skulls have been found at a number of sites in the Levant, along with burials of headless skeletons. Such care lavished on the dead was evidently a widespread burial custom and may be an indication of some form of ancestor worship.

Neolithic skull from Jericho
Palestine
c.6750–6250 BC
WA 127414; 1954–2–15,1
1. 20. 3 cm (8 in)
Excavated by Dame Kathleen Kenyon

FURTHER READING
J.R. Bartlett, *Jericho* (Guildford, 1982)
D. Collon, *Ancient Near Eastern Art* (London, 1995)

Judges of Hell

The belief in Hell entered China with Buddhism during the early first millennium AD. From the late Tang dynasty, judgement scenes in the underworld were common. The ten Judges of Hell and their assistants, before whom the dead would have to appear so that their virtues and vices could be assessed, became regular figures in secular folk literature. They appear in paintings of the eighth and ninth centuries AD from Dunhuang (p. 110) and also, much later, in Ming ceramic images. Despite their sometimes slightly humorous appearance, these figures combine features of Chinese magistrates with the duties required of the Buddhist world. The dead had to account to them for their deeds in the same way as the living did to their secular counterparts. The Judges' assistants would carry the rolls of documents required to support a case. In the novel by Wu Cheng'en, loosely based upon the pilgrimage of the monk Xuan Zang to India, and assembled under the title *The Journey to the West*, several encounters with the bureaucracy of the underworld are described. One underworld official tells how he made the transition from the position of magistrate in life to a similar one after death:

> When your humble servant was alive I used to serve His Late Majesty. I was magistrate of Cizhou and later made Vice-President of the Ministry of Rites. My name is Cui Jue. I have now been given office in the underworld as judge in charge of cases at Fengdu [translated W.J.E. Jenner].

Shown here is a fierce-looking Judge's assistant who holds a thick record of sins. The figure is of stoneware with aubergine, green and ochre glazes. The Museum also has a more benign assistant who carries the much slimmer record of good deeds.

FURTHER READING
J. Rawson (ed.), *The British Museum Book of Chinese Art* (London, 1992)

Assistant to a Judge of Hell
China
Ming dynasty,
16th century AD
OA 1927.11–6.1
h. 1.37 m (4 ft 6 in)
Given by the Friends of the British Museum and the National Art Collections Fund

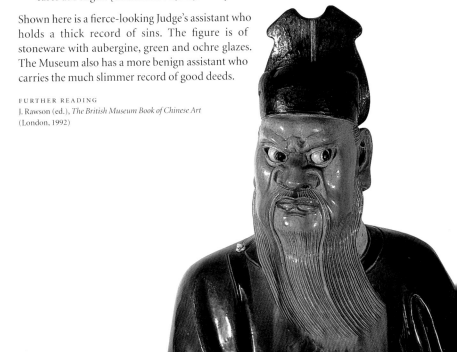

Kalabari screens

These funerary screens from the eastern Niger Delta of Nigeria (called Nduen Fobara or 'foreheads of the dead') were devised in the late eighteenth and early nineteenth centuries to commemorate the deceased leaders of powerful trading houses. The Ijos, originally simple fishermen, had become important middlemen between the African interior and the European traders of the coast. Commercial activity, exporting slaves and ivory, transformed them from a kinship based society to one organized around the competition between houses in commerce and war. Trading houses drew many of their members from slaves, who could rise to the leadership. Slaves could not approach traditional altars, so a new form of funerary memorial had to be devised.

The screens in the Museum were collected by P. Amaury Talbot, a British administrative officer, in 1916. They were made by the village that provided pilots for European vessels on the New Calabar River and drew heavily on European motifs and techniques. Their direct inspiration seems to have been European pictures of notables – the screens even incorporate a mitred frame. They show seated heads of houses in masquerade regalia with their retainers and trophy heads about them.

Shown here is a screen from the powerful Barboy group of houses, confirmed by the initials BB which appear on the frame. The European-style sailing vessel is the central figure's headpiece. It has been suggested that it represents the headdress used for the Bekinarusibi ('white man's ship on head') masquerade. Individuals on screens are often identified by depicting the masquerade costume with which they were particularly associated.

Ancestral screen
(Duein Fubara)
Nigeria
Wood, split vegetable
fibre, pigment, textile,
19th century AD
ETH 1950 Af.45.334
h. 1.16 cm (3 ft 9⅔ in)
Given by P. Amaury Talbot

FURTHER READING
N. Barley, *Foreheads of the Dead: An Anthropological View of Kalabari Ancestral Screens* (Washington, 1988)

The king of **Kandy** and his court

Ceylon (Sri Lanka), 18th–early 19th century AD

Kandy lies in the centre of Sri Lanka, an island known to the Greeks and Romans as Taprobane, and in later times as Serendib. The last king of Kandy, Sri Vikrama Raja Sinha, was deposed in 1815 and ended his days in exile. With him came to an end a long line of sovereigns whose pedigree may be traced back 2000 years. According to tradition the founder of the dynasty, Vijaya, landed in 543 BC from the Indian mainland. He married the daughter of a native chief, with whose aid he mastered the whole island and parcelled it out among his followers, some of whom formed petty kingdoms. By the nineteenth century only one king remained. An absolute monarch, he was supported by a conserva-

tive Buddhist establishment and a small number of powerful courtiers. The figures here represent (from left to right) a Buddhist priest, the wife of Dessave (a provincial officer), Dessave himself, the queen, the king, the king's umbrella bearer, a court official, Ratamahatmaya (a provincial officer) and finally the bearer of the king's betel box.

The Buddhist religion and the Sinhalese language both had their origins in North India. According to tradition Buddhism was introduced to Sri Lanka during the third century BC. In the eleventh century AD part of the island came under the control of the South Indian Chola kings and Hindu influence was marked. By the early sixteenth century Portuguese and then Dutch traders were settled in the coastal towns. Kandy, situated in the central mountains, hedged in by impenetrable forests and precipitous mountain ranges, became the focus of traditional Sri Lankan life. The British took control in 1803 but it was not until 1814–15 that the king was defeated and dethroned.

The Museum has an interesting selection of small Sri Lankan bronze sculptures and ivory carvings. The most outstanding item in the Museum's collection from Sri Lanka, however, is the solid cast gilt bronze image of the goddess Tara (p. 319).

The king of Kandy and his court
Kandy, Sri Lanka
Ivory carvings, 18th–early
19th century AD
OA 1985.111–15.14, 10, 5,
4, 1, 8, 3, 12, 7
h. (of tallest) 20.6 cm
(8¹⁄₁₀ in)

FURTHER READING
A.K. Coomaraswamy, *Medieval Sinhalese Art* (New York, n.d.)

173

King list of Ramesses II

The chronology of the rulers of Egypt is based on many sources – a list compiled by the historian Manetho in the third century BC, dated inscriptions and documents on papyrus, references to identifiable astronomical events, and lists of kings on papyrus and stone. This list was compiled for Ramesses II around 1270 BC. Not all of it has survived but it is similar to a complete list in the temple of Ramesses's father, Sethos I.

The list contains the names of those kings who were thought to be worthy of receiving offerings from the hands of Ramesses II. Thus it is partial, deleting from the Eighteenth Dynasty, for example, such non-persons as Hatshepsut (p. 290) and all those kings associated with the Amarna heresy (Akhenaten, Smenkhkare, Tutankhamun (p. 337) and Ay).

List of the kings of Egypt (detail)
Temple of Ramesses II, Abydos, Egypt
19th Dynasty, c.1270 BC
EA 117
h. 138 cm (54⅓ in)
Excavated by W.J. Bankes

Originally there were three lines of royal names, each contained in an oval cartouche, listing 76 of Ramesses's predecessors, in correct chronological sequence; his own two cartouches completed the third line, the lowest and most complete of those surviving. The top line is now lost. The second line, most of which has gone, contained the names of the Fifth- and Sixth-Dynasty kings, followed by 14 names which may be assigned to the Eighth Dynasty (c.2160 BC). The third line contained originally four Eighth-Dynasty kings, two of the Eleventh Dynasty, those of the Twelfth (c.1990–1785) and then a careful selection of Eighteenth-Dynasty kings and Ramesses II's two predecessors of the Nineteenth Dynasty.

The surviving names (which can be read from left to right) are: Twelfth Dynasty: Senwosret II, Senwosret III, Ammenemes III, Ammenemes IV; Eighteenth Dynasty: Amosis I, Amenhotep I, Thutmose I, Thutmose II, Thutmose III, Amenhotep II, Thutmose IV, Amenhotep III, Horemheb; Nineteenth Dynasty: Ramesses I, Sethos I, Ramesses II.

FURTHER READING
S. Quirke, *Who were the Pharaohs? A history of their names with a list of cartouches* (London, 1990)

174

The **King's Library** (Enlightenment Gallery) 19th century AD

The King's Library, described as 'one of the handsomest rooms in Europe', is the oldest and most ornate room in the Museum. Measuring 91.5 m (300 ft) in length with a width of 12.5 m (41 ft) and height of 9.2 m (30 ft), it was built in 1823–7 to house the library of King George III: over 60,000 volumes together with maps, unbound pamphlets, manuscripts, coins and medals.

The King's Library was designed by Sir Robert Smirke (1781–1867), architect of the British Museum, and was built in what was then the garden of Montagu House, a seventeenth-century mansion which was the Museum's first home. Over the next 30 years Smirke added north and west wings. Eventually Montagu House was demolished and replaced by the great south front, leaving a quadrangle into which the Reading Room (pp. 266–7) was later inserted. The great size of the King's Library called for the pioneering use of cast iron in the ceiling. In the centre are four columns of polished Aberdeen granite with capitals of Derbyshire alabaster and eight yellow scagliola (imitation marble) pilasters. The floor is oak inlaid with mahogany.

Below is a drawing of the Library in *c*.1875, showing table cases which remain today. The books have now been transferred to the new British Library building at St Pancras. The room has been restored to its former glory and houses an exhibition that reflects the visual splendour of the age in which the room was built. This focuses on the eighteenth and early nineteenth centuries, the great age of discovery and learning into which the British Museum itself was born in 1753.

FURTHER READING
K. Sloan (ed.), *Enlightenment: Discovering the World in the 18th Century* (London, 2003)

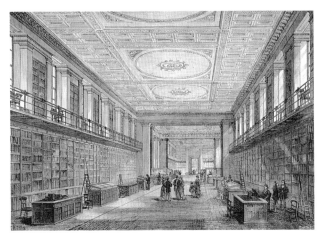

The King's Library,
c. 1875

Koryo ceramics

The Koryo dynasty (AD 918–1392), founded by Wang Kon (King T'aejo), from which the country's name 'Korea' is derived, was a cultural highpoint. Among its achievements during the tenth century was the development of beautiful green-glazed, high-fired ceramics, perhaps the finest expression of Korean art. Although the shapes and glaze colours were initially very similar to Chinese Song-dynasty celadons, the potters quickly created their own Korean style. Elegant vessels in the shape of fruit, animals and flowers showed the Korean love of natural forms, while decorative innovations included inlay (*sanggam*) and painting in copper red and iron brown under the celadon glaze and occasionally gold over it.

Celadon stoneware has a glaze which is green or blue due to the presence of a small amount of iron oxide. Koryo-dynasty celadon bodies were produced from a single raw material, an altered igneous rock or chinastone. The stone contained clay and mica, to make it plastic when pulverized and wetted, and feldspar, which caused it to fuse at temperatures of 1150°C or more. The glazes were produced by mixing body material with wood ash.

The potters lived in strictly controlled communities in the south-west, far away from the capital Songdo (present-day Kaesong). Sloping 'dragon' kilns seven metres (nearly eight yards) long with several chambers were used to fire the celadons in a reducing atmosphere, at temperatures of 1100–1200°C. There were 270 kilns in existence in the Koryo dynasty, of which around 246 were concentrated in the Cholla Province. The two main kiln areas were around Kangjin in South Cholla and Puan in North Cholla. From here the ceramics were shipped up the west coast to the capital, where they were used by aristocrats and also in wealthy Buddhist temples. Some were exported to China, where they were highly prized. After the end of the Koryo dynasty in 1392 celadon manufacture declined and was replaced by the coarser slip-decorated stoneware (*punch ong*).

Stoneware vase with incised floral decoration (lotus sprays)
Korea
Koryo dynasty,
early 12th century AD
OA 1973.7–26.390
h. 37 cm (14½ in)
Mrs B. Z. Seligman
Bequest

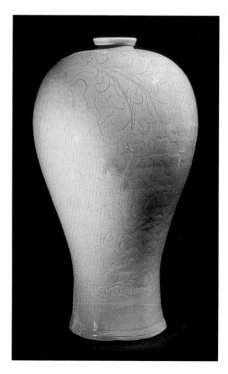

FURTHER READING
B. McKillop, *Korean Art and Design* (London, 1992)
J. Portal, 'Korean Celadons of the Koryo Dynasty' in I. Freestone and D. Gaimster (eds), *Pottery in the Making* (London, 1997)
J. Portal, Korea: *Art and Archaeology* (London, 2000)

The two main forms of free-standing sculpture that developed in Greece during the sixth century BC (the Archaic period) were figures of naked youths (*kouroi*, singular *kouros*) and clothed girls (*korai*, singular *kore*). Most *kouroi* and *korai* were made to be dedicated in sanctuaries, though some were markers over graves. In sanctuaries it is unclear whether they represented the deity or were in some sense servants or attendants. It was probably from Egypt that the Greeks learned the art of carving hard stone, but it is generally agreed that any resemblances between Egyptian standing youths and the Greek *kouroi* are largely superficial. Although both are shown in a proper walking position, the Egyptians have the withdrawn leg in an awkward vertical pose; since this does not occur even in the earliest *kouroi*, it seems that the idea of the *kouros* is distinctly Greek.

The Museum has a highly stylized example from Boeotia (*c.*560 BC) which is typical of the earlier Archaic period. Another found in Cyprus is some 40 years later in date and begins to show evidence of greater skill in portraying the human body. The 'Strangford Apollo' (right) spans the transition between the Archaic and the Classical periods of Greek art. Although he shares the strictly frontal pose of the earlier *kouroi* and the even snail-shell curls of his fringe are typical of the Archaic interest in formal pattern, there is a new confidence in the modelling of the contours of the face. The various parts of the body are now more correctly related to one another and we can sense the bone and muscle under the skin. Small holes were drilled on either side of the head and at the back for the attachment of a wreath or fillet (headband), probably made of bronze.

The 'Strangford Apollo'
Cyclades, Greece
Parian marble,
*c.*500–490 BC
GR 1864.2–20.1;
Sculpture B 475
h. 101 cm (39¾ in)
Purchased from the sixth
Viscount Strangford

FURTHER READING
J. Boardman, *Greek Sculpture. The Archaic Period*
(London, 1978)
G.M.A. Richter, *Kouroi* (London, 1960)

The siege of **Lachish**

Lachish was a town in southern Judah, on the borders with Egypt. The Assyrian king Sennacherib hoped to conquer Egypt, and his campaign against Hezekiah's kingdom of Judah in 701 BC was a preliminary to that conquest. The Egyptians, at that time ruled by a Nubian dynasty (p. 233), despatched an army to the aid of the Judaeans. Sennacherib did not succeed in capturing Hezekiah's capital Jerusalem, but he did capture the very important city of Lachish.

The relief sculpture (below) from Sennacherib's palace at Nineveh shows the power and savagery of the terrible Assyrian armies. A caption in cuneiform proclaims 'Sennacherib, king of the universe, king of Assyria, sat upon a throne, while the booty of Lachish passed before him'.

The city stands on hilly ground, depicted by a scale pattern, amid olive groves and vineyards. A great siege-mound, its surface covered with logs, has been thrown by the Assyrians against the city wall. Under the cover of a protecting fire of arrows, shot by archers advancing behind their shields, the siege machines climb up the mound to use their battering rams. Excavations at Lachish (modern Tell el Duweir) first took place in the 1930s. More recent excavations have identified the remains of the artificial ramp up which the Assyrian siege engines were brought to attack the town wall, and a counter ramp built by the inhabitants to strengthen the threatened fortifications on the inside.

The assault on Lachish
South-West Palace,
Nineveh, Iraq
c.700–692 BC
WA 124906; 1856–9–9,14
h. (of whole relief) 2.65 m
(8 ft 8 in)
Excavated by A.H. Layard

FURTHER READING
R.D. Barnett, G. Turner and E. Bleibtreu, *Sculptures from the Southwest Palace of Sennacherib at Nineveh* (London, 1998)

Lacquer

'Lacquer' is a broad term, used to describe a number of different processes. There are basically three main categories: 'true' lacquer (referred to here); 'resin' lacquer (also known as lac), which is insect-based; and substitute finishes, which can include japanning and modern lacquer paints.

'True' lacquer has its origins in East Asia, where it has for centuries been made from the sap of various indigenous species of the Rhus tree, found only in this part of the world – originally *R. succedanea* and later *R. verniciflua* – with the addition, in South-East Asia, of *Melanorrhioea laccifera* and *Musitata*. The sap of the tree is obtained by tapping in the same way as for rubber, with notches cut in the bark. The raw material has to be processed before use.

Although lacquer is tough, durable and resistant to water, acid, heat and insects, the materials to which it was applied were vulnerable and few examples of early lacquerwork have survived. Lacquer art appears to have originated in China, being used there since the Neolithic period. From the first it was used to give a colourful, durable coating to utensils and furniture made of wood or bamboo. Later, during the Eastern Zhou (770–221 BC) and Han dynasties (206 BC–AD 220), when lacquer was regarded as a prestigious material, it began to supplement and replace bronze.

Inscriptions on Han-dynasty lacquerware provide the first written evidence for mass production in China. Several processes were involved in creating good lacquer, which required many thin coats, each being allowed to dry in a humid atmosphere before the application of the next. During the fourteenth and fifteenth centuries AD in China, for example, between 100 and 200 layers of lacquer might be applied to a single piece before it was carved. It was thus more efficient to divide the work among a number of craftsmen.

Lacquer appeared in Korea following the establishment of Chinese political control after 108 BC. An indigenous lacquer-producing tree grows there, *Rhus trichocarpa*, but it is thought that *R. verniciflua* was transplanted from China. The Japanese had been using lacquer since the prehistoric late Jomon era. In the Nara period (AD 710–94), techniques using metal and mother-of-pearl were brought from Tang China and further developed in Japan. The use of lacquer spread throughout South-East Asia – to Vietnam, Thailand, Burma, Cambodia

Sutra box
Korea
Koryo dynasty,
13th century AD
OA 1966.12–21.1
l. 47.2 cm (18½ in)
Purchased with the aid of the Brooke Sewell Fund

Red lacquer eight-lobed dish
China
Ming dynasty,
early 15th century AD
OA 1974.2–26.20
diam. 34.8 cm (13⅔ in)

Lacquer

and the Ryuku Islands – although these areas did not have access to the sap of *R. verniciflua* as used in China, Korea and Japan. Today the Museum has ancient and modern lacquers.

Lacquer was applied to a variety of materials: wood, bamboo, pottery, silk, basketwork, metal. A number of techniques were used. Pigments were added. Inlay with turquoise and shell was used as early as the second millennium BC. Intricate pictorial designs were created with mother-of-pearl. Incised patterns were filled in with gold foil or powdered gold. Sometimes alternate layers of lacquer of different colours were carved through. In Japan craftsmen developed techniques using gold fillings (*makie*) in which the dust suspended in the lacquer can be revealed by suitable polishing to appear like gold.

On the previous page is a red lacquer dish from China with a Yongle mark (AD 1403–24) and an inscription saying 'Imperial Household, Department of Sweetmeats'. Wang Bo wrote the poem on the reverse of the dish and a prose piece to mark the renovation of the pavilion of the Prince of Teng, son of the Tang emperor, in the early seventh century AD. In the preface he refers to a drinking and poetry party held in the famous *lanting* (Orchard Pavilion) in AD 353, an occasion which may be shown on the front of the dish.

Kalat (covered tray)
Myanmar, Burma
Lacquered wood and
woven bamboo,
20th century AD
OA 1991.10–23.22
h. 65 cm (25½ in)

Also shown is a *sutra* box from Korea made of lacquer and inlaid with chrysanthemum scroll decoration in mother-of-pearl and bronze wire, one of only four examples known from this period.

Left is a piece recently acquired in Burma, a *kalat* (covered tray) used for carrying food offerings to the monastery.

FURTHER READING
J. Bourne et al., *Lacquer: An International History and Illustrated Survey* (New York, 1984)
Sir H. Garner, *Chinese Lacquer* (London, 1979)
R. Isaacs and T. R. Blurton, *Visions from the Golden Land: Burma and the Art of Lacquer* (London, 2000)
J. Portal, *Korea: Art and Archaeology* (London, 2000)

Lapiths and Centaurs

The fight between Greeks and Centaurs is a common theme in Greek art, symbolizing the triumph of Greek civilization over barbarism, order overcoming chaos. According to legend the Centaurs, a tribe of wild creatures, half horse, half man, lived on the wooded mountains of Thessaly, eating raw food. By classical times they were depicted as having four horse's hooves and two human arms. They appear in the legend of the hunt for the Erymanthian boar when, drunk with newly discovered wine, they attacked and were defeated by Herakles.

In the best-known story the Centaurs were invited to the wedding feast of Pirithous, king of the Lapiths (a neighbouring Greek tribe), and Hippodamia. Again, the Centaurs were unable to cope with alcohol. Frenzied with wine, the centaur leader Eurytion tried to carry off the bride, and a general battle ensued from which the Lapiths emerged victorious, driving the Centaurs out of Thessaly. In some versions of the story Theseus, king of Athens, was one of the wedding guests and is sometimes shown taking a prominent part in the battle alongside his host.

The battle between Lapiths and Centaurs can be seen both on the metopes of the Parthenon (pp. 245–6) and on the Bassae frieze (p. 52). Below is perhaps the finest of the surviving Parthenon metopes. The Centaur attempts to escape, pressing the right hand to a wound he has already sustained in the back. The Lapith stops him, tackling him by the throat with his left hand, the strain evident in his outstretched left leg and the tension of his abdominal muscles. At the same time he draws back his right arm for the death blow.

South metope XXVII from the Parthenon
Athens
c.447–442 BC
GR 1816.6–10.11;
Cat. Sculpture 316
h. 1.72 m (14 ft 1½ in)
Purchased by the British Government from Lord Elgin

FURTHER READING
J. Boardman, *Greek Sculpture. The Classical Period* (London, 1985)
B.F. Cook, *The Elgin Marbles* (2nd edn, London, 1997)

La Tène metalwork

L a Tène, on Lake Neuchâtel in Switzerland, gives its name to a phase of the European Iron Age (*c.*450 BC to the Roman mid-first century BC). It seems to have been the site of a water cult where objects were deposited as votive offerings. Engineering works and subsequent archaeological excavations during 1880–5 and 1907–14 produced more than 3000 swords and scabbards, spearheads, brooches, tools, coins and wooden objects. The name 'La Tène' (like 'Hallstatt', p. 142) is used because these sites produced artefacts considered typical of their respective periods: they are no more than type-sites and there is no suggestion that the cultures they represent originated at those sites. The term also covers the peoples of Britain at this time.

The Museum has a considerably smaller holding from the La Tène site than from the earlier Hallstatt. There are, however, extensive collections from elsewhere. Many of the Iron Age peoples of Europe buried their dead with great ceremony. Nowhere provides a better example of these rituals than Champagne in France, where the most spectacular finds are chariot burials in which the corpse was buried with a dismantled chariot or cart surrounded by harness and other offerings. It was customary to bury women with their jewellery – torc, bracelets and brooches – while warriors had an array of weapons and tools; both were accompanied by pottery, and animal bones suggest that food was included to sustain the dead.

In the second half of the nineteenth century many thousands of La Tène graves were excavated in Champagne, and one of the largest collections, amassed by Léon Morel of Rheims, was acquired by the Museum in 1901. It includes an elaborate chariot burial from Somme-Bionne (Marne), notable because it included a painted pottery cup and a bronze flagon, rare imports from Italy in the fifth century BC.

See also early Celtic art in Britain (pp. 72–3), the Basse Yutz flagons (p. 53) and torcs (p. 330).

Iron spearhead
La Tène, Switzerland
*c.*250–100 BC
PRB 1867 7–2 1
l. 42 cm (16½ in)
Given by Colonel Schwab

FURTHER READING
I. Stead, *Celtic Art in Britain before the Roman Conquest* (2nd edn, London, 1996)

The **Lewis chessmen**

These are the outstanding chessmen of the European Middle Ages, but since they were discovered in Uig on the west coast of Lewis, in the Outer Hebrides, in 1831, their origins have still not been satisfactorily explained. Why was a hoard of at least 93 pieces buried there? Accounts vary, but they were probably found in a sand-dune, possibly within a small drystone chamber with ashes on its floor. One version tells that their terrified discoverer thought that 'they were an assemblage of elves or gnomes upon whose mysteries he had unconsciously intruded'.

Eight kings, eight queens, sixteen bishops, fifteen knights, twelve rooks in the form of 'warders', and nineteen pawns are known. (The hoard also included fourteen plain discs for a game called *tabula*, the ancestor of modern draughts, and one belt buckle.) The National Museum of Scotland has two kings, three queens, three bishops, one knight and two warders. The remainder are in the Museum. Although every piece is different there appear to be four almost complete sets (lacking 44 pawns but only one knight and four warders), with parts of others. On arrival at the Museum, some of the pieces were described as being stained red.

It is unlikely that they were carved on Lewis. The style of carving is Scandinavian, probably Norwegian, since a very similar piece

Group of chessmen
Found in the Outer
Hebrides
Walrus-ivory, 12th
century AD
FROM LEFT TO RIGHT
MLA 1831,11–1,37
(knight), 47 (warder),
13 (bishop), 56 (pawn),
7 (queen), 1 (king),
50 (pawn), 38 (knight),
41 (warder)
h. (of king) 10.6 cm
(4⅘ in)

has been excavated at Trondheim. Various theories have been put forward to explain their travels to Uig. One suggestion is that they were the stock of a merchant, lost in unknown circumstances. Trade between Scandinavia, Iceland, Greenland and the Northern Isles of Britain flourished at the time; indeed, until 1266 the Outer Isles were politically subject to the kingdom of Norway.

FURTHER READING
I. Finkel, with illustrations by C. Hodgson, *The Lewis Chessmen and what happened to them* (London, 1995)
N. Stratford, *The Lewis Chessmen and the Enigma of the Hoard* (London, 1997)
J. Robinson, *The Lewis Chessmen*, British Museum Objects in Focus (London, 2004)

From the second half of the twelfth century to the early fourteenth century the most common type of champlevé enamelling is known as Limoges enamelling or *opus lemovicense*. Although the town of Limoges in south-west France was an early centre, it is unlikely that all Limoges enamels were made at Limoges itself. They were widely exported across Europe.

The works of Limoges were created for important ecclesiastical and royal patrons. The patronage of Henry II, king of England, and his queen Eleanor of Aquitaine was responsible for the many enamels in the Treasury of the Abbey of Grandmont, situated just outside Limoges.

The types of liturgical objects produced were reliquaries (often in the shape of chasses), book covers, processional crosses, candlesticks, pyxes and eucharistic doves. Secular objects include caskets, buckles and horse pendants. Gemellions (bowls for handwashing) were used both by priests at the altar and noblemen at table.

Champlevé enamelling is a technique by which the cells are cut out of the base metal plate (usually copper) leaving a design of fine round edges. The cells are then filled with enamel.

FURTHER READING
B. Drake Boehm and E. Taburet-Delahaye (eds), *Enamels of Limoges: 1100–1350* (New York, 1996)

Champlevé casket showing the Journey and Adoration of the Magi
Limoges, Haute-Vienne, France
*c.*1200 AD
MLA 1855,12–1, 8
h. 8.7 cm (3½ in)
Purchased (Bernal Collection)

Lindow Man

Lindow Man (sometimes known as 'Pete Marsh') is the oldest face so far known to have survived from British prehistory. He was found in 1984 by a peat-cutting machine (which destroyed his lower half) at Lindow Moss, near Wilmslow, Cheshire. His skin had been almost perfectly preserved by the acids of the peat-bog.

Scientists were able to establish much about his life and death, although dating the body was difficult, since there were no associated artefacts such as pots, brooches or coins. Instead, carbon-14 dating and pollen analysis suggest he lived in the first century AD. He probably weighed about 60 kg (132 lb) and was aged about 25 when he died. His neatly manicured fingernails and carefully trimmed beard and hair belong to a privileged class, so he may have been a priest or from a noble family.

First stunned by a couple of blows on the top of the head, he was garrotted with a fine length of animal sinew. The killers then cut his throat before dropping their victim face-down in the bog. A ritual killing is suggested by this elaborate sequence of death, but he could have been murdered and robbed. His stomach contents revealed that his last meal included finely ground wheat and barley, prepared as griddle cakes and cooked on an open fire, and that he suffered from roundworms. A hint at a druidic connection is the discovery of a small amount of mistletoe pollen in his gut – for the druids mistletoe was extremely sacred. If this came from flowering plants it suggests that he was killed some time in March or April, perhaps as a sacrificial victim linked with the rites of spring.

The Department of Conservation at the Museum has preserved the body by freeze-drying.

Lindow Man
From Lindow Moss,
Cheshire, England
mid-1st century AD
PRB P1984 10–2 1–2
h. 1.68 m (5 ft 6 in)

FURTHER READING
D. Brothwell, *The Bog Man and the Archaeology of People* (London, 1986)
I.M. Stead, J. Bourke and D. Brothwell, *Lindow Man: the body in the bog* (London, 1986)
A.T. Chamberlain and M. Parker Pearson, *Earthly Remains: The History and Science of Preserved Human Bodies* (London, 2004)

In the mid-seventh century BC in what is now Iraq lions were particularly common; Assyrian records claim that 'the hills resound with their roaring and the wild animals tremble'. It was the king's duty to protect his people from these and other enemies; hunting lions was thus a royal prerogative and the symbol of the king's care for his country. The royal seal showed the king killing a lion. But in the reliefs shown here the hunt is artificial, staged in an arena ringed by soldiers and huntsmen into which caged beasts are released to die.

The sculptures, which were originally painted, are largely from various rooms in King Ashurbanipal's (668–627 BC) North Palace at Nineveh, but some come from the earlier South-West Palace of Sennacherib (704–681 BC). They show a progression of events. We see the king's preparations for the hunt, with horses and grooms leaving the stables. In Ashurbanipal's hunt the royal chariot-horses are led by grooms towards an enclosure surrounded by servants holding screens. Within the enclosure is the king's chariot with men struggling to back one of the stallions into position; they push it backwards, and one of them grips it by the ear. The other horse is already harnessed; one man is tightening a strap while the charioteer pulls on the reins. There is a hill on the top of which stands a small building or monument, itself decorated with a scene of the king killing lions from his chariot. Men and women are scrambling up the slope, either in terror or to reach a point with a good view of the action that is about to begin. There are caged lions; one can be seen being released through a trapdoor opened by a small child, who has a miniature cage of his own in which to hide (opposite). The hunting-ground is surrounded by a double line of soldiers in front of whom keepers, with mastiffs, stand ready to drive back any lion that tries to escape.

The focus is on Ashurbanipal in his chariot. The king, like his

The king in his chariot
North Palace, Nineveh,
Assyria
c.645 BC
WA124867–8;
1856–9–9,16
h. 160 cm (63 in)
Excavated by H. Rassam

Lion being released from a cage before the hunt
North Palace, Nineveh, Assyria
*c.*645 BC
WA 124886–7;
1856–9–9, 51
h. of register 45 cm
(18 in)
Excavated by H. Rassam

charioteer and other personal attendants, wears magnificent clothes, embroidered with intricate patterns. He also wears the high Assyrian royal crown, earrings, heavy armlets above his elbows and bracelets on his wrists. A strap, fastened across his left thumb and forefingers, is designed to protect his hand when he is using his bow. The king despatches lions with spear, sword and bow. In one scene two guards beside the king deal with a wounded lion that springs at the chariot from behind. There are numerous lions and lionesses 'so uselessly brave, roaring and defiant or twitching in agony of death'. At the end of the hunt the king pours a libation before the gods.

The panels are some of the finest, perhaps the finest, animal sculptures to survive from the ancient world. They record a vanished species; the Mesopotamian lion survived into the nineteenth century AD but is now extinct.

FURTHER READING
J.E. Reade, *Assyrian Sculpture* (2nd edn, London, 1998)

Lions

The lion has attracted human admiration and has been adopted as a symbol perhaps more than any other animal. It is seen as proud, fierce and magnificent – characteristics which commend it to kings and countries. Indeed, as well as being the national symbol of England and Scotland, it is in many ways the symbol of the British Museum. It guards both entrances to the building. At the north entrance are the languid lions carved by Sir George Frampton; on the glass doors to the south are the cat-like beasts designed by Alfred Stevens in 1852.

Lions are to be found in the collections of all Departments of the Museum. The most famous are those portrayed with great sensitivity in the Lion-hunt of Ashurbanipal (pp. 186–7), fiercely brave but doomed. Assyrian gateways were guarded by colossal, generally winged, creatures, some of them human-headed lions. Stone and clay figures of lions placed as guardians in front of sacred buildings have a long history. Clay sculptures of lions were found at the entrance of the temple of Tell Hharmal near Babylon, dating to the second millennium BC. Overleaf (below) is one of a pair from the Temple of Ishtar at Nimrud. Lions fight with heroes on Mesopotamian cylinder seals of the third millennium BC.

In classical art lions guard the Mausoleum at Halikarnassos (pp. 292–3) and appear on other monuments. The myths about Herakles include his battle with the Nemean lion, invulnerable to all weapons. Herakles can be identified by his wearing of the skin which he had taken from this animal.

In Buddhism the royal lion came to stand for the Buddha himself, who is called the lion of the Sakyas, the clan to which he belonged, and his doctrine is the lion's roar. In later Buddhism the lion became the mount of *bodhisattvas* or saviour deities. Here is a

Lion
Dunhuang, Gansu
Province, China
Ink drawing on paper,
Tang dynasty,
8th–9th century AD
OA 1919.1–1.0169
29.8 × 42.8 cm
(11¾ × 16¾ in)
Collected by Aurel Stein

Lions

'Lioness'
Peter Paul Rubens
(1577–1640)
Black and yellow
chalk with grey wash
heightened with white
bodycolour, c.AD 1618
PD 1952–4–5–9
39.6 × 23.5 cm
(15½ × 9¼ in)

Colossal lion
Temple of Ishtar, Sharrat
Niphi, Nimrud, Assyria
c.865 BC
WA 118895;
1851–9–2, 505
w. 2.24 cm (7 ft 4 in)
Excavated by
A.H. Layard

Chinese drawing of a lion from a long-sealed library at the Buddhist cave-temple site of the Thousand Buddhas at Dunhuang (p. 110). There were no lions in China, and so no opportunities for artists to draw them from life or even repute. Figures of both crouching and pacing lions, inspired by Mesopotamian guardian lions, seem to have been introduced to China during the late Zhou and Han periods.

FURTHER READING
J. Rawson (ed.), *Animals in Art* (London, 1977)

Liu Hai, god of wealth

Below is a bronze figure of Liu Hai, an immortal associated by the Chinese with wealth. He holds a coin in one hand and a double gourd in the other. His three-legged toad, with whiskers, fangs, fins and bird feet, is linked with the concept of immortality. This belief has its origins in the mythology of the late first millennium BC, found in the classical text called the Huainanzi. The toad was thought to inhabit the moon, and lost one of its legs in order to correspond with the three-legged bird that inhabited the sun.

Liu Hai is a popular god. China's major religions – Confucianism, Daoism and Buddhism – all had both orthodox and popular strains. In Confucian orthodoxy at the highest level sacrifice was offered to Heaven and to the Earth. Lower down the hierarchy, temples were dedicated to Confucius himself. But in many localities heroes and prominent figures were drawn into the cycle of worship. The most popular and widely worshipped figure was Guandi, the apotheosis of the heroic general Guan Yu (d.AD 219), who was also worshipped as the god of the north.

Stellar gods and immortals were worshipped within the framework of Daoist beliefs as early as the Tang dynasty (AD 618–906), but it was not until the Ming (AD 1368–1644) that images of them became widespread.

From the Song dynasty (AD 960–1279) popular gods of the Buddhist pantheon also appeared in numerous media. Among these were the *bodhisattva* Guanyin, transformed into a female compassionate deity, and the Kings of the Underworld, before whom all had to appear to account for their deeds in this world.

Bronze figure of the
immortal Liu Hai
China
Qing dynasty, AD 1723
OA 1992.6–12.1
h. 79 cm (31 in)

FURTHER READING
M. Goedhuis, *Chinese and Japanese Bronzes,*
AD 1100–1900 (London, 1989)
R. Kerr, *Later Chinese Bronzes* (London, 1990)

The Lothar Crystal has led a charmed life. The inscription on it states that it was made for Lothar, King of the Franks. According-ing to the Chronicle of the Abbey of Waulsort, on the Meuse, the crystal belonged in the early tenth century to the wife of Eilbert, Count of Florennes, in present-day Namur. The Count pledged it with a canon of Rheims for a fine horse, but when he went to Rheims to redeem the jewel, the canon disclaimed all knowledge of it. The Count summoned his retainers and returned with a large force, whereupon the canon took refuge in the cathedral. Eilbert ordered the building to be set on fire, and the canon was driven out into the arms of the Count's men, who found the crystal on him. The Count, repenting in his old age of this sacrilege, presented the crystal to the Abbey of Waulsort, which he had recently founded.

The Lothar Crystal
Lotharingia, France
c.AD 855–69
MLA 1855,12–1, 5
diam. 11.4 cm (4½ in)
Purchased
(Bernal Sale)

The **Lothar Crystal**

For many years the crystal was worn as a brooch by the Abbots of Waulsort. In 1793, during the French Revolution, the Abbey was sacked and the crystal disappeared, re-emerging in the mid-nineteenth century when it was offered for sale by a Belgian dealer, minus its jewels, with the story that it had been fished up out of the Meuse. (If so, the crack may have been caused when it was thrown into the river). It was purchased by a French collector for 12 francs, and later acquired by the great English collector Ralph Bernal.

It is carved with eight scenes from the History of Susanna in the Apocrypha. These show how Susanna rejected the advances of two elders, was falsely accused by them and condemned to death. They claimed to have seen her lying under a tree with a young man. Her innocence was established by the youthful Daniel, who asked both accusers separately under what kind of tree the adultery took place, each naming a different species. The copper-gilt frame was added in the fifteenth century. The Latin inscription specifies that it was carved for Lothar, king of the Franks (*rex francorum*). There are two candidates: Lothar I (795–855), grandson of Charlemagne, is unlikely, since he used the title *imperator* (emperor), not *rex*. Lothar II (825–869), his son, had no other title than *rex*. Since, however, he spent much of his reign attempting to divorce his wife and marry his mistress, the topic of the faithful wife wrongly accused of adultery seems a little odd. The Susanna story might have been chosen for another aspect of his career such as justice and fair judgement, or it could have been imposed upon Lothar II by enemies who were fighting to make him take back his wife.

The Museum has a rich collection of precious objects of the Carolingian period, named for Charlemagne (742–814), who was crowned Emperor of Rome in AD 800 and united much of Western Europe, from Spain to Germany. From his capital at Aachen (Aix-la-Chapelle) he and his successors stimulated a religious, intellectual and artistic renaissance.

FURTHER READING
E. Kitzinger, *Early Medieval Art in the British Museum and British Library* (3rd edn, London, 1983)
G. Kornbluth, *Engraved Gems of the Carolingian Empire* (Philadelphia, 1995)

Lullingstone wall paintings

The Lullingstone wall paintings are very rare survivals of Roman painting in Britain. They were found at Lullingstone, Kent, in the Darenth valley, when the remains of a Roman villa were excavated in 1949. The villa had been built in the late first century AD, and altered and extended several times in the succeeding 300 years. There was evidence for pagan worship at the site well into the fourth century AD, but eventually the family which ran the estate adopted Christianity. A small suite of first-floor rooms (probably provided with external access) was set aside as a Christian place of worship. The walls were decorated with elaborate paintings on Christian themes.

The fallen plaster from the walls has been reconstructed and shown here is part of a restored frieze of praying figures. The figures pose with upraised hands in an attitude still used by Christian priests when praying before a congregation. Another panel bears the *chi-rho* monogram, the first letters of Christ's name in Greek, which was the standard symbol of Christianity at this period, together with the Greek letters *alpha* and *omega*. Whether this was a domestic chapel or part of a monastery we do not now know.

Wall painting showing praying figures
Lullingstone, Kent, England
4th century AD
PRB 1967 4–7 1
l. 4.5 m (14¾ ft)
Given by Kent County Council

FURTHER READING
G.W. Meates, *The Roman Villa at Lullingstone*, II: *The Wall Paintings and Finds* (Maidstone, 1987)
G. de la Bédoyère, *Roman Villas and the Countryside* (London, 1993)
C. Thomas, *Christianity in Roman Britain* (London, 1981)

Luohan

I n Chinese Buddhism *luohans* (otherwise known as *arhats*) were the followers of the Buddha (p. 65), his major apostles and patriarchs. It was believed that they were able to use their magical powers to remain alive indefinitely and so preserve the Buddha's teachings, even in times of trouble. A tradition of 16 *luohans* was known from the fifth century AD, and by the Tang period (618–906 AD) they were often depicted in groups of 18. At this time sets of *luohans* were made for the entrance halls of temples. The *luohan* below belongs to the Liao dynasty (907–1125 AD), and was found in a cave at Yi-xian in Hebei province along with seven others.

The surviving *luohans* from the set are so individually modelled that they have been considered portraits of eminent monks; however, as with pottery warriors, such images were not intended as depictions of individuals. The impression was created of a particular person in order to fulfil a religious purpose, in this case to promote the view that all mankind might aspire to the spiritual understanding represented by the *luohan*. Thus the figures are made in the tradition of Tang-dynasty portraiture of monks and priests and represent the aspirations of the educated man to obtain spiritual enlightenment.

The statue is made of three-coloured (*sancai*) lead-glazed earthenware. The bands on his yellow robe represent the patchwork traditionally worn by monks as a sign of humility.

Buddhism was introduced into China from India in the Han period (206 BC–AD 220). However, it did not become established as a powerful religious force until patronized by the Northern Wei dynasty in the fifth and sixth centuries AD.

Luohan
Yi-xian, China
Lead-glazed earthenware,
10th–12th centuries AD
OA 1913.11–12.1
h. 1.3 m (4ft 3 in)
Purchased with the aid of
the National Art
Collections Fund

FURTHER READING
M. Leidig Gridley, *Chinese Buddhist Sculpture Under the Liao* (New Delhi, 1993)
J. Rawson (ed.), *The British Museum Book of Chinese Art* (London, 1992)

The Iranian plateau is very rich in mineral ores and other natural resources, and the manufacture of gold, silver, copper, bronze and iron objects is a characteristic feature of Iranian cultures from at least the third millennium BC. During the Late Bronze and Early Iron Ages, a highly individual style of bronze-working developed in the remote highland valleys of Luristan, in the Zagros mountains of western Iran. Typical Luristan bronzes consist of horse-trappings and ornaments, 'standards' or finials, pins, weapons, tools and spouted sheet-metal vessels decorated with mythical winged beasts, animals or humans. Archaeological surveys and excavations indicate that many of the bronzes had been buried in graves, though some were deposited as votive offerings in shrines.

Horse bit with cheek-pieces in the form of winged goats
Luristan, Iran
late 2nd–early 1st millennium BC
WA 122930; 1930–8–6, 3
l. (side piece) 12 cm (4¾ in)

The first examples of these 'Luristan bronzes' reached the Museum during the nineteenth century. Many more were discovered by local tribesmen in the 1920s. There is uncertainty about the provenance of some of the bronzes, since some items coming on to the market at this time and later were incorrectly attributed to Luristan. Also, many forgeries exist.

These bronzes were probably manufactured in local settlements – Baba Jan is one of the few properly excavated examples. Simpler tools and weapons were made in open or in two-piece moulds; more elaborate items were produced by the 'lost-wax' process, in which clay moulds were formed around individually made wax models. These were sometimes carved out of a block of wax, but in other cases wax parts (themselves cast in simpler moulds) were

joined together so as to form the complete model. The need for new wax originals for each complicated item has meant that, although superficially similar, no two items are identical in detail.

FURTHER READING
P.R.S. Moorey, *Ancient Bronzes from Luristan* (London, 1974)

Cut from a single piece of glass coloured with manganese and colloidal gold, the Lycurgus cup appears opaque pea-green in reflected light and a rich translucent red-wine colour when light passes through it. This fourth-century AD masterpiece was probably carved in Rome, although the metal mounts are modern. It was probably a lamp.

The cup tells the story of the mythical Lycurgus, King of Thrace, and the terrible fate which befell him when he angered the god Dionysos (p. 105). There are a number of versions of the myth, but that shown here illustrates how, after driving Dionysos to take refuge with the goddess Thetis in the depths of the sea, Lycurgus attacked the Maenads who accompanied the god. One of them, Ambrosia, was saved by Mother Earth, who engulfed her. Ambrosia was transformed into a vine and strangled Lycurgus. The scene on the cup shows Lycurgus desperately struggling to escape from the clinging tendrils. Ambrosia reclines on the ground while a satyr threatens the king with a large stone. The angry Dionysos urges his panther and his follower Pan into the attack.

A thick blank of glass was blown and then cut away with a wheel to create an openwork design, connected to the body of the vessel by a number of 'bridges' that are strategically hidden behind the decoration.

The Lycurgus cup
Probably made in Rome
Glass, 4th century AD
MLA 1958,12–2,1
h. 15.9 cm (6¼ in)
Purchased with the aid
of the National Art
Collections Fund

FURTHER READING
D.B. Harden, *Glass of the Caesars* (Milan, 1987), pp. 245–9, no. 13
H. Tait (ed.), *Five Thousand Years of Glass* (paperback edn, London, 1995)

The **Mâcon hoard**

In 1764 a large hoard was found at Mâcon in France. Early descriptions indicate that it contained at least 30,000 gold and silver coins, jewellery, five pieces of plate and an unspecified number of statuettes. Today only eight silver statuettes and one large plate (below) are known.

These statuettes may have originated in either a public or a domestic shrine (*lararium*) in the late third century AD, since none of the coins was later than Gallienus (AD 253–68), and may have been buried after AD 260 when Gaul was in turmoil. Four of the statuettes represent Mercury, whose worship was widespread in Gaul. A cock, often associated with this god, stands next to one of the statuettes. Another shows Luna, the moon-goddess, and there is an image of Jupiter, the greatest of the gods, holding a thunderbolt. There is also a Genius, the guardian spirit of an institution or a place.

The most striking figure is a *tutela*, the personification of Chance or Fortune but also the goddess protecting a particular city. She is shown as a winged figure standing by an altar holding an offering dish in her right hand. Her role as city-goddess is indicated by the crown she wears, which takes the form of a miniature city-wall with seven towers and three gates. She carries numerous busts of gods and goddesses. Apollo and Diana spring from the cornucopia in her left hand. The Dioscuri (Castor and Pollux) are set halfway up her wings. Between her wing-tips are images of the gods of the days of the week: Saturn, Sol (the sun), Luna, Mars, Mercury, Jupiter and Venus.

FURTHER READING
D. Strong, *Greek and Roman Gold and Silver Plate* (London, 1966)

Items from the Mâcon hoard
Mâcon, Saône-et-Loire, France
Silver, *c*.AD 260
ABOVE Circular dish with fluted rim
GR 1878.12–31.1
diam. 22 cm (8⅔ in)
LEFT GR 1824.4–24.1 (*tutela*); 1824.4–26.5 (Luna); 1824.4–38.2 (Genius); 1824.4–53.9 (Jupiter); 1824.4–60.12, 13, 14, 16 (Mercury)
h. (*tutela*) 14 cm (5½ in)
Richard Payne Knight Bequest

Magical gems

It is often difficult to distinguish between ancient medicine and magic. In the late Roman period many doctors believed in the curative powers of certain precious and semi-precious stones and of particular images. Christianity became a state religion only in AD 324 and strong links continued to exist with the classical past. In a law of AD 318 Constantine the Great (c.AD 274–337) expressly permitted spells for the cure of illnesses; for those using magic to harm others, however, he prescribed severe penalties.

Magical gems were 'dispensed' by a gem-cutter to the 'prescription' of a magician. Engraved mainly in the eastern part of the empire, they usually bear the figures of gods whose help or power is sought. The language is generally Greek, the figures are often Egyptian, the names of the gods Hebrew-Aramaic, Egyptian or Greek. The god most commonly invoked is IAO, whose name renders the Greek pronunciation of the Hebrew YHWH, in English Yahweh or 'Jehovah'.

The collection contains some 650 magical gems. At the bottom of the page is a charm for backache, showing a reaper; on the reverse is a simple inscription, 'for the hips'. Perhaps the benefit was thought to result from the properties of the stone, since almost all amulets for backache are of haematite. On the right is a fifth- or fourth-century BC chalcedony scarab reused for magical purposes 800 years later. Chalcedony was credited with bringing victory, joy, intelligence and protection from shipwreck. The basalt stone (above left) shows the popular deity Chnoumis, believed to be effective against stomach-trouble. On the other side are his magical symbol and his name; along the edge are several of his titles, including 'giant-killer' and 'breaker of all things'.

Three magical gems
TOP
Basalt
MLA G46
2 × 3.1 cm (¾ × 1¼ in)
CENTRE
Chalcedony
MLA G206
3.4 × 2.5 cm (1⅜ × 1 in)
BOTTOM
Haematite
MLA G93
1.4 × 1.9 cm (½ × ¾ in)

Italian Renaissance **Maiolica**

The Museum has one of the world's great collections of Italian maiolica. This is the Italian name for earthenware covered in a glaze turned white by adding tin. In a new development after *c.*AD 1500 painters began to treat the whole of the white surface of tin-glazed pottery dishes as a medium for multi-coloured narrative painting, called *istoriato* ('story-painted') maiolica. Its most fashionable subjects were tales from classical mythology and history. Fired irreversibly in the kiln, the colours have come down to us in all their original freshness.

A luxury product of exceptional technical brilliance, *istoriato* maiolica was made for some of the wealthiest and most discriminating art patrons of the Renaissance, such as Isabella d'Este (1474–1539), Leo X (1475–1521, the first Medici pope), and the greatest patron of the French Renaissance, Anne de Montmorency (1493–1567), Grand Maître of France.

We know about the manufacture of maiolica from the *Three Books of the Potter's Art*, compiled by Cipriano Piccolpasso in *c.*AD 1557. Most of the best Renaissance maiolica was made from river clay that fired to a pale buff or pink. Dishes or vessels were made on a wheel, or sometimes using plaster moulds, and given a first firing to a temperature of *c.*1000°C. The ware was then dipped in a tin-opacified lead glaze. After painting, the surface was sometimes given a top coat of clear glaze, and the piece was then refired at about 950°C to its finished state.

The dish reproduced here shows Trajan stopping outside Rome to hear a petition for justice. On the tower in the background is a wreathed shield of arms, 'Gonzaga impaling Este'.

Maiolica dish on low foot
Nicola da Urbino
Urbino, Italy
*c.*1525
MLA 1855,12–1,96
diam. 26.9 cm (10½ in)
Purchased (Bernal Sale)

FURTHER READING
D. Thornton, 'Maiolica Production in Renaissance Italy' in I. Freestone and D. Gaimster (eds), *Pottery in the Making. World Ceramic Traditions* (London, 1997), pp. 116–121
T. Wilson, *Ceramic Art of the Italian Renaissance* (London, 1987)

Maori wood-carving New Zealand

Treasure box (*wakahuia*)
New Zealand
18th century AD
ETH NZ.113a–b
l. 59.5 cm (23½ in)
Cook Collection

Wood-carving is the most spectacular and prominent of the Maori arts. Prior to European contact, stone tools were employed. In the eighteenth century metal was introduced, although it was not until the early nineteenth century that this reached inland areas. European metal forms were modified to the carvers' purposes – ship's nails were beaten into chisels, flat hoop iron from barrels could be turned into adze blades.

Finished carvings might be left as plain wood or painted all over with *kokowqai* (red ochre) mixed with shark-liver oil. In some areas of the country, all-over red paint was relieved with black, either to pick out carved details or to colour whole carvings, as on canoe prows and sterns. Black paint was made by mixing shark-liver oil with powdered charcoal, obtained from certain resinous woods, or the soot of *kauri* gum.

Carving was a *tapu* activity, and had to be carried out under certain ritual restrictions to protect the artists, the intended users or owners, and the community at large from supernatural harm. The traditional carver worked with a fairly limited vocabulary of design forms and motifs which he combined according to well-established rules of composition. However, provided the artist understood and worked within these rules, he had a certain freedom in both the arrangement of major figures and their surface decoration. This enabled the classic Maori artists to elaborate a sweeping art expressed on large-scale constructions such as war canoes, store-houses, carved houses, mausolea, gateways and palisade figures. Even on small objects such as treasure boxes, bowls, ladles, feeding funnels, musical instruments and fighting clubs, almost every object displayed some difference, some new design touch that made it unique and individualized.

The Museum's collections are the most important outside New Zealand. They include a fine series of treasure boxes or *wakahuia*, among them one collected on one of Captain Cook's expeditions (left).

FURTHER READING
R. Neich, 'Wood Carving' in D.C. Starzecka (ed.), *Maori Art and Culture* (London, 1996)

The **Marlborough ice pails**

These are the only gold ice pails to have survived from the late seventeenth or early eighteenth century in the UK or abroad. They were bequeathed in 1744 by Sarah, Duchess of Marlborough (wife of John Churchill, the first Duke), to her grandson, the Hon. John Spencer, younger brother of Charles, who inherited the Marlborough title. They remained in the Spencer family seat at Althorp, Northamptonshire, until their acquisition by the Museum in 1981.

The introduction of ice pails which could be placed on the table is thought to have taken place at the French court towards the end of the seventeenth century and to have been rapidly copied in London by leading families. The Marlborough pails combine French elements, such as the ringed lions' masks on the upper part, with English-style decoration below. They were probably produced by Huguenot craftsmen in London (p. 155). There is no hallmark and date letter, but the form and decoration places them around 1700.

The Duchess was a favourite of Queen Anne and her husband was one of England's greatest military commanders. For a time the couple's stars were in the ascendant but in 1711 the Queen, wearied of the domineering Sarah, dismissed her, and her husband's position was undermined by intrigue. In the course of their careers the Churchills (ancestors of Sir Winston Churchill) amassed a great fortune. Family tradition suggests that the pails were a gift from Queen Anne, but this cannot be confirmed.

The Duke was restored to his honours by King George I but died in 1722. Sarah survived her husband by 20 years.

FURTHER READING
C. Blair (ed.), *The History of Silver* (London, 1987)
P. Glanville, *Silver in England* (London, 1987)
P. Glanville (ed.), *Silver* (London, 1996)
T. Schroder, *The National Trust Book of English Domestic Silver 1500–1900* (London, 1988)

The Marlborough ice pails
England
Gold, *c.*1700 AD
MLA 1981,12–1, 1 and 2
h. 26.7 cm and 26.9 cm
(10½ and 10⅗ in)
Purchased with the aid of the Worshipful Company of Goldsmiths, the National Art Collections Fund, the National Heritage Memorial Fund, the Pilgrim Trust and funds bequeathed by Mrs Katherine Goodhart Kitchingman

Masks

Masking is a near-universal phenomenon, but the uses and meanings of masks and masquerade have varied greatly between cultures. Many masks are objects of beauty, but decoration is seldom their major function. The splendid golden funerary masks of ancient Egypt were intended to equip the dead with divine power and attributes. Aztec codices (p. 207) frequently depict gods, or their priestly impersonators, wearing face paint or masks which serve to identify the divine being. Disguise or concealment is not necessarily the purpose of masks. In classical antiquity, masks worn in the drama actually assisted the actor's portrayal by displaying particular characteristics which the audience could interpret. In ritual and religious use, as today in Africa or Oceania, mask-wearers may be thought to be possessed by, and therefore to become, a spirit or god. It is not a performance: the mask is the spirit. Masks are often associated with rites of passage – birth, death and initiation – in which complex issues of transformation and identity are raised.

Masks may be constructed from precious metals, cloth, bark, basketry, papier mâché leaves, feathers and other perishable materials. Many are intended to survive permanently; others are made for temporary use only and may be considered too dangerous to keep.

The Museum has masks from ancient times to the present and from all over the world. Aztec masks include those of turquoise (pp. 335–6) and the stone representation of the mask of Xipe Totec (p. 362). Above is a mask used in the Japanese theatre, worn by Shikami, a male demon who appears in Kiri Nō plays such as *Rashomon* and *Momijigari*. Opposite (centre) is a mask in the form of a wolf, a clan crest of the Tlingit people of Northwest America, collected before 1867. Opposite (above) is a Malanggan mask from New Ireland, Papua New Guinea. The wooden helmet mask (opposite, below) comes from the Mende people of Sierra Leone. It would be worn by a member of the female Sande society.

FURTHER READING
J. Mack (ed.), *Masks: the Art of Expression* (London, 1994)

Nō mask
Japan
Lacquered wood with gilt teeth and eyes,
pre AD 1880
JA 1886.12–7. 9
h. 20.9 cm (8¼ in)

OPPOSITE ABOVE
Malanggan mask
New Ireland, Papua New Guinea
Wood, vegetable fibre, snail operculae and pigment, 1883
ETH 1884.7–28.25
h. 41 cm (16⅛ in)
Given by the Duke of Bedford

OPPOSITE CENTRE
Mask in the form of a wolf
Northwest America (Tlingit)
Painted wood, pre AD 1867
ETH 1939.Am.11.3
l. 24 cm (9½ in)
Given by P. I. Beeman

OPPOSITE BELOW
Wooden helmet mask
Sierra Leone, Africa
Date unknown
ETH 1981.Af.7.1

Medals

Medals are multiples, but unlike coins they are not means of exchange. They are small-scale, intimate sculptures and, like prints, they allow artists' work to be sold relatively cheaply. The two sides (obverse and reverse) complement and strengthen each other while never, by definition, being seen together. They can be struck from hand-engraved steel dies or cast in metal from a wax model and then finished and patinated by the artist.

The art of medal-making has its origins in the Italian Renaissance. Many early medallists, such as Pisanello, have left us superb likenesses of the appearance of notable contemporaries, such as John VIII Palaeologus, the Byzantine emperor (r.AD 1421–48) (left). Between about AD 1500 and the end of the nineteenth century there was a tendency to assimilate the style and technique of coins and medals, but the two have since separated once more, with medals losing much of their official character.

The Museum's collection of around 47,000 medals is drawn from every European and many non-European countries from the fifteenth century to the present day. The oldest medal in the collection, in fact the first modern medal, was struck to celebrate the capture of Padua by Francesco II da Carrara in AD 1390. There is a comprehensive collection of British medals of all periods, including two versions of Nicholas Hilliard's famous medal of the time of the Spanish Armada (p. 118), a fine series of portraits by Thomas and Abraham Simon, and a complete set of the medals engraved by John Roettiers after the Restoration of King Charles II. Italian Renaissance and Baroque medals are well represented, as are French and Dutch, Swiss and Scandinavian seventeenth- and eighteenth-century examples. The German medals of this period, accumulated by the Hanoverians, are particularly worthy of note, as are the outstanding collection of German First World War material, the wide-ranging, if not yet entirely representative, collections of late nineteenth- and early twentieth-century European and American medals and the growing number of late twentieth-century pieces. The collection also includes dies and models for medals, military medals and decorations.

Bronze medal of John VIII Palaeologus, Byzantine emperor
AD 1421–48
Pisanello
AD 1438
CM George III, Naples 9
diam. 103 mm (4 in)

Gwyniad
Bethan Williams
1993
CM 1995–3–41–5
84 × 80 mm
(3¼ × 3 in)

FURTHER READING

G. Hill, *Medals of the Renaissance*, revised and enlarged by Graham Pollard (London, 1978; first published 1920)

M. Jones, *The Art of the Medal* (London, 1979)

M. Jones, *Contemporary British Medals* (London, 1986)

This unique façade was discovered in July 1989 in the course of the excavation of a Roman villa near Meonstoke, Hampshire. The aisled, barn-like structure had been built in the early fourth century AD and collapsed soon after AD 353, sealing a coin of that year. The upper two storeys of the building survived almost complete, having become so deeply buried that they escaped damage from the plough and weather.

The surviving section of the façade was lifted from the ground and brought to the Museum. Subsequent excavation of the site and cleaning of the façade have transformed our knowledge of Romano-British architecture. The building was revealed to have been a highly elaborate basilica. It would have stood to a height of nearly 12 m (40 ft) with clerestory windows to light the main hall, and intricately decorated arcading in the gable. It was laid out in Roman feet, the *pes Monetalis* (29.6 cm/11⅝ in). It is 50 *p.M* wide and was almost certainly 40 *p.M* high.

An extraordinary amount of architectural detail survives on the façade. The general appearance of the building would have been highly colourful, with alternating red and white tiles, and pilaster capitals and bases, columns and quoins in greenstone. Carefully arranged courses of tile and flint separated by rendered areas where flints were exposed would have given an additional rusticated effect. The Meonstroke discovery thus demonstrates that, contrary to previous opinion, Romano-British domestic buildings could be of considerable height and of highly elaborate appearance.

Roman building façade
Meonstoke, Hampshire, Britain
4th century AD
PRB P 1988 11–11
h. 2 m (6½ ft)
Given by Mr and Mrs Bruce Horn

FURTHER READING
G. de la Bédoyère, *The Buildings of Roman Britain* (London, 1991)
T.W. Potter, *Roman Britain* (2nd edn, London, 1997)
A.L.F. Rivet, *The Roman Villa in Britain* (London, 1979)

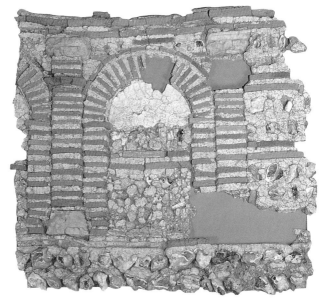

Madagascar is one of the world's largest islands and, thanks to its isolation, has evolved distinctive characteristics. It is the home of a people, the Malagasy, whose diverse ancestry has produced a rich and varied culture. The Merina, occupying the central highlands, are the most numerous of the 18 different peoples. Their language, like that of Madagascar's population as a whole, is of Malayo-Polynesian origin.

Handloom weaving on Madagascar remains a vigorous tradition. The characteristic textile of the Merina is a large rectangular cloth, worn as a shawl and known as a *lamba*. During the nineteenth century the manner of wearing the shawl varied according to age, rank and occasion. Apart from red, which denoted royalty, the use of pattern and colour was not restricted. The great complexity of some of the Merina patterned silks belies the rudimentary nature of the loom, still widely in use. The *lamba* also functioned as a burial shroud.

Merina textiles were produced using silk from the Chinese silkworm, with its fine, regular thread, originally brought by Arabs from India. Silk from the indigenous silkworm of Madagascar, by contrast, gave only a thick, uneven thread and was used to weave plain textiles. The Merina eventually developed their own silk industry with the aid of mulberry trees introduced in the early nineteenth century by British mission artisans. The characteristic vibrant colours were achieved by the use of imported dyes. *Lambas* tended to disappear after the late 1880s, but recently a significant revival in production has taken place, centred on the town of Arivonimamo.

The Museum has an extensive collection of objects from Madagascar. The most recent acquisitions of Merina textiles were made in 1990 and 1993.

Lamba (detail)
Madagascar
Silk, late 19th–early
20th century AD
ETH 1949.Af.10.1
Given by James Keeves

FURTHER READING
A. Hecht, *The Art of the Loom. Weaving, spinning and dyeing across the world* (London, 1989)
J. Mack, *Madagascar: Island of the Ancestors* (London, 1986)
J. Mack, *Malagasy Textiles* (Aylesbury, 1989)
J. Picton and J. Mack, *African Textiles* (London, 1989)

Mexican painted books

Bernal Diaz del Castillo, a companion of the Spanish *conquista-dor* Hernán Cortés, noted that the manuscript libraries of the Aztecs, the *amoxtli*, were of great size. When the ruler called for a manuscript, the bearer 'read' the book to him by pointing at the figures with small sticks or rods. There was no alphabet but rather pictures and ideographs (with some phonetic elements) to aid the recitation of what was essentially an oral tradition. The books and manuscripts, used by high priests and other officials, contained information concerning annual festivals, dreams and auguries, the names given to children, and marriage rites. They also recorded conquests, wars, the succession of principal lords, tempests and plagues, and the rulers' histories. Tragically, most of the hundreds, perhaps thousands, of books were systematically destroyed by the Spanish friars as manifestations of evil, and only 16 or so pre-Conquest texts survive.

The Museum has one, the Codex Zouche-Nuttall, which derives its name from Zelia Nuttall, who first published it in 1902, and the donor, Baroness Zouche. Painted on deerskin and designed to be read from right to left, it is made up of 48 screenfold pages, one of which is seen here. It was produced by scribes of the Mixtec peoples in mountainous northern Oaxaca. The Codex gives an historical account of a dynastic succession beginning in the eighth century AD or earlier and extending over six centuries. This page shows an expedition undertaken by four people: Four Serpent, Seven Serpent, One Rain and Seven Rain.

Scene from the Codex
Zouche-Nuttall
Mexico (Mixtec)
14th century AD
ETH 1902.3–8.1
h. 19 × 25.5 cm
(7½ × 10 in)
Given by Baroness Zouche
of Haryngworth

After the first fury of the conquest of the 1520s had abated, work was found again for the Indian scribes. The Indians explained their paintings to the Spanish priests in Nahuatl, the language of the Aztecs, which was then recorded in romanised script, from which a Spanish translation was made. Of these post-Conquest texts, several hundred survive, some in the British Library and the British Museum.

FURTHER READING
G. Brotherstone, *Painted Books from Mexico* (London, 1995)

Shown here is the only known complete large-scale cartoon by Michelangelo Buonarroti (1475–1564), probably executed between 1550 and 1553. ('Cartoon' is the term used for an immediate preliminary drawing on the same scale as an intended painting.) This particular work served as a basis for a painting, now in the Casa Buonarroti in Florence, by the artist's friend and biographer Ascanio Condivi (c.1525–74). The cartoon remained in Michelangelo's studio when he died and was then listed by the public notary as 'three large figures and two little boys'.

There has been some dispute as to the subject portrayed. The identification as an Epiphany – the Adoration of the Infant Christ by the Three Kings – has been discarded. It is now thought that the cartoon shows the Virgin and St Joseph with the brothers and sisters of Christ; the traditional title alludes to the fourth-century theologian St Epiphanias (c.AD 315–403), who held that these were the children of Joseph by a previous marriage.

Michelangelo is considered the most brilliant representative of the Italian Renaissance, a supreme sculptor and painter who was also poet, architect and military engineer. Born at Caprese, his family returned to Florence shortly after his birth. He was summoned to Rome by Pope Julius II in 1505, spending the years 1508–12 on the decoration of the ceiling of the Sistine Chapel. His subsequent career included work in both Florence under Medici patronage and in Rome.

The Museum has over 80 drawings by Michelangelo, the largest group outside Italy. Especially worthy of note are the study for a figure in the early cartoon of the 'Bathers', which formed part of the design for the unfinished 'Battle of Cascina'; the sketch of the first, discarded scheme for the Sistine Ceiling; the designs for the tombs in the Medici Chapel in S. Lorenzo in Florence; and the group of very late Crucifixion drawings. The Museum's collection was catalogued by Johannes Wilde in 1953. Three drawings have since been added. The collection also includes a number of prints after Michelangelo.

'Epifania'
Rome
Black chalk, AD 1550–3
PD 1895–9–15–518
232.7 × 165.6 cm
(91½ × 65¼ in)
Given by John Wingfield
Malcolm 1893

FURTHER READING
H. Chapman, *Michelangelo Drawings: Closer to the Master* (London, 2006)
J. Wilde, *Michelangelo and his Studio* (London, 1953)

The Mildenhall treasure is one of the most important collections of silver tableware from the late Roman Empire. The hoard, found during ploughing near Mildenhall in Suffolk in 1942 or 1943, consists of 34 pieces (dishes, cups, bowls, spoons and ladles), weighing about 25½ kilos (56 lb).

The style of the objects indicates that they were made in the fourth century AD. The treasure may have been hidden in the 360s at a time of harrassment by Pictish and Scottish raiders. The Greek name *Eutherios* was scratched on the underside of two small platters. An official of this name was one of the highest officials of the

Part of the Mildenhall Treasure
Roman, found in Mildenhall, Suffolk
Silver, 4th century AD
PRB 1946 10–7 1–32
diam. (of 'Great Dish',
TOP LEFT) 60.5 cm (24 in)
Treasure trove

Emperor Julian (AD 360–3). He is not known to have visited Britain, but he might have given the pieces to Lupicinus, a Christian general in Julian's entourage who was in Britain dealing with barbarian attacks in AD 360.

The decoration on the 'Great Dish' alludes to the worship and mythology of Bacchus (p. 105). Oceanus, his beard of seaweed fronds, dolphins in his hair, gazes from an inner circle of sea-nymphs riding mythological sea-creatures, a sea-horse, a triton, a sea-stag and a *ketos*, a dragon-like monster. The outer frieze features Bacchus himself. Round him dance and drink the hero Hercules, the goat-legged god Pan, satyrs and maenads. The greater part of the treasure has pagan decoration but three spoons are engraved with Christian symbols.

FURTHER READING
K.S. Painter, *The Mildenhall Treasure* (London, 1977)

Mirrors

'Mirror, mirror, on the wall, who is the fairest of them all?' enquires the wicked stepmother in the folk tale of *Snow White*. Humans have long been fascinated with their own appearance. Narcissus in classical mythology fell in love with his reflection in a pool of water. But mirrors are also powerful and mysterious objects associated with magic as, for example, in Lewis Carroll's *Alice Through the Looking-Glass*.

The Museum has a wide range of ancient mirrors, whole or fragmentary. Early mirrors usually consisted of a thin disk of highly polished metal, most frequently bronze. Polished minerals, for example obsidian (p. 100), have also been found. In Egypt mirrors occur from at least as early as the Old Kingdom (2686–2181 BC). They consist of a flat disk, usually of polished bronze or copper, attached to a handle, frequently represented as a papyrus stalk (below, left) or with motifs connected with Hathor, goddess of love. The Museum has mirrors from Egypt, from western Asia and from the classical world. One of the finest comes from Britain. Below (right) is the elaborately ornamented 'Desborough' mirror, so called from its find-place in Northamptonshire, made between 50 BC and AD 50. In characteristic Celtic fashion, fantastic owl-shaped faces emerge from the design.

In the Far East mirrors began to appear in Chinese tombs as early as the Shang dynasty (*c.*1500–1050 BC). These had a ritual function, illustrating a search for harmony with the cosmos and its gods. Inscriptions on mirrors often referred to a search for success in the present life and for harmony with spiritual forces. Round mirrors were introduced into Japan from China and Korea in the

Bronze mirror flanked by two falcons
Egypt
New Kingdom, *c.*1300 BC
EA 37175
h. 24 cm (9½ in)

RIGHT **The 'Desborough' mirror**
Britain
*c.*50 BC–AD 50
PRB 1924 1–9 1
l. 35 cm (13¾ in)
Given by the National Art Collections Fund

Mirrors

Three bronze mirrors from Japan
CLOCKWISE FROM RIGHT
Momoyama period,
early 17th century AD
JA 1944.4–1.5
l. 21 cm (8¼ in)

late 17th century AD
JA 1927.10–14.18
h. 10.9 cm (4¼ in)
Given by H. Yamakawa

Momoyama period,
16th century AD
JA 1944.4–1.7
diam. 9.1 cm (3½ in)
Given by Dr W. I.
Hildburgh

Yayoi period (300 BC–AD 300), probably with a religious function. Later, mirrors presented to the rulers of Japanese states during the third century AD were considered symbols of authority and handed on to succeeding generations. The mirror, together with the sword and the jewel, comprised the three objects of the Imperial regalia. Their makers were highly regarded craftsmen and were sometimes given honorary titles. Above is a group of three sixteenth- and seventeenth-century AD mirrors from Japan.

The Roman naturalist Pliny the Elder (first century AD) mentions mirrors made from glass coated with tin or silver, and by the Middle Ages the method of making mirrors by backing glass with thin sheets of metal was known. The making of glass mirrors on a commercial scale was first developed in Venice, a guild being formed in AD 1564. In 1835 a German chemist, Justus von Liebig, discovered the coating process called silvering, still in use. More recent mirrors in the Museum include some of all shapes and sizes in the Department of Africa, Oceania and the Americas.

Moche pottery

The Moche culture dates from around 100 BC to AD 700. During the height of their power in the sixth century AD, Moche lords held sway over a territory that extended for some 250 km (150 miles) along the Pacific coast of South America. Dense populations centred on the Moche, Chicama and Viru valleys in what is now Peru, surviving on irrigation agriculture combined with abundant offshore fishing. Moche artisans mastered the arts of textile weaving, metallurgy and ceramics, and much of this artistic production was devoted to depicting the ritual activities that took place against a backdrop of adobe pyramids, temples and compounds adorned with vibrant painted frescoes. The Moche are famed for their remarkable sculpted and painted ceramic art, which offers a glimpse of rulers, priests and warriors as well as commoners. Their portrait vessels surpass all others before the coming of the Spaniards in their realistic depictions of the human form. Below is a portrait vessel of a high-ranking Moche lord. He wears prominent earspools and his headdress is composed of two superimposed bands of woven textiles.

FURTHER READING
C.B. Donnan, *Ceramics of Ancient Peru* (Los Angeles, 1992)

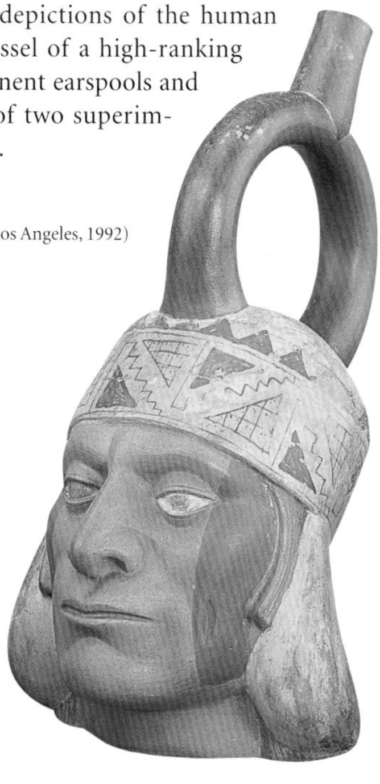

Ceramic portrait vessel
Peru
AD 100–700
ETH 1947.Am.16.12
h. 55 cm (21⅗ in)

The **Mold gold cape**

The Mold gold cape is one of the finest examples of Western European prehistoric sheet-gold working to be discovered. Dating perhaps to about 1800–1500 BC, it was found in 1833 around the bones of a skeleton in a grave at Mold, Clwyd (Flintshire), at a place known as 'Bryn-yr Ellyllon' (the Fairies' or Goblins' Hill). The skeleton was accidentally found by workmen digging for stones. It was contained in a stone burial chamber, beneath a mound of earth and stone. Also found were amber beads and fragments of bronze sheet.

Gold cape
Mold, Wales
*c.*1800–1500 BC
PRB 1836 9–2 1
h. 23.5 cm (9¼ in)
Given by the Revd George Rushleigh

The cape is made from a continuous piece of metal, beaten out over a former to obtain the shape. Its surface is decorated with bosses and ribs in a pattern that may imitate folds of cloth and multiple strands of beads. Holes which follow the upper and lower edges of the cape indicate that it was probably attached to an inner lining – possibly leather – which has not survived. The presence of bronze fragments in the grave also suggests that the flexible gold was stiffened internally at the base with a strip of sheet bronze. The cape was presumably for ceremonial use, since the wearer could barely have moved the upper arms once it was in place.

Some of the most lavish objects of the Early Bronze Age in north-west Europe were worn around the neck or shoulders. They are made from rare and exotic materials: gold, amber, jet and faience. At their simplest the ornaments were either strings or beads or the flat sheet-gold crescents known as *lunulae*. The working of sheet gold was taken over several centuries from simple beginnings to the high point of craftsmanship seen in the Mold cape.

FURTHER READING
'Gold British corselet found in a cairn at Mold in Flintshire', *Archaeologia*, xxvi (1836), pp. 422–31

Henry **Moore**

England, 20th century AD

The sculptor Henry Moore (1898–1986), one of the most original and powerful sculptors of the twentieth century, wrote in
1981: 'In my formative years, nine-tenths of my understanding and
learning about sculpture came from the British Museum.' He
subsequently declared: 'The Museum was a revelation to me. I went
at least twice a week for two or three hours each time, and one
room after another caught my enthusiasm. The wonderful thing
about the British Museum is that everything is stretched out before
you and you are free to make your own discoveries.'

He commented on the ethnographical collections: 'Although I
myself could not afford to collect. . . the displays for me were
wonderful; works were packed together in the glass show-cases,
often jumbled up, and so on every visit there always seemed to be
new things to discover. . . . It was obvious to me that these artists
were not trying – and failing – to represent the human form natu-
ralistically, but that they had definite traditions of their own. The
existence of such varied traditions outside European art was a great
revelation and stimulus.'

Among the pieces in the Museum which influenced Moore
were the colossal arm of a king, of which he wrote, 'when I saw the
"great arm" and imagined what the whole figure was like, which it
had only been a part of – then I realized how monumental, how
enormous, how impressive a single piece of sculpture could be.'
The link between the Museum's seated Egyptian figures of a high
official and his wife of the late Eighteenth Dynasty (EA 36) and
Moore's seated and reclining
figures is unmistakable.

The Museum possesses 22
mounted drawings by Henry
Moore and one of the two Shelter Sketchbooks (the pages now
individually mounted) which
show Londoners sheltering in
the Tube during the Blitz of
1940–1. Most of these were
presented by Moore himself, or
bequeathed by his long-time
friends and supporters, Lord
(Kenneth) Clark and his wife.

'Sleeping figures' (Shelter
Sketchbook)
Wax crayon with pen and
ink and washes of grey,
pink and yellow
*c.*AD 1940–1
PD 1977–4–2–1 (60)
18.8 × 16.3 cm
(7½ × 6½ in)
Lady Clark Bequest

FURTHER READING
H. Moore, *Henry Moore at the British
Museum* (London, 1981)
Henry Moore Shelter Sketchbook, with a
commentary by F. Carey (London, 1988)

Ancient **Mosaics**

Mosaics are composed of small pieces, usually cubes, of materials such as stone, tile or glass, laid closely together on a bed of mortar. These cubes are called tesserae, after the Greek word for 'four' or 'square'. Although normally associated with floor decoration, mosaics are also used for walls and ceilings. From the early fourth century BC mosaics constructed of pebbles were made throughout the Greek world in places such as Sicily, Egypt, Greece and Turkey, but the technique was most vigorously exploited by the Romans using tesserae, and is found throughout the Roman Empire.

Schools of highly skilled craftsmen flourished throughout the imperial provinces including Britain. Styles varied; black and white mosaics, for example, remained in fashion in Italy for much of the time of the Roman Empire. Many mosaics were evidently copied from the designs of woven carpets. Pictorial panels (*emblemata*), set within geometrically patterned floors, marked the most important points of a room. Fine shading was achieved by very small tesserae. Late imperial mosaics were often made of larger tesserae and the fashion arose for setting figures, buildings and plants individually against a plain background.

The Museum has good examples of the work of mosaicists from North Africa, where schools flourished from the second to fifth centuries AD. These created a distinctive African style which vividly reflects the tastes and interests of their wealthy patrons. One example is a fragment from Carthage of a mosaic illustrating months and seasons. Summer is portrayed wreathed with ears of corn. The figure of July stands picking mulberries from a glass bowl. The pavement, which would have been *c*.8.4 m (27 ft 6 in) square, must have adorned a large central room in a luxurious town house.

On the next page, from Italy, is a panel

Central roundel of a
mosaic pavement show-
ing Bacchus on a tiger
Roman, City of London
1st or 2nd century AD
PRB OA 290
diam. 1.12 m (3 ft 8 in)
Found in 1803

Ancient **Mosaics**

Panel showing edible fish
Said to be from
Populonia, near Rome
c.AD 100
GR 1989.3–22.1
h. 88.9 cm (35 in)
From the Victoria &
Albert Museum

from a floor (probably a dining room) showing edible fish from the Mediterranean Sea – octopus, spiny lobster, dentex, gilt-headed bream, red mullet, common bass, comba (*serranus*), green wrasse, rainbow wrasse, scorpion fish and moray eel.

In addition to mosaics from Italy and North Africa the Museum has some fine specimens from Western Turkey (Halikarnassos), France (Saint-Romain-en-Gal) and Britain. The latter include the Hinton St Mary mosaic pavement (p. 146), Bacchus riding on a tiger from Leadenhall Street, London (previous page); a bust of Oceanus from Withington, Gloucestershire; Venus rising from the sea from Hemsworth, Dorset; and a third-century AD foliate cross from the Bank of England site, London.

FURTHER READING
M. Blanchard, H. Slim, L. Slim and M. Ennaifer, *Roman Mosaics from North Africa* (London, 1996)
R. Ling, *Ancient Mosaics* (London, 1998)

The word 'Mosan' (from the River Meuse) is used to describe the style and technique of that area, whether or not an origin in the diocese of Liège is ascertained for the artefacts in question. The region between the Seine and the Rhine (Normandy excepted) inherited artistic traditions with Carolingian and Ottonian roots, which contrast strongly with the Southern Romanesque (see Limoges enamels, p. 184). By the second quarter of the twelfth century metal casting and *champlevé* enamelling was flourishing, in particular in the diocese of Liège, which had a long tradition of metalworking. Artists employed in the towns and monasteries of the Meuse valley also worked further afield, on the middle Rhine, in Champagne, the Ile de France, and even in England.

Front of an enamelled altar cross
'Mosan', France or Belgium
*c.*AD 1160–70
MLA 1856, 7–18, 1
h. 37.5 cm (14¾ in)
Purchased from William Maskell, previously Bouviers Collection

On the right is one of the finest Mosan enamels in the Museum, the front of a reliquary cross of *c.*1160–70 with five Old Testament scenes taken to be prophetic of the Crucifixion. The cross, made of copper alloy, was probably made to house a relic of the True Cross, since the reverse (in the Kunstgewerbe Museum, Berlin) is decorated with the legend of the Empress Helena's discovery of the Cross. The Museum's cross shows TOP Moses and Aaron with the brazen serpent; LEFT Elijah and the window of Sarepta; CENTRE Jacob blessing Ephraim and Manesseh; RIGHT the marking of the Tau on the houses of the Israelites during Passover; BOTTOM the return of the spies Joshua and Caleb bearing grapes from the Promised Land.

FURTHER READING
N. Stratford, *Catalogue of Medieval Enamels in the British Museum*, vol. II: *Northern Romanesque Enamel* (London, 1993)

Mughal miniatures

The Mughal school of miniature painting flourished in North India in the sixteenth and seventeenth centuries AD, chiefly under the patronage of the emperors Akbar, Jahangir and Shah Jahan. Rooted in a diversity of cultural, religious and artistic traditions, it became one of the richest and most productive schools in the whole history of Islamic art.

Akbar, grandson of Babur who had invaded India in AD 1526, consolidated the Mughal Empire. In a reign of nearly 50 years (AD 1556 to 1605), he succeeded in securing control of all northern India. It was Akbar's conception of the function of painting that determined the development of the Mughal school. He recruited both Muslim and Hindu artists to a studio which had been founded by his father, Humayun.

Akbar was succeeded by his son Prince Selim under the title Jahangir in 1605. A scene of stately court life is shown below as Prince Khusrau offers wine to the emperor Jahangir seated on a gold throne. Behind Prince Khusrau is Prince Parviz. Both Khusrau and a third son, Khurram, rebelled against their father, but Khurram succeeded as Shah Jahan in 1628.

The Museum has an important collection of Mughal miniature paintings, particularly those associated with the reigns of Akbar and Jahangir. There are portraits of courtiers; calligraphy by famous Mughal practitioners; illustrations to Hindu and Persian classics; books of fables; and illustrations from a brief life of Christ composed by the Jesuits for the emperor Akbar. There are also illustrations to the major chronicles of the reigns: *Babur-nama* and the *Tuzak-i Jahangiri*. Among the prizes of the collection is the fragmentary *Princes of the House of Timur*, possibly painted in Kabul around AD 1545–50; portraits of Akbar, Jahangir and Shah Jahan were added later. Equally fine are some of the pages from the late sixteenth-century *Hamza-nama*, a work of Akbar's studio. A Persian romance dedicated to the exploits of the Prophet's uncle Hamza, it comprised 1400 illustrations.

Jahangir in private audience
Painted on paper
By Manohar
Mughal Empire,
c.1605–6
OA 1920.9–17.02
21 × 15.5 cm (8¼ × 6 in)
Transferred from the
British Library
(Stowe Collection)

FURTHER READING
J.M. Rogers, *Mughal Miniatures* (rev. edn, London 200

Mummies and funerary equipment

The ancient Egyptians believed that it was necessary for the body to be preserved for the next life, in which the spirit of a man or woman who had safely passed the judgement of the gods would be transfigured, becoming a divine being. These *akhu* or blessed dead dwelt in a realm which included features replicating those of their earthly surroundings, and sampled the pleasures they had known on earth.

Methods of mummification developed over the centuries. The first preserved bodies, such as the Predynastic burial (p. 260), were the product of natural processes, buried in simple shallow graves in the dry sand, and this would continue to be the lot of most of the common people. Mummification in Egypt is now believed to have begun much earlier than once thought. As early as about 3500 BC there are clear signs that bodies were undergoing artificial preservation. During the Old and Middle Kingdoms (c.2686–1786 BC) various methods of preservation were tried, with limited success, but by the New Kingdom (c.1567–1085 BC) a basic formula had been evolved. Over a period of 70 days the corpse would undergo the following treatment: first the removal of the brain and viscera excluding the heart, then about 40 days' application of dry natron (a natural compound of sodium carbonate and sodium bicarbonate with sodium sulphate and chloride), leaving the body dehydrated but the skin relatively supple. After further treatment with ointments, spices and resins it was wrapped in bandages, into which jewellery and amulets of various kinds might be inserted. The internal organs, also treated, would be placed in four 'canopic' jars. Burial would then take place, perhaps in a nest of wooden coffins or a stone sarcophagus placed in a tomb.

The Museum's collection includes mummy cases, mummy masks and wooden coffins; equipment used by embalmers and the priests who ritually revivified the mummy before it was sealed in the tomb; sets of canopic boxes and jars. Among those whose remains or coffins are preserved in the Museum are Nesperennub, 'Opener of the two gates of Heaven in Karnak', who died around 850 BC; Ameniriirt, an official of the cult of the divine votaress Ameniridis, c.625 BC; Hor, an incense priest of the god Amun, who died c.850 BC; Hornedjitef, a priest at Thebes, c.200 BC; the 11-year-old Cleopatra, early second

Inner wooden coffin lid of the Libyan Pasenhor
Thebes, Egypt
22nd Dynasty, c.850 BC
EA 24906
h. 1.63 m (5ft 4½ in)

Mummies and funerary equipment

Wooden coffin and
mummy of an unnamed
Theban priestess
Thebes, Egypt
21st Dynasty, c.1000 BC
EA 48971–2
h. (coffin) 1.83 m (6 ft)
Given by Baroness
Amherst

century AD; Inpehefnaktu, Captain of the Divine Bark of Amun-Ra, c.1050 BC; Tjenthenef, Singer of Amun, c.1050 BC; Ahmose, Chief Doorkeeper of the Temple of Mut, c.950 BC; Sepi, the overseer of soldiers, c.1900 BC.

Mummification was not confined to humans – the collections include mummified bodies of sacred members of various species: cats, a gazelle, apes, ibises, crocodiles, fish, falcons, dogs and a calf.

See also: Artemidorus (p. 32); Egyptian Books of the Dead (pp. 61–2); Predynastic Burial (p. 260).

FURTHER READING
C. Andrews, *Egyptian Mummies* (2nd edn, London, 1998)

Musical instruments

The Museum does not aim to have a comprehensive collection of musical instruments and outside the ethnographic collections the most recent European piece is the English citole (p. 132) which dates from the thirteenth or fourteenth century AD. The collection does, however, range very widely and includes several important items. As well as the actual instruments there are numerous representations of the playing of music, for example on pottery and sculpture and in prints and drawings.

'Rubab player' signed by
Muhammad Ja'far
Persia
Safavid, Qazvin,
c.AD 1590
OA 1974.6–17.15 (23)
13 × 13 cm (5¹/₁₀ × 5¹/₁₀ in)

Asante slave drum
Virginia
Wood, cedar-root and
deerskin, pre 1753
ETH Sl.1368
h. 40 cm (15¾ in)
Sir Hans Sloane Bequest

The Egyptian collections include examples of harps, clappers, bells, cymbals, sistrum and reed pipes. The paintings from the tomb of Nebamun (p. 225) show musicians at a banquet playing the lute, a double oboe and a tambourine or drum. A Persian period bowl (c.450 BC) depicts a procession with musicians playing a tambourine, lyre, clappers and double flute. Lyres and harps from the earliest times appear in the Western Asiatic collections. The finds at Ur (pp. 341–2) include remains of two lyres and a harp, and the standard of Ur shows a court harpist. The Ancient Greek collections include cymbals, *auloi* (pipes) and a lyre with a tortoise-shell sound-box. Musicians are shown on vases; on a red-figured amphora (Vase E 271, c.440 BC), for example,

Musical instruments

FROM TOP TO BOTTOM
Maori bullroarer, trumpet and flute
New Zealand
Wood bound with *kiekie* roots
ETH Maori 4878
l. 34.3 cm (13½ in)
ETH LMS 147
l. 58.5 cm (23 in)
ETH 1692
l. 55 cm (21⅔ in)

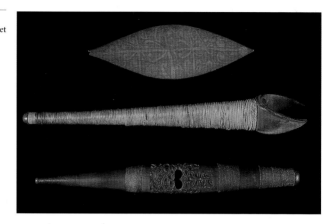

the archetypal musician Mousaios, holding a lyre, and Melousa a pair of pipes, listen while the Muse Terpsichore plays the harp. In the background hangs a kithara. The Roman collections include trumpet, sistrum, flutes and cymbals. The remains of an Anglo-Saxon lyre were found in the great ship burial at Sutton Hoo (pp. 312–13).

The Department of Ethnography has a wide collection of musical instruments from all over the world, in many instances supported by tape-recordings made on fieldwork expeditions. One of the finest sets is the Raffles *gamelan* (p. 263). Other oriental musical instruments include a fine selection from Tibet.

Mycenaean culture flourished on the Greek mainland in the Late Bronze Age, its name deriving from the site of Mycenae where the culture was first recognized by archaeologists. The earliest phase, the Shaft Grave Era, was characterized by rich burials, their contents strongly influenced by Minoan culture (p. 89). These were the graves excavated by Heinrich Schliemann in the nineteenth century AD which contained the gold masks (now in Athens) including the so-called 'Mask of Agamemnon'. In the fourteenth century BC the Mycenaeans built palaces similar to those of the Minoans, but characteristically centred on a *megaron*, or great hall. At this time too the huge fortifications of the Mycenaean citadels such as Mycenae, Tiryns and Midea were first constructed.

Clay tablets in the Linear B script show that the Mycenaeans spoke Greek. Linear B tablets at Knossos in its latest phase are evidence that the Mycenaeans, growing in power and prosperity, took control of Crete around 1450 BC, thereafter moving into previously Minoan spheres of influence.

Mycenaean pottery was greatly influenced by that of Crete, although the Mycenaeans did evolve their own distinctive shapes. For storing liquids they favoured the stirrup-jar, a closed vase with a false mouth (said to resemble a stirrup) and a separate spout beside it. Larger kraters (mixing-bowls) were designed for preparing the wine and jugs for pouring it out, while the favourite drinking-cup was extremely elegant in shape, with a shallow, delicate-handled bowl set at the top of a high, slender stem. One type of Mycenaean vase appears to have been particularly popular in Cyprus. These are distinguished by their designs of both animals and human figures. Bulls are particular favourites, for example the krater (right) which shows an egret picking parasites from the neck of a bull.

Krater (wine-bowl)
Greece (Mycenaean), found at Enkomi, Cyprus
c.1300–1200 BC
GR 1897.4–1.1150;
Vase C 416
h. 27.2 cm (10¾ in)
Miss E.T. Turner Bequest excavations

FURTHER READING
P.A. Mountjoy, *Mycenaean Pottery. An Introduction* (Oxford, 1993)

Nasca pottery

Nasca culture flourished on the arid Pacific coast of southern Peru between approximately 100 BC and AD 600. Here complex societies emerged, dependent on a combination of irrigated maize agriculture and marine resources for their subsistence.

Nasca ceramics are renowned for their bold polychrome slip-painted designs. The Museum's collection comprises a superb array of some 270 objects ranging from plates, bowls and goblets to large jars and effigy pots. They reveal a range of mythological beings, ceremonial scenes depicting seasonal festivals and striking images of felines, foxes, falcons, humming birds, killer whales and trophy heads, as well as readily recognizable plants and fruits.

The imagery on Nasca vessels is not easy to read at a glance because the designs are usually 'wrapped around' vessels of different shapes and sizes. Nevertheless, it is clear that there is a close correspondence between the zoomorphic motifs on the vessels and those found in the huge drawings or geoglyphs etched into the desert landscape alongside the mysterious Nasca lines. These images offer insights into coastal ecology and subsistence nearly two thousand years ago, and are likely to be closely linked to the ritual agricultural calendar. Studies now under way will show how the Museum's collection can be used to reconstruct aspects of Pre-Columbian ecology, ritual and cosmology. They will also point to the connections that exist between landscape art, archaeo-astronomy, and the natural phenomena such as the periodic El Niño event which profoundly affect Andean societies to this day.

FURTHER READING
C.B. Donnan, *Ceramics of Ancient Peru*
(Los Angeles, 1992)

Double-spout pottery bottle showing falcon deity with face mask and diadem
Nasca, Peru
100 BC–AD 600
ETH 1931.11–23.1
h. 31 cm (12¼ in)

Paintings from the tomb of **Nebamun** Egypt, late 15th century BC

The outstanding group of Egyptian paintings in the Museum, 11 in all, comes from the Theban tomb of an official whose name is not entirely certain but has been read from damaged inscriptions as Nebamun. On stylistic grounds the paintings are dated to the reign of King Thutmose IV.

Such paintings were meant to help the tomb-owner and his family achieve new and perfect life after death. There are details which indicate that these paintings were the work of a particularly talented and imaginative artist. In the banquet scene (p. 49, one of three fragments), to capture the beat and movement of dance and music, the artist – unusually in Egyptian art – presents the bodies of the dancing girls in pure profile and some of the musicians' faces frontally.

Below is the best-known painting of the series: Nebamun, his

Nebamun hunting birds in the marshes
Thebes, Egypt
18th Dynasty, *c.*1450 BC
EA 37977
h. 81 cm (32 in)

wife and daughter in a papyrus boat hunting in the marshes. The painting is teeming with incident and detail. Nebamun, dressed in a brief kilt and an elaborate collar, wields a throwing stick and grasps three decoy herons. In the papyrus thicket panic has over-taken the roosting birds but iridescent fish swim placidly in the water. Delicate butterflies flutter in the air. A ginger cat seizes birds with its teeth and claws.

Other scenes from the tomb show Nebamun's garden pool, geese and cattle being brought for inspection, crops being assessed for tax purposes and men bringing produce from the fields.

FURTHER READING
M. Hooper, *The Tomb of Nebamun* (Cambridge, 1997)

Nebuchadnezzar
The East India House Inscription

Inscription of
Nebuchadenezzar II
Babylon, Iraq
7th century BC
WA 129397; 1938–5–10, 1
h. 56.5 cm (22¼ in)
Given by the India Office

I am Nebuchadnezzar, King of Babylon, the exalted prince, the favourite of the god Marduk, the beloved of the god Nabu, the arbiter, the possessor of wisdom, who reverences their lordship, the untiring governor who is continually anxious for the maintenance of the shrines of Babylon and Borsippa, the wise, the pious, the chief son of Nabopolassar, King of Babylon. . . .

Thus begins the inscription of the great king Nebuchadnezzar II (604–562 BC). The king's boasts were no idle ones. During 625–605 BC Nabopolassar, founder of the Neo-Babylonian dynasty, and his famous son extended their rule from the Gulf to the Mediterranean. Today Babylon has disappeared but its surviving remains cover some 850 hectares (2100 acres), and it may originally have been twice that size. It has been estimated that 15 million baked bricks were used in the construction of official buildings. The outer defences included a wall stretching from the Euphrates to the Tigris. The city wall, which appears in some lists of the Seven Wonders of the Ancient World (pp. 292–3), was perhaps 18 km (11 miles) long and is said to have been wide enough to allow four-horse chariots to pass each other safely.

The 'East India House inscription', which describes the king's religious devotion and civic achievements, was found in the ruins of Babylon before 1803. It takes its name from the London headquarters of the East India Company, which previously owned it.

FURTHER READING
R.F. Harper, *Assyrian and Babylonian Literature* (London, 1901)
D.J. Wiseman, *Nebuchadnezzar and Babylon* (London, 1985)

The **Nereid Monument**

The Nereid Monument takes its name from the female figures with flowing drapery which stand between its columns. Thought to represent daughters of the sea-god Nereus, they appear to be skimming the waves, their thin clothes swirling around them. They may be there to convey the dead man, whose tomb this is, to the Islands of the Blessed, as they did the heroes of the Greeks.

This is the largest and most spectacular of a number of tombs brought back from Xanthos by Sir Charles Fellows in the mid-nineteenth century (pp. 360–1). It was commissioned by Lycians, a people native to Anatolia, although parts of the building and its sculpture are Greek in style. It originally occupied an imposing position on the brow of a steep hillside just outside the city of Xanthos.

It was probably built for Arbinas, a Xanthian dynast, and his family. Arbinas's exploits are likened to those of a number of Greek heroes, and the theme of the podium frieze is possibly taken from the life of one of those heroes. The smaller podium frieze probably reflects a real event from the life of Arbinas, who died *c.*380 BC.

When found the monument had long been demolished, possibly by an earthquake. The original place on the building of many of the sculptures is open to question, and the partial reconstruction of the east side in the Museum has been disputed. The building, a small temple in the Greek Ionic style, contained a burial chamber and stood on a high podium or platform. The larger of the sculptured friezes represents a battle between Greeks and Persians, the latter in distinctive clothing. The smaller frieze shows a successful attack on a walled city. Soldiers shelter behind battlements, a ramp is laid against the wall and attackers swarm up it, a woman wails and tears her hair in anguish. Inside the walls the garrison surrenders and two old men attempt to make terms with the victorious commander. The east pediment shows a bearded man and a woman enthroned, with standing figures, perhaps Arbinas and his family. A dog lies in the angle on the right.

The reconstructed façade of the Nereid Monument Xanthos, Lycia, Turkey *c.*390–380 BC GR 1848.10–20.33–258; Cat. Sculpture 850–944 h. 8.3 m (27¼ ft) Excavated by Sir Charles Fellows

FURTHER READING
W.A.P. Childs and P. Demargue, *Fouilles de Xanthos Tomb VIII: Le monument des Néréides. Le Décor Sculpté* (Paris, 1989)
A. Shapur Shahbati, *The Irano–Lycian Monuments* (Tehran, 1975)

Netsuke

The traditional outdoor dress of the Japanese, both men and women, consisted basically of a long wrap-around garment with sleeves, secured by a sash, and a shorter jacket with short sleeves over it, loosely secured at the front. There were no pockets and only the women's garment had places in the sleeves in which to keep small objects. Men needed to carry things around with them, including by the seventeenth century AD seal-cases (*inro*) used by the warrior class (samurai), tobacco pouches and pipes, purses and a combination of writing-brush with ink-well called a *yotate*.

While such objects could be hung from one of the two swords the samurai thrust through his sash, a more convenient way, the only one for the swordless classes, was to suspend the object on a cord from the sash. Such objects were called *sagemono* (hanging things). To stop the cord slipping a small toggle was necessary – a netsuke.

Such devices must have been used very early but were probably mostly pieces of wood – the word means 'root-fix'. Netsuke became an established form of miniature sculpture during the Edo period (1600–1868), and were made chiefly of wood or ivory. A few earlier ones have survived but these are mostly functional.

The poor man's netsuke was simply a piece of stone, a twig, a root, or a similar object requiring little fashioning. Everyday objects could be used, such as a pocket knife or a coin. On the other hand, the most elegant netsuke might well be the most valuable object a man possessed.

In the mid-nineteenth century the netsuke and pouch began to give way to the pocket and wallet with the introduction of Western dress, and unwanted netsuke were sold to Western enthusiasts. Purely decorative netsuke for export are still made today.

The Museum has an extensive collection of some 3300 netsuke.

Netsuke of a boy with a bag
Japan
Ivory and mother of pearl, 19th century AD
JA Franks 631
l. 3.5 cm (1⅓ in)
Given by A.W. Franks

Netsuke of a puffer-fish (*fugu*)
Japan
Wood and amber, no date
JA Franks 1074
l. 5.1 cm (2 in)
Given by A.W. Franks

FURTHER READING
R. Barker and L. Smith, *Netsuke: The Miniature Sculpture of Japan* (London, 1976)
V. Harris, *Netsuke, The Hull Grundy Collection in the British Museum* (London, 1987)

228

This large plaque, portraying a naked curvaceous figure now known as 'The Queen of the Night', probably depicts a goddess of the Underworld. Made of baked clay mixed with straw, it comes from the south of ancient Mesopotamia (present-day Iraq) and was made during the reign of the Babylonian king Hammurabi.

The 'goddess' was originally painted red against a black background. Her long multi-coloured wings hang downwards, indicating a connection with the Underworld. She wears the horned headdress of Mesopotamian deities and holds symbols of divinity: the rod and ring of justice. Her legs, perched on the backs of two lions, end in the talons of a bird of prey similar to those of the two owls that flank her. She could be an aspect of the goddess Ishtar, Mesopotamian goddess of sexual love and war, or Ishtar's sister and rival, the goddess Ereshkigal who ruled over the Underworld, or the demoness Lilitu, known in the Bible as Lilith.

The plaque is considered to be the most important surviving object of the period next to the Code of Hammurabi in the Louvre in Paris. At one time known as the 'Burney Relief' after a previous owner, it underwent scientific examination at the British Museum in 1933, but remained in private hands until 2003 when it was acquired to mark the British Museum's 250th anniversary.

The Queen of the Night
Babylonia
1800–1750 BC
ANE 2003-7-18,1
h. 49.5 cm (19⅔ in)
Purchased with the aid of the Heritage Lottery Fund, the British Museum Friends, the National Art Collections Fund (Art Fund) (with a contribution from the Wolfson Foundation), the Friends of the Ancient Near East, The Sir Joseph Hotung Charitable Settlement and The Seven Pillars of Wisdom Trust.

FURTHER READING
H. Frankfort, *The art and architecture of the ancient Orient* (London, 1970), pl.56
H.W. and A.F. Janson, *History of Art*, 6th edn (New York, 2001), p. 70, fig 3–15.
D. Collon, *The Queen of the Night*, British Museum Objects in Focus (London, 2005)

Ivory was widely used for decoration in the Near East. In the tenth century BC King Solomon is said to have made a 'throne of ivory' (I Kings 10:18), in the ninth century mention is made of Ahab's 'ivory house' (I Kings 22:39); the prophet Amos condemns those who lie on 'beds of ivory' (I Kings 22:39). The Museum has an outstanding collection from Nimrud, the Assyrian city of Kalhu (Biblical Calah).

The first to probe the site of Nimrud (the modern name) was Austen Henry Layard in 1849. In the first few days of his excavation of what proved to be the North-West Palace of Ashurnasirpal II (883–859 BC), he found two chambers on the western side of the site. Here he discovered abundant remains of exquisitely carved ivories. There were subsequent excavations in the nineteenth century, and the site was again explored between 1949 and 1962 by the British School of Archaeology in Iraq under the general direction of Sir Max Mallowan, who added to the earlier collection.

Most of the ivories were made by Syrian and Phoenician crafts-men and produced in the ninth and eighth centuries BC. They came to Assyria largely as booty or tribute but some pieces may have been traded or carved by craftsmen settled there. Furniture (beds, thrones, stools, and so on) was the major large product in ivory, although there is evidence that it was also used for inlaid wall-panelling in palaces and temples. Small ivory toilet articles (spoons, combs, ointment-boxes and vases) were also common. Initially ivory may have come from the elephants which lived wild in the area, but the last of these was probably killed in the eighth century BC. The alternative sources were then India and Africa. The ivory workers were highly skilled and used a variety of well-developed techniques, many closely allied with those of fine woodwork. Although some items, such as toilet-boxes, were made from a single piece of ivory, others were made in separate sections, fitted together with fine joints, and secured by small ivory pins.

In 614 BC the Babylonians and the Medes combined to attack the Assyrian Empire, when Nimrud was sacked and finally destroyed two years

Lioness and African
Fort Shalmaneser, Assyria
8th century BC
WA 127412;1954–5–8, 1
l. 10.2 cm (4 in)
Purchased from the British
School of Archaeology
in Iraq

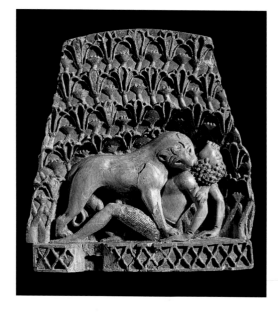

The **Nimrud ivories**

Woman at the window
Nimrud, Assyria
9th–8th century BC
WA 118156; 1848–7–2, 12
l. 10.79 cm (4¼ in)
Excavated by A.H. Layard

later. The ivory furniture was torn apart by looters eager for the valuable gold fittings, then tossed aside in the blazing buildings.

Opposite is the finest piece: a lioness in a papyrus and lotus thicket grips an African by the neck. It is one of a pair of identical plaques, perhaps from a miniature throne. Much of the surface of the ivory was once overlaid with gold leaf and inlaid with carnelian and lapis lazuli. Some of this survives and there are traces of the blue mortar into which the lapis lazuli inlays were pressed. The man's hair is formed by ivory pegs inserted individually. The two panels were discovered in 1951 embedded in damp sludge about 25 metres (82 feet) deep, near the bottom of a well into which they had apparently been thrown during the sack of Nimrud. The style is Phoenician but the theme is Egyptian in origin.

The piece shown above depicts a woman at a window. This is a popular Phoenician theme possibly connected with the goddess Astarte and ritual prostitution.

FURTHER READING
M. Mallowan, *The Nimrud Ivories* (London, 1978)

Northwest Coast art

In 1778 Captain James Cook found a rich society in the rainforest coast which extends some 1500 miles (2400 km) between southern Alaska and northern California. Archaeologists suggest that the area was first inhabited around 10,000 years ago. The abundant resources of timber and food are the product of a warm sea current and heavy rainfall. Together they provided resources for what was then one of the densest populations of any hunter-gatherer society, with perhaps as many as 200,000 people. Hierarchical societies had developed based on clans and stressing family lineages. Hereditary chiefs expressed their status by giving potlatches or feasts, at which masked dances were performed celebrating the status of the feast-giver. The northern tribes – Kwakiutl, Bella Coola, Haida, Tsimshian and Tlingit – were particularly prominent.

An abstract style of art was adopted more than 2000 years ago, enabling chiefs and leaders to be identified by crests. These, deriving from origin myths, are almost all in the form of animals. The animal crests are often shown with recognizable outlines, and also with specific characteristics: the dorsal fin of a killer whale, for instance, confirms the identity of that crest. Crests are carved and painted three-dimensionally, as on totem poles, or painted flat as on box fronts. In either case, usually the whole animal is depicted, much of it with an elaborate, abstract but highly disciplined series of formline designs, applied symmetrically, often to fill the whole of the available space. Chilkat blankets are twined by women, with abstract formline crests taken from pattern boards painted by men. They are worn at potlatches, fastened around the neck with ties.

Ceremonial wool robe
Tlingit, Alaska
c.AD 1900
ETH 1976.Am.3.28
w. 2.2 m (7 ft 2 in)

The Museum has important masks, feast bowls and ceremonial weaponry and clothing from the period of early contact at the end of the eighteenth century and later, including items from the voyages of Captain James Cook and George Vancouver.

FURTHER READING
D. Jensen and P. Sargent, *Robes of Power* (Vancouver, 1986)
J.C.H. King, *Portrait Masks from the Northwest Coast of America* (London, 1979)
J.C.H. King, *First Peoples, First Contacts. Native Peoples of North America* (London, 1999)
C. Samuel, *The Chilkat Dancing Blanket* (Seattle, 1982)
E. Wilson, *British Museum Pattern Books: North American Indian Designs* (London, 1984)

Nubian rulers of Egypt

The land of Nubia, stretching from south of Khartoum to the First Cataract of the Nile, was the vital link between the ancient Egyptian world and the cultures of Equatorial Africa. Upper Nubia was known as Kush in antiquity. The relationship between Nubia and Egypt changed repeatedly over the centuries: large areas of Nubia were annexed and ruled by Egypt as imperial possessions in the Middle and New Kingdoms. At other times the Nubians remained independent, strongest when Egypt was weak.

Taking advantage of instability in Egypt, the Kushite King Piye invaded c.728 BC. A second invasion under his successor Shabako (c.716–702 BC; p. 294) achieved complete control. Shabako and his three successors, Shabitqo, Taharqo and Tanutamani became the legitimate rulers of Egypt, as the Twenty-Fifth Dynasty.

The kings resided chiefly at Memphis, and Kushite princesses were appointed to the religious office of 'God's Wife of Amun' at Thebes. Each God's Wife adopted another young female member of the royal family as her successor, retaining political power in the hands of the ruling dynasty. The Kushite kings adopted Pharaonic costume and titularies, Egyptian language and royal burial practices.

The Twenty-Fifth Dynasty rulers fostered a revival of art, architecture and religious learning. The reign of Taharqo (690–664 BC) marked the Dynasty's highpoint. Between 674 and 663 BC, however, Assyrian invasions forced the Kushites to abandon Egypt. Tanutamani and his successors continued to rule their Kushite homeland, maintaining a pretence of being the rightful rulers of Egypt by their use of the title 'King of Upper and Lower Egypt'. The Egyptian Pharaohs of the Twenty-Sixth Dynasty evidently regarded the Kushite pretenders as a threat. In the reign of Psamtek II the Kushite rulers' names were erased from monuments and in 593 BC the Egyptians invaded and defeated Nubia.

On the right is a sphinx of Taharqo. The framing of the face with a lion's mane is a feature borrowed from Egyptian royal sculpture of the Middle and New Kingdoms. The double uraeus, the cap-like headdress and the vigorous carving of the king's facial features are purely Nubian in inspiration.

Granite sphinx of Taharqo wearing a skull cap and double uraeus
Kawa (Temple T), Nubia, Sudan
25th Dynasty,
c.690–664 BC
EA 1770
h. 42 cm (16½ in)
Excavated by Francis Llewellyn Griffith

FURTHER READING
D. A. Welsby and J.R. Anderson (eds),
Sudan: Ancient Treasures (London, 2004)

Every fourth year for well over a thousand years, from 776 BC (when according to tradition the Games were officially established) to AD 395, citizens from all over the classical world flocked to Olympia, situated on a grassy plain on the north bank of the River Alpheios in the Peloponnese. The Games were held in honour of the god Zeus, the supreme God of Greek mythology, and a visit to Olympia was also a pilgrimage to his most sacred place, the grove known as the Altis. The edict of Theodosius I in AD 393, banning pagan cults, put an end to the games and, not long after, earthquakes and floods devastated the site, which was silted over and almost forgotten until excavations began in 1875.

For the first 13 Olympiads the running race was the sole event. Gradually other contests were added, so that the Games increased from a one- to a five-day programme, including the pentathlon (running, the long-jump, javelin and discus throwing, and wrestling), combat sports and equestrian events. Central to the festival was the sacrifice to Zeus of 100 oxen, which took place following a grand procession of competitors, ambassadors and other officials and animals around the Altis.

The Museum has a large number of objects including vases, statues, coins and bronzes which illustrate the events of the Olympic Games and those held elsewhere in Greece. Opposite, a sprinter dashes across an amphora. The *stade* or short foot-race, a sprint of just under 200 metres, was always the most important contest, each particular Olympiad being named after the winner.

Discus-throwing was introduced as part of the pentathlon in 708 BC. About 20 ancient discuses have survived from various sites. The method of throwing is not precisely known, but it is probable that the athlete made a three-quarter turn and that the throw featured rhythm and grace. Shown here is a Roman copy of a lost Greek bronze original from the fifth century BC, perhaps the famous discus-thrower by the sculptor Myron.

A Syracusan coin, opposite, shows a figure of Victory flying down to crown the victor in a four-horse chariot race. Below is a set of armour, which

'Discobolos'
Roman marble copy of a
lost Greek bronze original
Found at Hadrian's Villa,
Tivoli, Latium (Lazio),
Italy
GR 1805.7–3.43;
Cat. Sculpture 250
h. 1.7 m (5 ft 7 in)
Purchased 1805 (Townley
Collection)

The ancient **Olympic Games**

was probably the prize at these particular games. The four-horse chariot race (*tethrippon*) was introduced in 680 BC. Charioteers were usually employees, the victory crown going to the owner.

Silver coin from Syracuse
4th century BC
BMC Coins, Syracuse 176
diam. 3.5 cm (1⅓ in)

The greatest achievement for an athlete in the ancient world was to win the Olympic crown. Wreaths were made from the leaves of the sacred olive tree behind the Temple of Zeus. Prior to the crowning, ribbons of wool were tied around the athlete's head, arms and legs as a mark of victory.

There were three other major national athletic festivals: the Pythian Games at Delphi, held in honour of Apollo; the Isthmian Games, held at Corinth for Poseidon; and the Games at Nemea, also in honour of Zeus. Important games were held at Athens as part of the Panathenaic festival, and over the centuries hundreds of other city-states established their own local games.

FURTHER READING
J. Swaddling, *The Ancient Olympic Games* (3rd edn, London, 2004)

Amphora decorated with a running man
Kamiros, Rhodes, eastern Greece
c.550–525 BC
GR 1864.10–7.156
h. 34.3 cm (13½ in)
Excavated by Auguste Salzmann and Sir Alfred Biliotti

The 'Oxborough Dirk', a kind of dagger, is one of only five weapons of this particular type so far discovered. It is an extremely large bronze blade modelled on the general style of Middle Bronze Age dirks. Its size, the lack of rivet holes for hafting and its bluntness indicate that it was produced not to be used, but for ritual or display purposes.

The dirk was discovered by accident in 1990 by a walker in My Lord's Wood, Oxborough, Norfolk. It was found set vertically in the soil with just the butt protruding above ground-level. Later inspection of the site suggested that the sub-soil was peat filling a small stream valley. Many ritual deposits are known to have been made in bogs and rivers during the Bronze Age.

These dirks are known as 'Plougrescant-Ommerschans' blades, taking their name from examples found in France and the Netherlands.

FURTHER READING
S.P. Needham, 'Middle Bronze Ceremonial Weapons: New Finds from Oxborough, Norfolk and Essex/Kent', *Antiquaries Journal*, 70 (1990), pp. 239–52
M. Parker Pearson, *Bronze Age Britain* (London, 1993)

The Oxborough Dirk
Oxborough, Norfolk, England
c.1500–1350 BC
PRB P 1994,100
l. 70.9 cm (27⁹/10 in)
Purchased with the aid of the National Art Collections Fund

The **Oxus treasure**

In May 1880 Captain F.C. Burton (1845–1931), a British political officer in Afghanistan, rescued a group of merchants travelling between Kabul and Peshawar who had been captured by bandits. They had with them a rich collection of fine gold and silver objects, said to have been found three years before on the banks of the Oxus River (now known as the Amu dar'ya). According to a later account the merchants allowed Burton to purchase a massive gold bracelet before continuing on their way. The treasure eventually emerged from the bazaars of Rawalpindi. Most of the objects now in the Museum were acquired by Major-General Sir Alexander Cunningham (1814–93), Director General of the Archaeological Survey of India, who sold them to Sir Augustus Wollaston Franks, a curator at the Museum; Franks also purchased items direct from India.

Gold armlet
Takht-i Kuwad (?), Oxus River, Tadjikistan
5th–4th century BC
WA 124017;
1897–12–31, 11
h. 12.3 cm (4¾ in)
A.W. Franks Bequest

The Oxus treasure is the most important collection of Achaemenid metalwork to have survived (p. 11), although some pieces show Greek or Central Asian influence. Dating mainly from the fifth and fourth centuries BC the treasure consists of about 170 objects – vessels, a gold scabbard, model chariots and figures, armlets, seals, finger-rings, miscellaneous personal objects, dedicatory plaques and coins. Indications are that the treasure was gathered together over a period of 200–300 years. It is probable that the Oxus treasure was a single find, although some coins may have been added later. The fact that the treasure is made of precious metals and includes coins and mutilated pieces suggests that it was buried as a hoard, having possibly been amassed by a temple.

Above is a gold armlet, one of a pair (the armlet purchased by Captain Burton was sold to the V&A). The terminals are in the shape of griffin's heads with ibex horns, originally inlaid with glass and precious stones. Similar bracelets are shown being presented to the king by a number of the delegations on the Persepolis reliefs (p. 248).

On the left is one of 51 gold plaques, the largest category of objects in the treasure.

Gold plaque showing a man holding a bundle of rods
Takht-i Kuwad (?), Oxus River, Tadjikistan
5th–4th century BC
WA 123949;
1897–12–31, 48
h. 15 cm (6 in)
A.W. Franks Bequest

FURTHER READING
J. Curtis, 'Franks and the Oxus Treasure' in M. Caygill and J. Cherry (eds), *A.W. Franks: Nineteenth-century Collecting and the British Museum* (London, 1997), pp. 230–49

The earliest art known in Europe seems to coincide with the appearance of fully modern humans about 35,000 years ago. From this time until about 10,000 years ago, paintings, engravings, bas-reliefs, sculpture and clay modelling form a fascinating part of the archaeological record. Animals are the theme of most compositions, although human representations including hands, female figures and therianthropes (humans with animal features), as well as abstract motifs, are also depicted. These subjects occur in both the mural art of the caves and rock-shelters of France, Spain, Italy and Russia and on portable objects found throughout mainland Europe. The Museum's collections are particularly rich in engraved stone and bone plaques, personal ornaments and decorated tools and weapons excavated from French sites in the nineteenth century. Some of the finest pieces come from La Madeleine and Les Eyzies (Dordogne) and Courbet and Montastruc (Penne-Tarn), and are about 12,500 years old. The ingeniously carved mammoth (above), made from a reindeer antler, formed part of a spear thrower. It was found at Montastruc in rock-shelter deposits which also contained a pair of reindeer (below), carved on ivory from the tip of a mammoth tusk. The larger male reindeer follows a female. Both have their heads tipped back as if swimming. The tapering form of the tusk may have suggested this pose to an artist seeking to represent the subject in the round.

Part of a spear thrower
carved in the form of
a mammoth
Montastruc, France
c.12,000 BC
PRB Peccadeau 551
w. 12.4 cm (4⁹/₁₀ in)
Puchased (Peccadeau de
l'Isle, 1887)

Male and female reindeer
carved on mammoth
ivory
Montastruc, France
c.12,000 BC
PRB Peccadeau 550
l. 20.7 cm (8¹/₇ in)
Purchased (Peccadeau de
l'Isle, 1887)

FURTHER READING

A. Sieveking, *A Catalogue of Palaeolithic Art in the British Museum* (London, 1987)
P.G. Bahn and J. Vertut, *Images of the Ice Age* (2nd edn, London, 1997)
P.G. Bahn, *The Cambridge Illustrated History of Prehistoric Art* (Cambridge, 1998)

Palestinian costume

The traditional costumes of the Palestinian villagers and Bedouin are of exceptional beauty and diversity, especially the festive costumes of the women, which feature lavish and particularly fine silk embroidery and patchwork and dramatic headdresses covered with coins. Much of the Museum's research into costumes has highlighted their significance as expressions of social status and regional identity. It has focused on wedding attire, since this ceremony is the key to an understanding of the language of Palestinian women's costume.

The Museum's earliest holdings were acquired from the Church Missionary Society in 1965. Further acquisitions came from other missionary societies, augmented by important pieces collected during fieldwork by the Museum from the late 1960s to the late 1980s, and by purchase and donation. The collection is now one of the finest in the world, numbering over 650 garments and 230 items of jewellery and amulets. It includes many exceptional pieces and is particularly rich in rare nineteenth-century items.

FURTHER READING
S. Weir, *Palestinian Costume*
(London, 1989)
S. Weir, *Embroidery from Palestine*,
Fabric Folios Series (London, 2006)

Palestinian dress
Southern plain
Cotton, with taffeta and
satin skirt, sleeve and
yoke panels, *c*.1920s
OA 1971.AS.101
l. 145 cm (57 in)

Afeature of the end of the Egyptian Predynastic period
(c.3250–3100 BC) was the production of large siltstone
palettes which were decorated in relief and apparently placed as
votive objects in temples. These ceremonial palettes seem to have
evolved from the earlier functional versions, which were intended
for grinding cosmetics. The Museum has fragments of two of the
best-known – the 'Battlefield' and the 'Hunters' palettes.

The Hunters palette may be the slightly earlier in date. Two
fragments survive in the Museum, plus a third in the Louvre. The
hunters, three of whom hold standards of individual clan groups,
are armed with spears, bows, maces, throwsticks and a lariat. The
earlier date is indicated by the technique of carving, particularly
the hollow eyes.

The Battlefield palette consists of two fragments, one of which
is in the Ashmolean Museum, Oxford. On one side are a pair of

The 'Hunters' palette
Provenance unknown
Late Predynastic–1st
Dynasty, c.3100 BC
EA 20790
l. 66.8 cm (26¼ in)

long-necked gazelles browsing on a date palm. The other side
shows the casualties of battle being preyed upon by scavengers. In
the top right-hand corner is the lower part of a figure wearing a
long cloak of foreign type, with a prisoner before him. Other
captives are shown restrained by the personified standards of
certain districts of Upper Egypt.

Little is known about the inhabitants of Egypt of the
Predynastic period, although it is thought that there eventually
existed two loose confederations, their leaders identified by their
distinctive crowns. The 'king' of Lower Egypt wore the red crown
and the 'king' of Upper Egypt wore the white crown. The late
Predynastic period seems to have been one of continuous struggle
until the final conquest of the north by the south, by a king known
to history as Menes. He is generally identified with Narmer, who is
shown on a palette in the Egyptian Museum, Cairo.

FURTHER READING
A.J. Spencer, *Early Egypt: The Rise of Civilisation in the Nile Valley* (London, 1993)

It is said that, as the three-year-old Samuel Palmer (1805–81) gazed out of the window at the moon with his nurse, she repeated these lines by the poet Edward Young:

> Fond man, the vision of a moment made,
> Dream of a dream, and shadow of a shade.

This scene remained with Palmer, who later wrote, 'I have never forgot those shadows, and am often trying to paint them.'

Palmer's fame rests chiefly on a small group of works painted from around 1826 to 1832 when he was living in seclusion in the village of Shoreham in the Darenth Valley, Kent, his 'Valley of Vision'. These drawings and paintings are characterized by a combination of almost visionary exaltation and the close study of nature and rural life, which he invested with a spiritual quality.

By 1833 the intensity in Palmer had begun to fade. His poverty was increasing and in 1835 he returned to London, married and struggled to make a living by teaching. He did, however, receive some recognition from the art establishment. In 1843 he was elected an Associate of the Society of Painters in Water-Colours, becoming a full member in 1854. In 1850 he became a member of the Etching Club and published his first etchings.

Already prone to depression, he was much affected by the deaths of two of his children and the struggle against poverty. In 1864 he began his series of watercolours to illustrate Milton's *Il Penseroso* and *L'Allegro* and worked slowly and laboriously on some of his finest etchings, perhaps the most notable of which were 'The Bellman' and 'The Lonely Tower'.

The Museum has two of Palmer's sketchbooks (the others were destroyed by his son) and impressions of all his etchings, several presented by the artist himself.

'A Cornfield by Moonlight with the Evening Star'
Watercolour with body-colour, pen and sepia ink, varnished, c.1830
PD 1985–5–5–1
19.7 × 25.8 cm
(7¾ × 10⅛ in)
Purchased with the aid of the National Heritage Memorial Fund, the Henry Moore Foundation, the Pilgrim Trust, the British Museum Society and public subscription

FURTHER READING
R. Lister, *Samuel Palmer and his Etchings* (London, 1969)
R. Lister, *The Paintings of Samuel Palmer* (Cambridge, 1985)
W. Vaughan, E.E. Barker and C. Harrison, *Samuel Palmer, Vision and Landscape* (London, 2005)

Palmyrene tomb portraits

Palmyra, a city in the Syrian desert, grew rich from the caravan trade. Its impressive ruins mark a site occupied since the Neolithic period (eighth millennium BC). In the first century BC the collapse of the vast Hellenistic Seleucid Empire, together with the expansion of trade routes between the Persian Gulf and the Mediterranean, allowed Palmyra to develop into a flourishing centre.

Palmyra was incorporated into the Roman Empire in the reign of Nero (AD 54–68). Later, under their famous queen Zenobia, Palmyrene troops wrested control of Syria from the Romans, conquered Egypt and embarked on the conquest of Asia Minor (now Turkey). However, in AD 272 the Emperor Aurelian (c.AD 212–75) defeated the Palmyrenes, captured Zenobia and took her to Rome, where she appeared in the Triumph wearing golden chains. Palmyra was destroyed following a second insurrection in AD 273.

Three types of tomb were built outside the city for the wealthier citizens: tomb towers of several storeys; single-storey house tombs; and underground rock-hewn tombs called *hypogea*. Towers were often added to *hypogea*, probably to cope with an overspill.

The tombs contained compartments (*cubicula*) set in the walls to hold the remains of the dead. Each *cubiculum* was sealed with a plaque bearing a sculptured portrait of the deceased, originally picked out in colour, and a brief dedicatory inscription. Contrary to the general trend in the Near East, women are dominant, proud in their finest jewels, which still bear traces of the paint once highlighting them.

Funerary bust of a woman
Palmyra, Syria
late 2nd century AD
WA 102612; 1908–4–17, 1
h. 51 cm (20 in)

An English traveller, Robert Wood, visited Palmyra in 1751 and afterwards published an account of his travels which encouraged visitors to the site. These early travellers were often avid collectors of antiquities, and a number of the Palmyrene funerary busts now in the Museum were acquired through their efforts. Altogether there are 38 in the collection, ranging in date between the first and third centuries AD.

Shown here is a limestone bust of a woman named Aqmat wearing her cloak (*himation*) over her headdress as a veil. The inscription, in Aramaic, reads 'Aqmat, daughter of Hagagu, descendant of Zebida, descendant of Ma'an, alas!'

FURTHER READING
M.A.R. Colledge, *The Art of Palmyra* (London, 1976)

Paper money

Money in the form of paper notes was introduced in China in the late tenth century AD, encouraged by the growth of commerce and inter-regional exchange during the Song dynasty (AD 960–1279). The early issues were private notes for remittance, credit or exchange, with a date limitation; closer parallels to the paper money we use today were the officially issued exchange notes without date limitation produced by the Jin in AD 1189. During the Mongol Yuan dynasty (AD 1206–1367), only paper money was used.

In the West, paper money appeared in the seventeenth century AD to supplement scarce or inconvenient coinage. The first banknotes were issued by Johan Palmstruch's Stockholm Banco in Sweden in 1661. The bank went out of business after only a few years, but its freely circulating notes anticipated future trends. In 1690 the province of Massachusetts Bay issued the first American paper money.

The earliest note issuers to continue successfully into modern times were the Bank of England and the Bank of Scotland, founded in 1694 and 1695 respectively. In several countries the growth of trade and industry in the later eighteenth and nineteenth centuries stimulated the rise of local banks, which issued their own notes. Then and later, banking and paper money also spread across the world as a by-product of European colonization. Over time, legislation to regulate banking practice and currency supply has restricted the right of note issue to centralized institutions such as state banks or treasuries.

The Museum's collection of banknotes and related items from over 200 countries is one of the foremost in the world. The collection includes not only state and privately issued notes, but also emergency and political issues, cheques, bills of exchange, printers' specimens and artwork for note designs.

The paper money collection of the Chartered Institute of Bankers is placed with the Museum on indefinite loan.

Board of Revenue note
for 1000 cash
China
Ming dynasty,
AD 1368– 1644 (notes
issued from 1374)
CM 1942–8–5–1

Modern banknotes
Canada, Oman, Uganda,
China and Bulgaria
CM 1991–5–28–1;
1988–1–18–1;
1995–8–35–3;
1997–3–12–10;
1995–8–54–3

FURTHER READING
E. Green, *Banking: An Illustrated History*
(Oxford, 1989)
V. Hewitt (ed.), *The Banker's Art: Studies in
Paper Money* (London, 1995)
W. Kranister, *The Moneymakers International*
(Cambridge, 1989)

From c.3100 BC onwards the papyrus plant provided an ideal surface for writing with a reed pen and pigments of carbon and red ochre. The papyrus is a tall flowering freshwater reed, *Cyperus papyrus*, which flourished in Egypt. Papyrus sheets were made from two layers of cut stems placed at right angles to each other and flattened. These sheets could be glued together with gum to form a roll.

The Museum has a particularly fine collection of Egyptian papyri, both religious and secular, including brilliantly illustrated Books of the Dead (pp. 61–2). Among the best known are the *Abu Sir Papyri*, Fifth Dynasty, c.2400 BC, comprising fragments of records from a temple attached to the Pyramid of King Neferirkare, probably the earliest written papyri to survive; the *Rhind Mathematical Papyrus* (below) of c.1550 BC, said to be copied from a Twelfth-Dynasty document of c.1850 BC, which shows arithmetical problems – multiplication and division of fractions, methods of determining the volume of a cylinder, the area of a square, a circle and a triangle, and the slope of a pyramid; the *Dream Book*, Nineteenth Dynasty, c.1250 BC, listing hypothetical dreams and their interpretations; the *London Medical Papyrus*, late Nineteenth Dynasty, c.1200 BC, a series of magical spells and prescriptions for remedying burns and diseases affecting the bones, eyes and female organs; the *Chester Beatty Medical Papyrus*, Nineteenth Dynasty, c.1200 BC, a medical treatise dealing with disorders of the anus and rectum, with prescribed remedies; the *Great Harris Papyrus*, Twentieth Dynasty, c.1198–1166 BC, written at the beginning of the reign of Ramesses IV, recording all the donations made by Ramesses III to the temples throughout Egypt (at 41 m (134 ft 6 in) it is the longest known); the *Harris Tomb Robbery Papyrus*, Twentieth Dynasty, c.1175 BC, containing depositions of eight thieves regarding objects stolen from a queen's tomb at Thebes; the *Abbot Papyrus*, c.1120 BC, recording an investigation into the robberies of royal tombs at Thebes during the reign of Ramesses IX; and the *Teaching of Amenemope*, Twenty-First Dynasty, c.1000 BC, parts of which agree very closely with passages in the Old Testament, paricularly the Book of Proverbs.

Rhind Mathematical
Papyrus (detail)
Thebes, Egypt
c.1550 BC
EA 10057
h. 32 cm (12½ in)
Purchased (collection of
Alexander Henry Rhind)

FURTHER READING
R. Parkinson and S. Quirke, *Papyrus*
(London, 1995)

The sculptures of the **Parthenon** Greece, late 5th century BC

The Parthenon was built on the Acropolis (the upper city or citadel) in Athens. Dedicated to the city's patron goddess Athena Parthenos, it contained an ivory and gold statue of the goddess, now lost. The term 'Parthenon' (which has been used since Roman times) means 'room of the maidens' and was originally applied only to a section of the building, probably intended for those who served the goddess.

Around 450 BC, the statesman Pericles induced the Athenians to divert for building purposes money collected from their Greek allies (the Delian league), originally to form a fleet for defence against the Persians. Earlier in the century the Persians had invaded Greece and sacked Athens, destroying the old temples on the Acropolis, before their decisive defeat at the naval battle of Salamis in 480 BC. The rebuilding was carried out under the overall supervision of the great sculptor Pheidias and the architects were Iktinos and Callicrates.

Riders in the procession
Athens
Marble, 5th century BC
North frieze slab XXXVIII
h. 99 cm (3 ft 3 in)

The frieze was set high up under the ceiling of the colonnade, facing outwards. Of its original 160 m (525 ft) two thirds survives, of which 60 per cent is in the British Museum, the rest is in Athens or in other museums. The traditional explanation is that the frieze shows the four-yearly procession of the 'Great Panathenaia', a festival in which the people of Athens brought a new woollen robe (*peplos*) for the statue of Athena on her birthday. (A less grand procession took place in the intervening years.) The west frieze shows preparations for the procession, the north and south friezes show the procession under way. The east frieze shows cult officials with the *peplos* and the Olympian gods.

The pediments are described in a second-century AD guidebook by Pausanias. The east represented the birth of Athena, just after she had sprung fully armed from the head of her father Zeus, which the smith-god Hephaistos had split open with his axe. In the

The sculptures of the **Parthenon**

Museum can be seen Helios (the Sun) driving his four-horse chariot out of the sea at daybreak; Dionysos reclining on a lion-skin; Demeter and her daughter Persephone; Hebe (the cup-bearer of Zeus); Hestia; Dione and her daughter Aphrodite; and finally the horse drawing the chariot of Selene (the moon) sinking into the sea. Substantial fragments remain of the west pediment, much of it in Athens; this portrays Iris, goddess of the rainbow, and the river-god Ilissos, among much else.

There were originally 92 metopes, carved by a number of sculptors, of which the 15 from the south side now in the British Museum illustrate the battle between centaurs and lapiths at the wedding of King Pirithous (p. 181). Others (not in the Museum) represented (east) the battle between the Olympian gods and the giants who tried to expel and supersede them; (west) Greeks fighting Amazons; (north) the Fall of Troy.

The building was badly damaged when it was converted into a Christian church, probably in the fifth century AD. In AD 1687 even worse damage occurred when it was used as a gunpowder magazine by defending Turkish forces and exploded following a direct hit by a Venetian shell. In 1799 Lord Elgin was appointed British Ambassador at Constantinople. He took with him a team of artists and moulders to record the remains of the antiquities of ancient Greece, then part of the Turkish empire (as it had been since AD 1458). When the continuing destruction of the Parthenon sculptures was brought to his notice, Elgin obtained a *firman* (permit) from the Turks allowing him to remove 'pieces of stone with inscriptions or figures', an operation which led him deeply into debt. By 1815 Elgin's financial position was so precarious that he was obliged to offer the sculptures to the British Government. Parliament agreed in 1816 to pay £35,000 (less than half the cost of their removal, plus interest on the sums so expended) and the sculptures, which included objects other than those from the Parthenon, were in 1816 deposited in perpetuity in the British Museum.

Two heavily draped female figures seated on rectangular chests, perhaps Demeter and her daughter Persephone
Athens
Marble, 5th century BC
GR 1816.6–10.94; Cat. Sculpture 303 E and 303 F
l. 1.6 m (5 ft 3 in)

Head of a horse of Selene from the east pediment
Athens
Marble, 447–432 BC
GR 1816.6–10.98;
Cat. Sculpture 303 O
l. 79 cm (2 ft 7 in)
Purchased from Lord Elgin by the British Government and deposited in the British Museum, 1816

FURTHER READING
S. Bird and I. Jenkins, *Second Sight of the Parthenon Frieze* (London, 1998)
B.F. Cook, *The Elgin Marbles* (2nd edn, London, 1997)
I. Jenkins, *The Parthenon Frieze* (London, 1994)

Parthian gold

Alexander the Great (p. 15) and his successors inherited the Achaemenid Empire (p. 11), which was divided between the Seleucids, who ruled Iran and much of the Near East, and the Ptolemies who ruled Egypt. The Seleucids established a capital in Mesopotamia at Seleucia-on-the-Tigris and ruled Iran using Iranian and Macedonian satraps (governors).

In *c.*238 BC a nomadic Iranian tribe, the Parthians, under their leader Arsaces, seized control of the province immediately east of the Caspian Sea. Arsaces' successors, notably Mithridates I (171–138 BC), gradually captured Iran and Mesopotamia from the Seleucids and established a new winter capital at Ctesiphon, opposite Seleucia. As the Parthians extended their western frontier to the Euphrates they came into conflict with the Roman Empire. Their control of the Silk Route brought them into contact with the Han dynasty of China. Later Parthian history was marked by periodic wars with Rome, but the Parthians held back Roman advances and ruled Iran until AD 224, when they were replaced by the Sasanian dynasty (p. 283).

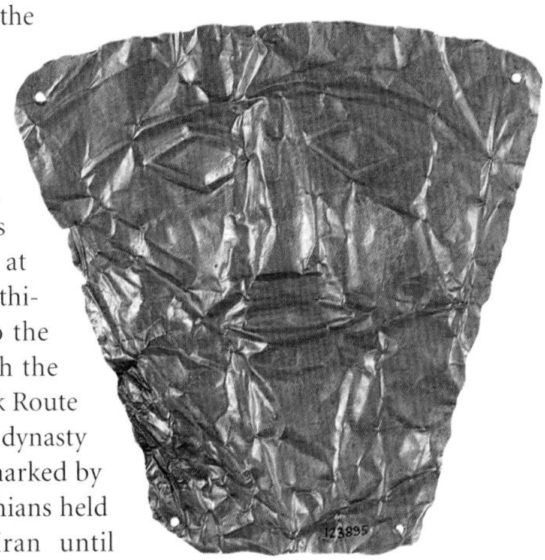

There was a cultural continuity between the Seleucid and early Parthian periods. Greek was replaced by Parthian as the official language only during the first century AD. Different dress and hairstyles were also adopted then and there was considerable regional variation in material culture and burial practices.

Shown here are two gold face masks from a Parthian settlement on the site of the old Assyrian capital of Nineveh, where excavations of the earlier citadel mound of Kuyunjik (p. 92) suggested the presence of imperial Parthian buildings: several rich graves were discovered in 1852. Gold masks were sometimes used to cover the faces of the dead, concealing the decay of features which would be needed in the afterlife.

Two gold face masks
Parthia, excavated at Nineveh
*c.*2nd century AD
WA 123894–5;
1856–9–9, 66–7
h. 16.5 cm, 13.9 cm
(6½ in, 5½ in)

FURTHER READING
J.E. Curtis, 'Parthian gold from Nineveh', *British Museum Yearbook*, I (London, 1976), pp. 47–66

Sculptures from **Persepolis**   Achaemenid Empire, 6th–4th centuries BC

In 550 BC Cyrus the Great (*r.*550–530 BC) overthrew Astyages, King of the Medes, and established the Achaemenid dynasty. Cyrus considerably expanded his new empire, first conquering western Anatolia, then the Neo-Babylonian Empire in 539 BC. He founded a capital at Pasargadae on the Iranian plateau. His successor after Cambyses (530–522 BC), Darius I ('the Great') (*r.*522–486 BC), began construction at the great royal centre of Persepolis – after Pasargadae and Susa the third of the great Achaemenid cities. It was continued by Xerxes (486–465 BC), Artaxerxes I (465–424 BC) and Artaxerxes III (359–338 BC) but destroyed by Alexander the Great in 334–332 BC.

Relief from the Apadana, Persepolis, showing guardsmen in Persian dress
Achaemenid Empire (Iran)
6th–5th century BC
WA 118838; 1825–4–21, 3
l. 102 cm (40⅛ in)
Given by Sir Gore Ouseley

Column base from the Throne Hall (Hall of 100 Columns), Persepolis
Achaemenid Empire (Iran)
5th century BC
WA 136209;
1974–12–10, 1
h. 98.5 cm (38¾ in)
Exchange gift from the Oriental Institute, University of Chicago (excavated 1932–3)

On a huge terrace cut into the natural rock were a whole series of palaces, columned halls and storerooms, reached by monumental stairways. The stone survives but the rest of the architecture, constructed from mudbrick and wood, has gone. The stairways were carved with reliefs showing the Persian king receiving tribute.

The Apadana, built by Darius and completed by Xerxes, was a square hall with 36 columns, three columned porticoes, a series of other rooms on the south side and four corner towers. Above is a relief from the north staircase of the east wing.

FURTHER READING
E.F. Schmidt, *Persepolis*, vols I–III (Chicago, 1953–70)
J.E. Curtis and N. Tallis (eds), *Forgotten Empire: the World of Ancient Persia* (London, 2005)

The term 'Pharaoh' is the Greek form of the ancient Egyptian phrase *per-aa* ('great house'), which was originally used to refer to the royal palace. From the New Kingdom (1550–1069 BC) onwards the term was often used to refer to the king himself. The kings of Egypt are traditionally divided into 30 dynasties or ruling houses, according to a system preserved in the work of Manetho, a priestly historian who lived in the third century BC.

Names of kings carried particular force. At birth a future king of Egypt would receive a personal name. Later names were acquired when the king came to power, in order to express his new identity. From the Pyramid Age to the last of the Ptolemies, the kings received five names, four at accession and one at birth. Initially names would be written in a rectangular panel. From the Fourth Dynasty (*c.*2613–2494 BC) the oval cartouche encircling the king's name appears. The cartouche is essentially an elongated form of the *shen* hieroglyph and signifies the concept of 'encircling protection' denoted by a coil of rope folded and tied at the end. The term *cartouche* ('gun cartridge') was introduced by the French in Egypt in the late eighteenth/early nineteenth century.

The king is portrayed wearing a number of different head coverings. The earliest is a tall conical head-piece ending in a bulb. This is the crown of Upper Egypt, or white crown (*hedjet*). The crown of Lower Egypt, or red crown (*deshret*), was a tall chair-shaped arrangement from which protruded a coil. Upon unification these two crowns were combined into the double crown (*pschent*). The king might also wear the *nemes* headcloth. This was a piece of striped cloth pulled tight across the forehead and tied into a kind of tail at the back while at each side of the face two strands or lappets hung down. The brow was decorated with the *uraeus* and the vulture.

The Museum has a rich collection of Egyptian royal sculpture. In addition there are many other links with the kings of Egypt – inscriptions, papyri, ivories and so on. Overleaf (top) is an ivory figure of an unidentified king from Abydos, wearing the white crown of Upper Egypt and a long robe which was worn at his jubilee (*heb-sed*).

Head from a monumental quartzite statue of Amen-hotep III wearing the red crown
Egypt
18th Dynasty, *c.*1425 BC
EA 6
h. 1.17 m (3 ft 10 in)
Purchased (Henry Salt, 1835)

Pharaohs of Egypt

Ivory figure of a king
Temple of Osiris, Abydos,
Egypt
Early Dynastic, c.2900 BC
EA 37996
h. 8.8 cm (3½ in)
Given by the Egypt
Exploration Fund

Colossal red granite head
Temple of Mut, Thebes,
Egypt
17th Dynasty, c.1390 BC
EA15
h. 2.9 m (9 ft 6 in)
Purchased (Henry Salt,
1835)

The sculpture comes principally from the great temples. Most of these were cult temples where the king, as high-priest of the deity concerned, performed, theoretically in person, the daily rituals of service. Statues of the king found in such temples were magical substitutes for the king himself and could participate in the personal relationship between god and king.

Below is a head from a colossal standing figure of a king wearing the double crown. His identity is disputed, although recent opinion favours Amenhotep III. There were also mortuary temples devoted to the funerary cults of individual kings. From these temples come statues of the king principally set up to participate magically in the regular mortuary services established after the king's death, and in the offerings prepared for his posthumous existence.

FURTHER READING
T.G.H. James and W.V. Davies, *Egyptian Sculpture* (London, 1983)
S. Quirke, *Who were the Pharaohs? A history of their names with a list of cartouches* (London, 1990)

By the beginning of the first millennium BC, the Israelites occupied most of Canaan except for the southern coastal strip, which continued to be held by the Philistines. To the north the powerful Aramaean kingdoms controlled most of central and northern Syria. The remaining Canaanite territory on the north coast – a loose confederation of city-states: Aradus, Byblos, Beirut, Sidon and Tyre in what is now Lebanon and Syria – became known as 'Phoenicia'. The name derives from the Greek word for 'purple' (phoinikeos), a reference to one of the principal industries of the region, the extraction of dye from murex shells and the production of purple-coloured fabrics.

The Phoenicians exploited their expertise in art and craftmanship, producing luxury items such as ivories (p. 230–1), metalwork, glassware and jewellery, which were sought after all over the Near East. Phoenicians are said to have been employed on Solomon's Temple in Jerusalem. It was ultimately to the sea, however, that they turned to make a living, becoming great seafarers and traders and transforming the small natural harbours into large ports capable of handling international trade. They established colonies as far afield as Tharros in Sardinia and Cádiz in Spain. The most famous was Carthage, in Tunisia, traditionally founded in 814 BC, whose importance long outlived the Phoenician homeland. The Romans knew the Carthaginians as Poeni (from which the adjective 'Punic' comes). During the three Punic Wars with Rome (264–241, 223–202 and 150–146 BC) Carthage lost much of her territory and was finally destroyed in 146 BC.

Phoenician gold bracelet or diadem
Tharros, Sardinia
7th–6th century BC
WA 133392
l. 13.2 cm (5¼ in)
Excavated 1853–5 by
G. Cara

The Greek alphabet was a successful adaptation of the Phoenician consonant script.

The Museum has material from excavations in and around Carthage in the 1850s, including a stele from the cemetery (*tophet*) where the remains of children sacrificed to the gods were buried. Phoenician merchants are shown on an Assyrian relief from the Palace of Ashurnasirpal II (883–859 BC) at Nimrud (WA 124562) bringing two monkeys as royal gifts. In 1856 the Museum bought a collection of antiquities excavated on the Tharros promontory of the west coast of Sardinia, including spectacular jewellery such as the bracelet or diadem shown here.

FURTHER READING
G. Markoe, *The Phoenicians* (London, 2000)

Photographs

Below is a scene familiar today – the entrance to the British Museum – but this is the Museum in the early morning of 1856. The Museum was one of the first public institutions to become involved in photography. As early as summer 1843 the pioneer photographer William Henry Fox Talbot (1800–77) carried out photographic 'experiments' there and corresponded with the excavator Charles Fellows in the hope, unfulfilled, of joining the Museum's archaeological expedition to Xanthos. In 1853 the Museum employed Roger Fenton (1819–69), who was to make his reputation photographing the Crimean War. The Museum now has some 250 Fenton prints of classical sculpture, Old Master drawings and cuneiform tablets, and also views of the building.

The rare Fenton print shown here was probably processed in his studio on the Museum roof. Since Fenton's time the Museum has amassed an archive of photographs of the objects in its collections.

Although the Museum has never aimed to illustrate the history of photography, its archival collection of some half a million items does include photographs of national and international importance, taken by various processes, the earliest dating from the 1840s. In addition to the record of its own history and collections, there is a considerable topographical collection, particularly photographs of archaeological sites and excavations in progress. The largest historical collection is that in the Department of Ethnography (over 200,000 items, the earliest from c.1854). This includes portraits of ethnic groups from all over the world. It is kept up to date by photographs of today's fieldwork expeditions.

The photograph above comes from the North American collection. A member of the Ute tribe, Tushaquinot, stands against an artificial background, resplendent in feather headdress, tightly grasping a revolver, his hair braided, defiant but with a touch of apprehension in his eyes.

'A Ute brave'
William Henry Jackson
(1843–1942)
Albumen print, c.AD 1880
ETH Am.A8.11
13.7 × 20.5 cm (5⅓ × 8 in)

The front of the British Museum
Roger Fenton
(AD 1819–69)
Salted paper print processed from a collodion negative on glass, c.AD 1856
Central Archive
CE114/652
33.1 × 4.21 cm
(13 × 16½ in)
Given by the British Museum Society

FURTHER READING
C. Date and A. Hamber, 'The Origins of Photography at the British Museum, 1839–1860' in *History of Photography*, vol. 14, no. 4 (London, Oct./Dec. 1990)
H. Gernsheim, *The Origins of Photography* (London, 1982)

Below is a Pictish symbol stone carved with the figure of a bull, one of a series from the vitrified fort at Burghead, Moray Firth. About 30 small specimens were found in digging the harbour during the nineteenth century, only some five of which survive today. The powerful bull symbol occurs only at Burghead and may indicate tribal or dynastic identity. It is thought that such symbol stones originated in a pagan context, but not necessarily any earlier than the seventh century AD. They consist of boulders and rough slabs like this one, incised with a range of symbols. In addition to the Burghead bulls, boars, birds, fish and abstract symbols have been found, the latter including stylized depictions of everyday objects such as combs and mirrors.

Picti is the term used in Roman writings to refer to the people north of the Antonine Wall between the Forth and Clyde estuaries. In Latin it means 'the painted ones', in accordance with classical writers' accounts of them as heavily tattooed, but it is probably derived from the Picts' own name for themselves. The Picts were culturally related to but distinct from other Celtic peoples. In the early medieval period they inhabited the northern part of modern Scotland. Much about their history is now obscure, although they are known to have been among the raiders who harried late-Roman Britain.

Pictish symbol stone
Burghead, Moray Firth,
Scotland
7th–8th century AD
MLA 1861,10–24, 1
Given by James de Carle
Sowerby

In the post-Roman period a number of kingdoms emerged in what is now Scotland. A limited migration of Scotti from Ireland led to the establishment of the Scottish kingdom of Dalriada along the coast of Argyll and its islands. Irish monks undertook evangelical work among the Picts, who had had contacts with sub-Roman Christianity. In the mid-ninth century Kenneth MacAlpin, King of the Scots, established himself in southern Pictland. From there Irish speech and influence spread across Scotland and thus the Scotti, not the Picts, came to give their name to the modern kingdom.

FURTHER READING
S.M. Foster, *Picts, Gaels and Scots* (London, 1996)

'Pieces of eight! Pieces of eight!' squawked the parrot of the sinister Long John Silver in Robert Louis Stevenson's *Treasure Island*. The coin in question, much sought after by the pirates who lurked in the approaches to the New World, was the Spanish *ocho-reales* (eight-real) piece. The coin of 1653 (left) shows the Pillars of Hercules and the motto *Plus ultra* ('There is more beyond'), symbols of Spain's empire.

In the 1540s rich silver deposits were discovered first in Mexico and then, greatest of all, at Potosi, the Silver Mountain itself, in Bolivia. The silver ingots from Potosi were taken overland to the coastal port of Arica, where they were loaded on to Spanish galleons and shipped up the west coast of South America to the Caribbean via Panama, and from there to Spain. Silver ingots and newly minted coins, mostly eight-real pieces, flowed into Spain in the later sixteenth and early seventeenth centuries and from there into the currency systems of Europe and the world. They were used to pay Spanish armies and to service loans from bankers and creditors in Genoa, Antwerp, Augsburg and Portugal. Much also went to buy goods, usually through Dutch intermediaries. American silver passed through traditional channels into the Middle East and from AD 1565 across the Pacific on Spain's 'Manila Galleons' or 'China Ships' to the Spanish Philippines, where it was traded for goods from China and South-East Asia. In the seventeenth century, however, the supplies from the Americas to Spain gradually diminished as mine output declined and more was retained for colonial use. But American silver remained significant right through the eighteenth century, when new discoveries and improved techniques revived mining productivity.

Silver *ocho-reales* of Philip IV (r.1621–65), King of Spain
Potosi mint, dated 1653
CM C0474
diam. 4 cm (1½ in)

FURTHER READING

P. Vilar, *A History of Gold and Money* (London, 1991)

J.L. Lázaro, *Reales de a ocho. Los Redondos de Lima, Mejico y Potosí y otras acuñaciones especiales* (Madrid, 1996), pp. 208–9

The Piranesi vase is not as it seems: a huge and magnificent ornament of Carrara marble of the Roman period. Closer inspection reveals that it was constructed in the eighteenth century from a great number of classical fragments with modern additions.

The vase was bought by the English collector Sir John Boyd (1718–1800) before 1778 from the Italian engraver, architect and antiquarian Giambattista Piranesi (1720–78). This was the period of the 'Grand Tour', when young Englishmen flocked to Italy to become acquainted with classical civilization. Many sought to put together their own collections from dealers such as Thomas Jenkins (1724–98) and Gavin Hamilton (1730–97). There was not, however, today's obsession with authenticity. To the dealers and their buyers it was almost unthinkable that a headless or armless torso should not have its missing parts skilfully replaced. If talented sculptor-restorers such as Piranesi succeeded in disguising modern additions so as not to detract from the overall effect, so much the better.

Piranesi began to operate in Rome from 1767/8 as a dealer in antiquities and marble decorative work. He was closely involved with Hamilton's excavation at Hadrian's Villa near Tivoli in 1769, acquiring a great number of classical fragments.

Thus some 70 per cent of the Piranesi vase is modern and there is no certainty that the base, support and vase ever belonged together. On the massive base, for example, two of the three bull's heads represent the only original antique component. The whole of the upper rim is modern, as is much of the relief. Flawed it may be, but it is a neo-classical sculpture of considerable merit.

Piranesi's work is also to be found in the Department of Prints and Drawings. There are 53 drawings of architectural subjects and examples of his etchings, including the *Views of Rome*.

The Piranesi vase
Rome
2nd and 18th centuries AD
GR Cat. Sculpture 2502
h. 271.8 cm (8 ft 11 in)
Purchased 1868

FURTHER READING
A.H. Smith, *A Catalogue of Sculpture in the Department of Greek and Roman Antiquities*, III (London, 1904), pp. 395–7
M. Jones (ed.), *Fake? The Art of Deception* (London, 1990), pp. 132–4

Playing cards

The Museum has around 1700 packs of playing cards, ranging in date from the fifteenth century to the present. The largest groups are from England, Germany, France and Italy, but there are others from elsewhere in Europe and from the East.

It is uncertain where cards originated – in Europe or the East. The earliest known European reference is in a manuscript (now in the British Library) dated AD 1377, written in Latin by a German monk living in a Swiss monastery. In 1378 we know that cards were prohibited in the German city of Regensburg; in 1379 the accounts of the Dukedom of Brabant record the purchase of cards. In 1392 there is a reference in the archives of King Charles VI of France to a payment being made to a certain Jacquemin Grigonneur for painting three packs of cards. The civic archives, guild books and registers of the German towns, particularly Nuremberg, Augsburg and Ulm, record early in the fifteenth century the names of both card-makers and card-painters.

Originally there were two types of cards, tarots and numerals. Tarot cards constitute a series of pieces, generally 22 in number, exceptionally 41 or 50. The designs vary according to time and country of origin, but are basically made up of: a Juggler, a Female Pope, an Empress, an Emperor, the Pope, the Lovers, a Chariot with a warrior; Justice, a Hermit, the Wheel of Fortune, Force, a Man hanging by his foot (Le Pendu), Death, Temperance, the Devil, a Tower struck by lightning, a large Star, the Moon, the Sun, the Last Judgement, the World, a Fool. The second, more familiar, type is the pack of numerals, 52 in number, divided into four suits each distinguished by a special mark or symbol. The latter vary at different times and in different countries – cups, money, swords and clubs; hearts, diamonds, clubs, spades; hearts, bells, leaves and acorns. There are three court cards, usually a King, Queen and Valet or Knave, which from the fourteenth century might sometimes take the name of historical or mythical characters such as David, Alexander, Rachel.

Two of clubs from a pack of playing cards made by John Lenthall of Fleet Street, London
Hand-coloured etching, 1665–85
PD 1982.U.4628, Willshire E. 203
88 × 57 mm (3½ × 2¼ in)

FURTHER READING
D. Hoffman, *The Playing Card* (Leipzig, 1973)
S. Mann, *All Cards on the Table* (Marburg, 1990)
R. Tilley, *Pleasures and Treasures: Playing Cards* (London, 1967)
W.H. Willshire, *A Descriptive Catalogue of Playing and other Cards in the British Museum* (London, 1876)

The audience for sophisticated and expensive works of art has always been limited, and since the beginnings of European printmaking in the fifteenth century the majority of prints have been relatively simple, cheaply produced images, answering the tastes and needs of the time. Such ephemera might serve a wide range of more or less utilitarian purposes: advertisement, decoration, education, entertainment, information, religious or political propaganda and titillation.

Until the development of photo-mechanical means of reproduction, the most cost-effective medium for a large print-run was the woodcut – cheap to produce and capable of printing thousands of impressions. Simple woodcut prints were widely distributed and would often be pasted or pinned to the walls of taverns and cottages. In the Catholic countries of continental Europe images of saints were probably the most commonplace. In England 'holy pictures' were rare before the nineteenth century, but there was no shortage of other subjects – great men and women, fashion, warfare, anti-establishment sentiments, morality, freaks of nature, advertisements for the lottery and insurance. In Germany such prints were long regarded as an important part of the history of the woodcut, while in France and Russia revolutions made every manifestation of popular culture a subject for serious consideration. Anonymous popular prints were not, however, systematically collected by the Museum until recently, but a number have found their way into the collection as part of larger gifts and bequests.

Below, a late eighteenth-century engraving entitled 'Cobler's Hall' shows how such prints might be used, with ballads and woodcuts pinned to the wall and a print of the Duke of Cumberland over the fireplace.

'Cobler's Hall'
England
Engraving, published by
Bowles & Carver, late 18th
century AD
PD 1875–8–14–2465
37.3 × 52 cm
(14⅔ × 20½ in)
Given by John Deffett
Francis

FURTHER
READING
T. Gretton, *Murders
and Moralities, British
Catchpenny Prints
1800–1860*
(London, 1980)
S. O'Connell, *The
Popular Print in
England*
(London, 1999)

The Portland Font is a unique survival in England of a gold bowl for private baptism. It was commissioned by the third Duke of Portland (1738–1809) on the occasion of the birth on 21 August 1796 of his first grandson, William Henry Cavendish-Scott-Bentinck, as a present to his eldest son, the Marquess of Titchfield. It comprises a bowl on a square plinth surrounded by the three Cardinal Virtues – Faith (standing with hand held over the bowl in the act of benediction), Hope (with symbolic anchor) and Charity (sheltering children).

The designer of this bold composition was the celebrated landscape gardener and architect Humphry Repton (1752–1818). It is the earliest example of English goldsmiths' work to use free-standing figures in the then fashionable neo-classical style and is the starting-point for the nineteenth-century English tradition of magnificent sculptural presentation plate. The modeller of these figures remains unknown but they are superbly executed: textured draperies contrast with the burnished gold. The underside of the bowl has a pattern of lilies, reflected in the shiny gold plinth as if on water. The Font was executed by the London firm of Paul Storr (1771–1844), who later joined with the Royal Goldsmiths, Rundell, Bridge & Rundell, and was to become the most famous of all English goldsmiths apart from Paul de Lamerie (p. 155).

The son for whose birth the font was made died unmarried in 1824 and thus did not succeed to the dukedom.

FURTHER READING
Exhibition catalogue, *Treasures for the Nation: Conserving our heritage* (London, 1998), no. 54

The Portland Font
Hallmarked London,
England
22-carat gold, AD 1797–8
MLA 1986,4–3, 1
w. (pedestal) 34.9 cm
(13¾ in)
Purchased with the aid of
a grant from the National
Heritage Memorial Fund
and with funds
bequeathed by George
Bernard Shaw

The Portland Vase, a technical masterpiece, is the most famous cameo-glass vessel to have survived from antiquity. Cameo-glass vessels are rare, presumably because they were extremely difficult to make. The cobalt-blue body of the vase was blown into a preliminary shape before being coated in opaque white glass. It was then blown to full size; the shoulders and rim were shaped and the handles attached. When it was cool, part of the outer white layer was carved away to create the design.

The bottom of the vase was apparently broken in antiquity; originally it may have had another frieze of decoration above a pointed base. A cameo-glass disc, of separate origin but equally ancient, is known since the early seventeenth century AD to have replaced the broken base, and may have been attached in antiquity.

The meaning of the scenes is much disputed, but the scenario seems to be one of love and marriage with a mythological theme in a marine setting, assuming that the serpent-like creature is a *ketos* (sea-snake). One interpretation is the betrothal of Peleus (the mortal father of Achilles) and Thetis, a Nereid (p. 227). The other figures might then be Eros, Hermes, Aphrodite and two sea deities – Doris, mother of Thetis, and her husband Nereus; or Tethys, her grandmother, and her husband Oceanus. A new interpretation suggests that the figure with the *ketos* is Cleopatra seducing Antony; on the other side Octavia, Antony's abandoned wife, reclines in her broken home and is consoled by her brother Octavian. The figure on the glass disc is usually identified as Paris, called upon to judge the contest of beauty between Hera, Athena and Aphrodite.

The Portland Vase
Italy
1st century BC–1st century AD
GR 1945.9–27.1
h. 24.5 cm (9⅓ in)
Purchased from the Duke of Portland with the aid of a bequest from James Rose Vallentin

The vase was owned by the Dukes of Portland from 1785 to 1945, when it was purchased by the Museum, where it had been on loan since 1810. It was smashed in 1845, but was successfully restored. It was dismantled and reassembled in 1947 and again in 1988/9. The modern repair, to replace discoloured earlier adhesives, has been made by epoxy resin fused by ultraviolet light. The vase itself has had a great influence in Britain. Josiah Wedgwood (p. 356) copied it in pottery in the late eighteenth century, and the popularity of Wedgwood versions, in various sizes and finishes, has continued ever since.

FURTHER READING
N. Williams, *The Breaking and Remaking of the Portland Vase* (London, 1989)
D.E.L. Haynes, *The Portland Vase* (London, 1975)
S. Walker, *The Portland Vase*, British Museum Objects in Focus (London, 2004)

Predynastic burial

From the earliest Predynastic age, over 5000 years ago, the Egyptians took care over the burial of their dead. Bodies were laid to rest in shallow graves dug in the desert, arranged with the knees drawn up and the hands in front of the face. They were often wrapped in animal skins or reed matting, but were not otherwise protected from the sand filling of the grave.

The bodies did not decay because the hot dry sand removed all traces of the moisture which bacteria need to live. Consequently, bodies of this period have survived, wizened and leathery, but recognizable as people who lived more than 3000 years before the birth of Christ. Whether or not the lifelike appearance of such corpses gave rise to the Egyptian belief in an afterlife, they certainly made the survival of the body in a recognizable form a basic tenet of subsequent Egyptian funerary belief. If the corpse decayed, the spirit which survived death also perished. That is why embalming or mummification, artificial preservation by removing the perishable internal organs and drying out the corpse, only came into being after bodies ceased to be buried in the preservative sand (pp. 219–20).

This body, sometimes known as 'Ginger' from the reddish colour of his hair, was found at Gebelein in Egypt in 1900 by, so it is said, the then Keeper of Egyptian and Assyrian Antiquities, Sir Wallis Budge, in a large grave nearly covered by two or three large lumps of stone. The stones were tightly jammed together and so the body had been preserved complete. It is well supplied with grave goods of the period: various styles of pottery, a mudstone palette, stone vase, flint knife and beads, and its continued preservation is ensured by the Museum's Department of Conservation.

FURTHER READING
A.J. Spencer, *Early Egypt: The Rise of Civilisation in the Nile Valley* (London, 1993)

Naturally preserved
body of a man in a
reconstructed grave pit
Gebelein, Egypt
Late Predynastic, Naqada
II, *c*.3400 BC
EA 32751
l. (unflexed) 1.63 m
(5 ft 4⅓ in)

Qing dynasty porcelain

The last dynasty of imperial China, the Qing (AD 1644–1911), was established by foreigners, the Manchu, from the northeast, but in its aspirations and accomplishments it was Chinese in character. The three great emperors Kangxi (1662–1722), Yongzheng (1723–35) and Qianlong (1736–96) were admirers of Chinese culture and patrons of the arts and literature. Qianlong's reign particularly has been termed one of China's golden ages. The emperor regarded himself as a patron of the arts, inscribing his name and sentiments over many works of art, as well as writing much poetry and sponsoring numerous catalogues of the royal collections. He was an ardent collector of antiquities and aimed to assimilate every famous old painting, bronze or other object into the imperial collection. Some of the most interesting decorative schemes devised for porcelain were created at this time, large quantities being commissioned for the emperor himself.

In ceramics the great technical breakthroughs had occurred long before, but the products of the Qing are remarkable for their technical virtuosity. Most porcelain was produced in Jingdezhen in Jiangxi province, the site of the imperial factories which were rebuilt in AD 1677. Master craftsmen created superior works of art for the court, like the exquisitely painted imperial porcelain. Among the skilled techniques were *famille verte*, which appeared in the Kangxi period in the late seventeenth century, and *famille rose*, which was developed around 1720, an enamel combination including rose-pink and white which replaced *famille verte*. It became popular during the Yongzheng and Qianlong periods for the finest imperial porcelains as well as for cheap export wares. Some of the most stunning of all Qing porcelains are the monochromes, which employed a wide variety of glazes and hues to satisfy both secular and sacral demands. The range of colours includes such hues as 'egg yolk- and buttercup-yellow', 'morello cherry- and liver-red', lime green, turquoise, raspberry and deep violet.

Porcelain wine-cup with lime-green enamel
China
Qing dynasty, Yongzheng mark and period
(AD 1723–35)
OA 1943.2–15.23
h. 5 cm (2 in)
Marjorie K. Coldwell Bequest

FURTHER READING
S.J. Vainker, *Chinese Pottery and Porcelain, from Prehistory to the Present* (London, 1991; 2nd edn 2005)

Quetzalcoatl, the feathered serpent Aztec, 14th–16th centuries AD

A ztec traditions told that the priest-king of the early Toltecs – Quetzalcoatl Ce Acatl Topiltzin, 'Feathered Serpent, One Reed, our venerated Lord', identified with the great god Quetzalcoatl – would one day return to claim the throne from which he had been driven. He was described as pale-skinned and bearded, and had promised to return from the east in the year *ce acatl*, one reed. The year of the landing of Hernán Cortés and his conquistadors, AD 1519, corresponded to this Aztec year, and from that point the Aztec empire was doomed.

The first creator gods of the Aztecs, Two Lord and Two Lady, entrusted the creation of everything to their four sons. Each of these four gods was a manifestation of the all-powerful Tezcatlipoca, the Smoking Mirror. The Red Tezcatlipoca was also known as the Flayed God, Xipe Totec (p. 362); the Blue Tezcatlipoca was the Aztec tribal god Huitzilopochtli; the White Tezcatlipoca was the equivalent of the Plumed Serpent, Quetzalcoatl; the Black Tezcatlipoca was the Lord of the Night Sky.

The Aztecs believed that five worlds had been successively created and four destroyed. Quetzalcoatl ruled in the second, called the Wind Sun, before its destruction by hurricanes. The Aztecs considered that they were living in the fifth world, overseen by Tonatiuh, the Sun God, which would eventually be destroyed by earthquakes. The gods might prolong it for a little longer but if they were not amply fed with sacrificial victims the world would end.

Below is one of the Museum's representations of Quetzalcoatl. In the Nahuatl language Quetzalcoatl means 'quetzal-feather snake'. The plumed serpent was seen as a metaphor for wind-borne rain. The iridescent feathers of the quetzal bird were widely used to symbolize the verdant sources of life-giving moisture. The profile of the god-hero is shown emerging from the jaws of a serpent atop a swirling mass of feathered coils. The figure of the quetzal bird is found on the back of the sculpture. The curved shell ear ornaments (*epcololli*) and the staff in his right hand are identifying insignia.

Jade bust of Quetzalcoatl
Aztec
AD 1300–1521
ETH 1825.12–10.1
h. 32.5 cm (12¾ in)
Purchased from Revd
Dr Buckland, 1825

FURTHER READING
R.F. Townsend, *The Aztecs*
(London, 1992)

A *gamelan* is an Indonesian orchestra, mainly of percussion instruments. The famous *gamelan* in the Museum, acquired by Sir Thomas Stamford Raffles (1781–1826), the founder of Singapore, consists of 19 instruments. The quality of the carving is so high and the gilding so lavish that it probably belonged to the ruler of one of the royal courts (*kraton*) of Java. The orchestras were treated with great care, often having a special storeroom set aside for them, but sets would from time to time be disposed of.

In his *History of Java* (1817) Raffles wrote:

> ... it is the harmony and pleasing sound of all the instruments united, which gives the music of Java its peculiar character. ... The sounds produced on several of the instruments are peculiarly rich, and when heard at a distance have been frequently compared to those produced on the harmonic glasses.

Gamelan first developed in the Indonesian area before the seventh century AD. The instruments mainly comprise tuned gongs and metallophones. Gongs lay down the structure of the music, while other instruments add melody and elaboration. Players communicate not by gesture but by music alone, to produce a kaleidoscope of sound. There are various kinds and sizes of *gamelan*, the main differences being the number and type of instruments and the tonal system employed. *Gamelan* traditionally accompany puppet shows, dance-dramas, feasts and ceremonies. In the performances of the shadow puppets (*wayang kulit* or *wayang purwa*), the orchestra highlights and accentuates the moments of drama, and music appropriate to the personality of the characters accompanies their appearance on the screen. Below is a *saron demong*.

Raffles was appointed Lieutenant-Governor on the capture of Java in 1811. A keen linguist and zoologist, he collected widely and travelled extensively. Together with the *gamelan* the Museum acquired from Raffles's family a large number of Javanese puppets (including probably the earliest to survive), masks and bronzes. It is thanks to Raffles that the Museum possesses the finest collection of Javanese sculpture outside Java and the Netherlands.

Saron demong
(xylophone, fish body
with monster head)
Java
Probably late 18th
century AD
ETH 1859.12–28.201
l. 100 cm (39½ in)

FURTHER READING
N. Barley (ed.), *The Golden Sword: Stamford Raffles and the East* (London, 1999)
W.B. Fagg (ed.), *The Raffles Gamelan; A Historical Note* (London, 1970)

Bust of **Ramesses the Great**
Egypt, 13th century BC

Perhaps the most impressive of the Egyptian royal sculptures in the Museum is the bust of Ramesses II of the Nineteenth Dynasty, from his mortuary temple at Thebes, known as the Ramesseum. It was transported by Giovanni Belzoni in 1816 on the commission of the Swiss explorer J.-L. Burckhardt and Henry Salt, the British Consul. Weighing 7.25 tons, it is cut from a single block of two-coloured granite. The king wears the *nemes* headdress surmounted by a cobra diadem. The statue is one of a pair and was, in the early nineteenth century, known as the 'Younger Memnon', from the supposed identification of one of the two famous colossi on the Nile at Thebes with the Homeric character Memnon, son of Eos.

Ramesses II succeeded his father Sethos I in *c.*1304 BC and ruled for 67 years. Much of his reputation rests on his penchant for erecting grandiose sculptures of himself and appropriating others. The bust with its fine features and enigmatic smile is in no way a naturalistic representation: rather, it is carved according to certain conventions, which include setting the eyes so that the royal gaze is directed not straight ahead, as was normal, but downwards. After its arrival in the Museum the statue was perhaps the first piece of Egyptian sculpture to be recognized as a work of art by connoisseurs accustomed to judging by the standards of Greek art.

The hole on the right of the torso is said to have been made by members of Napoleon's expedition to Egypt at the end of the eighteenth century in an unsuccessful attempt to remove the statue.

The imminent arrival of the head in England in 1818 inspired the poet Percy Bysshe Shelley to write *Ozymandias*:

...'My name is Ozymandias, king of kings:
Look on my works, ye mighty, and despair!'
Nothing beside remains. Round the decay
Of that colossal wreck, boundless and bare,
The lone and level sands stretch far away.

Upper half of a colossal seated statue of
Ramesses II
Ramesseum, Thebes, Egypt
19th Dynasty, *c.*1270 BC
EA 19
h. 2.67 m (8 ft 9 in)
Given by J.-L. Burckhardt and H. Salt

FURTHER READING
K.A. Kitcher, *Pharaoh Triumphant* (Warminster, 1982)
A. Siliotti (ed.), *Belzoni's Travels* (London, 2001)

Raphael

Italy, early 16th century AD

The Museum has about 40 drawings by Raffaello Santi, called Raphael (AD 1483–1520). There is also a collection of prints after Raphael and, on loan from HM The Queen, a collection of prints and photographs after Raphael's paintings and drawings assembled for Prince Albert between 1853 and 1861 by Carl Ruland.

Raphael was born at Urbino, the son of a minor painter attached to the court, from whom he received his first lessons. He seems subsequently to have studied under Perugino, then the leading painter of the Umbrian school, and his imitation of the master's style has made it difficult sometimes to distinguish the originator of works of this period. From AD 1504 to 1508 Florence was the principal centre of his activity, although he maintained his contact with Umbria. In Florence he came under the influence of Leonardo da Vinci and Michelangelo, who then dominated the artistic scene. In 1508 Raphael left Florence and went to Rome at the invitation of Pope Julius II on the recommendation of the pope's chief architect, Bramante, also a native of Urbino. In Pope Julius Raphael found a patron with the vision, the means and the opportunity to employ him on large decorative projects. Raphael's principal work was the decoration of two rooms, the *Stanza della Segnatura* and the *Stanza d'Eliodoro*, in the apartment on the second floor of the Vatican into which the pope had decided to move in 1507. After Julius II's death in 1513 Raphael was employed by the new pope, Leo X, for whom his most important work was the series of cartoons for the tapestries intended for the Sistine Chapel. In 1514 Leo X appointed him chief architect of St Peter's in succession to Bramante, and in the following year made him responsible for inspecting, and if necessary acquiring, all antiquities discovered in or near Rome. Raphael died at the age of 37, a friend of cardinals and princes, a position never before attained by an artist.

FURTHER READING

J.A. Gere and N. Turner, *Drawings by Raphael from the Royal Library, the Ashmolean, the British Museum, Chatsworth and other English Collections* (London, 1983)
P. Pouncey and J.A. Gere, *Raphael and his Circle* (London, 1962)
N. Turner, *Florentine Drawings of the 16th Century* (London, 1986)

'The Virgin and Child': cartoon for the Mackintosh Madonna
Rome
Black chalk, with a few touches of white heightening, c.1512–14
PD 1894–7–21–1
71 × 53.5 cm (28 × 21 in)

The **Reading Room** Britain, mid-19th century AD

The British Museum Reading Room is a haunted place. Here Karl Marx wrote and researched *Das Kapital*, making his way here daily for almost 30 years, sitting, it is assumed, somewhere in the vicinity of rows K to P, near the reference books he would have used. Vladimir Ilyich Lenin made two visits, first under the alias of 'Jacob Richter' and later under his real name (Oulianoff). The anarchist Peter Kropotkin was another reader. The ill-fated dancer Isadora Duncan obtained a reader's ticket in 1899. Among the many politicians who were readers and whose lives can be said to have changed the nineteenth and twentieth centuries were Sun Yatsen, M.A. Jinnah, W.E. Gladstone, and Sidney and Beatrice Webb. Perhaps equally influential were the writers, among them Gibbon, Carlyle, Thackeray, Swinburne, Shaw, Conrad, Forster, Hardy, Bennett, Kipling and Yeats, and musicians such as Elgar and Holst. The writer Angus Wilson was Deputy Superintendent from 1951 to 1955. In 1984 Mikhail Gorbachev, on his first visit to Britain, toured the Reading Room and declared that any blame for communism should be attached to the British Museum. Among the fictional characters are the hero of Jerome K. Jerome's *Three Men in a Boat* (1889), who after a session in the Room claimed to have every ailment listed in the reference books, and Max Beerbohm's unsuccessful poet Enoch Soames, who in 1897 sold his soul to the devil for the opportunity to visit the Reading Room a hundred years later.

The British Museum library has provided a reading room for scholars since 1759 and the Round Reading Room is the seventh in the series. The present Museum building, largely designed by Sir Robert Smirke, was begun in 1823. Since the collections had to be housed during construction the plan was to build three wings to the north of the old building (Montagu House), forming a courtyard, the house itself to be demolished and replaced by the great south front. In the event the courtyard, completed in 1847, was soon occupied. In 1852 the Keeper of Printed Books, Antonio Panizzi, made proposals for a reading room and bookstacks to be inserted there. These plans were refined by the architect Sydney Smirke (brother of Sir Robert). Work began in 1854 and the room opened in 1857.

The dome of the reading room is supported on 20 cast-iron girders enclosed in brick casings. Its height is 33 metres (90½ feet) and the diameter 43 metres (118 feet), giving a floor area of 1,350 square metres (14,531 square feet) and 35,375 cubic metres (1,250,000 cubic feet) of space. The inner lining of the dome is papier mâché, 1.5 cm (a little over ½ in) thick. The initial decoration was blue and cream with elaborate gilding.

There were originally places for 302 readers at 35 tables (including two tables reserved for ladies), but this number was

The **Reading Room**

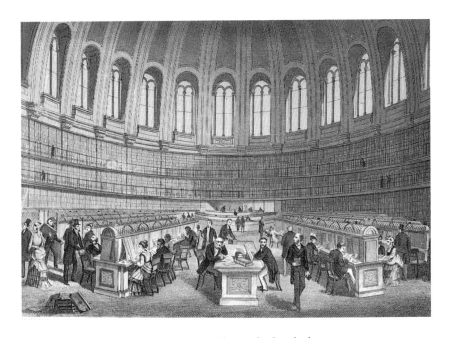

increased by extensions to some of the tables. Each place had an adjustable bookrest and a folding shelf for spare books, with space for an ink-stand and pen holders. The Superintendent sat in the 'keyhole' area in the northern segment, from which books were issued. Gaslight was never permitted and, before the introduction of electricity, it was common for the room to be closed early because of fog. The Museum's Trustees became involved in early experiments with electricity, starting in 1879, and in October 1880 four Siemens arc lamps of 5,000 candle-power each were in use.

The Reading Room
Built 1854–7, architect
Sydney Smirke
(1798–1877)

The bookstacks were demolished in 1998 in preparation for the redevelopment of the courtyard area following the departure of the British Library. The Reading Room was opened to all the Museum's visitors as a place for studying the collections and the societies which produced them. As the Walter and Leonore Annenberg Centre it now housed the Paul Hamlyn Library, with 25,000 books and a Collections Multimedia Public Access System (COMPASS), linking a computerized collections database with a sophisticated search facility.

FURTHER READING
P.R. Harris, *A History of the British Museum Library (1753–1973)* (London, 1998)
M. Caygill, *The British Museum Reading Room* (London, 2000)

The Museum's collection of over 80 of Rembrandt's drawings, one of the best-balanced in existence, has examples from every period of the artist's career. Rembrandt also experimented in both etching and drypoint prints, producing some 300 prints altogether, of every kind of subject. Impressions of almost all of them are held by the Museum, making this perhaps the best collection in the world. Where different states of the same print exist, the collection often includes examples of each. On the left is a drypoint of the Crucifixion. This is the fourth state, much changed from lighter and more worked earlier versions, and today generally regarded as a masterpiece. Some figures have been eliminated, but at the left a new figure on horseback has been introduced, wearing a mysterious hat, taken from the famous Renaissance medal of John Palaeologus by Pisanello (p. 204).

'Three Crosses'
Drypoint, 1653
PD 1973 U.942
37.9 × 43.8 cm
(15 × 17¼ in)
Clayton Mordaunt
Cracherode Bequest,
1799

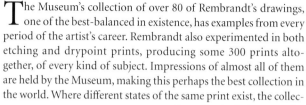

Rembrandt Harmensz. van Rijn (AD 1606–69) was born at Leiden in the Netherlands. In around 1621 he began a three-year apprenticeship with a local painter, Jacob van Swanenburgh, and subsequently studied for about six months in 1623–4 in Amsterdam with Pieter Lastman. Rembrandt settled permanently there in 1631 and was in considerable demand as a portraitist. He married Saskia van Uylenburgh in 1634. She died in 1642, a year after the birth of their son Titus, and by 1649 Rembrandt had become involved with a servant, Hendrickje Stoffels (left), who frequently modelled for him and remained his companion until his death.

'A Girl Sleeping'
(probably Hendrickje
Stoffels)
Brush drawing in brown
wash, c. 1655–6
PD 1895–9–15–1279
24.5 × 20.3 cm (9⅔ × 8 in)
Malcolm Collection

Throughout his career Rembrandt attracted students as both trainees and assistants. Their works can be hard to distinguish from Rembrandt's own. While agreement now surrounds the attribution of most of his prints, his drawings and paintings are still subject to debate.

FURTHER READING
M. Royalton-Kisch, *Drawings by Rembrandt and his Circle in the British Museum* (London, 1992)
E. Hinterding, G. Luijten and M. Royalton-Kisch, *Rembrandt the Printmaker* (London, 2000)

The **Ribchester helmet**

In 1796 a clogmaker's son, playing behind his father's house in Ribchester, Lancashire, discovered a mass of corroded metal-work. This proved to be a hoard of Roman military equipment, the most spectacular piece of which was a bronze face-mask vizor helmet with a scene of a skirmish between infantry and cavalry – today one of the most celebrated finds from Roman Britain.

During the Roman occupation of Britain, Ribchester, on the banks of the River Ribble, was the site of Bremetennacum Veteranorum, the largest Roman fort in Lancashire, standing at the junction of the roads to Chester, York and Carlisle.

Recent research has revealed that around AD 120 the helmet and the rest of the hoard seem to have been stored in a wooden box, probably beneath the floor of a barrack block. Until then the fort was garrisoned by a cavalry regiment, the Ala II Asturum. Auxiliary troops such as these served alongside the heavy infantry of the Roman legions. Their units were usually about 500 strong, normally recruited from new provinces or foreign tribes. The infantry regiments (*cohortes*) were always more numerous than the expensive *alae* of cavalry. A cavalry regiment would be led by a Prefect, the men divided into 16 troops under Decurions.

The hoard consists mainly of cavalry sports equipment and military awards. Cavalry sports – *hippika gymnasia* were flamboyant displays of military horsemanship and weapons drill. They served both to entertain the troopers and to keep them at peak performance. The most colourful events were mock battles among the elite riders of the unit, often in the guise of Greeks and Amazons (p. 19). Elaborate suites of equipment for both men and horses were worn on these occasions. The richly decorated metal fittings of the Ribchester suite include helmet, military awards, harness, discs and pendants, saddle plates and horse eye-guards.

Cavalry sports helmet
Ribchester, Britain
late 1st–early 2nd
century AD
PRB 1814 7–5 1
h. 27.6 cm (10⁹/₁₀ in)

FURTHER READING
R.P.J. Jackson and P.T. Craddock, 'The Ribchester Hoard' in B. Raffery, V. Megaw and V. Rigby (eds), *Sites and Sights of the Iron Age* (Oxford, 1995), pp. 75–102
B.J.N. Edwards, *The Ribchester Hoard* (Preston, Lancs, 1992)

Rings

A group of Anglo-Saxon
gold finger-rings
All found in England
9th–10th centuries AD
CLOCKWISE FROM TOP LEFT
MLA 55,11–15,1;
1829,11–14,1; AF 458;
1955,12–1,1; Ring Cat.184

A group of gold finger-
rings from the classical
world
CLOCKWISE FROM TOP LEFT
Roman
GR 1917.5–1.614;
BM Cat. Finger Rings 614
Western Greek
*c.*4th century BC
GR 1842.7–28.134;
BM Cat. Finger Rings 42
Roman, from Tarsus
3rd century AD
GR 1917.5–1.188; BM Cat.
Finger Rings 188
Mycenaean, from Tomb
93, Enkomi, Cyprus
GR 1897.4–1.546; BM Cat.
Finger Rings 7
Hellenistic
3rd century BC
GR 1865.7–12.55; BM Cat.
Finger Rings 95

Rings have been worn from ancient times to the present. Queen Pu-abi, who died almost 5000 years ago in the city of Ur (pp. 341–2), had ten of gold and lapis lazuli. Seianti Hanunia Tlesnasa, the Etruscan matron (p. 289), is portrayed wearing six on her left hand. The earliest Egyptian rings date from about the beginning of the Twelfth Dynasty (*c.*1800 BC).

The Museum has probably the most representative collection in existence (the Franks collection bequeathed in 1897 alone comprises over 3000). There is, for example, a sixteenth-century BC Minoan signet-ring from Crete engraved with a scene of two wild goats mating, and a third-century BC La Tène ring of silver wire, found in Britain.

Apart from decoration, rings have been worn for many purposes: for betrothal and marriage; as charms against the evil eye; as marks of rank, wealth or social status; in remembrance or support of people, events or causes; as credentials or signs of investiture; as seals; even to carry poison. Probably their earliest use was to make impressions upon clay, wax, or similar yielding material. At different times different fingers and joints were used. The Greeks and Romans used first the third finger, next the first finger, finally the little finger, but avoided the middle finger – the *digitus infamus*. In the medieval period the third was perhaps the most favoured, especially for betrothal and marriage rings. A thumb-ring was quite commonly worn by both sexes down to the sixteenth century AD. Archers in Europe and the Orient also wore these. The practice of wearing rings on the upper joints was not uncommon. Rings were worn over gloves, especially by ecclesiastics.

Rings are found in a variety of materials. The earliest Roman rings were of iron, gold being reserved for certain classes of persons or for special occasions. Other materials found over the centuries are silver, glass, ivory, bone, bronze, horn, precious and semi-precious stones and, rarely, lead, horn or amber.

FURTHER READING
F.H. Marshall, *Catalogue of the Finger Rings, Greek, Etruscan, and Roman, in the Departments of Antiquities, British Museum* (London, 1907)
O.M. Dalton, *Catalogue of the Finger Rings, Early Christian, Byzantine, Teutonic, Mediaeval and later bequeathed by Sir Augustus Wollaston Franks* (London, 1912)

Britain became a province of the Roman Empire in AD 43. For nearly 400 years (until AD 410) Britain's law, administrative system and currency were those of Rome.

The imperial culture was a vital factor in Roman military and civil administration, combining religious and political elements. Deceased rulers were often deified and though technically the living emperor, who was the state's chief priest, was not himself worshipped as a god, his *numen*, the spirit of his power and authority, was. The coinage was the primary means of disseminating both the image of the ruler and information about his achievements. In addition, statues and busts in stone and bronze and occasionally even precious metal, colossal, life-size and smaller, were placed in a variety of official and public settings. Such images symbolized the power of the state and the essential unity of the empire.

Below is a bronze head of Claudius (*r.*AD 41–54), part of a life-sized statue found in the River Alde at Rendham near Saxmundham, Suffolk, which may have come from a statue displayed in nearby Camulodunum (Colchester), a colony of army veterans. The conquest of Britain provided a military triumph for Claudius, a studious academic who had been unexpectedly elevated to power.

Above is Hadrian (*r.*AD 117–138), who was responsible for the building of the wall from the Solway to the Tyne. Found in the River Thames near London Bridge in 1834, the head is from a larger than life-size statue which probably stood in a public space in Roman London. The statue may have been erected to commemorate Hadrian's visit to Britain in AD 122.

The Museum also has a fine statuette of Nero (AD 54–68), Claudius' adopted son and successor, shown in the guise of Alexander. It is said to be from Barking Hall, Suffolk, but probably comes from Baylham Mill near Ipswich.

Hadrian (*r.*AD 117–138)
Britain
2nd century AD
PRB 1848 11–3 1
h. 43 cm (17 in)

Claudius (*r.*AD 41–54)
Britain
Bronze, 1st century AD
PRB 1965 12–1 1
h. 30 cm (11¾ in)
Found 1907

FURTHER READING
D.J. Breeze and B. Dobson, *Hadrian's Wall* (3rd edn, Harmondsworth, 1987)
T.W. Potter, *Roman Britain* (2nd edn, London, 1997)

The Rosetta Stone contains a copy of a decree passed by a general council of priests which assembled at Memphis on the first anniversary of the coronation of Ptolemy V Epiphanes (205–180 BC), King of all Egypt, on 27 March 196 BC. The text is in two languages, ancient Egyptian and Greek (53 lines). The Egyptian is written in two scripts, hieroglyphic (14 lines), the formal, monumental script of ancient Egypt, and demotic (32 lines), a later, cursive form.

The stone was discovered in AD 1799 by a detachment of French soldiers of Napoleon's army under the command of Pierre François Xavier Bouchard in the village of el-Rashid (Rosetta), in the Western Delta of the River Nile. When the British defeated the French the stone was ceded to the British king, George III, under the terms of the Treaty of Alexandria (1801) and given by him to the British Museum.

Knowledge of hieroglyphs had been lost in antiquity, and they were believed to be symbolic. A Swedish diplomat, J.K. Åkerblad (1763–1819), identified several proper names in the demotic

The Rosetta Stone
Fort Saint Julien,
el-Rashid, Western Delta,
Egypt
Ptolemaic, 196 BC
EA 24
h. (max) 1.14 m (3 ft 9 in)
Given by King George III,
1802

The **Rosetta Stone**

version of the Rosetta Stone, including that of Ptolemy, and a number of other words through knowing the equivalents in Coptic, the method of writing used by the Christian descendants of the ancient Egyptians from the turn of the third century AD.

The first to recognize that Egyptian writing (pp. 116–17) included alphabetic as well as non-alphabetic signs was Thomas Young (1773–1829). After studying a copy of the demotic section on the Stone in summer 1814, Young realized that the alphabetic theory for demotic already proposed by scholars such as Åkerblad was inaccurate. More importantly, Young grasped the fact that hieroglyphs and demotic were closely related. His method was to find a word in the Greek text which occurred more than once and then look for a group of signs in the demotic section which occurred approximately an equal number of times. From this probable identification Young compiled a Greek-demotic vocabulary amounting to 86 groups of signs, mostly correct in identification although nearly all incorrect in transliteration. He then demonstrated that the elongated ovals or cartouches in the hieroglyphic section contained the royal name Ptolemy. He also identified correctly the phonetic value of six hieroglyphic signs, and a further three signs partly correctly.

Young published his results in 1819. Jean-François Champollion (1790–1832), however, believed that hieroglyphs were symbolic and without phonetic value, until he saw in 1821 a copy of the inscriptions in hieroglyphs and Greek on an obelisk and its base excavated by W.J. Bankes at Philae in 1818. Bankes had rightly guessed that one of the cartouches contained the name Cleopatra.

Comparing the new cartouche with that of Ptolemy on the Rosetta Stone, Champollion saw that they showed three signs (P, O, L) in common, occurring in the right positions for an alphabetical spelling of 'Ptolemy' and 'Cleopatra'. This discovery convinced him that hieroglyphs, at least in some cases, had phonetic values. He then realized that phonetic signs wrote not only foreign names, such as Ptolemy, but the ancient Egyptian language. This realization marked the breakthrough in the decipherment of hieroglyphs.

In September 1822 Champollion presented to the French Academy his 'Lettre à M. Dacier', in which he corrected and greatly enlarged the list of phonetic hieroglyphs drawn up by Young. Subsequently he went on to formulate a system of grammar and to lay the foundations on which present knowledge of the language of the ancient Egyptians is based.

The grey granitoid stone weighs 762 kg (15 cwt). It is incomplete and was probably originally some 50 cm (20 in) higher, perhaps with a rounded top and carvings of the king.

FURTHER READING
R. Parkinson, *The Rosetta Stone,* British Museum Objects in Focus (London, 2005)

The Royal Gold Cup is one of the finest objects in the Museum. Made in Paris in *c.*1380 for the great patron Jean, Duc de Berry (1340–1416), and presented to his brother, the King of France Charles V (1337–80), it passed to his nephew Charles VI (1368–1422) and came into the hands of John of Lancaster, Duke of Bedford, third son of Henry IV of England. From the Duke it passed to his nephew Henry VI. The inserted collar in the stem with a rose records its ownership by the Tudors.

The cup was given by King James I of England and VI of Scotland (1566–1625) to the Spaniard Juan de Velasco, Duke of Frias and Constable of Castile, following the signing of a peace treaty between England and Spain in 1604. The Latin inscription in black enamel on the stem records its next change of ownership and can be translated: 'This cup of solid gold, a relic of the sacred trea-

The Royal Gold Cup
Paris
*c.*AD 1380
MLA 1892,5–1, 1
h. 23.6 cm (9¼ in)
Purchased with the aid of the Treasury, the Worshipful Company of Goldsmiths, the Duke of Northumberland, the Earl of Crawford, Lord Savile, Lord Iveagh, Sir Augustus Wollaston Franks, C. Drury Fortnum, S. Wertheimer

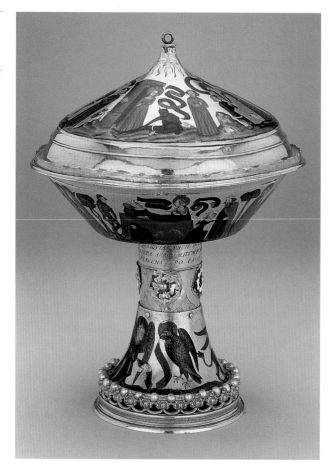

The **Royal Gold Cup**

sure of England and a memorial to the peace made between the kings, the Constable Juan de Velasco, returning thence after successfully accomplishing his mission, presented as an offering to Christ the Peacemaker'. This refers to de Velasco's gift of the cup to the nuns of the convent of Medina de Pomar in 1610. It remained there until it was sold in Paris in the late nineteenth century.

Made of gold, the cup is richly decorated with *pointillé* (punched work) and glowing translucent enamel *en basse taille* (in sunk or low relief). On the foot are the symbols of the Four Evangelists – Saints Matthew (angel), Mark (winged lion), Luke (ox) and John (eagle). Originally the cup stood on a gold tripod in the form of three winged serpents, the cover having a cresting of pearls similar to that around the foot, topped by an elaborate jewelled finial.

The scenes (which should be read anti-clockwise, beginning on the cover and ending on the bowl) depict the life and miracles of St Agnes, the daughter of a wealthy Roman of the time of the Emperor Constantine (*c.*AD 274–337). St Agnes first refuses marriage to Procopius, son of a high official, who approaches her with a rich jewel casket while his father looks on. She declares herself God's spouse. After being denounced as a Christian and condemned to life in a brothel, Agnes is attacked by Procopius, who is strangled by a demon. His father witnesses the scene. Agnes restores Procopius, who kneels before her. She tells him to go and sin no more, while his father declares her innocence. Agnes is then condemned to burn. The flames have no effect on her and she is finally martyred by a spear driven into her neck. Emerentia, her sister, is stoned for her faith before the martyr's tomb. Agnes, followed by three other virgin martyrs, appears to her parents at the tomb. Finally the leper Princess Constantia lies upon Agnes's tomb, which has become an object of veneration to the sick and crippled. Agnes appears and heals Constantia, who kneels before her father Constantine and tells him of the saint's virtues.

FURTHER READING
O.M. Dalton, *The Royal Gold Cup in the British Museum* (London, 1924)

O f the 'five great wares' designated during the time of the last two Chinese imperial dynasties, the Ming and Qing – Ding, Ru, Jun, Guan and Ge – only two, Ru and Guan, were exclusively made for imperial use, and of these Ru ware is today the rarest.

A grey-blue glazed ceramic, it was made in Henan province at a kiln site recently identified as Qing liangsi village in Baofeng county. It is thought to have been made for the Northern Song court for a very short time – a mere two decades from *c.*AD 1106 to 1126 – for the Emperor Huizong (*r.*AD 1100–26). These pieces were rare even then. With its simple forms and absence of decoration, Ru ware is perfectly understated. It is prized, like jade, for tactile quality, subtle colour variations and the unpredictable pattern of the crackle of the glaze. Until recently, when the kiln site was discovered with fragments of vessels, there were thought to be fewer than 40 examples surviving, more than half of them in Britain. The Museum has five pieces, plus a Ru-type vessel and one with an inscription which has been misfired.

Lotus-petal Ru ware cup stand, lavender-glazed
Henan province, North China
Northern Song dynasty, early 12th century AD
OA 1971.9–21.1
h. 7.6 cm (3 in)
Given by Sir Harry and Lady Garner

The Song dynasty (AD 960–1279) marked the summit of imperial China's intellectual achievements. It fell into two phases, the Northern (960–1126) and the Southern Song (1127–1279). Although China's borders were under constant threat from invading peoples, the Song did not, and perhaps could not, seek military victory. To keep the Qidan and the Tanguts at bay in the north they bribed them heavily. When the Ruzhen invaded in the 1110s the Song retreated southwards. Finally, when the Mongol armies swept through China in the thirteenth century, the Song dynasty ceased to exist.

FURTHER READING
S.J. Vainker, *Chinese Pottery and Porcelain, from Prehistory to the Present* (London, 1991; 2nd edn 2005)
Wang Qing-zheng, Fan Dong-qing, Zhou Lili (trans. L. Chin and X. Jie), *The Discovery of Ru Kiln: A Famous Song-Ware Klin of China* (Hong Kong, 1991)

Rubens (1577–1640) trained as an artist in Antwerp, his family's home, and in 1598 was registered as an independent master in the Antwerp Guild. He left for Italy in 1600, working for the Gonzaga family in Mantua and for other patrons in Rome and Genoa. When he returned to Antwerp in 1608 his reputation was established.

Rubens rapidly became the most favoured painter at the court of Archduke Albert. In 1609 he married Isabella Brant (*d.*1626), seen below in a portrait drawn *c.*1622. From 1612 he designed book illustrations for the Plantin Press in Antwerp. His contact with the English court began in 1612, when he painted the portrait of the Earl of Arundel. In the 1620s he worked for Charles I and the Duke of Buckingham, as well as a number of other royal patrons including Louis XIII of France, Marie de' Medici and Philip IV of Spain. A growing team of pupils and assistants collaborated on his paintings. His fame increased through engravings of his works made by professional printmakers working under his supervision.

In 1630 Rubens married the 16-year-old Hélène Fourment and in 1635 he bought a country house, the Château de Steen, where he spent much of his later life, the grounds inspiring several landscape paintings.

The Museum has a superlative collection of some 80 drawings by Rubens, as well as 40 drawings from his so-called 'Costume Book', an early compilation of study material from various sources, and a series of 28 rapid sketches after antique coins. All periods of his career and most aspects of his interests are represented. Only one print, an etching of St Catherine of Alexandria, is believed to be by Rubens himself, although the attribution is uncertain. The Museum has impressions of this print as well as a large series of the reproductive engravings made after his designs.

FURTHER READING
J.K. Rowlands, *Rubens, Drawings and Sketches* (London, 1977)

'**Portrait of Isabella Brant**'
The Netherlands
Black, red and white chalks on light brown paper, *c.*AD 1622
PD 1893–7–31–21
38.1 × 29.5 cm
(15 × 11⅗ in)

The manufacture of fine porcelain was well established in Imperial Russia. After the Revolution of 1917 the stocks of undecorated blanks held in reserve at the Imperial Porcelain Factory in St Petersburg were decorated with revolutionary designs and used to disseminate the new propaganda. The factory was renamed the State Porcelain Factory and its new art director, Sergei Chekhonin, recruited outstanding artists, whose designs were copied by the factory painters. St Petersburg itself was renamed Petrograd from 1914 to 1924, and then Leningrad.

This plate commemorates the assassination in 1918 of the Jewish revolutionary and commissar Mosei Uritzky. He is shown in Palace Square, renamed 'Uritzky Square' in his honour, but today again known as Palace Square. To the left is the Alexander Column and, behind, the General Staff Headquarters. The plate was designed by Alexandra Shchekotikhina-Pototskaya (1892–1967), who had previously studied in Paris and designed for Diaghilev. This is one of her most famous and characteristic designs for porcelain, with its deliberate disregard for perspective, its use of the whole surface of the plate and its lively imagery.

The Museum holds some eighteen pieces of revolutionary porcelain, many with propaganda slogans and illustrating a wide variety of styles, whether inspired by Russian folklore, by the dynamism of the Futurist style, or the abstract shapes of the Suprematist movement.

Porcelain plate,
'Petrograd, Uritzky
Square'
USSR
AD 1922
MLA 1990,5–6, 7
diam. 23.7 cm (9½ in)
Given by the British
Museum Society

FURTHER READING

J. Rudoe, *Decorative Arts 1850–1950. A Catalogue of the British Museum Collection* (2nd edn, London, 1994), cat. 2, 18, 34–5, 278–80, 337, 340–1, 343, 345, 350, 352–3, 356–7

N. Lobanov-Rostovsky, *Revolutionary Ceramics. Soviet Porcelain 1917–1927* (London, 1990)

Sakhmet

Sakhmet was a lion goddess who was regarded by the Egyptians as a bringer of destruction to the enemies of the sun-god Re, and also a goddess who could ward off dangers and diseases. Her name meant 'she who is powerful'. Because of the rise to power of the Theban rulers of the New Kingdom (1550–1609 BC), the Theban triad of gods (Amun, Mut and Khonsu) became correspondingly more important and began to absorb the attributes of other deities. Thus Sakhmet was increasingly represented as an aggressive manifestation of the goddess Mut. She appears to have been an object of special veneration to King Amenhotep III (1417–1379 BC), who caused an enormous quantity of statues of her to be erected in his mortuary temple in Western Thebes, later moved to the temple of Mut at Karnak.

Nearly 600 of these statues have now been accounted for; the Museum has fragments of over 20, the largest collection outside Egypt (where a considerable number of the original group can still be seen *in situ*).

In the four statues shown here the head of the goddess is surmounted by the solar disc and she clasps the symbol of life (the *ankh*) in one of her hands. The standing versions hold, in addition, a sceptre in the form of a papyrus. One of the seated statues is inscribed on the throne-front with the king's names and a dedication to 'Sakhmet, who smites the Nubians'.

FURTHER READING
G. Hart, *A Dictionary of Egyptian Gods and Goddesses* (London, 1986)

Four black granite statues of the goddess Sakhmet
Temple of Mut, Thebes, Egypt
18th Dynasty, *c.*1400 BC
EA 76, 57, 62, 80
h. *c.*2.18 m (7 ft 2 in)

Group of iron *tsuba*
Japan
CLOCKWISE FROM TOP
RIGHT
AD 1683
JA 1948.11–27.13
max. diam. 8.3 cm
(3¼ in)

17th century
JA 1948.11–27.57
diam. 7.2 cm (2¾ in)

18th century
JA 1948.11–27.43
diam. 7.9 cm (3 in)

The sword blade produced for the samurai or warriors of Japan is arguably superior to most others as a cutting weapon, and its technology demonstrates the skill of Japanese steel-making a millennium ago. The shape and surface texture of the steel of a finely polished blade have an intrinsic beauty.

The slight changes in sword shape over the ages, together with changing patterns on the tempered edge, indicate the time and province of manufacture of the blade. For around 1000 years swordsmiths have signed and dated their work on the tangs of the blades. In no other art was the individual allowed so early to mark his presence and personality, a telling proof of the extremely high prestige of the swordmaker in Japan.

AD 1845
JA TS 47
l. 8.5 cm (3⅓ in)

Muromachi period,
15th or 16th century
JA 1948.11–27.1
diam. 8.6 cm (3⅓ in)

17th century
JA TS 1
l. 8.5 cm (3⅓ in)

The special method of manufacture of the traditional sword involves first a repeated folding and hammering out, and finally a heating and quenching in water to harden the edge. The resulting blade has a tough and resilient core to withstand the shock of cutting hard objects, and an edge as hard as carbon steel can be while still retaining its strength. The main visual features of a finely polished blade are the grain of the body of the blade and the *hamon*, or pattern due to the hard crystalline structure along the cutting edge. The major types of grain are *masame* (straight longitudinal grain), *itame* (wood-plank grain) and *mokume* (a kind of wood grain with concentric contours). The *hamon* results from the special method of hardening the blade. The whole blade is covered

Samurai swords and sword guards

with a layer of clay which is partially scraped away along the edge, leaving it only thinly covered, and producing therefore a recognizable 'shadow' after tempering. The blade is then heated, according to tradition to the colour of the moon in February or August, and then quenched in water. The resulting more hardened structure of the edge is classified as of two types, according to the size of the crystals. *Nioi* ('fragrance') is a continuous white structure in which the individual crystals are not discernible. *Nie* ('boiling') is a continuous band of bright crystals, traditionally likened to frost on grass.

The Museum's collection of over 200 blades contains several fine items from the earliest periods. The earliest dates from the Heian period (AD 795–1285); the latest was made around the end of the nineteenth century. On the right is a shortened fourteenth-century *tachi* (long) blade attributed to the swordsmith Sa (Saemon Saburo). The *hamon* has bright lines of *nie* crystals.

Sword guards, known as *tsuba* (opposite) were kept separately. They were the subject of minute workmanship and were regarded as works of art in their own right. Some indicate the religious awareness of the samurai, with Buddhist or Shinto subjects; others depict the beauties of nature or poetic themes. Some, however, are more light-hearted, with references to folk stories or popular deities.

FURTHER READING
V. Harris, *Cutting Edge: Japanese Swords in the British Museum* (London, 2004)

Shortened *tachi* blade
Chikuzen Province, Japan
14th century AD
JA 1958.7–30.64
l. 70.1 cm (27½ in)
R.W. Lloyd Bequest

Sardinian bronzes

The 'Nuraghic' culture, named after the great *nuraghi* or towers built by the inhabitants of the Mediterranean island of Sardinia, was in existence by 1600 BC and lasted more than a thousand years. The rugged nature of the island, with its almost inaccessible interior, meant that its inhabitants maintained a strong individual identity throughout the period, though there is considerable evidence of foreign trade.

The culture is noted for its lively bronze statuettes. Many such figures, of warriors, musicians and women, were deposited as offerings in sacred wells. Shown here are two warriors: an archer, wearing a horned cap, draws his bow; he wears a rectangular breastplate and greaves to protect his shins, and is armed also with two daggers, one in his quiver and another behind his breastplate; a warrior, perhaps a chief, rests on a knotted staff.

Two Nuraghic bronzes
Sardinia, Italy
*c.*1000–900 BC
(resting chief)
GR 1974.12–1.1;
Bronze 338
h. 19 cm (7½ in)
(archer) GR 1974.12–1.2;
Bronze 337
h. 19 cm (7½ in)

Over six thousand *nuraghi* survive, constructed from massive stone blocks. The earliest were probably farmhouses, but defence seems always to have been a priority, with the later ones resembling complex fortresses. The nature of the earliest hostilities is unclear. From *c.*900 BC people from western central Italy traded with the island, and during the eighth century BC Phoenicians (p. 251) from Carthage in North Africa founded colonies there. The Phoenicians called the people the Shardana. It has been suggested that they may at one time have raided into Egypt. Before 500 BC, however, the Phoenicians had ransacked and destroyed many of the *nuraghi*, no doubt as part of an attempt to control the rich ore-bearing regions. Sardinia came under Roman rule after the First Punic War in 265–241 BC, but the Nuraghic people may have continued to inhabit the interior for several centuries.

FURTHER READING
M. Guido, *Sardinia* (London, 1963)
E. Macnamara, D. Ridgway and F.R. Ridgway, *The Bronze Hoard from Santa Maria in Paulis, Sardinia*, British Museum Occasional Paper no. 45 (London, 1984)
S. Moscari, *Italy before Rome: Greeks, Phoenicians, Etruscans, Italians* (Milan 1987), pt II, VI, 'Sardinia', pp. 135–63

Sasanian silver

'And Bahram, that Great Hunter – the Wild Ass Stamps o'er His Head, and he lies fast asleep.' So goes one of the stanzas in Fitzgerald's *Rubaiyat of Omar Khayyam*. Below is a link with this quotation, a silver bowl showing a Sasanian king hunting lions. Judging by the crown, this may represent Varahan V (also known as Bahram Gur; AD 421–39), whose hunting exploits became legendary. Royal hunting scenes such as this are a hall-mark of Sasanian art.

The Sasanian Empire was founded by Ardashir I (r.AD 224–40) from the province of Fars, just north of Persepolis, who led a successful revolt against the Parthian (p. 247) king Artabanus V, later commemorated on rock-cut reliefs in southern and western Iran. The dynasty takes its name from one of Ardashir's ancestors, who claimed descent from the last Achaemenid king. The Sasanian kings aimed to revive the glories of the Achaemenid Empire (p. 11). They adopted the Parthian capital of Ctesiphon, built up a strong army and centralized administration. Zoroastrianism was adopted as the state religion, although there were significant Christian, Jewish, Buddhist, gnostic and pagan religious communities.

Silver bowl
Sasanian
5th–7th centuries AD
WA 124092;
1897–12–31, 187
diam. 27.4 cm (10¾ in)
A.W. Franks Bequest

The empire extended from Mesopotamia into the Caucasus, Central Asia and Pakistan. There was heavy investment in large-scale irrigation, aimed at increasing taxable agricultural output. The Sasanian Empire was a major economic and military rival of Rome and later of Byzantium, and had contacts with the Far East via Central Asia. Gold and silver vessels were made in large quantities and these, together with high-quality cut glass, were traded as far east as China, Korea and Japan.

Weakened by internal strife and further wars in the West, the Sasanian Empire fell to repeated Muslim Arab attacks, culminating in the Islamic Conquest during the mid-seventh century AD. However, Sasanian art, administration and the economy continued to have profound effects on early Islamic developments.

FURTHER READING
R. Ghirshman, *Iran: Parthians and Sasanians* (London, 1962)

The Museum holds the national collection of single-sheet satires, prints published in large numbers from the seventeenth to the early nineteenth centuries. In the earlier period they were largely emblematic and allegorical in character; from the mid-eighteenth century they adopted the distortions of the Italian portrait *caricatura* to produce the type of print that is still familiar from the work of Gillray and Rowlandson. After the 1830s such prints stopped being produced singly, as the rise of the illustrated newspaper meant that the artists were now employed to make what today we call cartoons.

The most flourishing tradition of such prints was in Britain, and these satires are in many ways the most original British contribution to European art. The Museum has had an incomparable representation of British material since the purchase in 1868 of the collection formerly owned by Edward Hawkins (Keeper of Antiquities at the Museum 1826–60). The Museum now has over 17,000.

Below is a print by George Cruikshank featuring the Museum itself in Montagu House (now demolished). A frost-bitten procession headed by the Arctic explorer John Ross (1777–1856) extends from the coast, where huskies swim ashore from a boat, to the gate of the British Museum where Sir Joseph Banks, a Trustee, and Dr Leach, Keeper, can barely contain their excitement. The expedition, fresh from an 1818 attempt to find the North-West Passage, is laden with specimens for the natural history collections – a polar bear, worms found in seal intestines, red snow (melted), a sea-unicorn horn – while a citizen complains that 'I think we have Bears, Gulls, Savages, Chump wood, Stones and Puppies enough without going to the North Pole for them'.

'Landing the Treasures, or Results of the Polar Expedition!!!'
George Cruikshank
(AD 1792–1878)
AD 1819
PD George 13194
19 × 53 cm (7½ × 20⅞ in)

FURTHER READING
F.G. Stephens (I–IV, 1870–83) and D. George (V–XI, 1935–54), *Catalogue of Personal and Political Satires in the British Museum*

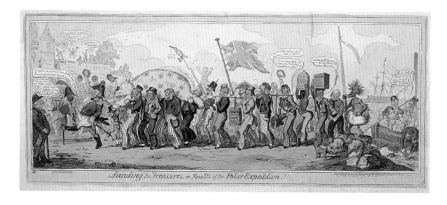

The **Savernake horn**

This ancient horn was last sounded officially when King George VI visited Savernake Forest in Wiltshire in 1940. The association of the horn with Savernake Forest was first made by the Elizabethan antiquary William Camden (1551–1623), who in 1610 recorded the horn as owned by the Seymours, Earls of Hertford. They kept it to mark their descent from the Esturmy family, bailiffs and guardians of the forest from the time of King Henry II (1133–89) until 1427, when the wardenship passed to the Seymours through marriage with the last Esturmy heiress.

Although perhaps originally a hunting horn, the Savernake Horn had become a symbol of office by the fourteenth century AD. It is made of elephant ivory, probably of eleventh- or twelfth-century date, and may have been produced in southern Italy. The two topmost silver bands were added in the fourteenth century. The band at the mouth and the one next to it are enamelled with hunting dogs and animals of the chase; the central panels of the band around the mouth show a king seated between a bishop and a forester. The leather baldric (the strap by which it was carried) is in two parts, decorated with silver discs bearing the arms of the first Scottish earldom of Moray, created in 1312 and extinct by 1347.

The horn and baldric were made separately but had come together by the early seventeenth century when they are shown on a pedigree of the Seymour family. It is not known why the arms of a Scottish earl are associated with a horn connected to the English forest of Savernake. One suggestion is that it might have fallen into Scottish hands during the wars of the early fourteenth century.

The Savernake Horn
Savernake Forest,
Wiltshire, England (horn
carved in southern Italy)
11th–14th centuries AD
MLA 1975,4–1,1
l. (along line of horn)
63.5 cm (25 in)
Purchased with the aid of
the National Art
Collections Fund, the
Pilgrim Trust and the
Worshipful Company
of Goldsmiths

FURTHER READING
R. Camber and J. Cherry,
'The Savernake Horn',
Collectors and Collections.
The British Museum Year-
book, 2 (London, 1977),
pp. 201–11

Scarabs

Gold rings with swivelling bezels, six with scarabs
Egypt
12th–22nd Dynasties,
c.1820–924 BC
MIDDLE AND BOTTOM ROWS,
FROM LEFT TO RIGHT
EA 49717; 14345; 36466;
65316; 37308; 2933
l. (of scarab, centre)
2.3 cm (⅞ in)

Colossal granite scarab
Egyptian, found at
Constantinople
c.200 BC
EA 74
h. 89 cm (35 in)
Purchased by the British
Government from Lord
Elgin, 1816

Scarabs are ubiquitous in Egyptian art. From the Sixth Dynasty they were the most popular subjects for amulets, and later functioned as seals. Perhaps the most magnificent in the Museum is the colossal granite scarab (below) brought back by Lord Elgin from Constantinople. This probably stood until Roman times in a court of a temple, perhaps the temple of Re at Heliopolis.

The Egyptian scarab (*Scarabaeus sacer*), or dung beetle, rolls a large ball of animal dung with its back legs to an underground hiding place, where it serves as a foodstuff. Such is the size of the ball that the beetle has to stand almost on its head while pushing, usually for a considerable distance. Since the scarab is unable to see where it is going, it often takes a route which is not only circuitous but beset with obstacles. The Egyptians likened the rolling of the ball of dung to the passage of the sun-disc across the heavens each day from east to west, pushed by a gigantic black beetle.

The Egyptians also regarded the scarab as a symbol of new life and resurrection. Scarab eggs are laid in a ball of dung which feeds the larvae when they hatch. This is created by the female from sheep excrement and is pear-shaped; the Egyptians, however, believed that baby beetles hatched out of the round type of ball. Mature scarabs sometimes appear to burst out of the earth from their empty underground larders when a new heap of dung is deposited in the vicinity.

As a hieroglyph the scarab has the phonetic value HPR (*kheper*), which as a verb means 'to come into being', 'to be created', and as a noun 'form' or 'manifestation'. According to the legend of creation centred on the city of Heliopolis, the new-born sun was called Khepri and usually took the form of a man with a scarab beetle for a head. However, it was always as a large black beetle that Khepri was depicted in funerary scenes, representing the passage of the sun god from night and darkness into the new day and new life.

FURTHER READING
C. Andrews, *Amulets of Ancient Egypt*
(London, 1994)

Seals and seal impressions

For 7000 years the act of sealing has guaranteed authenticity, marked ownership, indicated participation in a legal transaction or protected goods against theft. Some seals are a fascinating record of the religious beliefs of their owners, of contemporary fashions or developments in dress, architecture, transport, music, sport, festivals, myths, patterns and iconography. Seals and writing developed together, first emerging in ancient Mesopotamia. Some of the earliest stamp seals date to the seventh and sixth millennia BC and come from the sites of Buqras in Syria and Çatal Hüyük in central Turkey. The first administrative clay sealings (impressions)

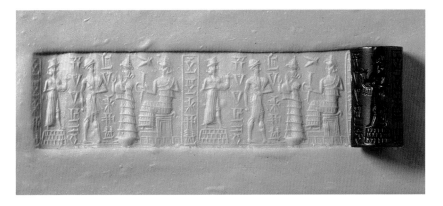

appear in the late sixth millennium BC at sites such as Arpachiyah in northern Iran and Tell Sabi Abiad in Syria.

Cylinder seal rolled out to leave an impression of the kilted king before deities
Haematite
Old Babylonian Period
WA 89002
h. 2.7 cm (1 in)

Seals are made of hard material which is carved with a design. This is generally recessed (carved in intaglio), so that when it is impressed on to clay or wax it will leave an impression in relief. Very occasionally the seal is carved in relief (cameo) so that the impression is recessed. The earliest seals were stamps; later a new form – the cylinder seal – was developed that covers a large area more swiftly. It was rolled across the clay to leave a continuous repeating impression of the carved design.

The use of seals spread into many cultures. The Museum has, for example, Minoan and Mycenaean seals of high quality dating from the second millennium BC. There are finely carved steatite seals from the great city culture which flourished in the Indus Valley between c.2500 and 2000 BC, mostly from Mohenjo-daro.

In China seals have been made since at least the late Zhou period (before 221 BC) for official, artistic, literary, commercial and personal purposes, and were commonly used instead of a signature. They were made from any material that could be carved or moulded, and varied in size from the huge imperial ones to small personal ones, bearing anything from one to twenty characters. At

Seals and seal impressions

first seals were impressed into clay, but from at least the Six Dynasties period (AD 265–589) a coloured ink paste, usually red, was employed.

In China seals were commonly attached to documents once they had been received or checked. In the same way they came to be applied to items of calligraphy and painting, so that as a work of art passed from one collector to another, each collector would add a personal inscription or colophon and print one or more of his personal seals.

The Museum holds the national collection of British seal dies (matrices) from the late Saxon period to the early twentieth century, and also has considerable collections of French, German and Italian seal matrices. From the medieval period they include those connected with trade and administration, such as customs seals, seals for the delivery of wool and hides, wool staple seals and seals of officials. There are seals belonging to ecclesiastical officials and institutions such as guilds and fraternities; an extensive series of colonial seals and many personal examples, some with coats of arms. The great seal matrices of the medieval kings of England do not survive, and from Tudor times the seals of state were often melted down and made into presentation plate. The earliest surviving great seal of an English king in the Museum is that of William IV (r.AD 1830–37), dated 1831. The obverse shows the king on horseback, wearing the robes of the Order of the Garter, with ships of war in the background; the reverse shows the king enthroned with Britannia, Neptune, Peace, Plenty, Justice and Religion.

The great seal of William IV, obverse (BOTTOM) and reverse (TOP)
London
Silver, engraved by Benjamin Wyon, 1831
MLA 1981,7–9,1
diam. 16.2 cm (6⅓ in)

FURTHER READING
D. Collon, *Near Eastern Seals* (London, 1990)
D. Collon, *7000 Years of Seals* (London, 1997)
D. Collon, *First Impressions: Cylinder Seals in the Ancient Near East* (London, 1993, rev. 2005)

Sarcophagus of
Seianti Hanunia Tlesnasa

Etruria (Italy), 2nd century BC

Seianti Hanunia Tlesnasa reclines for eternity upon a mattress and pillow, holding an open-lidded mirror in her left hand and raising her right hand to adjust her mantle. Her name is inscribed upon the base of the chest. She was obviously well-to-do, elegantly dressed in a tunic (*chiton*) with high girdle and a purple-bordered cloak, her jewellery comprising a tiara, earrings, necklace, bracelets and rings. She was Etruscan, buried at a time when the Etruscans, once independent, had been assimilated into the Roman world. They were undoubtedly the wealthiest and in many ways the most sophisticated of the peoples of pre-Roman Italy. Many features of their art, customs and religion were adopted by the Romans, so that their culture lived on even after their absorption into the Roman Republic.

Medical experts have been able to demonstrate that the skeleton inside the sarcophagus is that of the woman whose portrait we see. At the Unit of Art in Medicine at Manchester University soft tissue measurements were used to reconstruct her face on a plaster cast of the skull (above). The features of the model are strikingly similar to the face on the sarcophagus, although the ancient artist has made her somewhat younger and prettier. He may well have referred to the facial features of Seianti herself, or perhaps to an earlier portrait of her.

Examination of the dentine of her teeth by the University of Wales Dental School indicates an age of about 50. A defect in her jaw and other distortions down her right side may indicate severe injuries in adolescence. This damage and the strongly developed muscle attachments in her thighs have led a pathologist to suggest that she was a keen horse-rider who suffered a major accident, perhaps involving a horse falling on her. Over the years the resulting arthritis led to increasing inactivity and thus a gain in weight. The implication from this study is that some at least of the representations on Etruscan sarcophagi and cinerary urns bear true resemblances to the dead.

ABOVE **Reconstruction of the face by the Unit of Art in Medicine, Manchester University**

BELOW **Terracotta sarcophagus of Seianti Hanunia Tlesnasa**
Etruria (Poggio Cantarello, near Chiusi), Italy
*c.*150–130 BC
GR 1887.4–2.1; Terracotta D 786
l. 1.83 m (6 ft)

FURTHER READING
J Swaddling and J. Prag (eds), *Seianti Hanunia Tlesnasa: the Story of an Etruscan Noblewoman* (London, 2002)

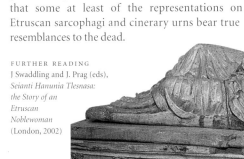

Senenmut appears to have been born at Armant of relatively humble parents. His rise in status is illustrated in the statue below, where he is shown holding the Princess Neferura, only daughter of Hatshepsut (1491–1479 BC), co-regent with Thutmose III and only the second woman to be crowned king of Egypt.

Senenmut entered royal service in the reign of Thutmose II (1492–1479 BC), who was married to his half-sister Hatshepsut, the daughter of Thutmose I (1504–1492 BC). The couple had no male heir. Thutmose II's son and heir Thutmose III was thus the son of a concubine. On the death of Thutmose II, Hatshepsut was appointed regent, and had herself crowned king.

There has been much speculation about the role of Senenmut. His numerous titles and positions included the role of steward of Amun and tutor to Neferura. He oversaw royal building works at Thebes and organized the transport and erection of the two great obelisks of Hatshepsut in the temple of Amun at Karnak. There is no evidence that he ever married and he is usually depicted only with his parents or with Neferura, leading to the suggestion, based on little evidence, that he was the lover of Hatshepsut.

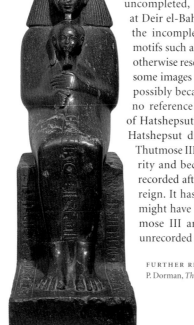

Statue of Senenmut with Princess Neferura seated on his lap
Karnak, Egypt
Black granite,
18th Dynasty,
c.1470 BC
EA 174
h. 76 cm (30 in)

An unusually large number of sculptures were made of Senenmut; there are three in the Museum. He built two tombs for himself, the second, uncompleted, near the temple of Hatshepsut at Deir el-Bahri. He was permitted to decorate the incomplete tomb with unusual religious motifs such as an astronomical ceiling and texts otherwise reserved for the tomb of the king. Like some images of him it was defaced in antiquity, possibly because of a fall from grace. There is no reference to Neferura after the 11th year of Hatshepsut's reign. It is not known whether Hatshepsut died or was forcibly removed by Thutmose III, who in due course reached maturity and became sole ruler. Senenmut is not recorded after the 19th year of Thutmose III's reign. It has however been suggested that he might have sought to ally himself with Thutmose III and survived his patroness as an unrecorded official.

FURTHER READING
P. Dorman, *The Monuments of Senenmut* (London, 1988)

The brilliant court creations of the Twelfth Dynasty range from sculpture and reliefs to the earliest written literary texts. Below are three life-size black granite statues of Senwosret III (1878–1843 BC), which were excavated from the site of the temple of his predecessor King Mentuhotep at Deir el-Bahri. They are among the most important statues in the Museum's collection, the one on the left being regarded as a masterpiece of Egyptian sculpture. Though all differ slightly, each demonstrates the new way of showing the facial features so characteristic of this reign. The king, wearing the *nemes* headdress, is shown with worn facial lines, in striking contrast to the idealized smooth, youthful appearance of the ruler in the art of other periods. His pose, with his hands placed flat on the front of his kilt, is also an innovation.

Senwosret III (also known as Senusret or Sesostris) of the late Twelfth Dynasty succeeded Senwosret II and was instrumental in reshaping Egypt's internal and foreign affairs. His domestic policy centred on the reorganization of the administrative system. Since the Old Kingdom the major threat to royal power had probably come from the provincial governors (*nomarchs*). A decline in provincial tombs for the elite, who seem now to have been tied more closely to the King's Residence, may indicate that Senwosret succeeded in reducing their authority drastically by removing many of their established privileges. The king also launched a series of campaigns to annex more thoroughly the Second Cataract region, and strengthened the chain of fortresses controlling Lower Nubia. So great was his hold on Nubia that by the New Kingdom the deified Senwosret was worshipped in the northern part of the province. The king seems to have personally led a campaign into Palestine.

Three statues of Senwosret III
Deir el-Bahri, Egypt
Black granite, 12th
Dynasty, c. 1850 BC
EA 684–6
h. (average) 1.40 m
(4 ft 7 in)
Given by the Egypt
Exploration Fund, 1905

FURTHER READING
J. Bourriau, *Pharaohs and Mortals. Egyptian Art in the Middle Kingdom* (Cambridge, 1988)

The list of the Seven Wonders varies. That most generally accepted today includes the pyramids of Egypt, the colossus of Rhodes, the hanging gardens of Babylon, the temple of Artemis (Diana) at Ephesus, the mausoleum at Halikarnassos, the lighthouse at Alexandria and the statue of Zeus at Olympia by Pheidias. The walls of Babylon sometimes appear on the list. Fragments of two of the Seven Wonders are in the Museum.

The Mausoleum takes its name from Maussollos, ruler of Caria (in modern Asia Minor) in the fourth century BC, whose tomb it is. Caria had been under the influence of Athens until the latter's collapse in the late fifth century BC. It then became part of the Persian Empire, but with a local ruler (satrap). Maussollos succeeded his father as satrap in 377 BC and married his sister Artemisia. He died c.353 BC but it is probable that work on his spectacular tomb had begun in his lifetime.

The Mausoleum at his capital Halikarnassos (modern Bodrum) must have been intact in the first century AD, when Pliny the Elder gave a partial description of it, and remained more or less undamaged until the thirteenth century AD when much of it collapsed, possibly because of an earthquake. In the late fifteenth century stones from the site were used by the Knights of St John of Malta to rebuild and extend their nearby castle, incorporating some sculptures. In 1856 Charles Newton discovered the site, establishing its ground plan and many of its architectural features. He also recovered a quantity of sculpture.

The Mausoleum consisted of a stepped colonnade of 36 columns. Above this was a pyramid of 24 steps surmounted by a four-horse chariot. There may have been as many as 330 other free-standing sculptures, all painted, perhaps from 56 to 72 lions at the base of the pyramid and 36 colossal portraits between the columns. There was room for 72 portrait figures on the middle step and 88 life-sized figures at the base.

The sculptures now in the Museum include two colossal statues once thought to be Maussollos and Artemisia but more probably members of the ruling dynasty of Caria. There is the head of one of the chariot horses, still with its bronze harness, and there are other fragments, among them the so-called 'Persian rider' from one of the groups of free-standing sculpture arranged along the steps of the podium. Of the three friezes, only that which shows the battle between

The **Seven Wonders of the ancient world**

Greeks and Amazons survives in any quantity.

From the later temple of Artemis at Ephesus, which replaced that destroyed in 356 BC, the Museum has a marble column drum and other fragments. Here it was that St Paul later preached to the Ephesians. Its precise appearance is not known, although some idea of the front elevation is given by Ephesian coins such as that shown below. Remains of the temple and its sculptures were discovered in 1869 by John Turtle Wood. Carved on the column drum (above) are a seated man (Pluton) and a standing woman (Persephone), gods of the underworld, who appear to be watching the preparations for departure made by a woman who stands muffled in a heavy mantle, a fold of which she draws out from her shoulder in a gesture often made by brides. Beckoning to her from her right is a youthful winged figure, whose sword suggests that he is Thanatos, Death; on her other side stands Hermes, the guide of the dead. The identity of the doomed woman is not known. She may be Iphigenia, lured to Aulis by a promise of marriage and then sacrificed by the Greeks to Artemis (the goddess of the temple) to win a fair wind for their passage to Troy; Alcestis, who offered to die in place of her husband Admetus; or Eurydice, wife of Orpheus.

The Hanging Gardens of Babylon have never been conclusively identified, nor has their existence been proved. They are generally assumed to have been of the time of Nebuchadnezzar II (604–562 BC). The Museum has illustrations of royal gardens from Mesopotamia which may give an impression of the Hanging Gardens. Among them are Ashurbanipal and his queen drinking in a garden on the outskirts of Nineveh (c.645 BC) (pp. 48–9).

FURTHER READING

P. Clayton and M. Price (eds), *The Seven Wonders of the Ancient World* (London, 1988)

G.B. Waywell, *The Free-standing Sculptures of the Mausoleum at Halicarnassus* (London, 1978)

OPPOSITE PAGE
Colossal statue from the Mausoleum
Halikarnassos (Bodrum), Turkey
mid-4th century BC
GR 1857.12–20.232 ('Maussollos'); Cat. Sculpture 100
h. 3 m (9 ft 10 in)
Excavated by Sir Charles Newton

Marble column drum from the south-west corner of the temple of Artemis
Ephesus, Turkey
c.325–300 BC
GR 1872.8–3.9; Cat. Sculpture 1206
h. 18.2 m (5 ft 11⅔ in)
Excavated by John Turtle Wood

Coin of Maximus showing sculptured drums at the foot of the columns of the Temple of Artemis
Ephesus, Turkey
AD 235–38
CM 1970–9–9–83 (v)
diam. 37 mm (1½ in)

The text carved on this slab of black basalt is the only surviving account of the creation by Ptah, god of Memphis, describing how he brings the world into being by giving names, thereby dividing land from water, light from darkness, heaven from earth, and so forth.

Also recorded on the stone, although much damaged, is the reason for the myth's survival. According to the text King Shabako (*r.*716–702 BC), of the expansionist Nubian dynasty whose capital was in the Sudan (p. 233), inspected the temple of Ptah at Memphis and was horrified to discover that its most sacred papyrus scroll was being devoured by worms. The king immediately ordered that the remaining undamaged text be incised in stone. The stone records:

> This writing was copied out anew by his Majesty
> in the Temple of his father Ptah-south-of-his-wall
> for his Majesty had found it to be a work of the ancestors
> which was worm-eaten
> and could not be understood from beginning to end.

The Shabako Stone
Memphis, Egypt
8th–7th century BC
EA 498
l. 1.37 m (4 ft 6⅛ in)
Given by Earl Spencer,
1805

The compiler of the text of the creation myth has reproduced the layout of early documents and introduced a number of archaisms, giving the piece an air of antiquity. Early scholars believed that the language pointed towards an Old Kingdom prototype (third millennium BC). More careful scrutiny has led to the rejection of this theory in favour of a Ramesside (*c.* thirteenth century BC) or later origin.

It is still a matter for dispute whether the text embodies a genuinely ancient religious tradition or whether it is purely a work of the Twenty-Fifth Dynasty, the story of its copying being a rhetorical device well known in Egyptian royal inscriptions and not a piece of genuine history. One theory is that, since the creation of the world was early ascribed to the god Atum of Heliopolis, this is an attempt by Memphis to give a prior claim to Ptah, patron god of that city. Alternatively, it may have been intended by Shabako to secure the allegiance of the priesthood of Memphis, an influential section of the recently conquered Egyptian populace, by giving new prestige to the city's patron deity.

The slab when discovered was in use as a millstone.

FURTHER READING
M. Jones (ed.), *Fake? The Art of Deception* (London, 1990), p. 60
S. Quirke, *Ancient Egyptian Religion* (London, 1992)

Shabtis

Shabtis, later known as *ushabtis* ('answerers'), are small figures placed in the tomb by the ancient Egyptians to carry out the hard agricultural labour required of their owner in the Afterlife. The Egyptians believed that, as in Egypt itself, there would be a regular need for work on the land such as was required after the annual flooding by the Nile. The intention of the *shabti*-figure was to act as the wealthy deceased's deputy for these labours in the Afterlife.

Shabtis first appeared in the early Middle Kingdom (*c.*2000 BC) and died out in the Ptolemaic period. The earliest *shabti*-figures were made of wood or wax in the form of a mummy and simply inscribed with the name of the deceased owner. In the New Kingdom the figures were usually carved in stone and inscribed with the *shabti*-text. At this time *shabtis* were first made with tools in their hands – baskets, mattocks, hoes. In the Eighteenth Dynasty glazed composition became the usual material.

Most *shabtis* are inscribed with Chapter 6 of the Book of the Dead (pp. 61–2), the spell to bring the figures to life and cause them to work. The basic form of the spell reads:

> [The deceased] says 'O *shabti*, if I be summoned or if I be detailed to do any work which has to be done in the realm of the dead; if indeed obstacles are implanted for you therewith as a man at his duties, you shall detail yourself for me on every occasion of making arable the fields, of flooding the banks or of conveying sand from east to west; "Here am I," you shall say.'

Painted wooden *shabti* box of the lady Henutmehyt containing eight painted *shabtis*
Thebes, Egypt
19th Dynasty, *c.*1290 BC
EA 41549
h. (box) 34 cm (13⅓ in)

The number of *shabtis* placed in the tomb gradually increased – at one point there was one for each day of the year, and 36 'overseers' with whips to control the gangs – and the figures came to be stored in elaborate boxes. Shown here are *shabtis* of the lady Henutmehyt and the box in which they were contained. The box shows the deceased adoring the jackal-headed Duamutef and the human-headed Imsety, two of the four Sons of Horus.

FURTHER READING
H.M. Stewart, *Egyptian Shabtis* (Aylesbury, 1995)

Portrait of George II by John **Shackleton**

King George II has a particular link with the British Museum since it was he who on 7 June 1753 gave the royal assent to the Act of Parliament by which it was established. He cannot be said to have been an enthusiastic supporter, but in 1757 he was responsible for a remarkable gift – the 'Old Royal Library' of the sovereigns of England which brought with it the privilege of copyright deposit enjoyed by today's British Library. As an acknowledgement of their debt to the King, the Museum's Trustees commissioned a full-length portrait from John Shackleton, 'Painter in Ordinary to His Majesty'. This was completed in 1762 and an elaborate frame procured in 1766.

There was a European tradition of displaying likenesses of eminent individuals as an adjunct to libraries and other collections. Thus throughout the eighteenth and much of the nineteenth century an increasing assembly of such portraits enhanced the Museum's exhibition galleries. When a new building, designed by Sir Robert Smirke, was begun in 1823 it was intended that the nation's collection of oil paintings should be housed in one of the upper galleries but the attempt to combine antiquities, natural history, a library and a picture gallery was opposed and the National Gallery established elsewhere. The British Museum Trustees retained ownership of a number of National Gallery paintings until 1868. In 1879 the best of the Museum's collection of portraits were transferred to the new National Portrait Gallery, leaving a collection largely consisting of donors such as George II, directors and foreigners.

The National Gallery and National Portrait Gallery are only two of the institutions to whose establishment the British Museum has contributed. The Natural History Museum was founded in 1881 when these collections were moved from Bloomsbury to South Kensington and did not become fully independent until 1963. The British Library was established in 1973 to incorporate the Museum's library collections and other libraries but did not move to its new building located near St Pancras railway station until 1998.

King George II
(1683–1760) in
Coronation Robes
John Shackleton (d. 1767)
England
Oil painting, 1762
h. 231 cm (91 in.)

FURTHER READING

Aileen Dawson, 'Collectors and commemoration: portrait sculpture and paintings in the British Museum', in Kim Sloan (ed.), *Enlightenment: Discovering the world in the eighteenth century* (London, 2003) J.R.F. Thompson and F.G. Roe, 'Some oil portraits in the British Museum', *The Connoisseur* (March 1961); 'More paintings at the British Museum', *idem* (April 1961)

Shang dynasty bronzes

Some of the most skilful pieces of metalwork the world has ever seen are the cast bronze vessels of the Shang dynasty (*c.*1500–1050 BC). The vessels were produced for religious ceremonies in which food and wine were offered to the ancestors. The dead were regarded as forming a part of the whole society, with offerings prepared and served as in a banquet for the living, using very elaborate forms of ordinary eating and drinking utensils. About 20 different shapes, derived from Neolithic ceramics, survived in ritual use long after the original forms had disappeared. Royal families owned the largest sets of vessels, more highly decorated than those of the lesser nobility. Ceramic copies were used lower down the social scale.

The Chinese method of casting bronze was the most complex ever developed. In most parts of the ancient world vessels of bronze were made by hammering. In China the ritual vessels with their extremely elaborate shapes were cast, using an alloy of copper and tin that was poured into fired clay moulds. To make the casting moulds, a model of the vessel was first made of clay, decorated with patterns and then allowed to harden. When dry the model was encased in the clay used for the mould. It was removed by cutting the clay wrapper into sections like orange peel. Before the vessel

Group of bronze ritual food and wine vessels
China
Shang dynasty,
12th century BC
h. (of *zun*, back right)
30 cm (11⅘ in)

was cast a core was made, and both core and mould were fired separately. The mould and core were then reassembled and the molten alloy poured in. Finally the mould was broken and the bronze vessel revealed.

Golden in colour when first made, they would have rapidly turned black in the humid summer climate of north central China.

FURTHER READING
J. Rawson, *Chinese Bronzes: Art and Ritual* (London, 1987)

Shields

Bronze shield
Moel Siabod, near Capel
Curig, Wales
Late Bronze Age, c.800 BC
PRB 1873 2–10 1
diam. 64.4 cm (25⅓ in)
Given by A.W. Franks;
found by W. Newcombe,
1784, and given to the
Meyrick Collection

The basic function of a shield was to protect the wearer, at the same time being sufficiently portable not to impede the soldier carrying it. It could be used to deflect missiles hurled from a distance or blows by weapons in hand-to-hand combat. A group of soldiers with interlocked shields like the Roman *testudo*, or tortoise, could be a formidable attacking vehicle, not unlike a modern tank. Some shields were utilitarian, others might be decorated both for ceremonial use and to identify their owners.

Various types of shield can be seen in the Museum. A relief depicting the attack on the Elamite city of Hamanu in the seventh century BC, for example, shows Assyrian soldiers crouching, their heavy round shields above their heads bristling with arrows fired by the defenders. In the Assyrian lion-hunt (pp. 186–7) a row of soldiers with shields protects the king. Greek vases depict the large round shields of bull's hide, with handgrip and forearm brace, sometimes faced with bronze, carried in classical times.

The finest in the Museum's collection came from Britain and were probably used for ceremonial purposes rather than actual combat. Above is a Late Bronze Age shield found in a bog at Moel Siabod, near Capel Curig, Wales. The raised decoration was beaten out from the back. The type differs considerably from continental forms. In the absence of body armour, the Celtic warrior defended himself with a shield that was usually made of wood or leather, although the finest might be faced with bronze. Recent discoveries include a unique bronze oval shield found at Chertsey in 1985. The two finest shields from the Celtic period are the one found in the River Witham near Washingborough, Lincolnshire, about 1826, and the Battersea

Shield of parade
Flanders
late 15th century AD
MLA 1863,5–1,1
h. 83 cm (32⅔ in)
Given by the Revd
J. Wilson

Shields

shield (p. 72). In the second and first centuries BC a new type was popular. It was equally long, but incurved at the ends, so that it had pointed corners and resembled the shape of a hide. A collection of miniature shields of this type was discovered recently.

The Sutton Hoo ship burial (pp. 312–13) included a shield with elaborate decoration, probably intended for display rather than combat. From the Middle Ages comes the highly decorated shield shown on the previous page. This would not have been used in battle but may have been a prize for a tournament. Made of wood with painted gesso, it shows a knight kneeling before a lady. In front of him lie the weapons of the tournament, the pole-axe, helmet and gauntlets, and from behind approaches a skeleton, the figure of Death. Above floats a scroll with the legend VOUS OU LA MORT (You or Death).

The introduction of sophisticated body armour and later of the musket, the rifle and heavy artillery led to the disappearance of shields in modern warfare, although they lingered on in remote areas and for ceremonial purposes. Today they are used by police. The Department of Ethnography has an extensive collection of nineteenth- and twentieth-century shields, including some particularly fine examples from the New Guinea Highlands acquired in the 1960s (right).

Wooden shield decorated with ochre, lime and soot
Telefomin area, Papua New Guinea
20th century AD
ETH 1964.Oc.3.81
h. 1.51 m (5 ft)

FURTHER READING
M. Parker Pearson, *Bronze Age Britain* (London, 1993)
S.M. Pearce, *Bronze Age Metalwork in Southern Britain* (Aylesbury, 1984)
M. Pfaffenbichler, *Medieval Craftsmen: Armourers* (London, 1992)
C. Spring, *African Arms and Armour* (London, 1993)
I. Stead, *Celtic Art in Britain before the Roman Conquest* (London, 1996)

Ships

The earliest travellers took to the water with buoyancy aids such as bundles of reeds, logs and inflated animal skins. The next step was the creation of rafts which, in forested regions, would have been constructed of bound logs. Along the Nile or in the marshy lower stretches of the Tigris and Euphrates they were probably made of batches of reed bundles bound together. Subsequently buoyed rafts were devised, consisting of a wooden frame supported by inflated animal skins or pots.

The crucial step in the development of water transport was the creation of the boat. One of the earliest forms could well have been the skin boat, fashioned by stretching hides over a light frame of branches and lacing them together. Where trees were plentiful the earliest boats were undoubtedly bark canoes and dugouts. Dugouts were adapted for use on open water, with protection against waves provided by adding planks, set on edge, along each side, with ribs running athwartship to brace them. Here we have in embryo the fundamental elements of the planked boat. The invention of the sail in Egypt in about 3500 BC resulted in ever faster and more efficient water transport and the nations that surrounded the Mediterranean in ancient times depended on ships and seafarers for their prosperity. Assyrian reliefs in the Museum of about 865 BC show that the boatmen of the Middle Euphrates were by that time using round skin boats – coracles – that had the size and strength to carry chariots. Massive loads of building stone in coracles on the Upper Tigris are shown on a relief of c.700 BC.

Some of the earliest boats in the Museum are the detailed models of passenger ships found in Egyptian Middle Kingdom tombs. Early ships are shown on Greek vases, for example a two-level Greek oar galley (above) of the eighth century BC. Probably the best-known ship in the Museum is that buried at Sutton Hoo in the seventh century AD (pp. 312–13). On the right is an extremely rare ship's prow discovered in the River Scheldt. The wood has been dated to AD 350–650 and it is thought on stylistic grounds to have been made in the fifth or sixth century AD.

FURTHER READING
L. Casson, *Ships and Seafaring in Ancient Times* (London, 1994)

Krater with a many-oared warship
Thebes, Greece
Geometric period,
c.735–720 BC
GR 1899.2–19.1
h. 30.5 cm (12 in)

Ship's prow of carved oak
River Scheldt at Appels,
near Termonde, Oost
Vlaanderen, Belgium
5th–6th century AD
MLA 1938, 2, 1
h. 149 cm (58⅔ in)
Purchased with the aid of
the National Art
Collections Fund and the
Christy Trustees

Shiva

For two millennia Shiva has been one of the great Hindu gods. His personality is mysterious and complex. He is the deity who controls the beginning and the end of time cycles and is concerned with elemental and often contradictory powers. He manifests five aspects of eternal energy: creation, preservation, destruction, concealment, favour. One of the most common depictions of him, even today, is as a standing pillar, the origins of which are phallic; such a pillar is known as a *lingam* and is often combined with the female symbol, *yoni*. In this form they are worshipped in a temple as powerful representations of the union of opposites, male and female, Shiva and his consort Parvati.

Shiva is also represented in sculpture and painting in human form. Sometimes, like many other Hindu gods, he may be multi-armed or multi-headed, suggesting his many qualities through the different attributes held in the hands, or the different characters of the faces. His main attributes are a leaping deer and a cobra, symbolic of his solitary life of meditation in the forests, a battle-axe, a trident and a flame or bowl of fire. His mount is the bull Nandi. Shiva is renowned as an ascetic or *yogi*; he is also a family man, residing at the sacred city of Benares with Parvati and their offspring Karttikeya and Ganesha (p. 131).

In the fine bronze of the Chola period (below), Shiva is seen as Supreme God and Lord of the Dance (Nataraja). The god is shown in the *anandatandava* position. In his upper right hand he holds a drum, representing the primordial sound of creation. The upper left hand holds a flame of destruction, indicating the overcoming of opposites in his nature, which are symbolized by both female and male earrings.

Shiva Nataraja
South India, probably
Tanjore District, Tamil
Nadu
*c.*AD 1100
OA 1987.3–14.1
h. 89.5 cm (35¼ in)

He makes the gesture 'have no fear' and points to his raised left foot, symbolizing release. He treads upon the prostrate dwarf of ignorance, Apasmara, and the diminutive figure of the goddess Ganga appears in his flowing hair. The god maintains an exquisite poise and equanimity at the centre of the whirling cycle of cosmic activity, symbolized by the flaming circle.

FURTHER READING
T.R. Blurton, *Hindu Art* (London, 1992)

Towards the end of the twelfth century AD in Japan the great warrior clans became increasingly active. For some 20 years the Taira clan eclipsed the Fujiwara at court, but they were themselves displaced by the head of the Minamoto clan, Minamoto no Yoritomo (1147–99). Yoritomo set up his government at Kamakura and in 1192 was awarded the title of *shogun* (leader of the army or commander-in-chief) by the emperor. For the first time Japan had a government which controlled the entire country, the 'Bakufu' (literally 'tent government') in Kamakura. The rule of the shoguns was to last until the restoration of imperial power in 1867.

Portrait of the first
Shogun, Minamoto no
Yoritomo, in court dress
Artist unknown
Japan
Hanging scroll; ink and
colours on silk
Kamakura period, early
14th century AD
JA 1920.7–13.1
145 × 88.5 cm
(57 × 34⅞ in)
Purchased with the aid
of G. Eumorfopoulos
and the National Art
Collections Fund

This portrait is based very closely on that attributed to the artist Fujiwara Takanobu (1142–1205), long preserved in the Jingoji Temple, Kyoto, with two other portraits (designated in Japan as 'National Treasures'). The identification of the subjects of these three has been traditional but was unproved; the inscription at the top of the Museum copy, however, provides important evidence. This inscription describes Yoritomo as the defeater of the

Taira family and the unifier and pacifier of Japan. It is probable that a number of copies, of which this is one, were made for use and suitable reverence in important political centres.

FURTHER READING
L. Smith, V. Harris and T. Clark, *Japanese Art: Masterpieces in the British Museum*
(London, 1990)

The cities of Sicily were colonized by Greeks attracted by the fertility of the island and by the possibilities of trade. The first foundations, such as Naxos and Syracuse, were established as early as the eighth century BC. The Sicilian cities maintained the closest relations with Greece, and during the sixth century BC achieved a high degree of material prosperity. However, they were subject to threats from Carthage, which had colonized the western tip of the island. Towards 500 BC the earlier oligarchic and aristocratic regimes of the Greek cities gave place to the sole rule of tyrants. Gelon, originally tyrant of Gela, made Syracuse his capital in 485 BC and transformed it into one of the classical world's greatest cities. Tyranny gave way to constitutional government and for 70 years Syracuse and the other cities had a relatively peaceful and prosperous existence. In 415 BC they survived an Athenian invasion, but Carthaginian incursions resulted in the destruction of several Greek cities; by 400 BC only Syracuse was left. By the third century BC Rome finally smashed the power of Carthage and took over Greek Sicily.

The coins were made by hand. The nugget of precious metal was first cast, while molten, into a lump and adjusted to the correct weight. The negative design was then worked on to a bronze or iron die. One die would be securely fixed in an anvil, the other held in the moneyer's hand. The prepared blank of metal was then reheated and placed on the anvil-die; the hand-held die was positioned above and struck into the metal blank with a hammer. The most important Sicilian coins came from Syracuse and like those of other cities were seen not only as functional objects but as works of art. The names of a number of engravers who produced and signed coins in Greek Sicily are known, mostly of the later fifth century BC. Below (left) is the so-called Demareteion, often dated to 480/479 BC because of a presumed connection with Queen Demarete, wife of Gelon, ruler of Syracuse.

FURTHER READING
G.K. Jenkins, *Coins of Greek Sicily* (London, 1976)

LEFT **Decadrachm or 10-drachmaeon (the Demareteion)**
(obverse) Four-horse chariot and running lion
Syracuse
*c.*480/479 BC or *c.*460 BC
CM BMC 63
diam. 3.5 cm (1⅓ in)

CENTRE **Tetradrachm**
(reverse) Silenus, with animal's ears and a bushy tail, holding a wine-cup (*kylix*)
Naxos
*c.*460 BC
CM BMC 7
diam. 2.6 cm (1 in)
C.M. Cracherode Bequest, 1799

RIGHT **Decadrachm**
(reverse) an eagle, the sacred bird of Zeus
Akragas
*c.*412 BC
CM CG Add. 29 L.817
diam. 3.5 cm (1⅓ in)
From the Naro Hoard

Opposite is a portrait of the founder of the British Museum, Sir Hans Sloane (AD 1660–1753), physician, natural historian and philanthropist. Sloane made his fortune in medicine – two of his major innovations were the prescription of milk chocolate and the promotion of vaccination against smallpox – but his great passion was collecting. Qualifying in France in 1683, in 1687 he was appointed physician to the Duke of Albemarle, the new Governor of Jamaica. After the duke's death he returned to London with a fine collection of West Indian natural history specimens and began to establish his medical practice, eventually including Queen Anne and Kings George I and II among his patients. Although not in the first rank of scientific enquiry, he was elected President of the College of Physicians in 1719 and succeeded Sir Isaac Newton as President of the Royal Society in 1719.

Meanwhile his collections grew as travellers looked out for rare things to bring back, first to No. 3 Bloomsbury Place and then to No. 4. In 1712, following his retirement, Sloane purchased the Manor of Chelsea, where his presence is still commemorated by such names as Sloane Square and Hans Crescent.

His land included a botanical garden established by the Society of Apothecaries of London in 1673. Sloane gave this to the Society, which in 1732 began a programme of building in the garden, including a greenhouse and two hothouses. The foundation stone was laid by Sloane. Eleven days later the Society's ruling body, the Court of Assistants, met and 'Ordered that the Statute [sic] of Sir Hans Sloane Bart be put up at the Greenhouse at Chelsea Garden'. The following March the Master told the court he had asked Sloane whom he would like as the sculptor, 'and Sir Hans Sloane had named Mr Ricebank'. This was actually Michael Rysbrack (1694–1770), who had come to England from Flanders (now part of Belgium) in 1720 and by 1733 had become the most fashionable sculptor in London.

Shown here is a terracotta model on which the head of the full-length statue is based. Presumably taken from life, although no record of sittings is known, it is also a highly finished portrait in its own right, although perhaps rather flattering to a man in his seventies. Sloane wears a full wig of a type that was rather old-fashioned by the 1730s. At the age of 23 Sloane was described as 'of medium height, hair very short, light chestnut, face rather long and grave marked with smallpox'.

For the full-length statue, which cost £280, Rysbrack portrayed Sloane wearing what may be the gown of the President of the Royal College of Physicians and holding out a scroll (perhaps the title deeds to the garden land).

The niche in front of the greenhouse in the Chelsea Physic Garden intended for the statue was found not to be strong enough

Sir Hans **Sloane** by Rysbrack

for its weight, so eventually, in the autumn of 1737, the statue was set up inside the greenhouse, part of the wall being dismantled to get it in. The greenhouse continued to present structural problems and in 1748 was in danger of collapse, whereupon the statue was transferred to the middle of the garden and began its long, losing battle with the London atmosphere.

Sloane bequeathed his collection to King George II for the nation. It was acquired by Act of Parliament in June 1753 in return for £20,000 paid to his two heirs, his daughters Lady Cadogan and Mrs Stanley. In turn, in 1756 they presented the terracotta bust to the Museum. In 1984 the Trustees of the Physic Garden deposited the statue on long-term loan.

The bust of Sloane is one of the finest of a substantial collection of English portrait busts of the seventeenth, eighteenth, nineteenth and twentieth centuries, including works by such noted sculptors as Louis-François Roubiliac, Joseph Wilton, Sir Francis Chantrey, Joseph Nollekens and others.

FURTHER READING
A. MacGregor (ed.), *Sir Hans Sloane: Collector, Scientist, Antiquary, Founding Father of the British Museum* (London, 1994)
A. Dawson, *Portrait Sculpture in the British Museum* (London, 2000)

Terracotta portrait bust of Sir Hans Sloane
Michael Rysbrack (1694–1770)
England
AD 1737
MLA 1756, 6–19, 1
h. 68 cm (26¾ in)
Given by Lady Cadogan and Mrs Stanley

The **Sophilos Vase**

The Sophilos Vase takes its name from the signature *Sophilos megraphsen* ('Sophilos painted me'): it is the work of the first Attic artist whose name is known to us. The *dinos*, a bowl and its stand, were designed to hold wine mixed with water for the feast.

The decorative technique is called black-figure; the artist's silhouettes, brush-drawn in clay slip, which becomes lustrous black after firing, stand in sharp contrast to the orange clay ground. Details are incised and the whole is enlivened by the use of added colours, a purplish-red and white.

The lower registers of the bowl and the whole of the stand are occupied by animals, real and fantastic. On the upper frieze we see the arrival of guests (their names given alongside them) at the wedding of Peleus and Thetis. Peleus stands alone at the door of his house holding out a *kantharos* (wine-cup) as a sign of welcome. The procession of deities is led by Iris, in winged boots, carrying her herald's wand; following her come several deities on foot. Of these, greatest prominence is given to Dionysos, god of wine (p. 105), who is in the centre of the scene on the front of the vase. Then come five chariots driven by deities in pairs and accompanied by Muses, Graces or Fates. Behind all these come slower-moving deities, including Okeanos, the river god, Eileithyia, the goddess of childbirth, and Hephaistos, the lame smith-god, on his mule.

The marriage of the beautiful sea-nymph Thetis to mortal Peleus was engineered by Zeus and Poseidon, both at first suitors of Thetis, because they learnt that her son would be greater than his father. It was at their wedding feast that the dispute between the goddesses as to who was the fairest broke out, thus setting in motion the sequence of events that was to culminate in the Trojan War.

FURTHER READING
D. Williams, *Greek Vases* (London, 1985), pp. 26–8
L. Burn, *Greek Myths* (London, 1990) pp. 31–3

The Sophilos *dinos*
Athens, Greece
*c.*580 BC
GR 1971.11–1.1
h. 71 cm (28 in)

Head of a poet, perhaps **Sophocles** Asia Minor, 3rd–2nd century BC

This is an imaginary portrait in bronze, once part of a full-length statue, perhaps a second-century BC version of a slightly earlier work. We know it represents a poet because of the ribbon that binds his hair. Long thought to represent Homer, it is now identified as a 'portrait' of the fifth-century BC Athenian tragedian Sophocles in middle age. Although realistic portraiture existed in the Hellenistic period, a continuing demand for portraits of famous men of the past was met, when no authentic example existed, by inventing a suitable type. The narrowed eyes, straight nose and set expression of the mouth convey a highly intellectual impression, but also a sense of authority and power.

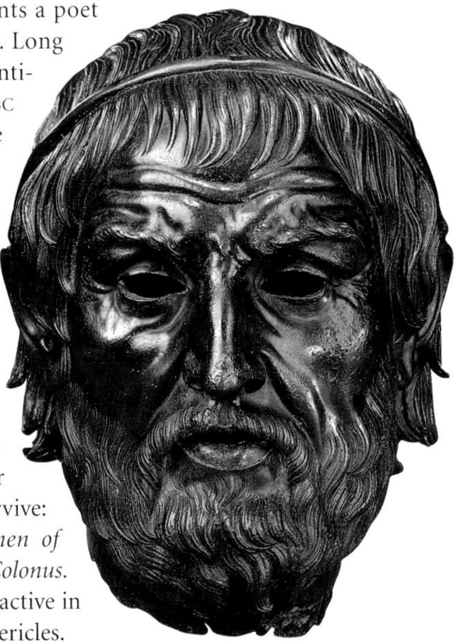

Sophocles (*c.*496–406 BC) was one of the great figures of Greek drama, author of over a hundred plays of which seven survive: *Ajax*, *Antigone*, *King Oedipus*, *The Women of Trachis*, *Electra*, *Philoctetes* and *Oedipus at Colonus*. He was known as a genial, popular figure, active in civic life and the friend of Herodotus and Pericles.

The portrait was brought to England from Constantinople in the early seventeenth century for the collection of Thomas Howard, Earl of Arundel (1585–1646). Subsequently it entered the possession first of Dr Richard Mead (1673–1754) and later of the Earl of Exeter, who in 1760 presented it to the Museum.

Head of a poet
Probably from Asia Minor (Turkey)
Bronze, 300–100 BC
GR 1760.9–19.1;
Bronze 847
h. 29.5 cm (11⅗ in)
Given by the Earl of Exeter

FURTHER READING

G. Hafner, *Späthellenistische Bildnisplastik*, 66 (Berlin, 1954), no. A12
K. Schefold, *Die Bildnisse der Antiken Dichter, Redner und Denker* (Basel, 1977), pp. 352–3

The ancient kingdoms of South Arabia owed their prosperity to the aromatic gums frankincense and myrrh, native to this area and to the Horn of Africa. An urban civilization grew up some time after 1000 BC on the basis of trade stimulated by the demand for these commodities, and such kingdoms as Saba (Biblical Sheba), Ma'in and Aataban rose to great wealth and power. It is thought that it was from Saba in the tenth century BC that the Queen of Sheba, 'with camels that bore spices and very much gold and precious stones', visited the Biblical King Solomon.

The details of South Arabian history are still uncertain. The first settlers probably arrived as nomads from the north during the second millennium BC, speaking a Semitic language which developed into the Minaean, Qatabanian and Hadrami dialects. Some centuries later, other tribes from the north speaking the forerunner of the Sabaean dialect moved into the area between Ma'in and Qataban, no doubt occupying territory previously controlled by these two groups.

Statue of a woman
Saba, South Arabia
c. 1st century BC–1st
century AD
WA 134693
h. 74.5 cm (29⅓ in)

Higher culture with cities and writing did not occur until well after 1000 BC. Towards the end of the first millennium BC a tribe called the Himyar began to come to prominence and eventually Himyarites ruled the whole of South Arabia.

South Arabia, recognized as a region of fabulous wealth, was the goal of an unsuccessful military campaign by the Romans under Aelius Gallus in 24 BC. The last centuries of this civilization saw conflicts between the adherents of Judaism and Christianity, the latter being championed by the Abyssinians of Aksum, who seized power in the sixth century AD. In the final decades before the Islamic conquest the area formed part of the Sasanian Empire.

The South Arabians had their own alphabetic script – Himyaratic – and a distinctive style of primitive sculpture. A local alabaster was used for sculptures of both men and women in temples, and for votive and funeral plaques.

The Museum also has a collection of bronzes, jewellery and seals from this area.

FURTHER READING
B. Doe, *Southern Arabia* (London, 1971)
St J. Simpson, *Queen of Sheba: Treasures from Ancient Yemen* (London, 2002)

Fragment of the beard of the **Sphinx** Egypt, early 15th century BC

The Museum has a small limestone fragment – about one-thirtieth – of the beard of the Sphinx. The largest surviving fragment is in the Cairo Museum.

The British Museum's fragment was presented in 1818 by Giovanni Battista Caviglia, a Genoese who regarded himself as a British subject. Caviglia excavated at Giza in 1817 and cleared parts of the Sphinx, which was then buried in sand up to the neck. Between the paws he found a number of fragments of the beard and the tip of the uraeus. His expenses were covered by Henry Salt (British Consul-General) and other British businessmen, with an agreement that finds be presented to the Museum. This was done according to a directive of Mohammed Ali Pasha, at that time virtual ruler of Egypt. Other parts of the beard were left *in situ*. When the Sphinx was cleared in 1925–6 the fragments then found – not, it seems, all of those left by Caviglia – were removed to the Cairo Museum.

Some archaeologists have doubted that the Sphinx, when first carved in *c.*2550 BC, had a beard. The probability is that the beard was subsequently added (possibly 1000 years later, during the Eighteenth-Dynasty restoration work), and fell off in antiquity. No estimate of the size of the original beard has ever been made, but it has been calculated that no more than one-third has survived.

It has sometimes been suggested that damage to the face was caused during the late eighteenth century by Napoleon's troops. In fact an early fifteenth-century Arab historian reported that the face had been disfigured in his time. This is borne out by seventeenth- and mid-eighteenth-century drawings executed prior to the French expedition to Egypt.

FURTHER READING
M. Lehner, *The Complete Pyramids* (London, 1997)

Fragment of the beard of
the Sphinx
Giza, Egypt
18th Dynasty, *c.*1420 BC
EA 58
l. 78.7 cm (31 in)
Given by Giovanni
Battista Caviglia, 1818

St Cuilean's bell

Irish priests and monks of the early Church used simple iron bells to summon their congregations to prayer. In the course of time many of these bells came to be regarded as holy relics and were encased in costly shrines. Below is the iron bell associated with St Cuilean, brother of Cormac, king-bishop of Cashel, who died in AD 908. The bell is coated with bronze and enclosed in a late eleventh-century shrine with enamel, niello and multicoloured wire inlays. It was found in a hollow tree at Kilcuilawn, Glankeen, Co. Tipperary, Ireland, and was used in the eighteenth century as a sacred object on which oaths were sworn. The original iron handle was missing, but the maker of the shrine added the traditional curve in openwork at the top.

Ireland, unlike Britain, never became a province of the Roman Empire, although merchants and mercenaries occasionally travelled there. The Scotti (as the inhabitants of Ireland were then known) raided the adjacent coasts of the empire for loot and slaves. Christian missionaries, among them Palladius and St Patrick, reached Ireland during the first half of the fifth century AD and during the sixth century monasteries were founded. Some were tiny, in isolated places, but there were also central foundations like Armagh which developed into populous monastic 'cities', renowned as centres of learning and craftsmanship. These became targets for Viking raiders.

During the early medieval period Irish craftsmen were amongst the most skilled in Europe, producing manuscripts and metalwork sculpture of superb technical and artistic quality. The Museum has an important group of Irish ecclesiastical metalwork dating from the eighth century onwards. In addition to a group of bells other important pieces include the 'Londesborough' brooch (eighth century AD) and the Kells crozier (ninth–twelfth centuries AD).

St Cuilean's bell (detail)
Ireland
late 11th century AD
MLA 1854,7–14,6
h. 30 cm (11⅘ in)
Purchased from
T.L. Cooke

FURTHER READING
F. Henry, *Irish Art in the Romanesque Period, 1020–1170 AD* (London, 1970), p. 102 ff.

The **Star Carr headdress**

The headdress of deer antlers (below) was used just over 9000 years ago by the hunter-gatherer inhabitants of what is now Yorkshire. It may have been worn to conceal the hunter when stalking deer, or as part of the costume used in social or religious ceremonies.

The prehistoric site at Star Carr, near Scarborough, Yorkshire, lay on what was then the edge of a reed swamp fringing a lake. Excavations in the 1950s revealed that the campsite extended out into the swamp on a raft of untrimmed birchwood. Here red deer carcasses were dismembered to provide both food and raw materials. Much effort went into the making of barbed spear-points from antlers, and flint skin-working tools showed that hides were also prepared on site. Other organic artefacts include elk-antler mattocks and a wooden paddle which may have been used in some sort of boat. Birch bark, found stored in convenient rolls, may have been processed to produce resin for fixing flint blades into hafts and handles to form weapons and tools.

A particularly interesting discovery was a series of skull frontlets from red deer stags with portions of antler still attached, which had been modified to make headdresses. The frontlet below has four holes made for its attachment, probably to a hood of leather or skin.

The Star Carr site was probably one of a number of places visited during the course of the year by a group of hunter-gatherers to exploit the seasonal sources of food within the area and to carry out specific manufacturing tasks. Red deer, roe deer and elk, the last now extinct in Britain, were the prime target of the hunt, providing the bulk of the meat consumed. Analysis of the age and sex of the deer remains suggests selective exploitation of animal resources.

FURTHER READING
J.G.D. Clark, *Excavations at Star Carr. An early Mesolithic site at Seamer near Scarborough, Yorkshire* (Cambridge, 1954)
A.J. Legg and P.A. Rowley-Conwy, *Star Carr Revisited* (London, 1988)
G. Smith, *Late Stone Age Hunters of the British Isles* (London, 1992)

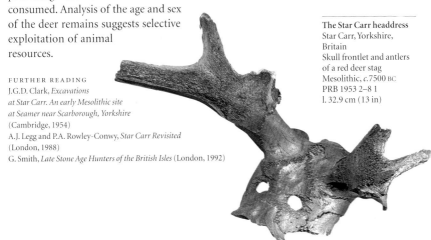

The Star Carr headdress
Star Carr, Yorkshire, Britain
Skull frontlet and antlers of a red deer stag
Mesolithic, *c*.7500 BC
PRB 1953 2–8 1
l. 32.9 cm (13 in)

The **Sutton Hoo ship burial**

The central enigma of the Sutton Hoo ship burial is the identity of the royal individual commemorated with such magnificence. This unique grave was discovered in 1939 in an area containing a series of mounds next to the River Deben at Sutton Hoo, Suffolk.

In the largest of the mounds the excavator Basil Brown found rusted iron rivets, which were the remains of a great ship, over 27 m (90 ft) in length. A specially constructed burial chamber roofed over by timber and turf had been erected on it; inside were objects which were to revolutionize scholars' views of the wealth and skills of Anglo-Saxon society. As well as the remains of a lyre, drinking horns, a helmet, shield and sword, there were two shoulder clasps, a purse lid decorated with intricately cut garnets, and a great gold buckle, bowls from Byzantium, Celtic hanging bowls, a bucket and three bronze cauldrons. One of the strangest finds was a ceremonial whetstone carved with brooding faces and fitted with metal mounts.

No bones were found, but excavations between 1965 and 1970 found a high concentration of phosphate indicating the presence of bone and body products in the burial chamber. The magnificence of the find indicates that it was almost certainly a royal personage who was being commemorated. The most often suggested candidate is Raedwald, High King of the Anglo-Saxon kingdoms south of the Humber, who died c.AD 624 or 625. Other

Two clasps, probably worn on the shoulders attached to a two-part garment
Sutton Hoo, Suffolk, England
Gold, decorated with *cloisonné*, garnets and *millefiore* glass, 7th century AD
MLA 1939,10–10, 4 and 5
l. approx 12.8 cm (5 in)

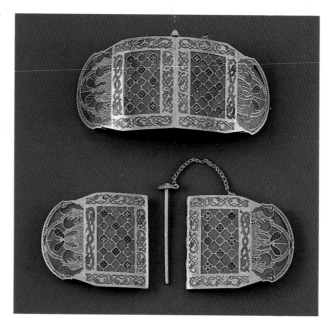

The **Sutton Hoo ship burial**

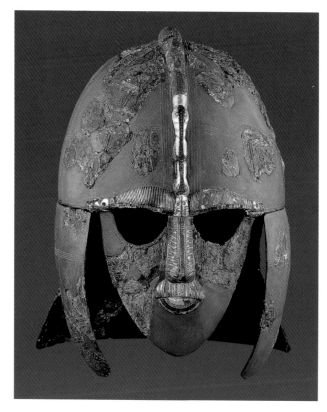

Reconstruction of the
ceremonial helmet, iron
and tinned bronze, with
original fragments
Sutton Hoo, Suffolk,
England
7th century AD
MLA 1939,10–10, 93 (51)
h. 31.8 cm (12½ in)
Given by Mrs Edith M.
Pretty

possibilities are Raedwald's son Eorpwald (*d.* 627/8) and Sigeberht
and Eric, who died together in battle against Penda of Mercia
in 636/7.

Mrs Edith M. Pretty, the landowner, gave the entire find to the
Museum – 'the most magnificent and munificent single gift made
in the lifetime of a donor'.

Further excavations of a large area of the cemetery were carried
out between 1984 and 1992, when seven mounds were examined.
All but one of the mounds had been gutted by sixteenth-century
robbers and later explorers. In the unrobbed mound were found
the graves of a young man and his pony, together with remains of
harness, weapons and vessels.

FURTHER READING

M. Carver, *Sutton Hoo: Burial Ground of Kings?* (London, 1998)

A.C. Evans, *The Sutton Hoo Ship Burial* (3rd edn, London, 1994)

R.L.S. Bruce-Mitford, *The Sutton Hoo Ship Burial*, vol. 1 (London, 1975), vol. 2 (London,
1978), vol. 3 (London, 1983)

M. Carver, Sutton Hoo: *A seventh-century princely burial ground and its context* (London, 2005)

This, the oldest of the prehistoric trackways in Britain, was constructed by the early farmers of a marshy area in Somerset, known today as the 'Somerset Levels'. Recent advances in the study of dating by means of tree-ring measurements (dendrochronology) have enabled its construction to be placed in the years 3807/3806 BC. It is named after the man who discovered it.

It is a surprisingly sophisticated piece of carpentry, using woods chosen for their different qualities. The three basic components are planks made of oak, ash and lime with rails and pegs mainly of hazel and alder. These were prepared on dry land and brought into the swamp. The rails (long poles) were laid end to end and secured by sharpened pegs driven slantwise into the soggy ground on either side. The planks were then wedged into place between the peg tops, parallel to the rails beneath and held firmly in position by vertical pegs. The track, two kilometres (1¼ miles) long, could have been assembled in a single day from the pre-shaped units, so neatly do they fit together.

Neolithic travellers dropped or hid a variety of objects alongside the track. Among these were flint and stone axeheads and the occasional pot.

Section of the Sweet Track
Somerset, Britain
3807/3806 BC
PRB P 1986 12–11 27
l. 3 m (10 ft)
Gift from Fisons plc and the Somerset Levels Project

FURTHER READING
B. and J. Coles, *Sweet Track to Glastonbury: the Somerset Levels in Prehistory* (London, 1986)

Tahitian mourner's dress

Tahiti, 18th century AD

O n Saturday 7 May 1774 Captain James Cook (1728–79) was
anchored off the island of Tahiti in HMS *Resolution* on his
second round-the-world voyage. He wrote in his journal:

> In the afternoon he [the King] and the whole Royal Family
> (Viz) his Father, Brother and three Sisters with their atten-
> dants, made me a Viset on board. His Father made me a
> present of a compleat Mourning dress, curiosities we most
> valued. . .

Such dresses were worn on the death of a high-ranking individual
by one of his close relatives or by a priest. Cook gave an account of
the ritual:

> . . . for several successive evenings after [the death] one of her
> relations dress'd himself in a very odd dress which I cannot tell
> how to describe or convey a better idea of it than to suppose a
> man dress'd with Plumes of feathers something in the same
> manner as those worn by Coaches, hearses, horses etc at the
> funerals in London, it was very neatly made up of black or
> brown and white cloth, black and white feathers and pearl
> oysteres shells, it cover'd the head, face and body as low as the
> Calf of the leg or lower and not only looked
> grand but awfull likewise. The man thus
> equip'd and attended by two or three more
> men or women with their faces and bodies
> besmeared with soot and a club in their
> hands would about sunset take a compass of
> near a mile running here and there and where
> ever they came the people would fly from
> them as tho they had been so many hobgob-
> lins not one daring to come in their way.

Mourner's dress
Tahiti
18th century AD
ETH Tah.78
h. 2.2 m (7 ft 2½ in)
Given by Captain James
Cook, 1775

Natural history specimens, drawings and other
objects from Cook's voyages came to the
Museum, some directly from his patron Sir
Joseph Banks or members of Cook's crew, other
items indirectly. This unique collection, made
during the first European contact with many
peoples, is now split between the Museum, the
British Library and the Natural History Museum.

FURTHER READING
B.A.L. Cranstone and H.J. Gowers, 'The Tahitian Mourner's Dress: A
discovery and a description', *British Museum Quarterly*, 32
(London, 1967–8), pp. 138–44
J.C. Beaglehole (ed.), *The Journals of Captain James Cook on his
Voyages of Discovery* (Cambridge, 1955, 1961, 1967): II. *The Voyage of
the Resolution and Adventure* (1961)

A t the time of Columbus's voyage to 'the Indies' the Taino Indians occupied much of the Greater Antilles, including the islands of Cuba, Jamaica, Hispaniola and Puerto Rico. Taino beliefs revolved around powerful spirit beings celebrated in myth and ritual. The Museum has an important group of Taino woodcarvings made before European contact. These include *duhos* (ceremonial stools) reserved for high-ranking males and *caciques* (chiefs). The elaborate designs and gold inlay on these sacred objects proclaimed their owner's power to enter the spirit domain and gain access to esoteric knowledge. There are also three rare wooden figures: a standing male (below) with tear-like channels running down the cheeks may be a deity or an ancestor figure. The 'tear channels' are associated in myth with twin *zemis* (spirit helpers), one related to the sun and one to the rain. A female figure, of great beauty, has a tray above her head. This was used to place bowls with offerings to the ancestral spirit world. These might have included harvest products and *cohoba*, a hallucinogenic snuff used in divination rites. A bird-headed figure is possibly a deity.

Little is known of the significance of the three pieces, or the date of their manufacture, except that they are of purely pre-Hispanic style and therefore were most probably manufactured before the arrival of Europeans. An account in the Society of Antiquaries' publication, *Archaeologia*, merely states:

Standing male figure
Taino, from the Greater
Antilles, Jamaica
*c.*1400–1600 AD
ETH Q 77 Am. 3
h. 1.40 m (4 ft 7 in)

April 11 1799
 Isaac Alves Rebello, Esq., F.A.S. exhibited to the Society Three Figures, supposed to be of Indian Deities, in wood, found in June 1792, in a natural cave near the summit of a mountain, called Spots, in Carphenter's [sic] Mountain, in the parish of Vere, in the island of Jamaica, by a surveyor in measuring the land. They were discovered placed with their faces (one of which is that of a bird) towards the east.

FURTHER READING
Archaeologia, xiv (1803), p. 269
I. Rouse, *The Tainos: the rise and decline of the People who greeted Columbus* (New Haven, 1992)

The terracotta figurines from Tanagra in Boeotia, produced in the late fourth and third centuries BC, are remarkable in that they show what appear to be ordinary people, dressed for shopping or travel, rather than the gods and goddesses of earlier years. Although there are many figures of children and youths, the typical 'Tanagra' figure is a slender and elegantly attired woman, generally dressed in a finely pleated *chiton* with a mantle drawn tightly over it. If she is bare-headed, her hair is usually drawn back into a knot at the nape of the neck; sometimes she wears a broad-brimmed sunhat, or pulls her mantle up to cover her head; often a fan or a wreath hangs from her hand. When compared with the stiff and formal terracotta goddesses of the sixth to mid-fourth centuries BC, their life-like appearance suggests that they must represent ordinary women. While their dress and hairstyles, however, are very probably modelled on contemporary fashions, many of the poses they assume are thought to imitate those of large-scale statues, and it is possible that they are in fact intended to represent Muses or divinities. Most of these figures are found in tombs, but similar objects have also been found in sanctuaries or decorating private homes.

The figures are technically accomplished – thin-walled and fully modelled. Frequently they retain traces of the bright pigments with which they were originally decorated; their hair may be coloured red, perhaps reflecting the use of henna, while their garments are rendered in shades of pink, red, blue and white, sometimes with touches of gold. The colours on the figure of the young man shown on the right are exceptionally well preserved.

Although terracotta figurines in this style are named after Tanagra, where large numbers were found in the 1870s, similar statuettes have been found elsewhere, and it is probable that the style originated in Athens.

Young man seated on a rock
Tanagra, Boeotia, Greece
c.300 BC
GR 1874.3–5.69
Terracotta C 274
h. 20 cm (7⁹⁄₁₀ in)

FURTHER READING
R.A. Higgins, *Tanagra and the Figurines* (London, 1987)
J.P. Uhlenbrock (ed.), 'The Hellenistic terracottas of Athens and the Tanagra style' in *The Coroplast's Art* (New York, 1990), pp. 48–53

The Taplow barrow, excavated in 1883, lay on a ridge overlooking the River Thames in the old churchyard at Taplow, Buckinghamshire. It consisted of a mound some 5 metres (5½ yds) in height and 75 metres (82 yds) in circumference. The lavish finds would have been even more spectacular, but the weight of the earth had crushed many of the remains and additional damage was caused by the fall of the stump of a yew tree during excavations.

The mound was constructed over an oaken chamber in which an adult male was buried accompanied by weapons, shields, jewelled belt and dress-fittings and clothing with gold-braided trim. He was equipped with quantities of fine drinking vessels: two pairs of drinking horns, four glass beakers and at least four

Four 'claw' beakers made of translucent light green glass
Taplow, Bucks, England
c.600 AD
MLA 1883,12–14,13–16
h. (of tallest) 30 cm
(12 in)
Given by Revd Charles Whately

mounted wooden cups, an imported bronze Byzantine bowl, large storage and cooking vessels, a lyre and gaming pieces.

The dead man was certainly a powerful local magnate, possibly even of royal status. The style of the objects indicates both a burial in the early seventh century and connections with the Kentish kingdom. This was a turbulent period, marked by the activities of warrior-kings and their followers, who rose and fell as more substantial kingdoms developed from looser tribal groupings.

About a dozen can be recognized between 550 and 650 AD. Among the more powerful were Kent, the West Saxons, to the north the kingdoms of the East Angles, the Hwicce, Mercia, Lindsey and, beyond the River Humber, Deira and Bernicia. This burial may be evidence of Kentish territorial expansion in the middle Thames region.

FURTHER READING
J. Blair and M. Lapidge (eds), 'The Taplow Barrow' in *A Companion to Anglo-Saxon England* (Oxford, 1998/9)

The **goddess Tara**

Sri Lanka is a bastion of Theravada Buddhism, a tradition of orthodoxy which lays primary emphasis on the historical Buddha and the spiritual succession of his enlightened (but still very human) followers. These perfected individuals are known as *arhats*. In contrast, Mahayana schools of Buddhism, associated most commonly with Tibet but found in Sri Lanka before the twelfth century, emphasize ideal heavenly worlds, transcendent cosmic Buddhas and semi-divine incarnations known as *bodhisattvas*. The *bodhisattvas* serve as intermediaries between the human and divine and often have female counterparts or consorts. These consorts are worshipped as 'saviouresses' in their own right.

In colossal rock-cut images at Buduruvagala in southern Sri Lanka, a female figure in a similar pose to the image shown here appears beside the *bodhisattva* Avalokiteshvara. This is the sole surviving sculpture in Sri Lanka which points to the identity of the Museum's image, the bronze itself having no specific features which tell us who she is.

The Tara has a tall tubular mass of hair. On the front of her tied-up locks is a fancy medallion with holes; these holes would have originally contained precious stones. The large central hole would have had a stone of immense size; it probably would have been engraved with a figure of Avalokiteshvara.

FURTHER READING
W. Zwalf (ed.), *Buddhism: Art and Faith* (London, 1985)

Figure of the Goddess Tara
Trincomalee, Sri Lanka
Gilded bronze,
8th century AD
OA 1830.6–12. 4
h. 1.43 m (4 ft 8¼ in)
Given by Sir Robert Brownrigg

The serving of tea in this special spirit in Japan has since the sixteenth century been called *cha-no-yu* ('hot water for tea'), but it is associated with a general philosophical and religious attitude called Chado (or Sado), the 'Way of Tea'. Its origins are in the tea ritual of Zen Buddhist temples in Tang dynasty (618–906 AD) China, but in its final form the tea ceremony is Japanese. The central concept is that everything – place, utensils, people – is unified by a common spirit which it is the host's duty to foster.

Since the sixteenth century AD the manner of preparation has varied among successive great masters, among them Shuko, Takeno Joo, Sen no Rikyu (1522–91), Furuta Oribe (1544–1615) and Kobori Enshu (1579–1647). The school of Rikyu separated in the seventeenth century into three, of which the largest today is Urasenke, 'the Rear House of Sen'. The Urasenke, which has sponsored a tea-house at the Museum, is the guardian of the traditions of 'Commoners' Tea'.

A tea-house in rustic style has walls of paper or mud and a ceiling of rush or bamboo. In a display alcove (*tokonoma*) is a scroll and/or flower arrangement. Because of the high prestige of Chinese ink-painting and Zen-style calligraphy, both of which traditionally used the hanging scroll (*kakemono*), the *tokonoma* was designed to suit that format.

The Museum has a fine collection of hanging scrolls in ink or restrained colour, especially those of the Kano and Nanga schools in the seventeenth to nineteenth centuries. There are also many hundreds of tea ceremony utensils dating mainly from the same period. A portable set for an outdoor ceremony is shown here.

FURTHER READING
L. Smith, V. Harris and T. Clark, *Japanese Art: Masterpieces in the British Museum* (London, 1990)

Portable set for an outdoor tea ceremony
Japan
Teabowl: painted Karatsu pottery (Hizen province); tea-caddy: probably Tekatori pottery (Chikuzen province) with turned ivory lid; napkin-holder: porcelain decorated in underglaze blue in *sometsuke* style; tea-whisk and holder: bamboo; container: black lacquer with gold *makie*
17th century AD (teabowl) and 18th century AD (remainder)
JA 1955.2–21.1
h. (container) 12 cm (4¾ in)
Given by Mr and Mrs D. Hewitt

Tell es Sa'idiyeh

The Museum has since the 1840s carried out excavations both in the United Kingdom and
abroad, and continues to do so today. One of the
more recent sites is Tell es-Sa'idiyeh (ancient
Zarethan) in the Central Jordan Valley. The site, a
large double mound or 'tell', lies on the south side
of the Wadi Kufrinjeh, about 1.8 km (1 mile) east
of the River Jordan. Excavations were undertaken
by the University of Pennsylvania in the 1960s and
in 1985 a new series of excavations was initiated by
the Museum.

Ivory pyxis
Tell es-Sa'idiyeh, Jordan
Late Bronze Age III
(1250–1150 BC)
WA 1998–3–30, 108
h. 5.1 cm (2 in)
Excavated in the 1987
season

Excavations on the lower tell have uncovered
parts of an extensive Early Bronze Age palace complex,
destroyed by fire in c.2700 BC, the function of which was the
industrial-scale production and commercial distribution of
commodities for export to Egypt. On the upper tell, below a series
of Iron Age city levels (eighth–tenth centuries BC), is an important
destruction level containing substantial and well-preserved architecture dating to the twelfth century BC. This, and the finds sealed
by the dense destruction debris, are strongly Egyptian in character
and it now seems clear that Sa'idiyeh in the twelfth century BC was,
like Beth-Shan or Gaza on the other side of the Jordan, an important centre for Egypt's control of its New Kingdom empire in
Canaan during its final phases under the pharaohs of the
Twentieth Dynasty. Towards the centre of the tell a 'Governor's
Residency' (a specific type of building known from Egyptian sites
in Canaan) has been excavated; parts of a massive city wall and a
large administrative complex have also been cleared. Over 420
graves were excavated, many showing strong Egyptian influence,
both in terms of the rich grave goods and also the burial practices,
which even include attempts at mummification.

The Museum has a considerable archive of objects from excavations available to researchers; much of it has been published.
Excavated material forms part of the permanent displays and it is
from time to time shown in temporary exhibitions.

FURTHER READING
J.N. Tubb, *Canaanites* (London, 1998)

This life-size terrapin of the species *Kachuga dhongoka*, endemic in the River Jumna, is made from a single piece of green Kashgar jade. It is related that it

> was brought from India by the late Lt General Kyd. . . While the General was employed, a number of years ago, as Engineer in the East India Company's Service, about the Fortifications at Allahabad, some Work People brought to him the said Tortoise which had been found at the bottom of a Tank [pond] and which it is most probable had been thrown in purposely by its worshippers to prevent its falling into the hands of the Enemy – General Kyd became possessed of this valuable Curiosity during the time that Marquis Cornwallis was Governor General of India [i.e. 1786–93].

The carving is thought to date from the reign of one of the Mughal emperors, either Akbar or Jahangir. Under the founder of the dynasty, Babur (AD 1483–1530), the Mughals, from Central Asia, swept into India. Babur's grandson Akbar (1556–1605) extended the Mughal empire from Gujarat to Bengal and from Afghanistan almost to the Deccan, with capitals at Agra and Fatehpur Sikri. Akbar fortified the sacred Hindu city of Piayag, renaming it Allahabad, and built a palace there. He designated it a capital in AH 991/AD 1583, but though it was appointed the residence of Crown Prince Shah Selim, Akbar never resided there. Selim became impatient to reign and set himself up in royal style, though he was briefly reconciled with his father in *c.*1605–27. In AH 1014/AD 1605 Selim succeeded and took the regal name of Jahangir (World-Grasper). After Jahangir's accession Allahabad was never again a royal residence.

Jade from eastern Asia (Kashgar) seems first to have been imported into Mughal India in the reign of Akbar. Mughal craftsmen became skilled in the art of carving hard stones and Jahangir is known to have patronized jade-carvers. It has been suggested that the terrapin, possibly an ornament from a garden pool or watercourse, may date from the period of Selim's rebellion before he became emperor.

Jade terrapin
Allahabad, India
17th century AD
OA 1830.6–12.1
l. 50.2 cm (19¾ in)
Bequest of Thomas
Wilkinson through James
Nairne

FURTHER READING
S.C. Welch, *India, Art and Culture
1300–1900* (New York, 1985)

The **Thetford treasure**

Although Christianity was well established in Britain in the fourth century AD, paganism continued to fight for existence. The Thetford treasure provides an illustration of this struggle. Among the 33 spoons found in the hoard, 31 were inscribed, 12 to the elusive Italian deity Faunus, a god of the countryside. Some spoons have Celtic bynames for Faunus, indicating that they were locally produced. There are also Latin personal names – Ingenuus, Primigenia, Silviola, Auspicius, Agrestis and perhaps Persevera.

The personal names indicate a family or group of people, and it may be that the spoons were used in the celebration of a religious ritual associated with the cult of Faunus. Their overtly pagan nature is exceptional at this late date, and the hoard's concealment may have been the result of anti-pagan legislation in the final decade of the fourth century AD. The spoons appear to come from a single work-shop, possibly in Gaul but perhaps local.

In addition to the spoons the hoard, which was found in 1979, included 48 other items. There were 22 gold rings set with garnets, emeralds, amethysts, other stones and glass (the largest and most important associated group of late-Roman rings yet discovered). The most striking object was a magnificent gold belt buckle (below) decorated with the figure of a satyr, with two horses' heads on the loop or bow. Other items of fine gold jewellery comprised necklaces and clasps, pendants, bracelets and beads.

Although one of the rings was probably designed for a man and the belt-buckle might also have been intended for masculine use, the jewellery as a whole is female. The pieces are almost entirely brand-new and at least two objects are unfinished. This, and stylistic similarities, suggest that this is a jeweller's or merchant's stock-in-trade of the second half of the fourth century AD.

The discovery was not immediately reported, and meanwhile the site was built upon. This has made it impossible for a proper archaeological investigation to be carried out. Thus we do not know whether the whole hoard was recovered or how it was buried.

FURTHER READING
C. Johns and T. Potter, *The Thetford Treasure: Roman Jewellery and Silver* (London, 1983)

Parcel gilt spoon (*cignus*) inscribed with a horn-blowing Triton and a dolphin
Thetford, Norfolk, Britain
4th century AD
PRB P 1981 2–1 50
l. 10.2 cm (4 in)
Treasure trove

Gold buckle
Thetford, Norfolk, Britain
4th century AD
PRB P 1981 2–1 1
h. 5.2 cm (2 in)
Treasure trove

Thoth is the ibis-headed god of Hermopolis, depicted also as a baboon; he was, traditionally, the scribe of the gods and the inventor of hieroglyphic writing. His ancient Egyptian name was Dejhuty; Thoth is the Greek rendering of his name (the Greeks equated him with their Hermes, messenger of the gods).

His major cult centre was at the ancient city of Khmun (Hermopolis Magna) in Middle Egypt, now known as El-Ashmunein, where vast but overgrown ruins remain of his temple. The site was excavated by the Museum in the 1980s.

Thoth appears in a variety of guises. He was closely associated with the moon and was regularly shown with a headdress consisting of a disc and crescent symbolizing the lunar phases. He was keeper of the divine archives and patron of history. During the ceremony of the judgement of the dead it was Thoth who proclaimed and registered the verdict when the heart was weighed (pp. 61–2).

The statue above shows him as a crouching baboon, probably from Hermopolis, where several colossal baboon-like statues, also of quartzite, were erected by Amenhotep III. This pharaoh's names are incised on the pedestal of this small figure.

Below is the ibis-headed Thoth offering the signs for 'all life and dominion' to Osiris (not shown), from the Book of the Dead of Hunefer.

Quartzite figure of a
baboon
Probably from
Hermopolis, Egypt
18th Dynasty, c.1390 BC
EA 38
h. 67 cm (26⅓ in)

Hieroglyphic Book of the
Dead of Hunefer
Egypt
19th Dynasty, c.1310 BC
EA 9901/2
h. 45 cm (17¾ in)
Purchased 1852, collected
by Antoine Barthélemy
Clot, Bey

FURTHER READING
G. Hart, *A Dictionary of Egyptian Gods and Goddesses* (London, 1986)

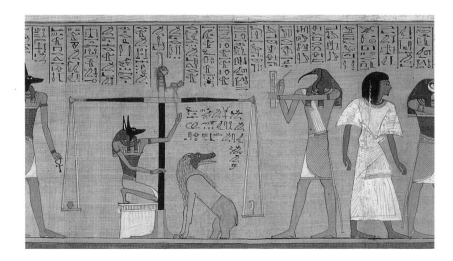

Tigers

The tiger is the great cat of Asia, the largest member of the cat family (*Felidae*). Although it is now endangered in many parts of the wild, its range extends from Siberia and Turkistan south to Djawa and Sumatra. It is to be seen in a few places in the Museum, but probably the most ferocious representation is that shown below, painted in the late eighteenth century AD by the Japanese artist Kishi Ganku. A wild tiger has climbed on to a jagged outcrop of rock beside a foaming mountain torrent and bares its teeth in a fierce snarl. The artist could not have seen a live tiger, which may explain why the head is strangely flattened, suggesting that he was drawing from the skin of a dead animal.

Another tiger far from its natural habitat is that shown above from the Romano-British Hoxne hoard (p. 154). One of the finest of the silver objects in the hoard is the solid-cast statuette of a prancing tigress whose stripes are inlaid in niello (black silver sulphide). The tigress is a handle from a large silver vase, and would originally have had a matching companion, perhaps a male tiger.

Tigers appear on Greek gems. The Department of Ethnography has model tigers and objects made of tiger teeth and claws. There are tiger masks and tiger puppets. Tigers are shown on items from the Sutton Hoo and Carthage treasures (pp. 312–13 and p. 68). They are modelled in English and continental porcelain; they emerge in large numbers in oriental painting. In the Mughal Empire the greatest importance was attached to the hunting of the tiger, the killing of which was ceremonially restricted to the emperor himself.

FURTHER READING
J. Rawson (ed.), *Animals in Art* (London, 1977)

Tigress
Hoxne, Britain
Silver, with stripes inlaid in niello
5th century AD
PRB P 1994 4–8 30
l. 15.9 cm (6¼ in)
Treasure trove
Acquired with the aid of the National Heritage Memorial Fund, the National Art Collections Fund, Lloyds Private Banking and private donations

Tiger
Kishi Ganku (1749–1838)
Hanging scroll; ink and colour on silk,
c.AD 1784–96
JA 1931.4–27.01 (Japanese painting ADD 79)
169 × 114.5 cm
(66½ × 45 in)

Tiles

Tiles, thin slabs of baked clay for roofs, pavements, walls and so on, have been used for millennia. They range from the rough and utilitarian to brilliantly decorated works of art. The Museum has particularly fine collections from the Islamic world and the English Middle Ages, to which have been added a number of outstanding tiles from the nineteenth century.

Ceramic tiles have been produced for over 1000 years in the heartlands of the Islamic world, from Iraq in the ninth century AD to Turkey in the nineteenth. The wealth of designs and colours later provided inspiration for European artists and designers. Together with mural painting and stucco, tiles brought colour and lavish designs to mosques and shrines, palaces and private houses. The Museum's collection is rich and varied and strong in several areas, particularly medieval Iran and the Ottoman Empire. There are rare types and dated pieces, as well as archaeological fragments, all of which are of great value to the student. Opposite are three underglaze tiles from sixteenth-century AD Syria, from a panel painted in delicate underglaze blue, turquoise and sage green. The narrow border has a scrolling design of rosettes and lotus blossoms against a blue ground which contrasts with the central motif of flowers entwined around wavy bands on a white ground.

In medieval England decorated tiles formed vivid patterned floors for royal palaces, ecclesiastical and monastic buildings, and prosperous merchants' houses. Although some decorated tiles were used in England in the tenth and twelfth centuries AD, the period of their greatest popularity was from the thirteenth to the mid-sixteenth century. The Museum has an unrivalled collection of some 14,000 medieval decorated tiles, including a complete pavement from a private dwelling, Canynges House, Redcliffe

Wall-tiles
Tring, Hertfordshire, England
early 14th century AD
MLA 1922, 4–12,1–8
32.5 × 16.3 cm
(12¾ × 6⅖ in)
Purchased in 1922 with the aid of the National Art Collections Fund

Tiles

Three underglaze tiles
Syria
16th century AD
OA G.1983.98
average 29 × 37 cm
(11²⁄₅ × 14½ in)
Bequest of Frederic
Ducane Godman

Street, Bristol, probably laid between AD 1480 and 1515. Shown opposite are tiles from Tring Church, Hertfordshire, incised with apocryphal stories of the childhood of Christ. In the two upper scenes boys who attack Jesus fall dead but are miraculously restored to life. In the lower (left), a father locks up his son to prevent him playing with Jesus, who helps the boy out of the tower; Jesus is chastised by his teacher Levi (right), but to the amazement of his teachers heals the infirm. The tiles were saved during restoration work in the nineteenth century. Ten complete tiles are known, eight in the Museum.

FURTHER READING

E. Eames, *English Mediaeval Tiles* (London, 1985)

E. Eames, *Medieval Craftsmen. English Tilers* (London, 1992)

V. Porter, *Islamic Tiles* (London, 1995)

In *c*.658–7 BC war broke out between Assyria and Elam in what is now southern Iran. The kingdom of Elam lay uncomfortably close to Assyria's Chaldaean and Babylonian provinces; disturbances there frequently involved the Elamites and there was a temptation for the Assyrians to interfere in the complicated policies of Elam. The king of Elam was Tepti-Human-Insushnak, a name abbreviated by the Assyrians to Teumman. He had apparently come to power in 664 BC. The sons of the previous king went to Assyria as refugees. Teumman requested their extradition but the diplomatic exchange ended in insults. Teumann's subsequent defeat and death at the battle of Til-Tuba (also known as the Battle of the River Ulai) were recorded with relish in these carvings.

The battle of Til-Tuba
(detail)
South-West Palace,
Nineveh, Assyria
c.660–650 BC
WA 124801; 1851–9–2, 8
h. 1.82 m (5 ft 11⅔ in)

The episodes, shown in 'strip-cartoon' form and partly explained by cuneiform inscriptions, record (from left to right): the chariot of Teumman crashes and an arrow hits him in the back. His son urges him to hurry away but Teumman and his son are surrounded by Assyrian soldiers. One Assyrian hits Teumman's son with a club while the second cuts off Teumman's head; a third picks up the royal headdress. Elamites in a tent are identifying heads brought by Assyrian soldiers. Teumman's head with its distinctive receding hairline is held out towards them. This is carried off to Assyria in an Elamite cart for presentation to Ashurbanipal. His son-in-law, seriously wounded, asks an Assyrian to behead him. Ituni, an Elamite officer, cuts his own bow in despair. Scene of triumph in Assyria.

FURTHER READING
J. Reade, *Assyrian Sculpture* (2nd edn, London, 1998)

Below is a group of tomb figures said to have come from the tomb of the general Liu Tingxun, who died in AD 728 and was buried at Luoyang. They include two earth spirits, two *Lokapalas* (Buddhist guardian figures) and two civil officials. The Museum also has two horses (which would probably originally have had leather harnesses with gilt bronze trappings), two camels (one laden with a pack guarded by animal masks and with a parrot, a pilgrim's flask, a ewer and some meat attached to it) and three grooms. The figures would have been displayed on a cart as part of Liu Tingxun's funeral cortège, then lined up outside the tomb until the coffin was in place, and finally positioned appropriately within the tomb before it was sealed. The official position of the tomb

Ceramic tomb figures
China
Tang dynasty,
*c.*AD 700–750
OA 1936.10–12.220–5
h. (largest) 1.09 m (43 in)
Purchased from the
George Eumorfopoulos
Collection with the aid of
public subscription

occupant apparently governed the size and number of the figures.

For a period of just over 50 years, from the end of the seventh to the middle of the eighth century AD, brightly glazed, vigorously modelled figures were produced in huge quantity in and around the Tang capitals Chang'an (present-day Xi'an) in Shaanxi province and Luoyang in Henan province, as well as in further-flung parts of the empire, for the tombs of those who could afford them. They are described as *sancai* (three colours), referring to the green, amber and cream glazes, but this is somewhat inexact, since the Tang *sancai* palette also included blue and black glazes. Tripod trays and incense burners, bottle vases with ribbed necks, ewers and other vessels were also produced by this method. Similar glazing techniques were employed in architectural ceramics and on later wares of the Song and Ming periods.

FURTHER READING
S.J. Vainker, *Chinese Pottery and Porcelain* (London, 1991; 2nd edn 2005)

Torcs, or torques, are ornamental neck rings, so named because the earliest versions were made of twisted metal rods or wire. Some of the most spectacular were made of gold or a gold/silver alloy, and their weight and rarity suggest that they were very highly prized.

Classical writers describe the Celtic warriors of Europe wearing gold torcs in battle, while classical sculptors portray both warriors and women with torcs. Archaeology provides a different picture: warriors were buried with iron torcs, women and girls with bronze ones and very rarely gold. At the battle of Telemon the writer Polybius wrote that 'all the warriors in the front ranks were adorned in gold necklaces and bracelets'.

Prior to 1948 the Museum could display only two torcs and a terminal, none from East Anglia. The 'Gold Field' at Ken Hill, Snettisham, Norfolk, has over the past half-century revolutionized the situation, being the site where at least 12 and perhaps 14 hoards were buried about 75 BC. These comprised 75 more or less complete torcs and pieces of 100 more. The first indication of the richness of the site was the discovery of five hoards during deep ploughing in 1948 and 1950. Between 1964 and 1973 four isolated torcs were found, and it was assumed that the site was exhausted, but in August 1990 a huge deposit of broken torcs, bracelets, ingots and coins was discovered and an archaeological excavation brought to light five more hoards. The entire treasure, some 20 kg (44 lb) of silver and 15 kg (33 lb) of gold, the largest deposit of gold and silver from Iron-Age Europe, seems unlikely to have belonged to an individual and may be a tribal treasury. Shown here is a 'nest' of torcs discovered in 1990, prior to its being moved.

Hoard of gold torcs photographed as found
Found at Snettisham, Norfolk, Britain
Buried 1st century BC, found 1990
PRB 1991 4–7 23–39
Treasure trove

FURTHER READING
I. Stead, *Celtic Art* (2nd edn, London, 1996)
R. Hobbs, *Treasure: Finding our Past* (London, 2003)

The **Towcester head**

This carved limestone head from Towcester (pronounced 'toaster'), Northamptonshire, is of particular interest in that it shows a mixture of native British and Roman styles. Britain became a province of the Roman Empire in AD 43. Although there had been previous contact with the Roman world, the conquest brought profound changes. For nearly 400 years Latin was the official language, and Britain's law, administrative system and currency were those of Rome. Towns, imposing stone and brick buildings, roads and bridges, classical religion and art, all became familiar. The vastly increased choice of everyday goods, including many imports, and settlers from other provinces in Europe, the Middle East and North Africa helped to create a richer and more diverse society.

Yet the Roman way of life did not wholly supplant its fore-runner. The degree of Romanization varied in different regions, but nowhere was the native heritage completely lost or suppressed. Over many generations the traditions of Iron Age society inter-acted and combined with classical elements to form a distinctive Romano-British cultural identity.

The head, which shows the continuation of Celtic influences, is probably from a funerary monument or enclosure alongside Watling Street (the Roman road which ran from London to Wroxeter), outside the Roman town of Lactodurum (Towcester). Its Celtic style indicates that it was probably made by a local craftsman. It represents a woman, larger than life-size, her hair worn in thick strands secured by a narrow band or diadem. Two curled locks descend on to the cheeks. The flatness of the face recalls Roman theatre masks.

Stone female head
Towcester, Northampton-
shire, England
2nd–4th centuries AD
PRB 1903 11–21 1
h. 57 cm (22½ in)
Given by Sir T. Fermor-
Hesketh, Bart.

FURTHER READING
J.M.C. Toynbee, *Art in Britain under the Romans* (Oxford, 1964), pp. 111–12
M. Henig, *The Art of Roman Britain* (London, 1995), pp. 99–100

Charles Townley (AD 1737–1805) spent much of his youth and early manhood abroad and while in Rome became an enthusiastic collector of antiquities. Returning to England, he bought a house in Park Street, Westminster, and filled it with sculpture. He wrote several catalogues of his collection, often recording the date and place of discovery or the date of purchase. As the collection grew it attracted considerable public interest.

Townley was a Trustee of the Museum and it was understood that he intended to bequeath the collection to it, but before his death in 1805 he decided instead to add a sculpture gallery to the family seat, Townley Hall, at Burnley, Lancashire. However, funds to build a gallery were not forthcoming and the collection was purchased by Parliament for the Museum.

The sculpture collection of Charles Townley in the dining room of his house in Park Street, Westminster
Drawn by William Chambers
Pen and grey ink and watercolour, 1794
PD 1995 5–6 8
39 × 54 cm
(15⅓ × 21¼ in)

Portrait bust of a woman, long identified as 'Clytie', who pined for the love of Helios. Possibly Antonia (*d.*AD 38), daughter of Mark Antony and Octavia
AD 40–50 (recut in the 18th century)
GR Cat. Sculpture 1874
h. 68.5 cm (27 in)
Townley Collection

The collection consists largely of Roman sculpture, with a few Greek originals. In the mid-eighteenth century Rome had become the destination for rich Englishmen on the Grand Tour. Old Roman collections were being broken up and sold by the impoverished descendants of the great families. The Roman art market developed under the direction of such British dealers as the artist Gavin Hamilton (1730–97) who, to feed demand, began 'excavations' of nearby sites including the villa of the Roman Emperor Hadrian (AD 76–138) at Tivoli.

FURTHER READING
B.F. Cook, *The Townley Marbles* (London, 1985)

Children's **Toys**

Children have amused themselves with toys of various sorts for millennia. Contrasting with the grander items in the Museum there are a few toys, some, rather poignantly, found in children's graves. Toys appear not to have survived particularly well. No doubt, as in modern times, they were made of ephemeral materials and received hard usage. They can, however, be hard to identify, since in some instances it is difficult to decide whether a model object is a child's toy or a votive offering.

The Egyptian collections include spinning tops (of a style still found today, rare before the Roman period), Roman-period balls of linen and reeds, and a model feline with an articulated jaw, inlaid crystal eyes and bronze teeth which may date from the New Kingdom.

Greek toys
FROM LEFT TO RIGHT
Terracotta whip-top
8th century BC
GR 1875.3–9.31

Terracotta dancing-doll
Corinth, c.350 BC
GR Terracottas 973

Baby-feeder
Southern Italy
Black-glazed pottery
4th century BC
BM Cat. Vases F 596

Miniature wine jug
Athens, c.425–400 BC
BM Cat. Vases E 549

Terracotta rattle
Cyprus, 3rd–2nd century BC
GR 1926.4–19.4

Shown here is a group of toys from the classical world. The whip-top dates from the eighth century BC and is very similar to those from Egypt. There is a terracotta dancing-doll holding castanets, a baby-feeder of black-glazed pottery with an inscription in Greek, 'drink, don't drop', a miniature *chous* (wine jug) showing an infant crawling towards a table and a terracotta rattle from Cyprus in the form of a pig. Children with toy carts are depicted on Greek pottery.

The Department of Ethnography has a large collection of toys from all over the world, among them model elephants, birds, weapons, canoes, camels, soldiers and carts. Toys used by Japanese children can be glimpsed in the large collection of Japanese prints. In the Department of Prints and Drawings is a toy theatre collection, acquired in 1886, with pantomimes, tragedies, popular dramas, naval and military battles and portraits.

Joseph Mallord William Turner's great achievement was to transform landscape painting from a topographical exercise to an accepted subject of imaginative expression of the highest order, informing his work with a wealth of references to literature, classical mythology and the art of the past. The son of a London barber, Turner (1775–1851) rapidly attained a prominent position in the artistic life of London, becoming a Royal Academician in 1802 and Professor of Perspective at the Academy from 1807 to 1837. He travelled extensively on the Continent between 1802 and 1845.

Turner sketched constantly, mainly in pencil, but he also made quick, slight watercolours, capturing his impressions, or 'colour beginnings', in which he worked out the main tones and shapes for the final works he had in mind. The finished works were for sale, exhibition or for use as the basis for engravings.

In the late 1820s Turner planned to leave the contents of his studio to the nation, with the intention that a special gallery should

'The Vale of Ashburnham'
One of a group of watercolours depicting views in Sussex commissioned by John Fuller, MP for the county. Beachy Head is visible in the centre distance.
Watercolour, AD 1816
PD 1910–2–12–272
37.9 × 56.3 cm
(15 × 22⅛ in)
George Salting Bequest

be built for their display by the Trustees of the National Gallery. This did not happen until the Clore Gallery was opened in 1986 as an adjunct to the Tate Gallery, and the 19,000 drawings, watercolours and sketchbooks which had been housed in the British Museum since 1931 were united with the oil paintings from the Turner Bequest. The Museum still has one of the finest collections of Turner's finished watercolours, nearly 80 magnificent unfaded examples, and it also houses virtually the complete collection of prints after Turner, nearly 900 compositions.

FURTHER READING
J. Gage, *Turner, 'A Wonderful Range of Mind'* (London and New Haven, 1987)
K. Sloan, *J.M.W. Turner Watercolours in the R.W. Lloyd Bequest* (London, 1998)
A. Wilton, *Turner in his Time* (London and New York, 1987)

For the Aztecs turquoise was among the most valued of all green stones (*chalchihuites*), which together symbolized life-giving water and the sources of fertility. The mineral was precious not only on account of its scarcity, but through its identification with the rain gods Tlaloc and Chalchiuhtlicue and with Tonatiuh and another aspect of the sun, Huitzilopochtli. Turquoise was reserved for ritual objects and ceremonial regalia worn by priests and rulers to signify their embodiment of the creative powers that governed all human life. Aztec trading emissaries (*pochteca*) sought far afield for this precious stone, securing much of it from mines in what is now the south-west USA.

The Aztecs lived around Lake Texcoco in the valley of Mexico, ruling what became an extensive empire from the island metropolis of Tenochtitlán. They forged an imperial dynasty based on military prowess and a network of long-distance trade and tribute routes that stretched from the Caribbean to the Pacific. The crafts-

men who produced the turquoise masks were most probably Mixtec, a people who during the fifteenth century AD resisted the Aztec imperial advance but offered the skills of their craftsmen in the service of the Aztec kings.

Only about 55 turquoise mosaics are known to have survived; of these, nine of the finest are in the Museum. They were acquired from various sources on the Continent of Europe, and it is thought that they may have formed part of the tribute given by the Emperor Moctezuma II to the Spanish conquistador Hernán Cortés upon his arrival on the coast of Mexico in AD 1519.

One of the finest, a mask formed on the base of a human skull, represents Tezcatlipoca, 'Smoking Mirror', in his quadruple aspect

Double-headed serpent
Mexico (Mixtec-Aztec)
AD 1400–1521
ETH 1894–634
h. 20.5 cm (8 in)
Purchased (Christy Fund)

one of the powerful creator gods in the Aztec pantheon. His distinguishing emblem, an obsidian mirror, symbolizes his control over the hidden forces of creation and destruction. The mask is also decorated with lignite and shell; polished iron pyrites have been used to fashion the eyes.

Opposite is a double-headed serpent, perhaps worn on the chest or as part of a headdress ensemble.

Below is a sacrificial knife with a blade of chalcedony, the handle carved in wood in the form of a crouching 'eagle knight' and covered with a mosaic of turquoise and other stone. The Aztecs practised several forms of human sacrifice, the most characteristic being the removal of a pulsating heart from a living victim.

In addition, the Museum's collection includes another mask (of Quetzalcoatl, p. 262), a ceremonial shield, a small animal head, a helmet and a bowl supported by an animal.

FURTHER READING
C. McEwan, *Ancient Mexico in the British Museum* (London, 1994)
C. McEwan, A. Middleton, C. Cartwright and R. Stacey, *Turquoise Mosaics from Mexico* (London, 2006)

Sacrificial knife
Mexico (Mixtec-Aztec)
AD 1400–1521
ETH St.399
l. 31.7 cm (12½ in)
Christy Collection
(acquired 1860–9)

Tutankhamun

The treasures from the tomb discovered by Howard Carter in 1922 are in Cairo, although they were shown outside Egypt in the spectacular exhibition at the Museum in 1972. The Museum has a number of items related to Tutankhamun, although nothing as fine as the Cairo collection. There are a number of rings and pendants with his prenomen, but the most impressive piece is a red granite lion, one of a pair, both attributable to Amenhotep III, who installed them as images of himself in front of his temple at Soleb in Nubia. While one bears an original inscription naming Amenhotep 'lion great of strength', the other appears to have been left unfinished, to be later inscribed by Tutankhamun. They were subsequently transported south to Gebel Barkal in the third century BC by the Meroitic ruler Amanislo, who had his names carved on the lion's chests. These are now located near the entrance to the Egyptian Sculpture Gallery.

Black granite royal statue of Hapy with the facial features of Tutankhamun
Thebes, Egypt
18th Dynasty, c.1320 BC
EA 75
h. 1.68 m (6 ft 6 in)

Shown here is a black granite royal statue with the attributes of the Nile-flood deity, Hapy. It is inscribed with the names of Horemheb, last king of the Eighteenth Dynasty, who usurped many monuments of Tutankhamun, but the statue preserves the features commonly associated with the boy king. The Museum also has a door jamb from Horemheb's tomb at Saqqara which shows him standing with hands uplifted in adoration, wearing a long-braided wig and the *uraeus* (perhaps added after his elevation to the kingship).

Tutankhamun, originally known as Tutankhaten, succeeded to the throne as a child. One of his chief advisers was General Horemheb. After his death Ay, an elderly noble, succeeded for a short period and may have married Tutankhamun's widow. When Ay died in c.1323 BC Horemheb became king.

FURTHER READING
N. Reeves, *The Complete Tutankhamun: the King, the Tomb, the Royal Treasure* (London, 1990)

Below is a selection of Tiffany objects made around 1900 from the Museum's collection of applied art covering the period from 1900 to 1950, which has largely been built up in the past two decades. The particular strengths of the collection include Continental Art Nouveau, applied art in Germany from *c*.1900 to 1930 (including the work of the Bauhaus school of design), Russian revolutionary porcelain (p. 278) and American decorative arts of the 1930s and 1940s. The collection comprises metalwork, jewellery, ceramics and glass. Twentieth-century furniture and textiles may be seen at the Victoria & Albert Museum.

The Tiffany group shown here comprises two vases, one deep blue with inlaid wave pattern and iridescent surface, another in the form of a jack-in-the-pulpit flower, one of Tiffany's most famous creations; a bronze candlestick in the form of a stylized tree with glass shade; a 'bud' candlestick; and one of Tiffany's early electric table lamps with 'mushroom' base and 'spider and web' shade.

Louis Comfort Tiffany trained as a painter before turning to interior decoration in 1879. In 1892 he formed his own company, with a factory for glassware and studios for the production of bronze candlesticks and lamps. Tiffany's work embodies the Art Nouveau style in America, and his is perhaps the most famous name in American decorative arts of the early twentieth century.

Glassware by L.C. Tiffany
USA
c.1896–1928
MLA 1980,11–9,1;
1980,11–8,1; 1981,7–12,1;
1981,7–13,1; 1984,7–4,1
h. of table lamp with
shade 45.5 cm (17 9/10 in)

FURTHER READING

D.C. Johnson, *American Art Nouveau* (New York, 1979)
J. Rudoe, *Decorative Arts 1850–1950* (London, 1994), cat. 284–8
A.C. Freylinghuysen, *Louis Comfort Tiffany at the Metropolitan Museum* (The Metropolitan Museum of Art Bulletin, New York, Summer 1998)

Ukiyo-e – 'pictures of the floating world' – was a school of popular art which recorded the life, fashions and entertainments of Japan's urban population in the seventeenth, eighteenth and nineteenth centuries, a world on the edge of conventional society:

> living only for the moment, turning our full attention to the pleasures of the moon, the snow, the cherry blossoms and the maple leaves; singing songs, drinking wine, diverting ourselves in just floating, floating; caring not a whit for the pauperism staring us in the face . . . [trans. Richard Lane, 1978].

Ukiyo-e belonged mainly to the great city of Edo (now Tokyo), the seat of government of the Shoguns from 1603 to 1868. Its artistic origins, however, lay in the ancient city of Kyoto, the cradle of both courtly and bourgeois culture. In January 1657 a great fire occurred in Edo, causing considerable destruction. The pleasure quarters were subsequently moved away from shrines, temples and the residences of the feudal lords. These districts became pockets of freedom and classlessness; their inhabitants adopted the gloomy Buddhist word *ukiyo* (the dark, shifting world of existence), changing its meaning to the 'floating world' of pleasure.

The lively publication of critiques of courtesans and actors and other illustrated books about the Floating World was carried out by the ancient woodblock printing technique. The erotic element was never far away where the subject-matter was the great courtesans and their activities. Single-sheet prints were rather less important than illustrated books until the decade 1740–50. Among artists of particular note were Suzuki Harunobu (*d.*1770), the leading artist of full-colour 'brocade prints' in the 1760s; Katsushika Hokusai (1760–1849) (p. 151) and Utagawa Hiroshige (1797–1858), the leading landscape artists of the school; and Kitagawa Utamaro (*d.*1806) (p. 345), the most celebrated artist of beautiful women and erotica. The Museum's collection of around 8000 ukiyo-e prints, illustrated books and albums is one of the finest and most comprehensive outside of Japan.

The Kabuki actors
Nakamura Wadaemon
and Nakamura Konozo
Toshusai Sharaku
(*fl.* AD 1794–5)
Japan
AD 1794
JA 1909.6–18.53
35 × 24.2 cm
(13¾ × 9½ in)
From the collection of
Sir Ernest Satow

FURTHER READING

L. Smith (ed.), *Ukiyo-e: Images of Unknown Japan* (London, 1988)
J. Reeve, *Floating World: Japan in the Edo Period* (London, 2006)

Honoratus to the holy god Mercury. I complain to your divinity that I have lost two wheels and four cows and many small belongings from my house. I would ask the Genius of your divinity that you do not allow health to the person who has done me wrong, nor allow him to lie or sit or drink or eat, whether he is man or woman, whether boy or girl, whether slave or free, unless he brings my property to me and is reconciled with me. With renewed prayers I ask your divinity that my petition may immediately make me vindicated by your majesty.

So runs one of around 100 rolled-up sheets of lead (*defixiones*) found on the site of the temple of Mercury at Uley, Gloucestershire. Often referred to as 'curses', they are petitions for divine intervention against wrongdoers. They shed light on the personal possessions of ordinary people as well as the timeless problems of petty theft and crime.

Excavations at West Hill, Gloucestershire, in 1977–9 revealed evidence of a religious site which was probably in use from Neolithic times to the early medieval period; in its Roman phase it can be identified as a temple to Mercury. An Iron Age shrine and surrounding enclosure were replaced in the early second century AD by a stone-built Romano-Celtic temple, which was in turn enlarged in the fourth century. Around the temple were other buildings including living quarters, guest accommodation and shops. By the fifth century AD pagan worship at the site appears to have been replaced by Christianity.

The principal cult statue of Mercury was a little larger than life-size (approximately 2m/6ft 6 in tall). Fragments only remain; the head (left) is carved in local Cotswold stone in the Roman style. Technical and stylistic details indicate that it was made in the later second century AD. The statue stood on a base with two of the god's animal companions, a ram and a cockerel. Bones of sacrificial animals, mainly domestic poultry, sheep and goats, were also found on the site.

Head of Mercury
Uley, Gloucestershire,
England
2nd century AD
PRB P 1978 1–2 1
h. (of statue) *c.*2 m
(6½ ft)

FURTHER READING
A. Woodward and P. Leach, *The Uley Shrines. Excavation of a ritual complex on West Hill, Uley, Gloucestershire: 1977–9* (London, 1993)

The city of Ur lay in southern Mesopotamia, close to the ancient shoreline of the Gulf. Excavations by Leonard Woolley in 1927–32 uncovered a unique cemetery with hundreds of graves, most dating from c.2800–2370 BC. Below the simple graves of the common people lay the elite of Ur, buried with magnificent treasures. Among the richest tombs was that of Pu-abi, her name recorded on a fine cylinder seal of lapis lazuli. She lay on a wooden bier, a gold cup near her hand, the upper part of her body entirely hidden by multi-coloured beads. Over her crushed skull she wore an elaborate headdress. Buried with her were 25 attendants. An adjacent tomb with no principal occupant had 65 attendants. Even more bodies were found in the tomb known as the Great Death-Pit, which was occupied by six servants, four women harpists and 64 other women, dressed in scarlet and adorned with gold, silver, lapis lazuli and carnelian. It was surmised that the attendants had voluntarily taken poison and been buried while unconscious or dead.

The identity of the people buried in these graves is uncertain. The original supposition was that they were kings and queens, but there is nothing like these burials elsewhere in Mesopotamia and only one written reference to human sacrifice. Such personal titles as have been found do not appear on Mesopotamian king-lists. The occupants may be officials, especially priestesses, of the Moon God of Ur. The practice of human sacrifice might then have been restricted to this particular cult, which would explain its absence elsewhere. Other possibilities are that the principal occupants are priests and priestesses killed after sacred marriage ceremonies, or even substitute kings and queens killed to avert bad luck.

In addition to a large collection of jewellery, weapons, armour, harness and stone vessels a number of spectacular pieces were found. The 'Ram in the thicket' (right), is more accurately a goat perched up against a bush. It is one of a pair, used to support an item of

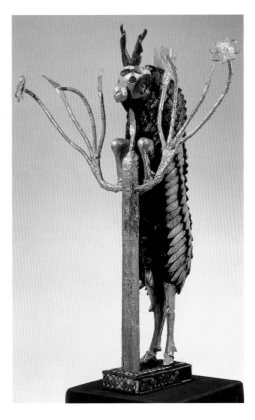

The 'Ram in the thicket'
Mesopotamia (Iraq)
c.2600 BC
WA 122200; 929–10–17,1
h. 45.7 cm (18 in)
Excavated by Sir Leonard Woolley

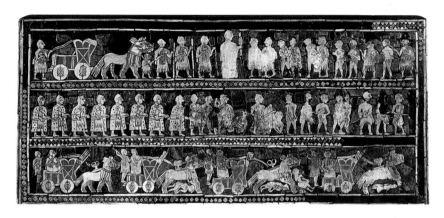

The 'Standard of Ur'
Mesopotamia (Iraq)
*c.*2600 BC
WA 121201;
1928–10–10,3
l. 49.5 cm (19½ in)
Excavated by Sir Leonard
Woolley

furniture. The goat has a face and legs of gold leaf. The horn, eyes
and shoulder fleece are of lapis lazuli and the body fleece white
shell. Above is the so-called 'Standard of Ur', a hollow box of
unknown function inlaid with mosaic scenes made from shell, red
limestone and lapis lazuli, set in bitumen. On one side can be seen
peace and prosperity, with a procession of men bringing animals,
fish and other goods. At the top the king banquets among his
friends, entertained by a singer and a man with a lyre. On the other
side (shown here) a Sumerian army, with chariots (the earliest
known representations of wheeled vehicles) and infantry, charges
the enemy. The prisoners are then brought before the king. In addition there are the remains of gold vessels, lyres and board games
(pp. 58–9).

The finds from the excavation were split equally between Iraq,
the University of Pennsylvania Museum in Philadelphia and the
British Museum.

FURTHER READING
L. Woolley, *Ur 'of the Chaldees': the Final Account, Excavation at Ur*, rev. and updated by
P.R.S. Moorey (London, 1982)
L. Woolley, *Ur Excavations*, 10 vols, 1927–76; *Texts*, 8 vols, 1928–74
(London and Philadelphia)

L ittle is known of the early history of the mountainous area of eastern Anatolia. In the first millennium BC the mountain clans united and founded the kingdom of Urartu, which was centred on Lake Van but extended north and east across the modern frontiers; the ancient name survives in that of its highest mountain, Ararat. Between 640 and 590 BC the kingdom was over-run by Medes or Scythians from the east.

The Urartians built impressive fortresses to guard the mountain passes into their kingdom. Their craftsmen sought inspiration from the cultures of their neighbours (particularly Assyria) but created a distinctive art of their own. Urartian metalwork became famous, and Assyrian texts tell of huge treasures stored in the temples. Some of the scenes on the Balawat Gates (p. 45) show Assyrians campaigning in Urartu.

The Museum has a number of objects found at Toprakkale (Rusahinili), the site of a major Urartian temple of the god Haldi outside the capital, Tushpa (now Van). These include bronze figures and ivories. Urartian temples, built of stone and mud-brick, were square with buttressed corners. Shields and spears decorated the façade. In front stood tall bronze statues and tripods support-ing cauldrons with massive handle attachments. The floor at Toprakkale was inlaid with stone circles; a decorated bronze band and pegs for hangings probably adorned the walls, and a bronze model of a city (below) was displayed before the god.

The city has a high arched doorway flanked by towers. There were at least three upper floors, with two further ones in the turrets. Above the decorated parapets are stepped crenellations. The lower part of the walls and the door- and window-frames would have been made from beautifully cut and fitted stone blocks, with the upper wall of mud-brick and the parapets resting on pairs of jutting beams. The function of the model is not known. It could have been dedi-cated in the temple to ensure the deity's protec-tion, or presented by a vassal city.

Model of a city and turret
Toprakkale (Rusahinili),
Turkey
Bronze, late 8th
century BC
WA 91177, 91250;
1877–12–18,1 and 2
h. 28 cm (11 in)
Purchased from
A.H. Layard

FURTHER READING
B.B. Piotrovsky, *The Ancient King-dom of Urartu* (London, 1969)

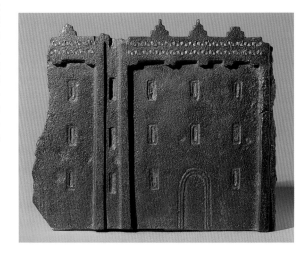

Mesopotamia, the land between the Rivers Tigris and Euphrates, including much of modern Iraq and eastern Syria, has been called the cradle of civilization, home of some of man's first experiments in agriculture and irrigation. A series of prehistoric communities slowly becoming more reliant on domestic rather than wild resources for their food occupied the area from before 8000 BC. Successful adaptation led to increased density of population, and large towns evolved before 3500 BC. By 3000 BC the development of writing and the mass production of goods reflected the complexities of social organization.

One of the major centres was Uruk in southern Mesopotamia, which grew until it covered over five square km (nearly two square miles). Power seems to have been concentrated in the temples or religious organizations, but the eventual building of a city wall is ascribed to a king, Gilgamesh. Massive temple buildings were constructed and reconstructed over the centuries. Elaborate administrative organizations existed, with specialist craftsmen classified by rank. Workers may have been paid in rations of food. International trade and other links flourished.

The Uruk Trough
Uruk (Warka), Iraq
c.3300–3000 BC
WA 120000; 1928–7–14,1
l. 96.52 cm (38 in)
Purchased with the aid of
the National Art
Collections Fund

While pottery for common use was mass-produced, magnificent examples of stone carving were created for dedication in the temples. The working of metal became widespread.

The Uruk Trough, which is made of carved gypsum, comes from this late prehistoric period. Since it is impractical – if raised high enough for its relief decoration to be visible it cannot readily be used as a trough or basin – it was probably a cult object in the temple of Inanna, goddess of love and fertility, the supreme goddess of Uruk and a version of Ishtar.

The carving shows a procession of ewes and rams approaching a reed building of a type still found in southern Iraq, and two lambs emerging from it. The reed bundles with streamers on the building and at the ends of the scene appear later as a symbol of Inanna. The precise meaning of the scene is unknown, but it probably reflects the fecundity of flocks under her protection. The Uruk ceremonial trough is among the earliest examples of formal religious art from Mesopotamia.

FURTHER READING
D. and J. Oates, *The Rise of Civilisation* (Oxford, 1976)

Utamaro's women

The Japanese artist most famous outside Japan is Hokusai (p. 151; next comes Kitagawa Utamaro (1753–1806), the most celebrated artist of women of the whole ukiyo-e school (p. 339).

Pictures of beautiful women had always been the most important category of subject-matter for most ukiyo-e artists, but Utamaro's preoccupation with the appearance and moods of women of all types and classes was obsessive. The largest category of his subjects was the elite group of high-ranking courtesans in the single government-licensed pleasure quarter, the Yoshiwara. They constitute perhaps 30 per cent or so of the approximately 1900 designs for sheet prints currently known. Other series show ordinary townswomen of various classes engaged in trades or housework, particularly looking after children.

Utamaro's obsession with women manifested itself in many ways. He excelled at sensuous depictions, at conveying the sense of the glistening skin of the female body and capturing the most delicate nuances of emotional states. Sometimes all male figures will be excluded from a scene in which they would normally be found; sometimes their presence is only hinted at beyond the edge of the composition. Women may be shown impersonating the roles or work normally performed by men.

In the early 1790s Utamaro and his publisher Tsutaya introduced the innovation of half-length portraits of beautiful women set against a background of silvery-white ground mica. Shown here is a half-length portrait of Ohisa, the beautiful daughter of the proprietor of a chain of cake shops and tea-houses, the Takashimaya. Her role was to draw patrons to the tea-houses, and she was the subject of colour prints by several ukiyo-e artists during the 1790s. Inscribed on the print is a poem by Karabana Tadaaya which begins, 'Though love and tea are overflowing, neither grows cold'.

FURTHER READING
S. Asano and T. Clark, *The Passionate Art of Kitagawa Utamaro* (London, 1995)

Half-length portrait of Ohisa holding a fan
Japan
Colour woodblock print, *c.*AD 1792–3
JA 1927.6–13.6
37.6 × 24.7 cm
(14⅘ × 9¾ in)
Given by R.N. Shaw

Venetian glass

Venetian glass of the Renaissance represents an astonishing technological achievement. By experimenting with raw materials and techniques in the course of the fifteenth century, Venetian craftsmen were able to produce glass which was famous for its thinness and clarity. Some Roman techniques, such as *millefiori*, were revived; others were developed in the sixteenth century, for example the imitation of semi-precious stones such as chalcedony and opal. Venetian glass was collected and exported to princely courts and aristocratic consumers throughout Europe.

Because of the risks of fire and for greater ease of control, the Grand Council of Venice had decreed in AD 1292 the removal of all Venetian glass-houses to the island of Murano, about an hour across the Lagoon in a rowing-boat.

Even before the end of the fifteenth century the Venetian glass-makers had succeeded in making monumental armorial covered standing cups of clear, gilded *cristallo* and betrothal goblets of sapphire-blue, emerald-green and turquoise, on which gold and enamels were lavishly applied. Below is a *lattimo* (opaque-white glass) vase painted with a portrait of Henry VII, king of England (1485–1509), and his personal badge (a portcullis with chains). Another magnificent item in the Museum's collection is the so-called 'Deblin' standing cup and cover, with a diamond-engraved inscription in Czech which can be translated 'Praise the Lord and drink cool wine to the health of the masters [lords] of Deblin'; it was perhaps made in Murano for a member of the Bohemian or Hungarian nobility.

'Ring-handled' vase of Henry VII
Venice, Italy
*c.*AD 1500–9
MLA 1979,4–1, 1
h. 19.8 cm (7¾ in)

FURTHER READING
H. Tait, *The Golden Age of Venetian Glass* (London, 1979)
H. Tait (ed.), *Five Thousand Years of Glass* (London, 1991; paperback edn 1995)

Victorian illustrated books

The 1860s were unique in the history of British illustration. There was a remarkable increase in the scale of publishing of both books and magazines, which could be cheaply illustrated by means of wood-engraving. At the same time several of the greatest artists, led by the Pre-Raphaelites and those influenced by them (often termed the Idyllic School), produced large numbers of memorable and moving designs. Two great wood-engraving businesses dominated publishing in London at this date – those of the Dalziel Brothers and Joseph Swain. The Museum has both the Dalziel Archive (purchased in 1913) and a collection given by Robin de Beaumont in 1992. The Dalziel Archive consists of albums containing almost every print engraved by the Dalziels – some 54,000 impressions. The de Beaumont collection comprises over 300 illustrated books and magazines, proofs, wood-blocks, letters and original drawings. The books in this collection are unequalled for their remarkable state of preservation.

The collection includes works by many of the most distinguished artists active during the period. Precursors in the 1840s included Richard Dadd (p. 97), John Tenniel and Charles Keene, while in the next decade John Everett Millais, Dante Gabriel Rossetti, Edward Burne-Jones, Ford Madox Brown and William Holman Hunt began their careers. At the same time women artists, notably Jane Benham (Hay), Eleanor Vere Boyle (working as EVB) and Mary Ellen Edwards became popular and admired. The 1860s proper saw the ranks of illustrators swelled by Frederic Shields, Frederick Sandys, Arthur Hughes, James McNeill Whistler, Arthur Boyd Houghton and Matthew Lawless among many others.

Shown on the right is 'Shadow and Substance' by G.J. Pinwell, described as the most intensely poetic of the Idyllic artists for his ability to produce haunting and sometimes disturbing images with an air of mystery about them. Very few of his figures look directly out of the designs, while many hide their features with a hat.

'Shadow and Substance'
from *Wayside Posies*, i. 8
G.J. Pinwell (1842–75)
England
AD 1867
PD 1992-4-6-395
16.9 × 12.5 cm
(6⅔ × 4⁹/₁₀ in)
Given by Robin de Beaumont

FURTHER READING
P. Goldman, *Victorian Illustrated Books 1850–1870* (London, 1994)
P. Goldman, *Victorian Illustration. The Pre-Raphaelites, the Idyllic School and the High Victorians* (Aldershot, 1996)

The Vikings' love of ostentatious display is revealed in the lavish goods found in pagan burials and by the many ornaments buried in silver hoards. Women wore dresses suspended from shoulder-straps in the form of paired loops held together by two brooches. A third brooch might fasten a shawl and a small round brooch at the neck the opening of a chemise. During the ninth and tenth centuries AD the commonest shoulder-brooches were domed and oval in shape. Men used brooches and pins, often massive, for fastening cloaks of furs, hides and shaggy wool. Smaller cloaks were fastened with simpler pins of bronze or bone on the right shoulder, so that the sword arm could be kept free. Pendants on chains, such as Thor's hammers, were also worn.

Art historians discern in Viking jewellery, and in their art generally, a series of overlapping styles. The earliest is Broa (eighth century AD, called after the motifs on a series of gilt-bronze bridle-mounts found in a grave at Broa on Gotland); then come Borre (ninth to second half of the tenth century AD, from a lavishly ornamented bridle in a barrow-burial at Borre in Vestfold, Norway); Jellinge (late ninth to late tenth century AD, called after the ornament of a silver cup from the Danish royal burial-mound at Jelling in Jutland); Mammen (second half of the tenth to early eleventh century, named after the designs on an axe from the grave of a

Pair of bronze oval brooches from a burial mound
Møre og Romsdal, Vestnes, Norway
10th century AD
MLA 1894,11–5, 2, 3
l. 10.79 cm (4¼ in)

Danish Viking); Ringerike (first half of the eleventh century, named after the carved slabs of a rich district north of Oslo); and Urnes (mid-eleventh century, from the wooden carving of the church at Urnes in western Norway).

FURTHER READING

J. Graham-Campbell and D. Kidd, *The Vikings* (London, 1980)
J. Graham-Campbell, *The Viking World* (London, 1980)
D.M. Wilson, *The Vikings and Their Origins* (London, 1980)

Between 1973 and 1997, excavations directed by Robin Birley at the Roman fort of Vindolanda (modern Chesterholm), Northumberland, close to Hadrian's Wall, brought to light hundreds of fragments of wooden writing tablets – the oldest group of handwritten documents known from Britain. They were deposited between about AD 92 and 120 and consist mainly of official military documents. There are also many personal letters to and from the serving soldiers and officers – several hundred have been identified – which provide an unparalleled insight into military life at that time. There are inventories, memoranda, a military intelligence report; personal letters of recommendation; an entertainment account; and even a birthday invitation from the wife of one fort commander to the wife of another.

Britain was the most northerly outpost of the empire. The first, brief, Roman military expeditions in 55 and 54 BC were led by Julius Caesar. In AD 43 the Emperor Claudius made Britain a province. Roman rule was gradually extended north in the last three decades of the first century AD, when the frontier was established on the so-called Stanegate Line, a road and ditch system connecting the main frontier forts, Stanwix, Nether Denton, Chesterholm (Vindolanda) and Corbridge. It retained its importance until the building of Hadrian's Wall a few miles further to the north *c.*AD 122–5.

There seem to have been two auxiliary cohorts stationed at Vindolanda during the period of the letters. One was the Ninth Cohort of Batavians (probably 500 soldiers), part mounted. The other was the First Tungrian Cohort (1,000 strong). Both were raised in an area which is now in Belgium or the Netherlands.

Most of the tablets consist of wafer-thin leaves of wood (birch or alder), a type hardly recognized before because of its tendency to decay, but one probably in common use in antiquity, in addition to the better-known wax-holding tablets. The texts are written in ink in a cursive Latin script, with small, simple characters used for documents and letters, as opposed to 'literary bookhands' which used capital forms of the letters. They are extremely difficult to read.

FURTHER READING
A.K. Bowman, *Life and Letters on the Roman Frontier: Vindolanda and its People* (3rd edn, London, 2003)

FAR LEFT
The 'Aeneid Fragment', ink writing tablet
Vindolanda (modern Chesterholm), Northumberland
Wood, late 1st–early 2nd century AD
PRB P 1986 10–1 128
w. 10 cm (4 in)

LEFT
Intelligence report
Fragment of what was probably a memorandum, possibly left by a commanding officer for his successor, describing the fighting habits of the Britons
Vindolanda, Northumberland
Wood, late 1st–early 2nd century AD
PRB P 1986 10–1 34
w. 7.8 cm (3 in)

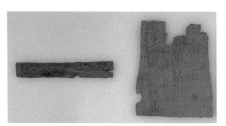

Vishnu

Vishnu is, with Brahma and Shiva (p. 301), one of the three great gods of the Hindu pantheon. Most Hindus worship either Vishnu or Shiva as the supreme deity, and few temples are dedicated to Brahma. The gods can be identified by particular attributes, and if there are many the god may be given several pairs of hands to hold them. One unmistakable attribute, though not always shown, is the real or mythical animal mount of the more important gods.

Vishnu is the preserver of the order of the universe and its protector. His consorts are Lakshmi and Shri, both goddesses of good fortune, and Bhu, the earth goddess. He is the god of love and of emotion. He may be identified by his mount – a creature, half-man and half-bird, called Garuda – and by his tall, conical jewelled crown. He has four hands and usually carries a conch shell and a lotus, with two distinctive weapons, the club (*gada*) and the discus (*chakra*). Sometimes one hand is empty, shown either in the position of boon-granting (*varadamudra*) or fearlessness (*abhaya-mudra*). The qualities of Vishnu as saviour are manifested in his incarnations on earth (*avataras*) at times of spiritual and political decline, guiding erring mankind. There are generally accepted to be ten incarnations (*dashavatars*): Matsya (the fish), Kurma (the tortoise), Varaha (the boar), Narasimha (the lion), Vamana (the dwarf), Parashurama (Rama with the Axe), Rama, Krishna, Buddha and Kalki (the incarnation still to come).

Krishna is the most widely worshipped of all the *avataras* of Vishnu (save perhaps Rama). There are many different strands in Krishna's personality: a god-child involved in practical jokes; a cowherd god renowned for his erotic dalliance with the milkmaids (*gopis*), above all Radha; a pastoral deity who plays the flute with magical effect; a god who controls the snake deities (*nagas*); a philosopher; and an urban ruler.

On the left is an illustration of Krishna dancing with the milkmaids in a circular dance known as the *rasamandala*. The flute-playing god in the centre magically causes each of the milkmaids to imagine that he is dancing with her alone.

Krishna dancing with the *gopis*
Mewar, Rajasthan, India
Manuscript page,
AD 1630–40
OA 1959.4–11.7
25.1 × 18.6 cm
(9¾ × 7⅓ in)
Purchased with the aid of
P.T. Brooke Sewell

FURTHER READING
T.R. Blurton, *Hindu Art* (London, 1992)

This collection, from Waddesdon Manor in Buckinghamshire, was bequeathed by Baron Ferdinand de Rothschild (1839–98) and forms the nearest equivalent to be found in Britain of the varied *Schatzkammer* (treasure chamber) of a Renaissance prince. It comprises a glittering, spectacular display of goldsmiths' work, jewellery and precious *objets d'art*.

The nucleus of the collection was formed by Baron Anselm de Rothschild of the Austrian branch of the family. His son Ferdinand, who as a child had delighted in handling his father's collection, moved to England in 1860, where he fell in love with and married Evelina, the daughter of Baron Lionel de Rothschild of the English branch. His wife died shortly after the marriage. Baron Ferdinand never remarried but turned to charitable and public work. In 1874 he embarked on a lifetime project – the construction and furnishing of a fine house at Waddesdon in Buckinghamshire. He became a Trustee of the Museum in 1896 and bequeathed the contents of the New Smoking Room in the Bachelor's Wing at Waddesdon to the Museum on condition that it be permanently displayed in a room known as 'the Waddesdon Bequest Room'.

The bequest, which was in 1900 valued at £325,000, comprises over 250 objects, most dating from the European Renaissance. In the tradition of the *Schatzkammer* there are older pieces. The oldest items are four Hellenistic bronze medallions of unknown origin and use found in a tomb in the province of Trebizond. From the Middle Ages comes a *champlevé* enamelled reliquary, probably manufactured at Limoges in France in the decade 1170–80, which depicts the martyrdom of Saint Valerie. There is a fourteenth-century enamelled glass mosque lamp from Syria.

The most spectacular object in the collection is the gold enamelled reliquary of the Holy Thorn, made in *c*.1400–10 for Jean, Duc de Berry, uncle of Charles VI of France (right). The Holy Thorn, supposedly from Christ's Crown of Thorns, is set in a cabochon sapphire behind a 'window' of rock crystal. Around the relic is the scene of the Second Coming and below it the Resurrection of the Dead.

The Holy Thorn reliquary
France
c.AD1400–10
MLA WB 67
h. 30.5 cm (12 in)
Baron Ferdinand de
Rothschild Bequest

FURTHER READING
H. Tait, *Catalogue of the Waddesdon Bequest in the British Museum*, vol. I: *The Jewels* (London, 1986); vol. II: *The Silver Plate* (London, 1988); vol. III: *The 'Curiosities'* (London, 1991)

When and where the first watch was made is not known; no surviving example can be dated before the second quarter of the sixteenth century AD. There is some written evidence suggesting a fifteenth-century origin in Italy or an early sixteenth-century origin in Nuremberg, but this is inconclusive. As with clocks (p. 81), the most important development was the use of a spring as a power source, but another technological breakthrough probably occurred before the middle of the fifteenth century, when a totally different form of construction was adopted in clockmaking. The movement was placed horizontally and all the mechanism except the balance wheel was contained between two plates held apart by four pillars. The plates were used as a basis on which to build the mechanism. In consequence there was no longer a frame into which the mechanism was suspended and fixed. Clockmakers gradually learnt how to execute mechanisms on a very small scale, eventually creating what we call 'watches' – miniature portable timepieces that could be worn on the person.

By AD 1512 spring-driven timepieces small enough to be carried in pouches (or purses) were being made in Nuremburg – the inventor of the mechanism was Peter Henlein (*c*.1497–1542) – but these may have been merely miniature table-clocks. In 1524 the Nuremberg archives record a gilt musk-ball with a timepiece, and

Six early watches, all *c*.1550–1650

BOTTOM LEFT a German 'tambour' watch, with iron 'stackfreed' movement, shown below ?Nuremberg, Germany MLA CAI–2203 diam. 5.54 cm (2¼ in)

TOP CENTRE a striking watch signed '*Jaecques bulck(e)*', with the movement shown below ?England or the Low Countries MLA CAI–2242 diam. 6 cm (2⅓ in)

TOP RIGHT steel-cased watch, outer case of leather and *piqué* ornament, signed '*Richard Crayle fecit*' England MLA CAI–2300 diam. 5.35 cm (2 in)

BOTTOM RIGHT Silver shell-shaped watch signed '*Jo. Willowe in Fleetstreet*' England MLA CM 1888, 12–1, 204 5 × 3.5 cm (2 × 1⅓ in) Octavius Morgan Bequest

RIGHT striking and alarum watch with pierced floral case signed '*Sam. Shelton*' (died 1648) England MLA 1874, 7–18, 62 diam. 4.45 cm (1¾ in) Fellows Bequest

TOP LEFT 'stackfreed' watch with striking mechanism made by Hans-Jakob Zurlauben for Beat Jakob Zurlauben Zug, Switzerland MLA 1888, 12–1.167 5 × 4.4 cm (2 × 1¾ in) Octavius Morgan Bequest

Watches

the inventory of jewels given by King Henry VIII to Catherine Howard in 1540–1 lists a gold pomander 'wherein is a clocke'. These seem to be the earliest mention of 'watches' in our sense of the word.

The Museum's collection of over 4200 watches comprehensively covers every aspect of the history and development of the watch as a portable timekeeper and is probably the finest in the world. It ranges from examples of the German 'stackfreed' watches of the mid-sixteenth century to the advent of quartz technology in the early 1970s. On the previous page are six early watches of *c*.1550–1650. Bottom left is a German (perhaps Nuremberg) 'tambour' watch, with iron stackfreed movement shown below it. Top centre is a striking watch signed 'Jaecques bulck(e)', perhaps English or Low Countries, with the movement shown below. Top right is an English steel-cased watch, outer case of leather and piqué ornament, signed 'Richard Crayle fecit'. Bottom right is an English silver shell-shaped watch signed 'Jo. Willowe in Fleet Street'. Right is an English striking and alarum watch with pierced floral case signed 'Sam. Shelton' (*d*.1648). Top left is a Swiss 'stackfreed' watch with striking mechanism made in Zug by Hans Jakob Zurlauben for his relative Beat Jakob Zurlauben in *c*.1615. Above, by contrast, is a group of modern watches.

FURTHER READING

H. Tait, *Clocks and Watches* (London, 1983)

H. Tait and P.G. Coole, *Catalogue of Watches in the British Museum*, vol. 1: *The Stackfreed* (London, 1987)

A. Randall, rev. R. Good, *Catalogue of Watches in the British Museum*, vol. VI: *Pocket Chronometers, Marine Chronometers and Other Portable Precision Timekeepers* (London, 1989)

Six modern watches
CLOCKWISE FROM LEFT
Sports wrist-watch
Stainless steel case and strap, 1975–80
MLA 1988,10–13,1
case: 3.8 × 4.4 cm
(1½ × 1¾ in)

Swatch wrist-watch
Plastic case and strap, 1988
MLA 1990,5–8,1
case: 3.4 × 3.8 mm
(1⅓ × 1½ in)

Gold-plated cased pin-pallet lever watch
Brass case with stainless steel, black leather and plastic strap, 1965–70
MLA 1983,10–12, 200
case: 3.3 × 4.1 mm
(1¼ × 1½ in)

Mickey Mouse wrist-watch
Base metal case with steel strap, *c*.1960
MLA 1987,10–12,18
case: 3.4 × 4.1 cm
(1⅓ × 1½ in)

Chrome-plated wrist-watch
Stainless steel case and strap
MLA 1989, 4–6, 9
case: 3.4 × 4.1 cm
(1⅓ × 1½ in)

Gold-plated octagonal wrist-watch
Brass case with black enamel dial and leather strap
MLA 1987, 10–12, 20
case: diam. 4 cm (1½ in)

The Water Newton Treasure is the earliest group of Christian liturgical silver yet found in the Roman Empire. It was discovered in a recently ploughed field at Water Newton, Cambridgeshire, the Roman town of Durobrivae, in February 1975. The treasure contains nearly 30 objects, some badly damaged. Nine items are vessels – bowls, jugs, a two-handled cup and a strainer – while the rest are small triangular plaques of thin metal, representing stylized leaves. Except for one small gold plaque, everything is made of silver. Many of the objects bear the Greek letters *chi* (X) and *rho* (P), standing for Christ's name, and also *alpha* and *omega*, the first and last letters of the Greek alphabet (see Revelation 1: 8: 'I am Alpha and Omega, the beginning and the

The Water Newton
Treasure
Water Newton, Cambs,
England
4th century AD
PRB P 1975 10–2 1–28
h. (central vase) 20.3 cm
(8 in)
Treasure trove

end, saith the Lord'). Plaques of the type found here are well known from pagan temples bearing dedications to deities such as Mars, Minerva and Jupiter, but the Water Newton examples are the first to demonstrate the practice within a Christian congregation.

Two bowls and one plaque have longer inscriptions in Latin. One of these, on a bowl, reads: 'I, Publianus, honour your sacred shrine, trusting in you, O Lord.' Other inscriptions give the names of three female dedicators: Amcilla, Innocentia and Viventia, who must also have belonged to the congregation.

The individual pieces were probably made at different times and it is impossible to establish accurately the date when they were hidden, though it would have been in the fourth century AD. The concealment of the treasure may have been in response to specific persecution of Christians or to more general political instability.

FURTHER READING
K.S. Painter, *The Water Newton Early Christian Silver* (London, 1977)

Antoine **Watteau**

W atteau (1684–1721) is generally regarded as one of France's most fluent draughtsmen, but there are few documented facts about his life. His career began as the pupil of a local painter in his native town of Valenciennes, and from around 1703 to 1709 he was in Paris, where he worked with Claude Gillot (1673–1722) and Claude Audran III (1658–1734). After a spell in Valenciennes, painting mostly military subjects, he returned to Paris, where he rapidly gained patrons for his *fêtes galantes* (paintings depicting actors of the *commedia dell'arte* in idealized landscape settings). He died aged 37, possibly of tuberculosis – a visit to the physician and collector Dr Meade in London in 1719–20 may have been prompted by his search for a cure.

The Museum's collection is one of the two best in existence, with 59 sheets and a number of prints after Watteau's paintings and drawings. The drawings cover a wider range than most other collections and include some of his finest masterpieces. They include studies of musicians and actors, informal portraits, nudes, hands, women's dress, landscapes from nature or from older masters, details of paintings by Rubens – his main inspiration – and ornamental design. Below is a sheet with four studies of a young woman's head. Watteau made several comparable studies of heads, adding them to the stock of drawings that he used for his paintings. No painting related to this sheet is, however, known.

Four studies of the head of a young woman, her hair tied with a ribbon
France
Two shades of red chalk, black and white chalks
18th century AD
PD 1895–9–15–941
33.1 × 23.8 cm
(13 × 9⅓ in)
Purchased (Malcolm Collection)

FURTHER READING
P. Hulton, *Watteau Drawings in the British Museum* (London, 1980)
P. Stein, *French Drawings: Clouet to Seurat* (London, 2005)

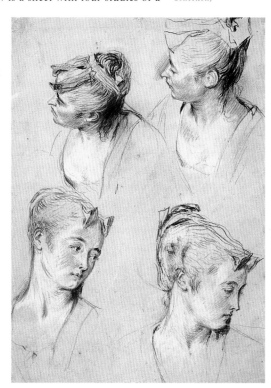

Wedgwood pottery

The Staffordshire potter Josiah Wedgwood (AD 1730–95) is often considered to be the most remarkable of all English potters. Not only did he take full advantage of growing markets in the late eighteenth century to build up an immensely successful business, which continues today; he is also noted for his innovative experiments, including those on green glazes, and he later formulated many new varieties of unglazed stoneware, details being recorded in code in his 'Experiment Book'.

Staffordshire at this time had a well-established pottery industry, based on the proximity of clays, with outcrops of coal for fuel. Salt and lead supplies, which formed the basis of glazes for stonewares and earthenwares respectively, were also reasonably accessible. In 1759 Wedgwood began business on his own account, taking a lease on the Ivy House, Burslem, and its adjoining potworks. In 1769 he began a partnership for ornamental wares with Thomas Bentley. A new model factory near Stoke-on-Trent was opened, named Etruria after the classical Greek and Roman pottery recently excavated in Italy and thought to be Etruscan. Here Wedgwood perfected his famous black basalt (c.1767) and jasperware (1774), the latter a fine white stoneware hard enough to be polished on a lapidary wheel like the semi-precious stone. Jasperware could take a colour throughout and was frequently tinted blue. The firm's greatest commercial success, however, came from its creamware, made by Josiah in partnership with his cousin Thomas Wedgwood and later called 'Queen's Ware' following Wedgwood's appointment as potter to Queen Charlotte in 1765.

The collection of Wedgwood pottery in the Museum is the oldest and one of the most extensive in Britain. The Pegasus vase (left), presented by Wedgwood himself in 1786, was considered by him to be his finest vase and takes its current name from the flying horse on the top of the cover. The main scene was designed in 1778 by J. Flaxman jnr and shows the crowning of a poet (called by Wedgwood the 'Apotheosis of Homer'); it was copied from a Greek painted earthenware vase in the collection of Sir William Hamilton, which was purchased by the Museum in 1772.

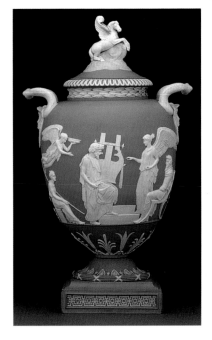

The 'Pegasus' vase, pale blue jasperware with white reliefs, designed by John Flaxman jnr
Etruria, Stoke-on-Trent, Staffordshire, England
AD 1786
MLA 1786,5–27,1;
Pottery Cat. I 712
h. 46 cm (18 in)
Given by Josiah Wedgwood

FURTHER READING
A. Dawson, *Masterpieces of Wedgwood in the British Museum* (London, 1984)
A. Finer and G. Savage (eds), *The Selected Letters of Josiah Wedgwood* (London, 1965)

The medieval palace at Westminster is one of the great lost buildings of London. Here the sovereigns of England held court and council from the end of the eleventh century AD, when the Great Hall was constructed for the Norman King William Rufus. The palace largely survived accidents and alterations, including the attentions of Victorian restorers. But on 16 October 1834 a devastating fire destroyed most of the surviving buildings. These were replaced by the present Houses of Parliament.

In 1323 two Irish friars wrote of 'the celebrated palace of the kings of England, in which is that famous chamber on whose walls all the warlike stories of the whole Bible are painted with wonderful skill, and explained by a complete series of texts accurately written in French to the great admiration of the beholder and with the greatest royal magnificence'. Although the appearance of the 'Painted Chamber' had been recorded by antiquaries, it was thought that the paintings themselves had been entirely destroyed in the fire of 1834. However, in 1993 two panel paintings, removed during restoration work in 1816, were rediscovered in Bristol. They had been concealed beneath the geometric panels (*paterae*) which studded the wooden planks of the ceiling of the chamber. It seems likely that they were part of an initial scheme executed immediately after the fire of AD 1263 for King Henry III, later abandoned in

Panel painting of a seraph
Palace of Westminster, London
13th century AD
MLA 1995, 4–1,1
l. 45.3 cm (17¾ in)

The medieval palace at **Westminster**

Fragment of wall painting with scene from the Book of Tobit
Palace of Westminster, London
14th century AD
MLA 1814, 3–12, 2
h. 78 cm (30⅔ in), including inscription below
Presented by the Society of Antiquaries of London

favour of the *paterae*. On the previous page is a seraph enveloped in flaming wings. The other panel shows a grim-faced prophet holding a scroll. They are the earliest surviving English panel paintings, among the masterpieces of Henry III's court style, created during one of the greatest periods of English medieval art.

The Museum also has relics from another lost masterpiece, St Stephen's Chapel, the private royal chapel within the palace which was founded by King Edward I and built between AD 1292 and 1348 in the style of the Sainte Chapelle in Paris. The building consisted of two storeys, and in the years following 1348 King Edward III had the upper storey richly decorated with sculpture, stained glass and wall paintings. A huge cycle of Biblical and other scenes ran round the chapel. From 1548 the upper floor was used as the chamber and lobby of the House of Commons. By 1651 the side walls with the paintings had been covered. In 1692 and again in 1707 the interior was remodelled for the Commons by Sir Christopher Wren. During work in 1880–1 to remove Wren's panelling, the architect James Wyatt (known as 'the destroyer') discovered a whole series of fourteenth-century wall paintings. The few fragments exhibited in the Museum were saved by antiquaries. Above are shown scenes from the apocryphal Book of Tobit showing the Marriage of Tobias to Sarah and the Departure of the Archangel Raphael. Other fragments in the Museum, the largest to survive, are from the Book of Job.

FURTHER READING
P. Binski, *The Painted Chamber at Westminster* (London, 1986)

Many artists before John White (*fl.*1585–93) sailed to North America with voyages of discovery, but it was White who left the first convincing record we have of the lands he explored. He is known to have made a number of voyages: he sailed as draughts-man-surveyor with the first expedition to colonize Roanoke, Virginia, organized by Sir Water Raleigh in 1585; with its successor in 1587; and with the failed relief expedition of 1590.

There is no certain mention of White before 11 July 1585. His drawings are unsigned, but their first engraver and publisher, Theodor de Bry, printed on the title-page of the Indian engravings illustrating Thomas Harriot's *A brief and true report of the new found land of Virginia* (1590) the words 'Diligently collected and draowne by Ihon White who was sent thiter speciallye and for the same purpose by the said Sir Walter Relegh the year abouesaid 1585'.

White became governor of the second, 1587, colony at Roanoake, but returned to England to attempt to secure supplies, leaving behind his daughter and grandson. Eventually, in March 1590, he was able to return with two supply ships. They found the colony deserted, with an indication that the settlers had moved to a safer place; unable to make contact, they returned to England. White never went back to the 'Lost Colony'.

'Indian man and woman eating'
PD 199a.1
20.9 × 21.4 cm
(8¼ × 8½ in)

White painted the Carolina Algonquians, the Inuit of South Baffin Island, creatures and plants. He drew maps, of which five survive. The Museum has 75 drawings from an album formerly in the library of Lord Charlemont (purchased in 1866). A volume from the founding collection of Sir Hans Sloane (acquired in 1753) includes a number of drawings in different hands, among them copies of White's drawings. Above is a drawing of Indians squatting to eat a bowl of hominy, maize kernels swollen by soaking and boil-

'Indians dancing'
PD 199a.2
27.4 × 35.6 cm
(10¾ × 14 in)

ing. On the right men and women of the village of Secoton dance round a circle of posts, probably in a green corn or harvest ritual such as was widespread throughout the Indian tribes of eastern North America about mid-July.

FURTHER READING
P. Hulton, *America 1585: The Complete Drawings of John White* (London and Chapel Hill, 1984)

Throughout antiquity the people of the mountainous land of Lycia retained a distinct identity and a unique style of funerary architecture. The Greeks called the people Lycians, supposedly after Lycos, the exiled son of King Pandion of Athens. The Lycians, however, called themselves Termilai in texts written in Lycian, a language which is even today only partially understood. Despite heroic Lycian resistance at Xanthos, the Persians under their general Harpagos overran Lycia in 546–545 BC. From 468 BC the Lycians were absorbed into the Athenian Empire. From the end of the fifth century BC they once again came within the Persian orbit.

The Payava tomb
Xanthos, Lycia, Turkey
c.375–360 BC
GR 1848.10–20.142;
Cat. Sculpture 950
h. 1.05 m (41¼ in)
Excavated by Sir Charles
Fellows

Under the Persians the Lycian cities were ruled by local dynasts, whose monumental tombs commemorated their aristocratic status and their success in war. No such tombs survive from the period under Athenian control, but the monuments of the later Persian period reflect the influence of contemporary Greek design and suggest the presence of Greek sculptors.

The majority of the tombs were built as tall pillars, the burial concealed in the decorated chest at the top of the shaft. The largest and most spectacular of the tombs, the Nereid Monument (p. 227), is however in the form of a small Ionic temple. The earliest of the 'pillar' tombs in the Museum is the 'Lion Tomb', which dates from about the second half of the sixth century BC and is decorated with sculptures of a lion (opposite), a lioness with cubs, a man fighting a panther and a warrior and horseman. The Harpy Tomb (p. 143) is similar but larger, and dates from c.470–460 BC.

The Payava Tomb (left) had a barrel-vaulted design, its projecting beams and curved roof suggesting the influence of wooden buildings. It takes its name from the inscription on it in the Lycian language which states: 'Payava built this monument'. Another damaged inscription refers to 'Payava, son of Ad..., Secretary of A...rah, by race a Lycian'. Lycian used an alphabet of 29 characters, some borrowed from

Xanthian tombs

Sculpture from the 'Lion Tomb'
Xanthos, Lycia, Turkey
c.600–575 BC
GR 1840.10–20.31; Cat.
Sculpture B 286
h. 95 cm (37½ in)
Excavated by Sir Charles
Fellows

Greek. The figures carved on the walls of the tomb display a typi-cally Lycian blend of Greek and Persian elements: the representation of a naked athlete receiving a victory wreath is entirely Greek, while on the adjoining wall a dignified seated figure in full Persian court regalia is shown receiving a delegation. This may be the satrap (governor) Autophradates, named in the inscription as having made a presentation to the tomb-owner Payava. Projecting from the curving roof are the heads and forepaws of lions, a favourite Lycian royal symbol. A similar tomb, of which only the lid survives, is that of Merehi, which bears the inscription 'Merehi, son of Cydalos Kandalos, of the race of Triatarbas Playtos, built this monument for his household. He was Captain of Caricas'. Among the sculptures are a four-horse chariot and the fabulous two-headed Chimaera, crouched ready to spring.

FURTHER READING
Sir C. Fellows, *Travels and Researches in Asia Minor, more particularly in The Province of Lycia* (London, 1852)
P. Demargne, *Fouilles de Xanthos I, Les Piliers funéraires* (Paris, 1958)
A. Shapur Shahbati, *The Irano-Lycian Monuments* (Tehran, 1975)

H orror and disgust mixed with bafflement were the Spaniards' reactions to the human sacrifices of the Aztecs. However, to the Aztecs such practices were regarded not as cruel but as essential. Their religion was an anxious one. The world faced a constant threat of destruction and could only be kept in being, even momentarily, by the shedding of human blood. The victims, usually war captives, were no longer enemies but at the moment of death might become living incarnations of the gods. One of the most terrible of these was the Flayed One, Xipe Totec. In a ceremony marking the second of the Aztec 20-day months a prisoner would be tied to a special stone and armed with a wooden club covered with feathers. Pitted against him were a series of knights dressed as eagles and jaguars, carrying wooden clubs fitted with blades of hard obsidian. After the victim's death his skin would be removed and worn by the priests for the next 20 days. Thus flayed skins of victims sacrificed during the springtime planting festivals were worn to ensure the renewal of life. The mask of dead skin was likened to dead vegetation concealing new life beneath it.

Mask of Xipe Totec
Mexico (Aztec)
Stone, AD 1300–1521
ETH 1902.11–14.1
h. 22 cm (8⅔ in)
Christy Collection

On the inner surface of the mask is a full-figure representation presumed to be of Xipe Totec. The god has four arms, one holding a rattlespear, one a shield, a third carrying an inverted skull (probably representing a container for incense) and the fourth held across the breast, with drapery covering the forearm. Some doubts have been raised about the authenticity of the mask (there is another like it in the collection), since there appear to be no multiple-armed deities in the Aztec pantheon. Other aspects of the carving are unusual. While the mask might be a much later piece, it is more probable that it is a genuine idiosyncratic work of the period.

FURTHER READING
M. Jones (ed.), *Fake? The Art of Deception* (London, 1990), p. 298
R.F. Townsend, *The Aztecs* (London, 1992)

Xiuhtecuhtli and Xiuhcoatl,
fire god and fire serpent

The Aztecs thought of heat and fire in many guises. The fire of the sun could upset the balance of nature by causing drought and famine. From the bowels of the earth the Fire God, Xiuhtecuhtli (right), one of the oldest deities of ancient America, provoked outpourings of molten lava from volcanic eruptions, and in many aspects he overlaps with the old god Huehueteotl. Xiuhtecuhtli is closely identified with youthful warriors and rulership, and is often depicted in the Aztec codices (p. 207) wearing a fire serpent (Xiuhcoatl) on his back. The figure shown here wears a pleated fan made in bark paper (*amacuexpalli*) at the back of his head. Vestiges of yellow pigment and a black line around the eyes are still visible. The sculpture may have been used as a temple brazier.

Xiuhtecuhtli's name also means Turquoise Lord, and he is shown in the codices adorned with turquoise mosaic. One of his emblems is the butterfly, which can be seen on one of the Museum's turquoise mosaic ritual masks (pp. 335–6).

On the right is a fire serpent, Xiuhcoatl, sculpted in basalt as a jagged, serpentine bolt of lightning striking earthwards from the sky.

The Aztecs settled around Lake Texcoco in the Valley of Mexico, ruling from the island metropolis of Tenochtitlán which, by the fifteenth century AD, formed the heart of an empire that embraced much of non-Maya Central America. It was this civilization that was to fall to the Spaniard Hernán Cortés and his conquistadors in 1521.

FURTHER READING
R.F. Townsend, *The Aztecs* (London, 1992)

Stone figure of
Xiuhtecuhtli
Mexico (Aztec)
AD 1300–1521
ETH 1849.6–29.8
h. 32 cm (12⅗ in)
Purchased from John
Wetherall, 1849

The fire serpent
Xiuhcoatl
Mexico (Aztec)
Basalt, AD 1300–1521
ETH 1825.12–10.1
h. 77 cm (30⅓ in)

Yaxchilan, the 'Place of the Split Sky', is located on the banks of the Usumacinta River, close to the present border between Mexico and Guatemala. The city was constructed in phases between AD 400 and AD 800 by successive Mayan rulers.

Maya civilization developed in southern Mexico, Guatemala and parts of the adjacent countries, attaining in its classic phase (*c.*AD 300–900) an organizational complexity and cultural sophistication unsurpassed in Central America. The invention of hieroglyphic writing allowed the recording of names, birth dates, marriage alliances, coronations and the deaths of rulers. Inscriptions place major events within repeated cycles of time using a complex and precise calendrical system. The Maya believed that the world had been created and destroyed at least three times and that the last cycle of creation began on 13 August 3114 BC.

Two buildings in Yaxchilan contain a series of panels commemorating the accession rituals of Lord Shield Jaguar and Lord Bird Jaguar, who reigned during the seventh and eighth centuries AD. The scenes depict the rituals performed to invoke powerful ancestral spirits, ensure success in battle and secure captives for sacrifice. These ritual deeds legitimized the lords' authority and ancestral right to rule. Each panel formed the upper lintel of a doorway so that the participants in the ritual passed beneath them.

Lintel 16
Maya, from Yaxchilan,
Mexico
Limestone, *c.*AD 755–70
ETH 1886–318
h. 76.2 cm (30 in)
Transferred from the
Victoria & Albert
Museum

In the scene portrayed below Bird Jaguar stands over a captive noble who, judging from the beaded droplets on his nose and cheek, has already let blood. Eight days later, when his heir, Shield Jaguar II, was born, Bird Jaguar and one of his other wives performed ritual bloodletting in celebration. Seventy-five days later, on 3 May AD 752, Bird Jaguar was officially installed as king, an event which took place only after the capture of noble prisoners and, in this case, the birth of a male heir. The lintels were painted; there are vestiges of red and blue pigment still visible on the surface.

The lintels were collected by Dr A.P. Maudslay, who made a number of expeditions to Maya sites between 1881 and 1894.

FURTHER READING
C. McEwan, *Ancient Mexico in the British Museum* (London, 1995)

The Ziwiye treasure is an enigma. A rich burial was discovered at the hill-top site of Ziwiye in what is now north-west Iran in about 1946, but the exact details of the find are obscure. The body and grave-goods were in a bronze coffin of Assyrian type which can be dated to around 700 BC. However, so many objects since have been attributed to this burial that they would have filled several coffins, and it is now impossible to isolate those which were genuinely associated with it.

Little is known about the identity of the various groups who lived in Iron Age Iran. Distinctive types of burnished grey-ware pottery appeared in northern Iran during the second half of the second millennium BC. These mark the beginning of the Iron Age in the region, during which people arrived speaking new Indo-European languages. During the ninth and eighth centuries BC Late Assyrian armies campaigned in western Iran and inscriptions refer for the first time to the Medes and Persians.

By the seventh century BC the Medes controlled a large region around their capital at Ecbatana (modern Hamadan), while the Persians were restricted to the province of Fars. Cyaxares, King of the Medes (625–585 BC), allied with the Babylonians and over-threw the Late Assyrian Empire in 612 BC. The Medes then ruled over much of Iran until the rise of the Achaemenid dynasty (p. 11). Another group of people living between Media, Assyria and Urartu were the Mannaeans, whose centre lay near Lake Urmia.

Below is one of the objects attributed to the treasure, a frag-ment of gold sheet, probably from a belt. Resting stags and goats are set within an interlaced design incorporating lions' faces. Simi-lar compositions occur on contemporary Urartian belts, seals and seal impressions. The stags resemble those of the so-called Animal Style of Central Asia used by the Scythians, who made their appearance in the history of the Near East at this time.

Fragment of gold sheet
Said to come from Ziwiye, north-west Iran
c.8th–7th century BC
WA 132825; 1960–5–14, 1
l. 16.5 cm (6½ in)

FURTHER READING
A. Godard, *Le Trésor de Ziwiyé*
(Haarlem, 1950)
J. Curtis, *Ancient Persia*
(London, 2000)

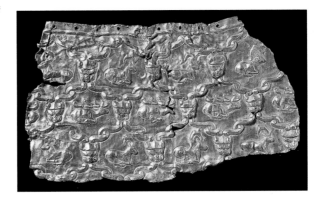

The **Zodiac**

In astronomy and astrology the zodiac is a belt of the heavens extending about eight degrees on either side of the ecliptic: the band of sky which includes all apparent positions of the sun, moon and planets as known to the ancient world, and is divided into twelve equal parts, in the West Aries, Taurus, Gemini, Cancer, Leo, Virgo, Libra, Scorpio, Sagittarius, Capricorn, Aquarius and Pisces.

The source of some of these images, and also of the relevant astronomical observations, was Mesopotamia. Cuneiform documents giving lists of the names of stars and constellations are known from the early second millennium BC onwards. Many of the Babylonian equivalents of the names of constellations occur in the star lists, and on a cuneiform tablet of about 500 BC the twelve names are listed in the order in which they are known today. It was in the fourth century BC that the zodiac, in the modern astrological sense, was established. The innovation, introduced for accuracy of reference, was the division of the ecliptic into its twelve 30-degree sections. These sections were named after the twelve zodiacal constellations, and the progress of the sun, moon and planets could be charted by reference to them. Some of the earliest representations of zodiac signs in today's astrological sense appear on Roman coins.

FURTHER READING
C.B.F. Walker (ed.), *Astronomy before the Telescope* (London, 1996)

Silver coin of Augustus (r. 27 BC–AD 14)
He was born 23 September 63 BC, with the moon in the constellation of Capricorn (shown here). Modern horoscopes would place him under Libra.
Minted at Ephesus in Ionia, Asia Minor
CM BMC 696
diam. 2.7 cm (1 in)

'The celestial globe – Northern Hemisphere'
Albrecht Dürer
(AD 1471–1528)
Woodcut, 1515
PD 1895–1–22–734
43.5 × 43.1 cm
(18 × 17 in)
Given by W. Mitchell

Zulu beadwork Africa, 19th century AD onwards

The Museum's collection of Zulu beadwork dates from the nineteenth century AD to the present, but glass beads were traded along the East African coast for at least two millennia. Arab and Roman traders were supplied from Egypt and Iran, also looking to lands as distant as China for 'trade-wind beads'. From the sixteenth century the Portuguese gradually imposed a monopoly on this trade, and beads were increasingly drawn from Europe, particularly Venice and Amsterdam. Before glass beads became widely available, beadwork was made from natural materials such as seeds, ostrich eggshell and animal claws. A number of Ndebele and Xhosa-speaking peoples produced decorative beadwork, but it is perhaps among the Zulu that the greatest variety of form, colour, use and significance of beadwork is to be found.

The earliest depictions of the wearing of beadwork are the paintings made by A.F. Gardiner at the court of King Dingane in 1835. Beadwork of a uniform pattern and colour may have been used as a means of unifying the many clans in the newly formed Zulu kingdom of the early nineteenth century. A formal, courtly style of communication through beadwork was developed, but the destruction of centralized Zulu power led to the development of various regional styles, each with its own colour conventions. During the 1960s and 1970s many of these older-established patterns and colour conventions gave way to a modern style (*isimodeni*). A relatively cheap and plentiful supply of glass and plastic beads from Czechoslovakia and Japan contributed to a spectacular blossoming of beadwork in South Africa.

Zulu beaded panel
Kwazulu, Republic of South Africa
Collected between 1940–80
ETH 1997 Af.6.34

A.F. Gardiner, *Narrative of a Journey through the Zoolu Country* (London, 1836)
M. Wood, 'Zulu Beadwork' in *Zulu Treasures* (Durban, 1996), pp. 143–70

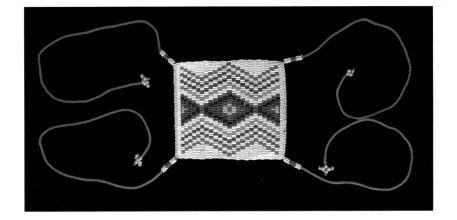

Plans of the Museum

- Africa
- Americas
- Ancient Near East
- Asia
- Egypt
- Europe
- Greece and Rome
- Money
- Prehistory
- Prints and Drawings
- Roman Britain
- Temporary exhibitions

North

West

East

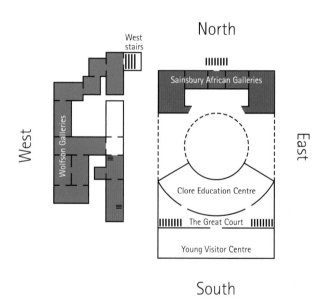

West stairs

Wolfson Galleries

Sainsbury African Galleries

Clore Education Centre

The Great Court

Young Visitor Centre

South

Lower floors

Plans of the Museum

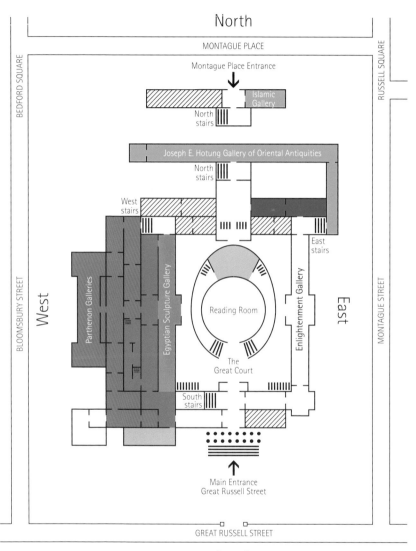

North

MONTAGUE PLACE

BEDFORD SQUARE

RUSSELL SQUARE

Montague Place Entrance

Islamic Gallery

North stairs

Joseph E. Hotung Gallery of Oriental Antiquities

North stairs

West stairs

East stairs

West

Parthenon Galleries

Egyptian Sculpture Gallery

Reading Room

Enlightenment Gallery

East

BLOOMSBURY STREET

MONTAGUE STREET

The Great Court

South stairs

Main Entrance
Great Russell Street

GREAT RUSSELL STREET

South

Main floor

Plans of the Museum

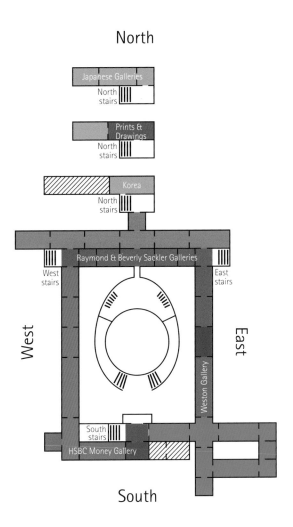

North

Japanese Galleries

North stairs

Prints & Drawings

North stairs

Korea

North stairs

Raymond & Beverly Sackler Galleries

West stairs

East stairs

West

East

Weston Gallery

South stairs

HSBC Money Gallery

South

Upper floors

Appendices

Kings of Assyria

These are the kings of Assyria from 1132 BC. A few dates are uncertain, but are unlikely to be wrong by more than one or two years. Overlaps indicate joint or rival reigns. Those represented on sculptures in the Museum are marked thus (*):

1132–1115 Ashur-resh-ishi I
1114–1076 Tiglath-pileser I
1075–1074 Asharid-apil-Ekur
1073–1056 Ashur-bel-kala*
1055–1054 Eriba-Adad II
1053–1050 Shamshi-Adad IV
1049–1031 Ashurnasirpal I*
1030–1019 Shalmaneser II
1018–1013 Ashur-nirari IV
971–967 Ashur-resh-ishi II
966–935 Tiglath-pileser II
934–912 Ashur-dan II
911–891 Adad-nirari II
890–884 Tukulti-Ninurta II
883–859 Ashurnasirpal II*

858–824 Shalmaneser III*
823–811 Shamshi-Adad V*
810–783 Adad-nirari III*
782–773 Shalmaneser IV
772–755 Ashur-dan III
754–745 Ashur-nirari V
744–727 Tiglath-pileser III*
726–722 Shalmaneser V
721–705 Sargon II*
704–681 Sennacherib*
680–669 Esarhaddon*
668–627 Ashurbanipal*
630–623 Ashur-etel-ilani
623–612 Sin-shar-ishkun
611–609 Ashur-uballit II

The final collapse of the Assyrian Empire came in 614 BC when a joint force of Medes and Babylonians attacked Ashur. In 612 BC this alliance captured and sacked Nineveh.

Source: J.E. Reade, *Assyrian Sculpture* (2nd edn, London, 1998)

Babylonian chronology

Akkad	2334–2154 BC
Ur III	2112–2004 BC
Isin	2017–1794 BC
Larsa	2025–1763 BC
First Dynasty of Babylon	1894–1595 BC
First Dynasty of the Sealand	?
Kassite Dynasty	? – 1155 BC
Second Dynasty of Isin	1157–1026 BC
Second Dynasty of the Sealand	1025–1005 BC
Bazi Dynasty	1004–985 BC
Elamite Dynasty	984–979 BC
Undetermined or mixed dynasties	978–626 BC
Neo-Babylonian Dynasty	625–539 BC
Achaemenid Dynasty	538–331 BC
Macedonian Dynasty	330–307 BC
Seleucid Dynasty	305–164 BC

Source: C.B.F. Walker, 'Mesopotamian Chronology' in D. Collon, *Ancient Near Eastern Art* (London, 1995), pp. 234–8

History and organization of the British Museum

One of the greatest museums of the world, the British Museum at Bloomsbury was founded by Act of Parliament in 1753 and is now governed under the British Museum Act 1963. General management and control are vested in a Board of twenty-five Trustees (one appointed by the Sovereign, fifteen by the Prime Minister, four nominated by learned societies and five elected by the Trustees themselves). The Museum is largely funded by a government grant-in-aid administered by the Department of Culture, Media and Sport. Additional income is also secured through sponsorship and a wide range of commercial and fund-raising activities. The British Museum Company is responsible for the sale of publications and replicas. There are a number of active supporters' groups including the British Museum Friends (formerly the British Museum Society) and its Young Friends, Patrons, Associates, the Townley Group, Caryatids, Friends of the Ancient Near East and Japanese Friends.

The Museum now holds national collections of antiquities; coins, medals and paper money; ethnography; and prints and drawings. Its natural history collections were transferred to South Kensington in the 1880s, becoming the Natural History Museum. The library collections (Printed Books, Manuscripts, Maps, Music and Stamps) became part of the British Library in 1973 and have now gone to a new building at St Pancras.

The main Museum buildings are in Bloomsbury. The core consists of buildings of a floor area of c.600,000 sq. ft designed by Sir Robert and Sydney Smirke and erected between the 1820s and 1850s. Major subsequent additions totalling c.340,000 sq. ft consist of the Classical and Assyrian Sculpture Galleries (1850s–1870s), the White Wing (1884), the King Edward VII Building (1914), the Duveen Gallery (1939/62) and the New Wing (1979/80). With the departure of the British Library the Museum embarked upon a programme of development leading up to its 250th anniversary in 2003. The glass-covered Great Court, completed in 2000, is the centrepiece of the project. The King's Library has been refurbished and houses a permanent exhibition entitled 'Enlightenment: Discovering the World in the Eighteenth Century'.

The Departments of the British Museum

The approximate number of items in each collection is given in brackets.

Africa, Oceania and the Americas (AOA), formerly Ethnography (ETH) (300,000) is concerned with studying and collecting from the cultures of recent and contemporary small-scale indigenous societies (and a number of complex state systems) of Africa, the Americas and Oceania. It is also deals with the archaeology of the Americas, Oceania and the post-Quaternary (most recent) archaeology of sub-Saharan Africa. The collection is among the best in the world in these fields.

Ancient Egypt and Sudan (AES), formerly Egyptian Antiquities (EA) (6 million) has the largest and most comprehensive collection of its kind outside Cairo, and illustrates every aspect of ancient Egyptian culture (including Nubia) from the Predynastic period down to the Coptic (Christian) period, a time-span of over 5000 years from about 4000 BC to the 12th century AD. The collection includes a significant amount of material from Sudan.

Asia, formerly **Oriental Antiquities (OA)** and **Japanese Antiquities (JA)** (207,000) covers the cultures of Asia from the Neolithic period up to the present, with the exception of the ancient civilizations of the Near East. The collection includes paintings and prints as well as antiquities and sculpture. In many areas such as Chinese antiquities, Islamic pottery and Indian sculpture, the collection is the most important in the West. The collection of Japanese decorative arts and paintings is among the finest and most comprehensive in Europe.

Coins and Medals (CM) (750,000) have one of the largest collections in the world. It is the most representative of world coinage, with a high proportion of significant rarities. It also includes paper money, tokens, modern plastic cards, badges and items associated with manufacture such as coin dies.

Greek and Roman Antiquities (GR) (150,000) covers the Greek world from the beginning of the Bronze Age; Italy and Rome from the Bronze Age; and the whole of the Roman Empire except Britain until the Edict of Milan in AD 313, with pagan survivals later. The collection is one of the most comprehensive in the world.

Middle East (ME), formerly **Western Asiatic Antiquities (WAA)** and **Ancient Near East (ANE)** (282,000), deals with the civilizations of the ancient Near East and adjacent areas (Mesopotamia, Iran, the Arabian Peninsula, Anatolia, the Caucasus, parts of Central Asia, Syria, Palestine and Phoenician settlements in the western Mediterranean) from the prehistoric period until the coming of Islam in the 7th century AD. It is one of the most comprehensive collections of ancient Near Eastern material in the world.

Prehistory and Europe (P&E), formerly **Prehistoric and Romano-British Antiquities (PRB)** and **Medieval and Later Antiquities (MLA)** (2,850,000), has Quaternary material from all over the world. Neolithic and Bronze Age antiquities derive largely from sites in Europe. The finds from Roman Britain form one of the best illustrations of provincial culture within the Roman Empire. The collections also cover European art and archaeology to the present day, with the exception of the material held in the Department of Greek and Roman Antiquities (see above). These includes national collections of Anglo-Saxon antiquities and archaeology, icons, seal-dies and medieval pottery, as well as the most comprehensive horological collection in existence.

Prints and Drawings (PD) (3,500,000) has one of the most representative collections of Western prints and drawings in existence. The prints cover in a comprehensive way the development of print-making from its beginnings in the 15th century up to modern times. The collection of drawings is probably the most diverse extant, including many works of the highest quality by most of the leading artists of the European schools from the 15th century onwards. The Department has a large number of trade cards and the definitive Wharton-Tigar collection of approximately 1 million cigarette cards.

Conservation, Documentation and Science
The Department comprises one of the largest museum conservation facilities in the world; its main role is to clean, repair and restore the objects in the Museum collections and also to ensure that they have the best possible environmental conditions. Conservation scientists are involved in research into why objects deteriorate, methods of arresting deterioration, methods for cleaning, repairing and restoring, and the properties of new materials for use in conservation. Other scientific research carried out by the Department focuses on the composition, technology of manufacture, provenance and date of objects.

Ceramics: technical terms

BISCUIT When glazed ware is fired twice, the initial firing before the application of glaze is known as the biscuit firing. French biscuit porcelain (and the term is of French origin) is literally twice-fired, since the soft-paste, or glassy, type has undergone an initial firing of the frit (see below) and the hard-paste type is often fired at a low temperature to drive off any remaining moisture, before it undergoes its first true firing at a high temperature.

blanc de chine French name denoting white glazed porcelain made in the factories at Dehua in Fujian province in south-eastern China.

BODY 1. The mixture of raw materials which is shaped to be fired into a ceramic.
2. The interior of the ceramic, as distinct from the glaze or paint.

CHINA Commonly used term that broadly and inexactly refers to any ceramic tableware.

CHINOISERIE Term generally used to describe the European interpretation of Far Eastern shapes or decorative motifs on objects made from the 18th century.

CLAY A fine-grained natural material, which when wet is characterized by its plasticity. This allows it to be formed without cracking, and to keep its shape. Its main constituents are alumino-silicates, together with quartz; other minerals such as feldspar, calcite and iron oxide may also be present. When heated to around 600 °C or more, soft clay hardens to a durable ceramic.

EARTHENWARE Opaque and coarse ceramic body which is not fully vitrified and remains porous, requiring glazing to make it impervious to liquids. There are many types of earthenware, from low-fired common pottery to high-fired cream-coloured earthenware, known as creamware, such as that made from the 1760s by Josiah Wedgwood I in partnership with his cousin Thomas.

ENAMEL A colour consisting of a pigment derived from a metal oxide and a glass flux which is painted over a pre-fired glaze and then fired at a low temperature.

FAIENCE French term for tin-glazed earthenware made in Europe from the Renaissance, which is derived from one of the chief manufacturing centres in Italy, Faenza, and usually applied only to French pottery. The term also denotes a glazed ceramic, its body composed of crushed quartz, which is common in the Near East and Mediterranean. It was initially confused with earthenware which had a white tin-opacified glaze, and the word faience, incorrectly applied, has remained in use.

FIRING Process of exposing a clay body to intense heat, initially to harden the clay and then to melt the applied glaze. Several firings may be needed before the piece reaches its final state. Different types of clay require different degrees of heat for successful firing: earthenware in the region of 700 to 1200 °C; stoneware around 1150 to 1350 °C; porcelain around 1250 to 1450 °C. Firing is usually done in a kiln, the size and shape of which vary from culture to culture; in those where gas, oil and electricity are not readily available, firing may be done in the open in a large bonfire.

FLUX A substance which lowers the melting point of another. Lead or alkalis are commonly used fluxes for melting glazes. Other fluxes will vitrify porcelain or clay bodies. Fluxes are added to ground metal oxides used as colouring agents to lower their melting point when they are painted over glazes.

FRIT Partially fused glassy material usually employed in glaze- or glass-making. Frit can also be added to a ceramic body, such as porcelain.

FRITWARE Pottery made from a stone paste body, consisting chiefly of crushed quartz to which about 10% glass and 10% clay were added. Fritware was widely used by Islamic potters from around the 10th century.

GLAZE Glassy coating fused to a ceramic body either to seal it against moisture or to decorate it. Glazes are typically applied by dipping in a water-based suspension, by brushing, or in the form of a vapour.

LUSTRE Iridescent decoration on ceramic, achieved by depositing a metallic film on to glazes. Ground salts of silver or copper combined with an inert carrier are painted on to a cold glazed pot and fired in a reducing, or smoky, atmosphere, which converts the metallic salts to metal.

MAIOLICA Italian tin-glazed earthenware.

PORCELAIN A white vitreous and translucent ceramic, of which there are several types. Translucent porcelain was first made in China around the 10th century. In Europe soft-paste porcelain, a glassy substance, was first made in the 16th century at the Medici court in Florence. 'True' or hard-paste porcelain, similar to the Oriental type, appeared in Saxony around 1708, but was not made in England until more than sixty years later. Bone china, a type of 'artificial' porcelain containing calcined ox bones, was made in England from the end of the 18th century and became the foundation of the modern English tableware industry.

SALT GLAZE A glaze which results from a chemical reaction between a ceramic body and salt vapour when salt is thrown into the kiln at the peak of the firing cycle. Only pottery made with clays capable of withstanding 1100 °C can be glazed in this way.

SGRAFFITO Type of decoration of pottery in which designs are scratched through a light-coloured slip to expose the darker body beneath.

SLIP Potter's clay mixed with water to form a smooth creamy liquid used to decorate ceramics.

SLIPWARE Coarse earthenware decorated with slip which may be trailed or swirled over the surface. The term often denotes large dishes and other vessels with complex but usually naive decorative schemes made in 17th- and 18th-century Staffordshire.

STONEWARE Dense non-porous pottery, typically firing to a grey colour at temperatures in excess of 1100 °C. European stoneware is commonly salt-glazed, with a dark brown finish; fine pale grey stoneware, often moulded, was made in Staffordshire in the eighteenth century.

TERRACOTTA Low-fired earthenware, usually red and unglazed.

TERRA SIGILLATA Slip-covered pottery which is a glossy red colour, made in Italy and Gaul during the Roman period, and sometimes termed samian ware.

TIN GLAZE An opaque white glaze used to cover the colour of the underlying clay body and as a ground for painting. The technique was first adopted by Islamic potters and involves the addition of 5 to 10% tin oxide to the glaze, which makes it opaque.

WHEEL-ENGRAVED DECORATION Designs achieved using the gem-cutter's wheel to incise or cut away the surface of the fired clay.

Sources: I. Freestone and D. Gaimster (eds), *Pottery in the Making: World Ceramic Traditions* (London, 1997)

D.H. Cohen and C. Hess, *Looking at European Ceramics: A Guide to Technical Terms* (London, 1993)

Chinese chronological periods

NEOLITHIC CULTURES	*c.*6500– 1900 BC
EARLY DYNASTIES	
Shang	*c.*1500–1050 BC
Western Zhou	1050–771 BC
Eastern Zhou	
Spring and Autumn	770–475 BC
Warring States	475–221 BC
IMPERIAL CHINA	
Qin	221–207 BC
Han	
Western Han	206 BC–AD 9
Xin	AD 9–25
Eastern Han	AD 25–220
Three Kingdoms	
Shu (Han)	221–263
Wei	220–265
Wu	222–280
Southern Dynasties (Six Dynasties)	
Western Jin	265–316
Eastern Jin	317–420
Liu Song	420–479
Southern Qi	479–502
Liang	502–557
Chen	557–589
Northern Dynasties	
Northern Wei	386–535
Eastern Wei	534–550
Western Wei	535–557
Northern Qi	550–577
Northern Zhou	557–581
Sui	589–618
Tang	618–906
Five Dynasties	907–960
Liao	907–1125
Song	
Northern Song	960–1126
Southern Song	1127–1279
Jin	1115–1234
Yuan	1279–1368
Ming	1368–1644
Qing	1644–1911
REPUBLICAN CHINA	
Republic	1912–1949
People's Republic	1949–

Source: J. Rawson (ed.), *The British Museum Book of Chinese Art* (London, 1992)

Classical architecture

The British Museum building, designed by Sir Robert Smirke and begun in 1823, is the largest Neo-classical building in the United Kingdom. The colonnade which visitors see on arrival is in the Ionic order, a modified version of that belonging to the Ionic temple of Athena Polias at Priene; the column bases were probably modelled on the Temple of Dionysos at Teos. Within the Front Hall the order is Doric.

Within the Museum's galleries are illustrations of classical architecture from some of the greatest buildings of the ancient world. These include the 4th-century BC Temple of Athena Polias, already mentioned, dedicated by Alexander the Great in 334 BC (p. 15); two of the Temples of Artemis at Ephesus, that built in the 6th century BC whose cost was partly defrayed by the fabled King Croesus, and the 4th-century BC temple, later considered one of the Wonders of the ancient world (pp. 292–3). Another Wonder is the 4th-century BC Mausoleum at Halikarnassos (pp. 292–3). From the Acropolis in Athens there are fragments of the Propylaea, the Hephaisteion, the Erechtheion and the Temple of Athena Nike.

Certain special terms are used to describe Greek and Roman architecture, some of which are shown opposite. There are three basic 'orders' or styles of architecture: Ionic, Doric and Corinthian. Composite is a later Roman development, a variation linking Corinthian and Ionic.

FURTHER READING

J.J. Coulton, *Greek Architects at Work. Problems of Structure and Design* (London, 1977)

J. Mordaunt Crook, *The British Museum: A Case-Study in Architectural Politics* (London, 1972)

D.S. Robertson, *Greek and Roman Architecture* (2nd edn, Cambridge, 1943)

R.A. Tomlinson, *Greek and Roman Architecture* (London, 1995)

I. Jenkins, *Greek Architecture and Its Sculpture* (London, 2006)

Classical architecture

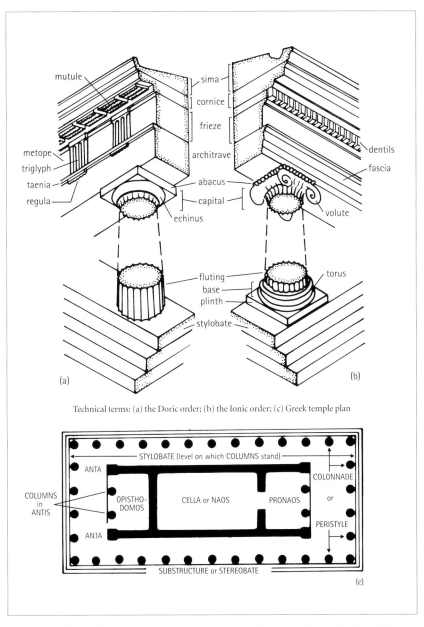

mutule
sima
cornice
frieze
metope
triglyph
architrave
taenia
regula
abacus
capital
echinus
volute
dentils
fascia
fluting
base
plinth
torus
stylobate

(a)

(b)

Technical terms: (a) the Doric order; (b) the Ionic order; (c) Greek temple plan

STYLOBATE (level on which COLUMNS stand)

ANTA
COLUMNS in ANTIS
OPISTHO-DOMOS
CELLA or NAOS
PRONAOS
COLONNADE
or
PERISTYLE
ANTA

SUBSTRUCTURE or STEREOBATE

(c)

Adapted from J.J. Coulton, *Greek Architects at Work. Problems of Structure and Design* (London, 1977)

Terms used for drawings and watercolours

BODYCOLOUR Any type of opaque pigment.

CARTOON A drawing of the principal forms of a composition made to the same scale as the painting or fresco for which it is preparatory.

CHIAROSCURO/GRISAILLE Works executed in grey or other monotones, bodycolour, washes or oils, sometimes to give an impression of low relief.

CONTE CRAYON A mixture of refined graphite and clay invented in the 19th century.

CRAYON A colour combined with an oily, waxy or greasy binding medium or with a combination of water-soluble and fatty binders in the form of a stick.

FRESCO A method of wall or ceiling painting. The paint used, of the distemper/tempera type in which the colours are mixed with some binding substance soluble in water, was applied to wet plaster. As the plaster dried, the pigment became sealed within it.

GOUACHE A method of painting with colours made opaque by mixing them with chalks or whites in a medium of gum and honey. Today used to describe any drawing made entirely in bodycolour.

LEAD POINT Lead or an alloy of lead and tin was used in the 15th and 16th centuries as an underdrawing for a work intended to be completed in pen and ink. A conveniently portable implement before the invention of the graphite pencil.

METALPOINT An instrument with a point of gold, silver or other metal was used for drawing on a prepared paper. A ground composed of powdered bones or lead white mixed with gum-water or size had been applied to the paper in several coats. The metal point reacted chemically with the ground on the paper, thus producing a line.

MODELLO A finished study, on a reduced scale, made in preparation for a large work.

POUNCE A fine powder used in the transference of the principal outlines of a drawing to another support, e.g. a wall or another sheet of paper. Small prick-holes were made in the paper along the lines, and dust was pounced or rubbed through these holes, leaving a dotted outline underneath.

RECTO The front, or more fully worked face of a sheet drawn on both sides. Also the right-hand page of an opening of a bound volume.

SEPIA Pigment, ranging from black to yellow-brown, extracted from the ink bag of the cuttlefish.

TEMPERA (DISTEMPER) A method of painting in which dry colours are made usable by mixing them with some glutinous substance soluble in water, e.g. egg yolk, usually on a ground of chalk or plaster mixed with gum.

VERSO Opposite of recto.

VIGNETTE A small ornamental engraving or design chiefly used in book illustration and with no defined border.

WASH When used in connection with watercolour denotes a covering with a broad layer of colour made by continuous movement of the brush. When applied to ink drawings often means the use of a dilute ink.

WATERCOLOUR A pigment for which water and not oil is used as a medium, and gum arabic added as a binder. The brilliancy of pure watercolour occurs because its translucent nature allows the white surface of the paper to be used as the lighting agent.

Source: P. Goldman, *Looking at Prints, Drawings and Watercolours: A Guide to Technical Terms* (London, 1988)

Egyptian dynasties

The kings of Egypt are traditionally divided into thirty dynasties or ruling houses, according to a system preserved in the work of Manetho, a priestly historian who lived in the 3rd century BC. This dynastic period lasted from the time of the unification of all Egypt by a king known as Menes in *c*.3100 BC until the invasion by Alexander the Great in 332 BC. The time before the First Dynasty is known as the Predynastic period and the rule of the Macedonian Greek successors of Alexander as the Ptolemaic period. In 30 BC Egypt became a province of the Roman Empire.

Successive groups of dynasties are given the following names:

Period	Dynasty No.	Dates (some approximate)
Early Dynastic	I–II	3100–2686 BC
Old Kingdom	III–VI	2686–2181 BC
lst Intermediate	VII–X	2181–2050 BC
Middle Kingdom	X–XII	2050–1750 BC
2nd Intermediate	XIII–XVII	1750–1550 BC
New Kingdom	XVIII–XX	1550–1070 BC
Late Dynastic	XXI–XXX	1070–332 BC

Source: Department of Egyptian Antiquities

FURTHER READING

S. Quirke, *Who were the Pharaohs? A history of their names with a list of cartouches* (London, 1990)

S. Quirke and J. Spencer (eds), *The British Museum Book of Ancient Egypt* (London, 1992)

I. Shaw and P. Nicholson, *The British Museum Dictionary of Ancient Egypt* (London, 1995)

Egyptian gods

The gods who played some part in the daily religious life of the ancient Egyptians were very varied in character and infinitely various in form, their importance and character changing over time. There were immense numbers of divine beings, in early times worshipped in the forms of animals and inanimate objects, later many were shown with human bodies and animal or other heads. In many of the important religious centres, for political reasons, the principal god was associated with two other local deities to form a divine family, known as a triad.

Those whose likenesses can be seen throughout the Museum include: *Amun*, the great god of Thebes, of uncertain origin, who is represented as a man, his sacred animals being the ram and the goose; *Anubis* the jackal-god, patron of embalmers, the great necropolis-god; *Bastet*, the cat-goddess; *Hathor*, goddess of many functions and attributes, represented often as a cow or a cow-headed woman, or as a woman with horned head-dress; *Horus*, the falcon-deity, originally the sky-god, identified with the king during his lifetime, also regarded as the son of Osiris and Isis, for the former of whom he became the avenger; *Isis*, the divine mother, wife of Osiris, one of the four 'protector'-goddesses, guarding coffins and canopic jars, sister of Nephthys, with whom she acted as a divine mourner for the dead; *Khepri*, the scarab-beetle god, often represented as a beetle within the sun-disk; *Osiris*, the god of the underworld, identified as the dead king, also a god of the flood and vegetation, represented as a mummified king; *Ptah*, the creator god of Memphis, represented as a man, the patron god of craftsmen; *Re*, the sun-god of Heliopolis, supreme judge; *Re-Horakhty*, a god in the form of a falcon, embodying the characteristics of Re and Horus; *Sakhmet*, a lion-headed goddess worshipped in the area of Memphis, wife of Ptah, regarded as the bringer of destruction to the enemies of Re; *Seth*, the god of storms and violence, brother and murderer of Osiris; *Thoth*, the ibis-headed god of Hermopolis, the scribe of the gods and the inventor of writing.

Four minor gods provided protection for the embalmed organs of the dead contained in 'canopic jars'. Known as the Sons of Horus, these comprised the human-headed *Imsety* (the liver), the baboon-headed *Hapy* (the lungs), the jackal-headed *Duamutef* (the stomach) and the falcon- headed *Qebehsenauref* (the intestines).

Source: Department of Egyptian Antiquities

FURTHER READING
G. Hart, *A Dictionary of Gods and Goddesses* (London, 1986)
G. Hart, *Egyptian Myths* (London, 1990)
G. Pinch, *Magic in Ancient Egypt* (London, 1994)
S. Quirke, *Ancient Egyptian Religion* (London, 1992)

Periods of Greek art

Greek art is divided for the convenience of scholars according to the following broad scheme. The dates are approximate and there are further subdivisions. The exact dates are subject to constant revision, especially in the earlier periods.

Early Bronze Age	*c.*3200–2000 BC
Middle Bronze Age	*c.*2000–1600 BC
Late Bronze Age	*c.*1600–1100 BC
Dark Age	*c.*1100–900 BC
Geometric period	*c.*900–700 BC
Orientalizing period	*c.*720–600 BC
Archaic period	*c.*600–480 BC
Classical period	*c.*480–323 BC
Hellenistic period	323–31 BC

Source: Department of Greek and Roman Antiquities

FURTHER READING
L. Burn, *The British Museum Book of Greek and Roman Art* (2nd edn, London, 1999)

Greek vases

The shapes of Greek vases varied considerably over time. Some forms disappeared and were superseded by others. The following is a guide to the principal terms used.

ALABASTRON A perfume-jar, sometimes made of alabaster or glass but more frequently of fired clay.

AMPHORA A jar with two handles used for transporting or storing liquids, especially wine; various forms are distinguished, such as the 'neck-amphora' with neck offset from the body or the 'pointed amphora' with lower body drawn into a point.

ARYBALLOS A perfume-jar usually made of fired clay (the ancient Greek word *aryballos* can mean 'bag' or purse').

ASKOS A low, often squat vase, used for pouring oil.

DINOS A round bottomed bowl, usually bronze or fired clay, for mixing wine and water.

HYDRIA A water-jar with two horizontal handles at the shoulder for lifting and carrying and a vertical handle at the neck for pouring.

KANTHAROS A drinking cup, often with a tall stem and two handles that sometimes curve up high above the rim.

KRATER A wide-mouthed bowl (of bronze or, more commonly, fired clay) for mixing wine and water; the four main types are defined and named by the position and shape of their handles as volute-, calyx-, bell- and column-kraters.

KYLIX A shallow drinking cup with two handles, often on a tall stem.

LEKYTHOS An oil- or perfume-bottle with a narrow neck through which only a little liquid could be poured at a time; often used in a funerary context.

LOUTROPHOROS An elongated form of amphora, traditionally used to carry the water for the ritual ablutions of a bride; also used for funerals.

OINOCHOE A jug used for pouring wine into cups.

OLPE A special type of oinochoe, tall and thin with a circular mouth.

PELIKE A two-handled jar, a heavy, rather sagging version of an amphora.

PSYKTER A mushroom-shaped vessel used for cooling wine; wine was put into it and it was then set to float in a krater of ice-cold water and ice.

PYXIS A cylindrical box with a lid, used for cosmetics and jewellery.

SKYPHOS A deep drinking cup with two handles.

STAMNOS A two-handled, round-mouthed storage jar, more squat than an amphora.

Source: L. Burn, *The British Museum Book of Greek and Roman Art* (2nd edn, London, 1999)

FURTHER READING
D. Williams, *Greek Vases* (2nd edn, London 1999)

Greek gods

The Greeks traditionally recognized twelve Supreme Gods who made their home on Mount Olympos. Many Roman gods had much in common with them, or acquired similar characteristics. This did not, however, mean that they were identical. There were a number of mountains in Greece called Olympos, the best known in Thessaly. Over time, however, Olympos was regarded as a heavenly dwelling place.

The Olympian gods (Roman equivalents in brackets) were *Zeus* (Jupiter), the father of gods and men, ruler of the gods on Mount Olympos and lord of the sky, bringer of rain and thunderstorms; *Hera* (Juno), wife and sister of Zeus, goddess of marriage and maternity, the personification of virtue and honour; *Demeter* (Ceres), a corn-goddess who governed the fruits of the earth; *Poseidon* (Neptune), god of the sea, who could cause storms and earthquakes, patron of horses; *Ares* (Mars), son of Zeus and Hera, patron of smiths; *Aphrodite* (Venus), daugher of Zeus, goddess of love and beauty; *Apollo* (Apollo), personification of reason and high moral principles, who also cared for flocks and herds, concerned with music and archery; *Artemis* (Diana), sister of Apollo, goddess of the hunt, the moon and night, a deity of fertility and childbirth; *Athena* (Minerva), the personification of courage and wisdom, usually shown with helmet, spear and shield; *Hermes* (Mercury), messenger and herald of the Olympian gods, dressed in broad-brimmed hat and winged sandals; *Dionysos* (Bacchus; p. 105), god of wine and revelry, patron of the dramatic arts.

The underworld was ruled by *Hades* (Pluto), grim and merciless but not evil, and by *Persephone* (Proserpina), the daughter of Demeter, whom Hades kidnapped and made his queen, obliged to remain with him for half the year.

FURTHER READING
W. Burkert, *Greek Religion* (Oxford, 1985)
T.H. Carpenter, *Art and Myth in Ancient Greece* (London, 1991)

Indian chronology

India was rarely ruled as a single unit. What follows is, therefore, a selective and simplified chronology for the Indian subcontinent. Dates are approximate.

Periods

Indus Valley (north-west)	mid 3rd–2nd millennium BC
Protohistoric (north)	mid 2nd–mid lst millennium BC
Maurya (north)	4th–2nd century BC
Shunga (north)	2nd–lst century BC
Satavahana (Deccan)	1st century BC–3rd century AD
Kushan (north)	1st century BC–4th century AD
Gupta (north)	4th–6th century AD
Pallava (south)	7th–9th century AD
Pala and Sena (north-east)	8th–13th century AD
Chalukya (Deccan)	6th–12th century AD
Chola period (south)	mid 9th–13th century AD
Chandella and other medieval dynasties (central)	mid 10th–early 13th century AD
Hoysala (Deccan)	early 12th–mid 14th century AD
Vijayanagara (south)	mid 14th–16th century AD
Mughal (north)	mid 16th–18th century AD

Source: Department of Oriental Antiquities

FURTHER READING
R. Blurton, *Hindu Art* (London, 1992)
B. Brend, *Islamic Art* (London, 1991)

Chronology of the Islamic world

The Islamic religion was founded by the *Prophet Muhammad* who was born in Western Arabia *c.*AD 570. Muhammad's flight (*hijra*) from Mecca to Medina in AD 622 marks the beginning of the Islamic era and is the first year of the Muslim calendar (AH 1).

What follows in this appendix is a partial chronology, listing some of the major dynasties and empires. By AD 710 the empire of Muhammad's successors, the first caliphs or rulers of Islam, stretched from Spain to Central Asia, absorbing the lands of the Roman Empire in the west and the Sasanian Empire in the east. The *Umayyads* (AD 661–750) established their caliphate in Damascus. In 750 they were overthrown by the *'Abbasids* (AD 750–1258) whose capital was Baghdad, although military unrest caused them to move temporarily to Samarra between AD 836 and 883. In Iran local dynasties sprang up largely outside 'Abbasid control. The most important of these were the *Samanids* (AD 819–1005) and the *Ghaznavids* (AD 977–1186) in eastern Iran and Afghanistan, and the *Buyids* or *Buwayhids* (AD 932–1062) who invaded Iraq in AD 945, leaving the 'Abbasid caliphate in place but powerless.

The *Fatimids* (AD 909–1171) first gained power in North Africa, but in AD 969 founded a new capital at Cairo. From Egypt the Fatimids extended eastward into Syria and the Hijaz. The *Zengids* (AD 1127–1223) were the most important of a number of small dynasties ruling the Jazira and northern Syria after the *Seljuk Turks* ousted the Fatimids from the area. They were based at Mosul. The *Ayyubids* (AD 1169–1260) began in the service of the Zengids but in AD 1171 Salah al-Din (Saladin) conquered the Fatimids in Egypt. From AD 1250 to 1517 Egypt and Syria were ruled by the *Mamluks*, an hierarchical military regime of Turkish origin, with their capital at Cairo. By

the early 14th century the *Ottomans* were established as a small Turcoman principality in north-west Anatolia with their capital at Bursa. In the later 14th century they overran a large part of the Balkans and transferred their capital to Edirne (Adrianople). In AD 1453 Sultan Mehmed II captured Constantinople, bringing to an end the Byzantine Empire. The city, renamed Istanbul, became for almost five centuries the capital of the Ottoman Empire which extended through Egypt, Syria, the Balkans and Arabia.

In AD 1083 the invasion of *Seljuk Turks* from Central Asia marked the beginning of a long period of Turkish rule in Iran. The 12th century witnessed the decline of Seljuk power and the struggle for domination of Iran between the *Khwarazm Shahs* (AD 1194–1231) and the *Ghurids*, who ruled in eastern Iran (AD 1147–1215). The Khwarazm Shahs prevailed in the early 13th century, pushing the Ghurids eastwards into India. The *Mongol* invasions under Genghis Khan and his successors from AD 1219 onwards brought widespread destruction but the invasion of Timur (Tamerlane) at the end of the 14th century reunited Iran under *Timurid* rule (AD 1378– 1506). His successors were unable to maintain control and the west was lost to two Turcoman tribes. The ancestor of the *Safavids* was a Sufi dervish, Shaykh Safi (*d.*AD 1334). He founded a dervish order at Ardabil in north-west Iran, which during the next hundred years became steadily more powerful. The first Safavid Shah, Isma'il I (AD 1501–24) established his capital at Tabriz and rapidly brought all Iran under his control. In the later 17th century the dynasty weakened.

Source: Department of Oriental Antiquities

FURTHER READING

B. Brend, *Islamic Art* (London, 1991)

Japanese historical periods

Jōmon	c.10,000 BC–c.300 BC (variously divided by different archaeologists)
Yayoi	c.300 BC–c.AD 300
Kofun ('Great Tombs')	c.AD 300–mid 6th century AD
Asuka	mid 6th century–AD 710
Nara	AD 710–794
Heian (Fujiwara)	AD 794–1185
Kamakura	AD 1185–1333
Muromachi (Ashikaga)	AD 1333–1568 (the period 1333–92 is sometimes separately listed as Nambokuchō – 'the Northern and Southern Courts')
Momoyama	AD 1568–1600
Edo	AD 1600–1868
Modern	
Meiji era	AD 1868–1912
Taishō era	AD 1912–1926
Showa era	AD 1926–1989
Heisei era	AD 1989–

Source: L. Smith, V. Harris and T. Clark, *Japanese Art: Masterpieces in the British Museum* (London, 1990)

Korean historical periods

Neolithic	c.6000–1000 BC
Bronze Age	c.1000 BC–c.400 BC
Iron Age	c.400 BC–mid/late lst century BC
Three Kingdoms	
Silla	57 BC–AD 668
Koguryo	37 BC–AD 668
Paekche	18 BC–AD 668
Unified Silla	AD 668–935
Koryo dynasty	AD 918–1392
Choson dynasty	AD 1392–1910

Source: Department of Oriental Antiquities

Techniques used in jewellery manufacture

ANNEALING Reheating worked metal to remove its brittleness.

CABOCHON A precious or semi-precious stone which is merely polished without being cut into facets.

CALIBRE-CUTTING A stone cut into a specific shape to fit its setting exactly.

CAMEO A hardstone or gem into which a design is cut in relief, often making use within the design of the contrasting colours occurring naturally in the stone.

CHASING A technique of working metal from the front using a tool with a rounded end so that the pattern is modelled in relief or indented into the surface.

CIRE-PERDUE The 'lost-wax' process of casting. A wax or wax-coated model is embedded in clay which is then baked so that the wax melts and is lost, leaving a mould into which the molten metal can be poured. The mould has to be broken to retrieve the object.

CLOISON A cell formed of thin strips of metal soldered to a metal base. In inlaid work the cloison is designed to hold the inlay of stone or glass (or a man-made imitation). A design made up of a network of cloisons for inlays or enamels is described as cloisonné.

ENAMEL A coloured glass, or a combination of vitreous glazes, fused on to a metallic surface.

ENAMELLING 1. Cloisonné – a technique in which a network of cloisons forming the outlines of a decorative pattern or a picture is soldered to a metal surface; the coloured enamels are laid into the cloisons in powdered form and fired.
2. Champlevé – a technique in which the surface of the metal is gouged away to create troughs and channels, each separated from the other by a thin ridge. The coloured enamels are laid into the troughs in powdered form and fired.
3. Basse-taille – a sophisticated version of champlevé enamelling. Within an area that has been cut away to receive the enamels a design or scene is chased in low relief. The translucent enamels used 'flood' the chased

work, so that they lie in varying thicknesses. Light is reflected back through the enamels from the metal in varying degrees, producing rich tonal effects.

ENGRAVING A technique of cutting patterns into a surface with a sharp tool. The metal (or glass) is removed in the process (as distinct from chasing where the metal is pushed but not removed).

FAIENCE A glazed composition used in the ancient world; formed from a fused mass of crushed quartz and glazed in various colours, often imitating semi-precious stones.

FILIGREE A decorative pattern made of wires, sometimes soldered to a background, but often left as openwork.

GILDING The application of gold to the surface of an object made of another material, usually silver or other metal.

INTAGLIO A sunk pattern or a design cut into a flat surface, usually metal or a hardstone.

NIELLO A black compound of silver, lead, copper and sulphur – the exact composition varies; fusible at low temperatures, it is applied to metal (usually silver) in much the same way as enamel but is not vitreous.

PARCEL-GILT A term used to describe silver objects which have been partially enriched with gilding.

POUNCING The surface patterning produced by the technique of stippling.

REPOUSSÉ (Also called embossing) a technique of working sheet metal from behind with punches to raise the pattern, which stands in relief on the front.

Source: H. Tait (ed.), *Seven Thousand Years of Jewellery* (London, 1986)

FURTHER READING
C. Andrews, *Ancient Egyptian Jewellery* (London, 1996)
J. Mack (ed.), *Ethnic Jewellery* (London, 1994)
J. Rudoe, *Cartier: 1900–1939* (London, 1997)
H. Tait (ed.), *Seven Thousand Years of Jewellery* (London, 1986)
D. Williams and J. Ogden, *Greek Gold: Jewellery of the Classical World* (London, 1994)

Common numismatic terms

Æ	*aes* (copper or bronze)
AR	*argentum* (silver)
N	*aurum* (gold)
billon	A base metal, an alloy of silver with a high copper content.
blank	The blank piece of metal before a coin is struck.
die	The block of metal, with design cut into it, which actually impresses the coin blank with the design.
electrum	An alloy of gold and silver, used in the earliest coins.
field	The flat part of a coin between the main design and the inscription or edge.
flan	The whole piece of metal after striking.
legend	The inscription.
obv.	Obverse. Now used to mean the side that bears the most important design, e.g. the Queen's head on a pound coin.
pattern	A coin of a new design that was not adopted.
rev.	Reverse – opposite of obverse.
type	The main, central design.

FURTHER READING

J. Williams (ed.), *Money. A History* (London, 1997)
G. Williams (ed.), *World of Money CD-ROM* (London, 1998)

Prehistory

The term 'prehistory' broadly covers the great unrecorded sweep of humanity's past which precedes the written record. For much of our knowledge of this period we are dependent on the results of archaeological excavation, and theories change rapidly, particularly following scientific advances such as dating techniques, the more recent development of DNA testing and the discovery of new sites.

The 'Three Age System' (Stone, Bronze, Iron) was developed in Denmark in 1816 by C. Thomsen and J.J. Worsaae. At a time when the extent of human antiquity was only just being realized it provided a means of measuring time by reference to human technology. The system has been considerably refined but is still in use today. It should not, however, be taken too literally, since technologies overlap and thus the periods shade into each other, often imperceptibly. Also the time scale varies, often widely, in different parts of the world.

It is currently thought that tool-making humans emerged some 2,500,000 years ago. Various types appeared but eventually, some 130,000 years ago, *homo sapiens* emerged in Africa and is thought to have reached Europe around 35,000 years ago. There were a number of glacial periods, the most recent ending around 8000 BC, when the Neolithic period saw the emergence of farming and eventually of the first literate societies in the Middle East.

Below is a guide to time periods in Britain according to current evidence.

Palaeolithic (Old Stone Age) beginning some time before 500,000 years ago (Often divided into Lower, Middle and Upper Palaeolithic periods)

Mesolithic (Middle Stone Age) beginning *c.*8000 BC

Neolithic (New Stone Age) *c.*4000 BC–2000 BC

Bronze Age *c.*2500 BC–700 BC

Iron Age from *c.*800 BC

In Britain the Roman invasion (AD 43) is taken as the point at which the 'prehistoric' period ends.

Source: Department of Prehistoric and Romano-British Antiquities

FURTHER READING
S. Bowman (ed.), *Science and the Past* (London, 1991)
M. Ehrenberg, *Women in Prehistory* (London, 1995)
A. Schnapp, *The Discovery of the Past* (London, 1996)

Terms used in printmaking

AQUATINT A variety of etching. Tone process used to imitate the appearance of watercolour washes. The plate is covered with a ground of powdered resin which is bound to it by heating. The acid bites tiny rings around each resin grain, and these hold sufficient ink when printed to give the effect of a wash. The printmaker will 'stop out' parts of the ground where he wishes to obtain pure white with a protecting varnish.

DRYPOINT A type of intaglio print. The line is scratched directly into the plate with a metal point, which is pulled across the surface, not pushed as in engraving. The metal displaced from the scratched line is thrown up on either side (the burr). This is left on to retain ink during printing. This gives the line a rich velvety texture, but the effect is weakened with each impression.

ENGRAVING Intaglio print made with a graver or burin, a small metal rod with a sharpened point. It is pushed across the plate, forcing the metal up into slivers in front of the V-shaped line. These pieces are removed with a sharp-bladed scraper.

ETCHING Intaglio print in which the lines in a metal plate are bitten by acid. The polished surface of the plate is first covered with a thin layer of ground, composed of waxes, gums and resins. The etcher draws through the ground with a metal point which exposes the metal. The plate is then immersed in a bath of acid. The depth of the line and thus its darkness when printed, is determined by the length of time the plate remains in the bath and the strength of the acid solution.

INTAGLIO A metal plate is incised or roughened, then inked and wiped so that the ink remains in the incisions or hollows and is forced out by being printed under pressure. The way in which the incisions are made on the plate defines the different intaglio processes, which include etching, drypoint, mezzotint, stipple, aquatint, engraving.

LITHOGRAPH A drawing is made on a suitable surface, e.g. limestone or zinc, with some greasy medium. The surface is dampened with water, which settles on the unmarked areas only. It is then rolled over with greasy printing ink, which will adhere only to the drawn marks, the water repelling it from elsewhere. The ink is transferred to a sheet of paper by running paper and printing surface together through a scraper press.

MEZZOTINT A type of intaglio print in which a metal plate is roughened or ground all over using a tool with a curved and serrated edge (rocker), producing an overall burr. The artist scrapes down the burr in proportion to the lightness of tone required.

MONOTYPE The artist paints his design in printing ink on a plate and transfers it to a sheet of paper by running it through a press while the ink is still wet. Only one strong impression can be made and one weak.

RELIEF The type of surface matrices that includes woodcut, wood-engraving, metalcut and lino-cut. White areas are cut away so that the parts of the block that are left in relief print black.

SCREENPRINTING A gauze screen, fixed tautly on a rectangular frame, is laid directly on top of a sheet of paper. Printing ink is spread over the upper side of the mesh on which a design has been drawn in a waxy or other impermeable medium, and forced through it with a squeegee (rubber blade) so that it transfers to the paper on the other side (also known as silk-screen or serigraphy).

STATE The printed impression from a plate or block is known as 'first state'; second state, third state and so on are used for subsequent impressions which show additional working on the plate.

STIPPLE ENGRAVING An intaglio process in which the tone is produced by a profusion of tiny dots, either etched or engraved.

WOODCUT The design is drawn directly on the surface of the block, which is cut parallel to the grain. The parts which are to print white are cut away, leaving the black lines in relief. The tool used is usually a knife. The block is then printed on a relief press.

Source: For these and other more detailed definitions see P. Goldman, *Looking at Prints, Drawings and Watercolours: A Guide to Technical Terms* (London and Los Angeles, 1988)

Index